PENGUIN SOUP FOR THE SOUL

Also by Tom Tomorrow:

Greetings from This Modern World
Tune in Tomorrow
The Wrath of Sparky

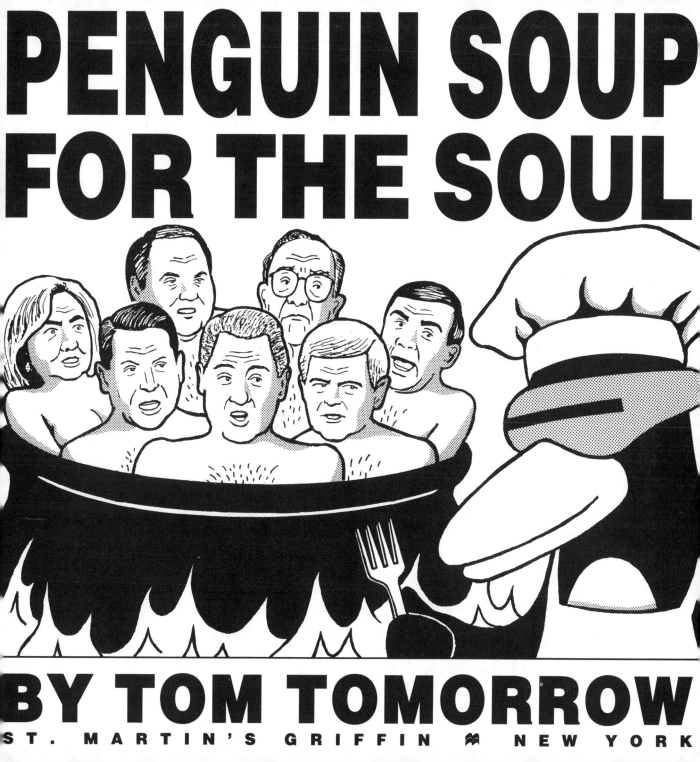

PENGUIN SOUP FOR THE SOUL

BY TOM TOMORROW

ST. MARTIN'S GRIFFIN ⚓ NEW YORK

"Stick a fork in their ass and turn 'em over, they're done."
—Lou Reed

PENGUIN SOUP FOR THE SOUL. Copyright © 1998 by Tom Tomorrow (Dan Perkins). All rights reserved. Printed in the United States of America. No part of this book may be used or reproduced in any manner whatsoever without written permission except in the case of brief quotations embodied in critical articles or reviews. For information address St. Martin's Press, 175 Fifth Avenue, New York, N.Y. 10010.

E-mail Tom Tomorrow at tomorrow@well.com or visit the Tom Tomorrow web site at
www.well.com/user/tomorrow
or www.thismodernworld.com.

Library of Congress Cataloging-in-Publication Data

Tomorrow, Tom.
   Penguin soup for the soul / Tom Tomorrow.
      p. cm.
   ISBN 0-312-19316-5
   1. United States—Politics and government—1993– —Caricatures and
cartoons. 2. American wit and humor, Pictorial. I. Title.
E885.T647 1998
973.929'022'2—dc21   98-28821
                                              CIP

First Edition: September 1998

10 9 8 7 6 5 4 3 2 1

Design and cover by Dan Perkins

The cartoons on pages 2, 3, 20, 21, 30, 31, 36, 37, 52, 53, 75, 80, 81, 100, 101, and 111 originally appeared in *The Nation.*

The cartoons on pages 85, 89, 90, 94, 95, 98, and 105 originally appeared in *U.S. News & World Report.*

"Those Wacky Republicans" (pages 55–57) originally appeared in *The New Haven Advocate.*

The panels on page 79, drawn by Matt Wuerker, Mark Alan Stamaty, John Backderf, Bill Griffith, and Tom Toles, are copyrighted by the respective artists.

FOREWORD

Why was *Primary Colors* (the movie, I mean) such a flop at the box office? And why does *This Modern World* continue to get itself clipped and passed on by a growing number of readers who are too cheap to send their friends a proper subscription to the ever-fewer mainstream, and shamefully few nonmainstream, magazines that continue to run the work of Tom Tomorrow?

a) Tom Tomorrow has the nerve to run captions and bubbles as long as, if not longer than, the preceding sentence.

b) Tom Tomorrow features a penguin, while *Primary Colors* was a flapping, gobbling, flightless bird of another kidney.

c) People may make their own private excuses for Clinton, but find themselves repelled when Hollywood comes up with a sickly, self-pitying version of lesser-evilism. They don't want to hear their own pathetic reasoning played back to them as "entertainment," thanks very much.

d) People do readily recognise the absurdity and falsity of official and even unofficial propaganda when it is rendered deadpan.

In other words, all the answers above are correct. *This Modern World* is a continuous "yeah, right" to the stream of sinister piffle that is directed at us from page and screen. It takes the pifflers literally and at face value, and is thus—to rescue a degraded term—always committing irony.

When I was a lad, the sturdy penguin was a symbol of learning, a paperback guarantee that the treasure-house of the world's finest minds was available to all for pennies. More progress followed, and by election year 1992, for example, members of my own uniquely favored generation had been so cognitively empowered that they were able to say things like "Time for a change" and "It's the economy, stupid" as if they had thought of these all by themselves. Some of us felt the need for a touch of market correction: a slight uptick in the critical faculty quotient that isn't, but should be, one of our leading indicators. And

the hour brought forth the man. You've tried "Monday, Monday" and "Ruby Tuesday" and *The Man Who Was Thursday* and Man Friday and Billy Sunday. But Señor Mañana and Monsieur Demain will always be one news cycle ahead. Yet Mr. Tomorrow achieves this effect by a form of *in retro* fertilisation, drawing his images and characters from the epoch of trust and innocence and artless advertising—the time when Walter Cronkite could say "That's the way it is tonight," and schoolchildren could be taught the duck-and-cover drill for those thermonuclear episodes that might spoil your whole day.

To mine the age of credulity in order to satirise our own present (so smart and so wised up, and yet so stupid and so superstitious) is to show some interest in history and even tradition. Well, mercy me. I live in "historic" Washington, and the cartoonist of our hometown rag feels he's done *that* job if he shows the reproachful ghost of Abe Lincoln in a stovepipe hat—plus the word "Lincoln" written on his pants to make sure nobody misses it—or shows a donkey and an elephant in mortal combat to illustrate the latest "partisan" sham-fight. Over the braying jackass and the trumpeting pachyderm, who should never be depicted except when writhing in obscene and unlawful congress, give me a sardonic penguin every time. Or a talking stomach—which may be (I can dream, too, can't I?) Mr. Tomorrow's publishable version of the eloquent sphincter that spoke so feelingly in *Naked Lunch*.

Let me call your attention to the fact that many of these cartoons represent reportage, and that Tom Tomorrow actually took his pad and pencil out to the field, and listened as well as drew, and in this respect also put many fashionable doodlers, like the overrated houseboy who brought us the innocuous *Dilbert,* to a shame they will probably never feel.

These drawings will help preserve the record of the Clinton-Gingrich copresidency, and will show future generations that there was a sort of united front against bullshit, and that all you had to do was volunteer. If I have a criticism, it is that the punchline in these following frames is often unnecessary. Let the bastards hang themselves with their own rope, is what I tend to say. Yet who can quarrel with the view that it's best to ensure that the rope is tightly knotted?

I have spent much of a lifetime vainly trying to prove that one word is worth any number of pictures, but the united front of words and pictures in the ensuing pages is as vital as the other united front I mentioned above. May Tomorrow always come.

Christopher Hitchens
May Day, 1998

INTRODUCTION

I'm a weekly cartoonist. I produce fifty-two cartoons a year, which are syndicated primarily throughout the alternative press. I also am an occasional contributor to *The Nation,* and—improbably enough—briefly had a regular spot in that most staid of mainstream news magazines, *U.S. News & World Report.*[1] But that's about it. I've always resisted increasing my output much beyond this level for fear of becoming what I loathe, another banal cartoonist forced by the pressure of imminent deadlines into churning out superficial jokes about the day's events. The trade-off, of course, is that I'll never be a contender for the title of World's Most Prolific Cartoonist, but I can live with that. And anyway, I've got Wordiest clinched, hands down.

The point is, these books of mine only come out once every two years, after I've accumulated enough work to fill 119 pages—and in many ways, these two-year intervals have come to demarcate the phases of my life. Two years ago, I was not a particularly happy camper. I was swamped, spending my days rushing to beat *The Wrath of Sparky*'s publication deadline, while spending my evenings sorting through the accumulated detritus of more than ten years in San Francisco—and those who know me can attest to the fact that I am quite the accomplished accumulator, so this was no mean feat—in preparation for a rapidly approaching cross-country move.

I probably love the Bay Area more than any place on earth, and indeed, after two years away, I still dream at night about the intensity of the light, the perpetual hint of an ocean breeze hanging in the air, the sheer physical beauty of the place. But ten years anywhere can leave you ready for a change, particularly when a vague yet chronic sense of low-level dissatisfaction is coupled with that old standby of life-altering events, the long-distance relationship. There's more to the story, of course—there always is—but what it boils down to is this: at the ripe old age of thirty-five, I put my cats on an airplane and my photocopier in the trunk of a rental car and took a blind leap of faith into an uncertain future because, well, it seemed like a good idea at the time.

And so this time around, I'm sitting in a sunny Tribeca studio on a glorious spring day in New York City, mulling over what is, it suddenly occurs to me, the last Tom Tomorrow collection of the millenium. Some of these cartoons really stirred up some shit over the past couple of years, which is gratifying in theory—it is better to be denounced than ignored, after all. Unfortunately, the controversies have either revolved around utterly inconsequential topics, such as my less-than-earth-shattering argument that Scott Adams may not be the hero of the information-age working class he is widely perceived to be (p. 38),[2] or they've been the result of a complete misreading of the cartoon in question, such as the time my intentionally ironic use of the word "Negroes" (p. 35) led politicians in Connecticut to denounce me as a racist.

But far and away the most ludicrous controversy of the past two years—of what I laughingly refer to as my career, for that matter—was triggered by a recent meditation on the media's excessive coverage of the presidential sex scandals (p. 114) . . . or more accurately, triggered by the visual metaphor with which I attempted to represent these excesses, an admittedly envelope-pushing orgy scene taken from eighteenth-century engravings. Papers across the country received a deluge of complaints from readers shocked and appalled by this "so-called comic"; as one typical correspondent noted, "If this is what the modern world is about, I can see Satan is having a field day." And while the cartoon in question ended with a mocking reference to "media elitists (who) seem to believe that Americans won't pay attention to anything unless it involves sex," hindsight forces me to acknowledge that the disproportionately vehement response of these readers has rendered my point invalid. Satire has been

---

[1]Editor Jim Fallows was a fan of my work, though as it turned out, publisher Mort Zuckerman was not, and I was quickly given the boot. Apparently there were irreconcilable differences between my worldview and that of a wealthy New York real estate magnate. Go figure.

[2]That one first ran in January of '97, but to this day I still get e-mail from outraged Dilbert fanatics taking me to task for such daring to speak such heresy, which leads me to the inescapable conclusion that some of you people have way too much time on your hands.

transformed into a simple statement of fact: as it turns out, there really are a lot of people out there who don't pay attention to anything unless it involves sex. Ironically, most of them seem to be conservative Christians.

The center of the storm was in Oklahoma City, where oddly named state representative Forrest Claunch, along with a group of knuckleheaded right-wingers calling themselves Oklahomans for Children and Family,[3] went so far as to file an obscenity complaint with the local police against the paper that ran my cartoon there, the Oklahoma Gazette. (The district attorney, apparently having some passing familiarity with the Constitution, declined to prosecute.) And while OCAF executive director Bob Anderson admitted to a reporter that the cartoon did not in fact arouse *his* prurient interest—one legal definition of pornography—he worried that it might appeal to others. "It might teach a girl to try oral sex with another girl. Or someone might say, 'I haven't tried anal sex.' It might turn someone else on." (Impressionable readers may at this point wish to either carefully avoid page 114 of this book, or to turn quickly to it, depending on personal preference.)

The paper, in what I believe to be a seriously misguided attempt to placate these simpletons, dropped my cartoon soon thereafter (and one thing I sure wouldn't have anticipated two years ago was that I would someday be banned in Oklahoma City as a pornographer)—but it didn't end there. The Gazette's publisher is an attorney whose firm represents school boards, and as of this writing he's lost at least one major client as a result of community pressure. As OCAF's Anderson helpfully explained to Salon magazine, "If he is representing the school and a little girl is raped in the restroom and he's the type of guy that runs this cartoon in the newspaper, whose side do you think he'll be on? I think he'd be very biased."

As Sparky might say, you just can't argue with logic like that.

Finally, while there are many people to whom I am immeasurably indebted for their friendship and support, I particularly want to thank all the editors who continue to give me the space each week to do what I do, even when it occasionally blows up in their faces. Since I'm not really qualified to do much of anything else at this point, they're basically all that stands between me and a job at the local copy shop.

Special thanks are also due to reader Bill Lennan (who keeps up with This Modern World online from his home in London, England) for suggesting the title of this book.

And as for that cross-country relationship, which by all rights should have crashed and burned within weeks once we were forced to discard our long-distance fantasies and confront the day-to-day reality of one another—it has instead flourished and grown, and although it is an inadequate gesture that does not begin to convey the sheer astonishment I feel each day, this book is nonetheless dedicated to Beverly, whose wit and insight inform my work and grace my life.

Dan Perkins
("Tom Tomorrow")
New York City
May 1998

---

[3]OCAF is the same group which convinced an Oklahoma judge that the Academy Award–winning film The Tin Drum was pornographic. It was pulled from local video store shelves, and Oklahoma City's finest were actually dispatched to retrieve rented copies from people's homes. In one of those bizarre twists that serve to remind us that reality is stranger than satire, one of the copies had been rented by the development director of the local ACLU, who of course promptly filed suit.

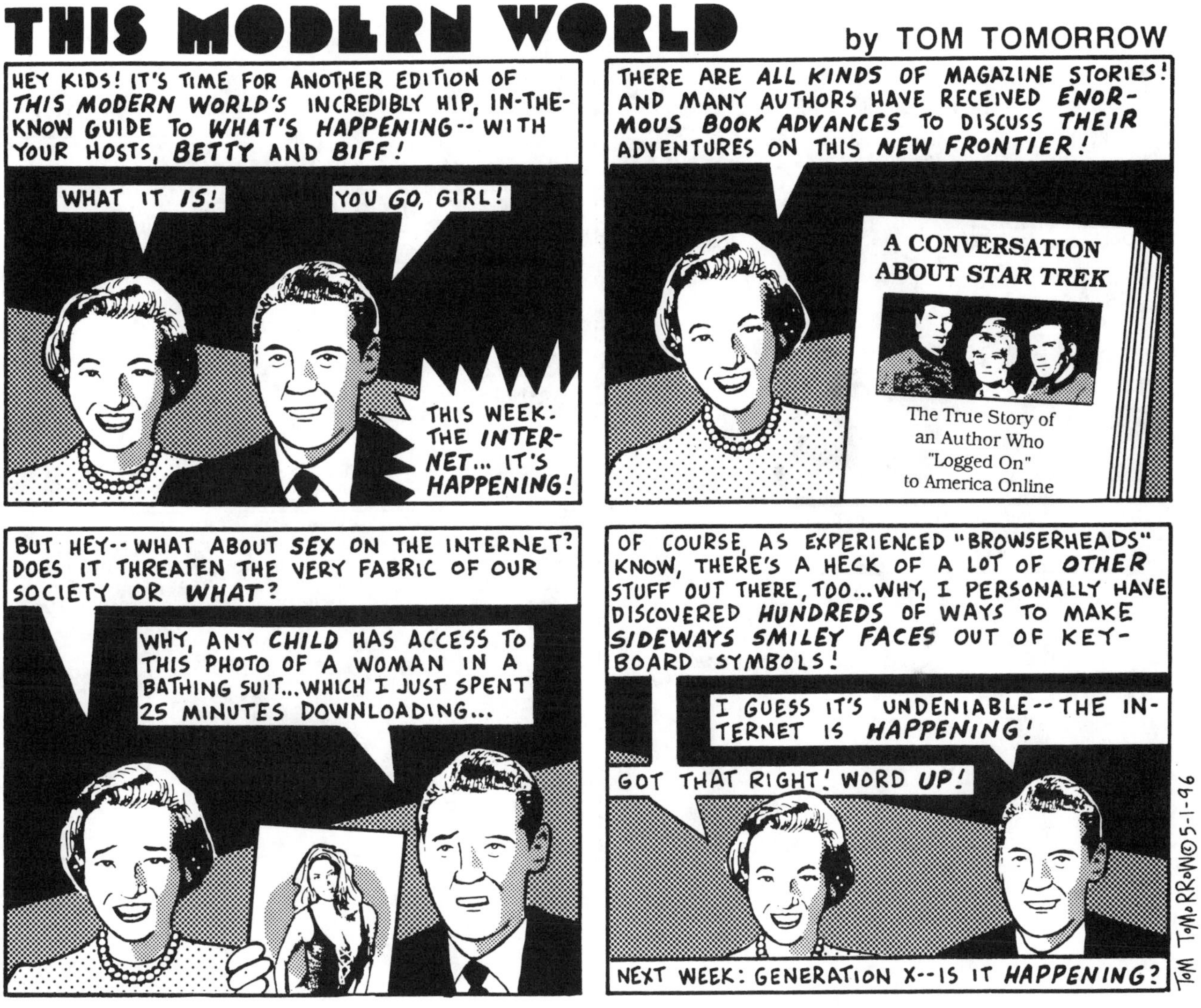
THIS MODERN WORLD
by TOM TOMORROW
HEY KIDS! IT'S TIME FOR ANOTHER EDITION OF THIS MODERN WORLD'S INCREDIBLY HIP, IN-THE-KNOW GUIDE TO WHAT'S HAPPENING-- WITH YOUR HOSTS, BETTY AND BIFF!
WHAT IT IS!
YOU GO, GIRL!
THIS WEEK: THE INTERNET... IT'S HAPPENING!
THERE ARE ALL KINDS OF MAGAZINE STORIES! AND MANY AUTHORS HAVE RECEIVED ENORMOUS BOOK ADVANCES TO DISCUSS THEIR ADVENTURES ON THIS NEW FRONTIER!
A CONVERSATION ABOUT STAR TREK
The True Story of an Author Who "Logged On" to America Online
BUT HEY-- WHAT ABOUT SEX ON THE INTERNET? DOES IT THREATEN THE VERY FABRIC OF OUR SOCIETY OR WHAT?
WHY, ANY CHILD HAS ACCESS TO THIS PHOTO OF A WOMAN IN A BATHING SUIT... WHICH I JUST SPENT 25 MINUTES DOWNLOADING...
OF COURSE, AS EXPERIENCED "BROWSERHEADS" KNOW, THERE'S A HECK OF A LOT OF OTHER STUFF OUT THERE, TOO... WHY, I PERSONALLY HAVE DISCOVERED HUNDREDS OF WAYS TO MAKE SIDEWAYS SMILEY FACES OUT OF KEYBOARD SYMBOLS!
I GUESS IT'S UNDENIABLE-- THE INTERNET IS HAPPENING!
GOT THAT RIGHT! WORD UP!
NEXT WEEK: GENERATION X-- IS IT HAPPENING?
TOM TOMORROW©5-1-96

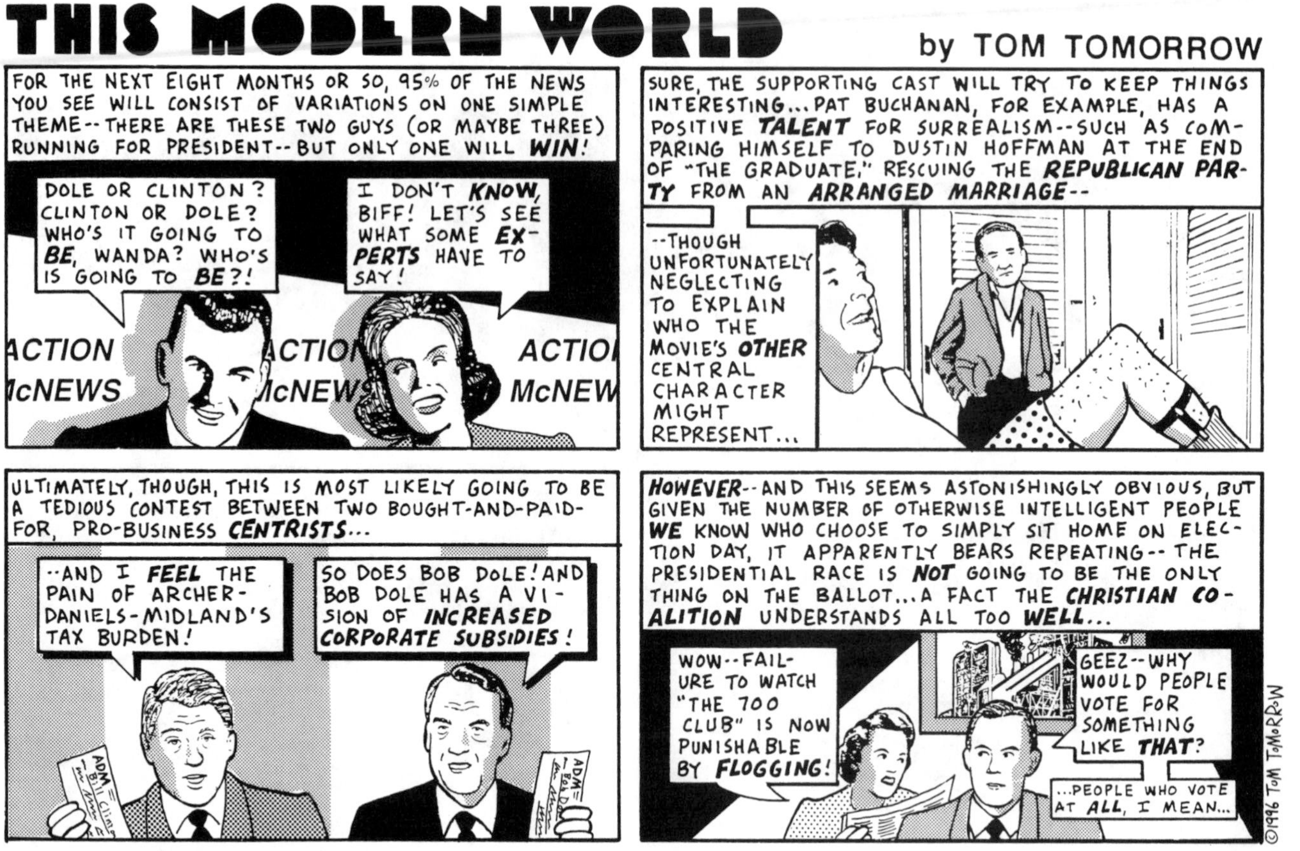
THIS MODERN WORLD
by TOM TOMORROW
FOR THE NEXT EIGHT MONTHS OR SO, 95% OF THE NEWS YOU SEE WILL CONSIST OF VARIATIONS ON ONE SIMPLE THEME-- THERE ARE THESE TWO GUYS (OR MAYBE THREE) RUNNING FOR PRESIDENT-- BUT ONLY ONE WILL WIN!
DOLE OR CLINTON? CLINTON OR DOLE? WHO'S IT GOING TO BE, WANDA? WHO'S IS GOING TO BE?!
I DON'T KNOW, BIFF! LET'S SEE WHAT SOME EXPERTS HAVE TO SAY!
ACTION McNEWS
SURE, THE SUPPORTING CAST WILL TRY TO KEEP THINGS INTERESTING... PAT BUCHANAN, FOR EXAMPLE, HAS A POSITIVE TALENT FOR SURREALISM--SUCH AS COMPARING HIMSELF TO DUSTIN HOFFMAN AT THE END OF "THE GRADUATE," RESCUING THE REPUBLICAN PARTY FROM AN ARRANGED MARRIAGE--
--THOUGH UNFORTUNATELY NEGLECTING TO EXPLAIN WHO THE MOVIE'S OTHER CENTRAL CHARACTER MIGHT REPRESENT...
ULTIMATELY, THOUGH, THIS IS MOST LIKELY GOING TO BE A TEDIOUS CONTEST BETWEEN TWO BOUGHT-AND-PAID-FOR, PRO-BUSINESS CENTRISTS...
--AND I FEEL THE PAIN OF ARCHER-DANIELS-MIDLAND'S TAX BURDEN!
SO DOES BOB DOLE! AND BOB DOLE HAS A VISION OF INCREASED CORPORATE SUBSIDIES!
HOWEVER-- AND THIS SEEMS ASTONISHINGLY OBVIOUS, BUT GIVEN THE NUMBER OF OTHERWISE INTELLIGENT PEOPLE WE KNOW WHO CHOOSE TO SIMPLY SIT HOME ON ELECTION DAY, IT APPARENTLY BEARS REPEATING-- THE PRESIDENTIAL RACE IS NOT GOING TO BE THE ONLY THING ON THE BALLOT... A FACT THE CHRISTIAN COALITION UNDERSTANDS ALL TOO WELL...
WOW--FAILURE TO WATCH "THE 700 CLUB" IS NOW PUNISHABLE BY FLOGGING!
GEEZ--WHY WOULD PEOPLE VOTE FOR SOMETHING LIKE THAT?
...PEOPLE WHO VOTE AT ALL, I MEAN...
©1996 TOM TOMORROW

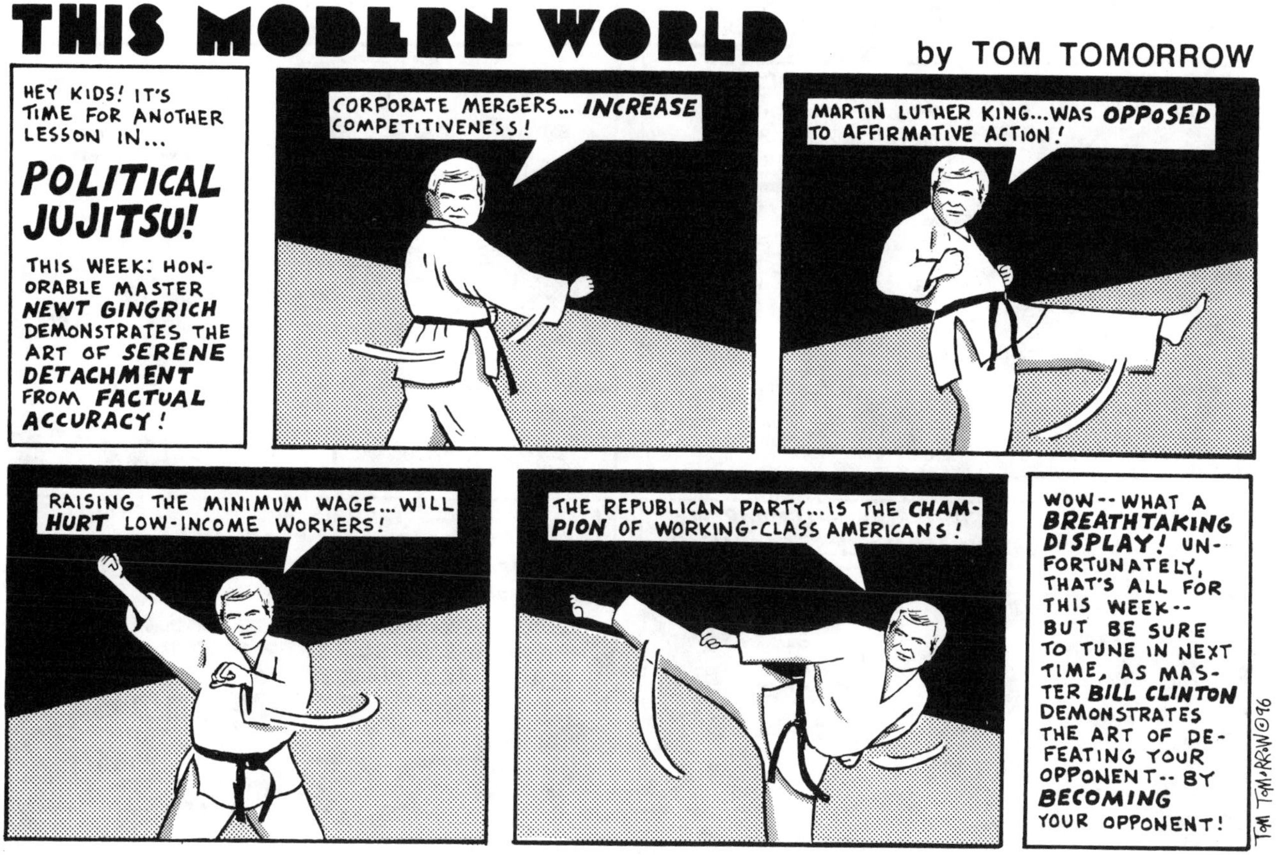
THIS MODERN WORLD
by TOM TOMORROW
HEY KIDS! IT'S TIME FOR ANOTHER LESSON IN...
POLITICAL JUJITSU!
THIS WEEK: HONORABLE MASTER NEWT GINGRICH DEMONSTRATES THE ART OF SERENE DETACHMENT FROM FACTUAL ACCURACY!
CORPORATE MERGERS... INCREASE COMPETITIVENESS!
MARTIN LUTHER KING...WAS OPPOSED TO AFFIRMATIVE ACTION!
RAISING THE MINIMUM WAGE...WILL HURT LOW-INCOME WORKERS!
THE REPUBLICAN PARTY...IS THE CHAMPION OF WORKING-CLASS AMERICANS!
WOW--WHAT A BREATHTAKING DISPLAY! UNFORTUNATELY, THAT'S ALL FOR THIS WEEK--BUT BE SURE TO TUNE IN NEXT TIME, AS MASTER BILL CLINTON DEMONSTRATES THE ART OF DEFEATING YOUR OPPONENT--BY BECOMING YOUR OPPONENT!
TOM TOMORROW©96

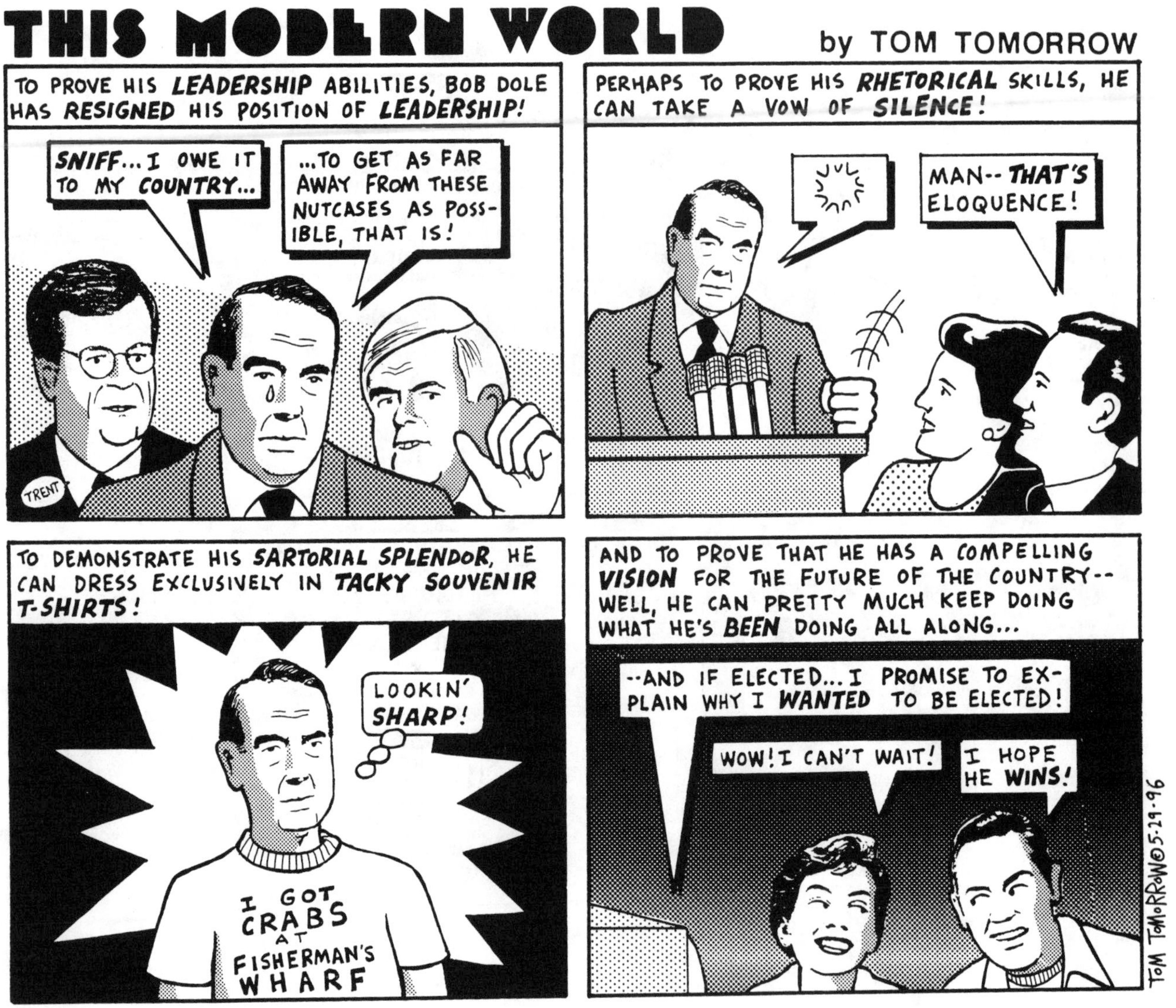
THIS MODERN WORLD
by TOM TOMORROW
TO PROVE HIS LEADERSHIP ABILITIES, BOB DOLE HAS RESIGNED HIS POSITION OF LEADERSHIP!
SNIFF... I OWE IT TO MY COUNTRY...
...TO GET AS FAR AWAY FROM THESE NUTCASES AS POSSIBLE, THAT IS!
TRENT
PERHAPS TO PROVE HIS RHETORICAL SKILLS, HE CAN TAKE A VOW OF SILENCE!
MAN-- THAT'S ELOQUENCE!
TO DEMONSTRATE HIS SARTORIAL SPLENDOR, HE CAN DRESS EXCLUSIVELY IN TACKY SOUVENIR T-SHIRTS!
LOOKIN' SHARP!
I GOT CRABS AT FISHERMAN'S WHARF
AND TO PROVE THAT HE HAS A COMPELLING VISION FOR THE FUTURE OF THE COUNTRY-- WELL, HE CAN PRETTY MUCH KEEP DOING WHAT HE'S BEEN DOING ALL ALONG...
--AND IF ELECTED... I PROMISE TO EXPLAIN WHY I WANTED TO BE ELECTED!
WOW! I CAN'T WAIT!
I HOPE HE WINS!
TOM TOMORROW©5-29-96

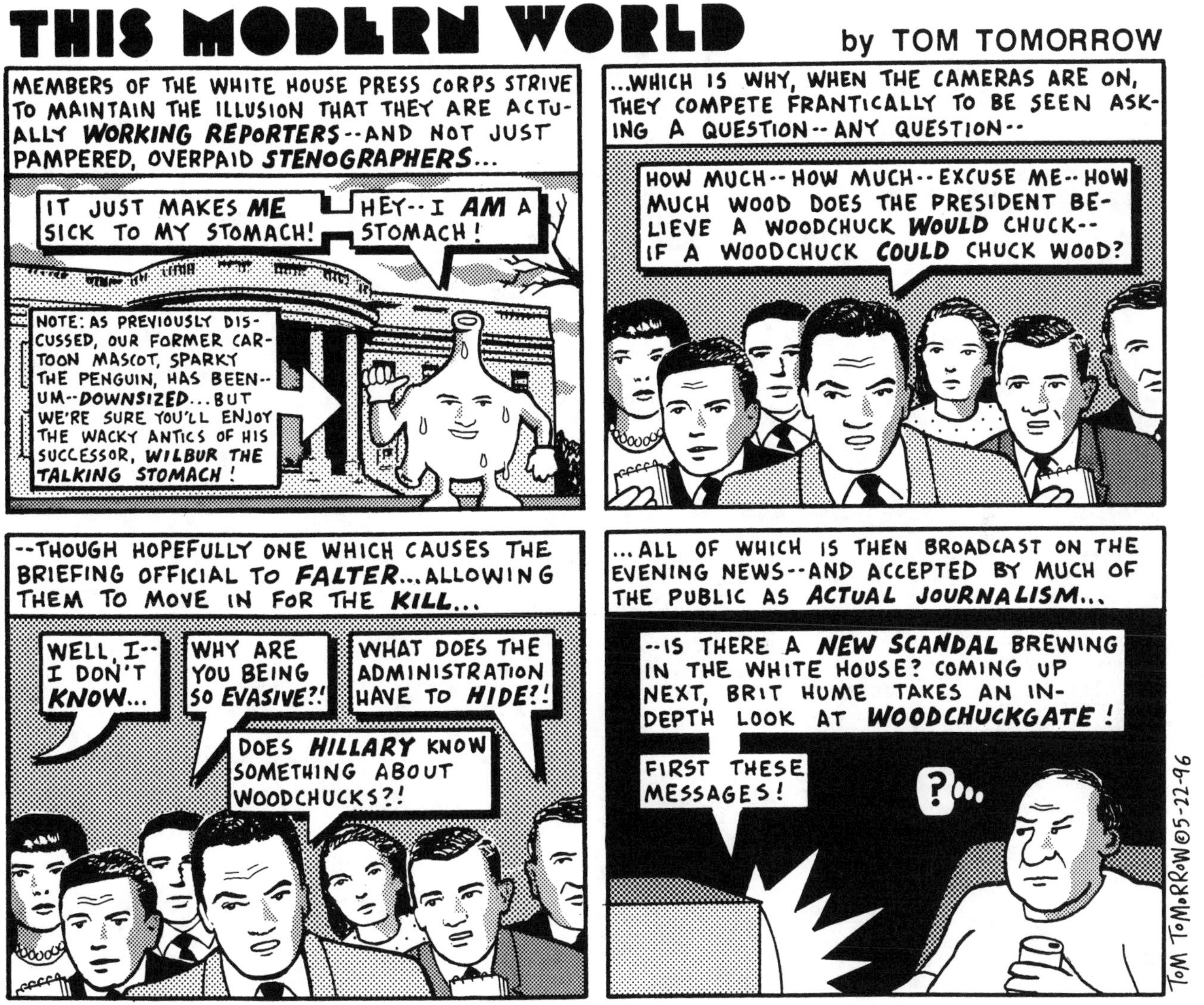
THIS MODERN WORLD
by TOM TOMORROW
MEMBERS OF THE WHITE HOUSE PRESS CORPS STRIVE TO MAINTAIN THE ILLUSION THAT THEY ARE ACTUALLY WORKING REPORTERS--AND NOT JUST PAMPERED, OVERPAID STENOGRAPHERS...
IT JUST MAKES ME SICK TO MY STOMACH!
HEY--I AM A STOMACH!
NOTE: AS PREVIOUSLY DISCUSSED, OUR FORMER CARTOON MASCOT, SPARKY THE PENGUIN, HAS BEEN--UM--DOWNSIZED...BUT WE'RE SURE YOU'LL ENJOY THE WACKY ANTICS OF HIS SUCCESSOR, WILBUR THE TALKING STOMACH!
...WHICH IS WHY, WHEN THE CAMERAS ARE ON, THEY COMPETE FRANTICALLY TO BE SEEN ASKING A QUESTION--ANY QUESTION--
HOW MUCH--HOW MUCH--EXCUSE ME--HOW MUCH WOOD DOES THE PRESIDENT BELIEVE A WOODCHUCK WOULD CHUCK--IF A WOODCHUCK COULD CHUCK WOOD?
--THOUGH HOPEFULLY ONE WHICH CAUSES THE BRIEFING OFFICIAL TO FALTER...ALLOWING THEM TO MOVE IN FOR THE KILL...
WELL, I--I DON'T KNOW...
WHY ARE YOU BEING SO EVASIVE?!
WHAT DOES THE ADMINISTRATION HAVE TO HIDE?!
DOES HILLARY KNOW SOMETHING ABOUT WOODCHUCKS?!
...ALL OF WHICH IS THEN BROADCAST ON THE EVENING NEWS--AND ACCEPTED BY MUCH OF THE PUBLIC AS ACTUAL JOURNALISM...
--IS THERE A NEW SCANDAL BREWING IN THE WHITE HOUSE? COMING UP NEXT, BRIT HUME TAKES AN IN-DEPTH LOOK AT WOODCHUCKGATE!
FIRST THESE MESSAGES!
?...
TOM TOMORROW©5-22-96

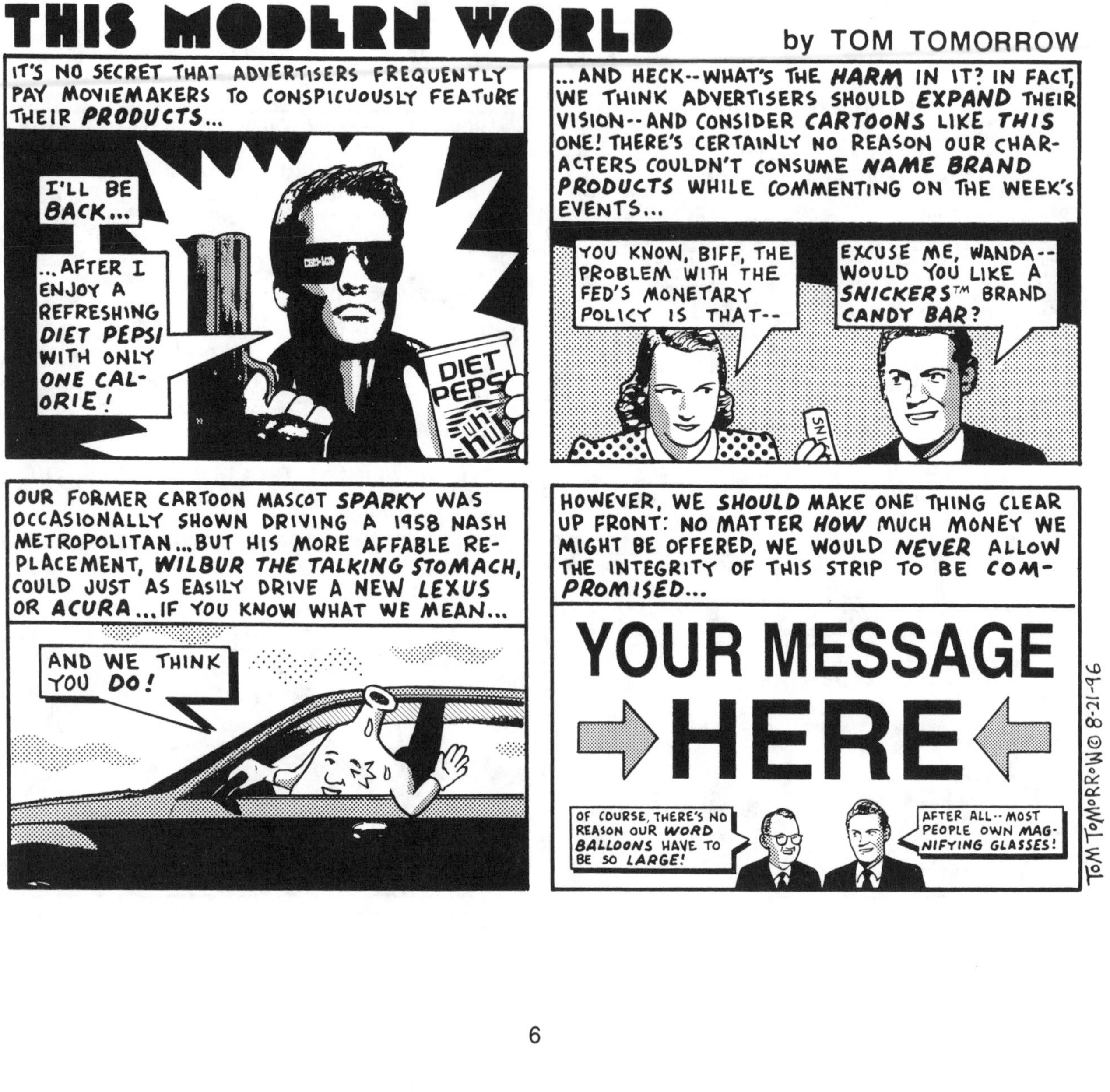

THIS MODERN WORLD
by TOM TOMORROW
IT'S NO SECRET THAT ADVERTISERS FREQUENTLY PAY MOVIEMAKERS TO CONSPICUOUSLY FEATURE THEIR PRODUCTS...
I'LL BE BACK...
...AFTER I ENJOY A REFRESHING DIET PEPSI WITH ONLY ONE CALORIE!
DIET PEPSI
...AND HECK--WHAT'S THE HARM IN IT? IN FACT, WE THINK ADVERTISERS SHOULD EXPAND THEIR VISION--AND CONSIDER CARTOONS LIKE THIS ONE! THERE'S CERTAINLY NO REASON OUR CHARACTERS COULDN'T CONSUME NAME BRAND PRODUCTS WHILE COMMENTING ON THE WEEK'S EVENTS...
YOU KNOW, BIFF, THE PROBLEM WITH THE FED'S MONETARY POLICY IS THAT--
EXCUSE ME, WANDA--WOULD YOU LIKE A SNICKERS™ BRAND CANDY BAR?
OUR FORMER CARTOON MASCOT SPARKY WAS OCCASIONALLY SHOWN DRIVING A 1958 NASH METROPOLITAN...BUT HIS MORE AFFABLE REPLACEMENT, WILBUR THE TALKING STOMACH, COULD JUST AS EASILY DRIVE A NEW LEXUS OR ACURA...IF YOU KNOW WHAT WE MEAN...
AND WE THINK YOU DO!
HOWEVER, WE SHOULD MAKE ONE THING CLEAR UP FRONT: NO MATTER HOW MUCH MONEY WE MIGHT BE OFFERED, WE WOULD NEVER ALLOW THE INTEGRITY OF THIS STRIP TO BE COMPROMISED...
YOUR MESSAGE
HERE
OF COURSE, THERE'S NO REASON OUR WORD BALLOONS HAVE TO BE SO LARGE!
AFTER ALL--MOST PEOPLE OWN MAGNIFYING GLASSES!
TOM TOMORROW© 8-21-96

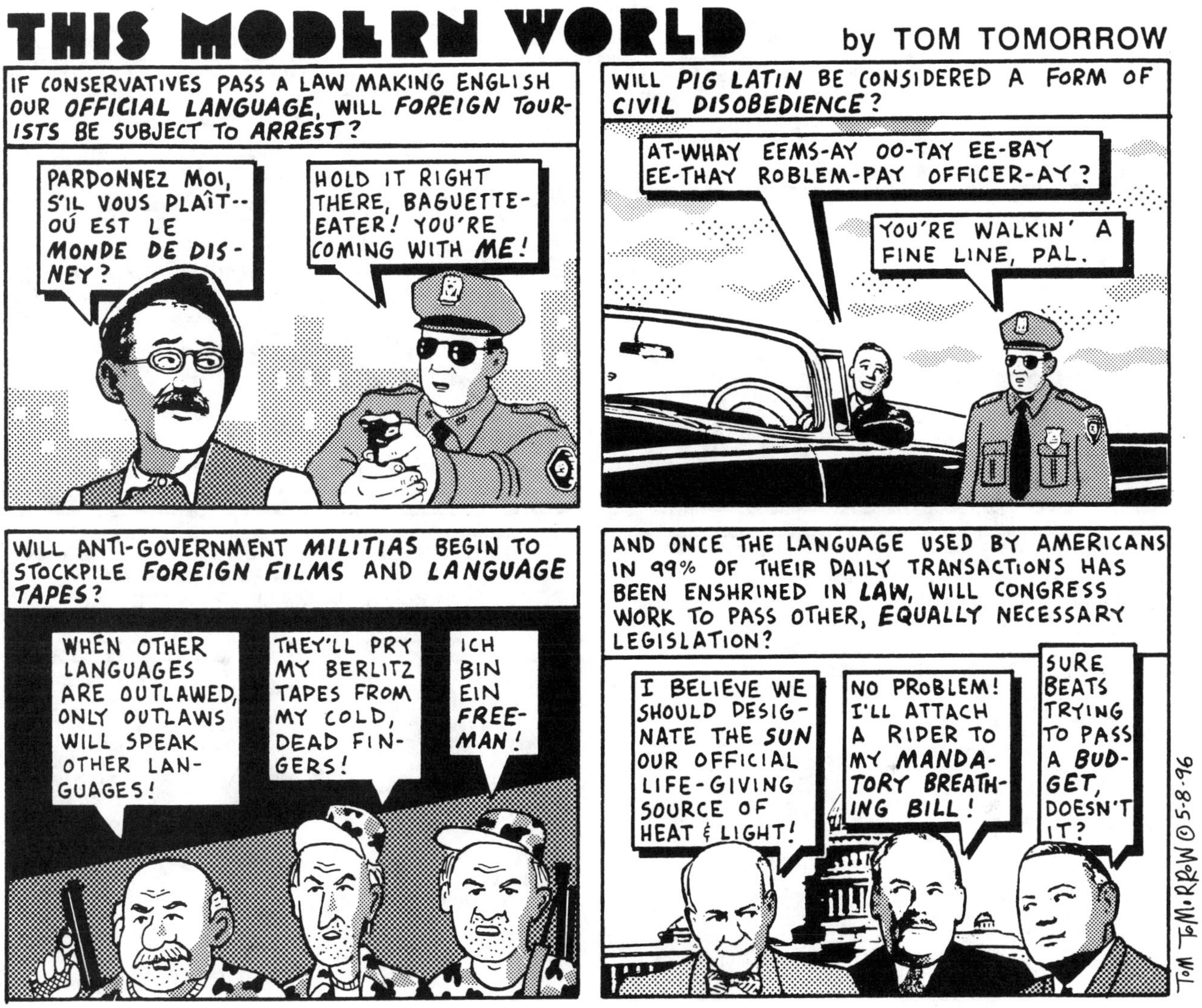
THIS MODERN WORLD
by TOM TOMORROW
IF CONSERVATIVES PASS A LAW MAKING ENGLISH OUR OFFICIAL LANGUAGE, WILL FOREIGN TOURISTS BE SUBJECT TO ARREST?
PARDONNEZ MOI, S'IL VOUS PLAÎT-- OÚ EST LE MONDE DE DISNEY?
HOLD IT RIGHT THERE, BAGUETTE-EATER! YOU'RE COMING WITH ME!
WILL PIG LATIN BE CONSIDERED A FORM OF CIVIL DISOBEDIENCE?
AT-WHAY EEMS-AY OO-TAY EE-BAY EE-THAY ROBLEM-PAY OFFICER-AY?
YOU'RE WALKIN' A FINE LINE, PAL.
WILL ANTI-GOVERNMENT MILITIAS BEGIN TO STOCKPILE FOREIGN FILMS AND LANGUAGE TAPES?
WHEN OTHER LANGUAGES ARE OUTLAWED, ONLY OUTLAWS WILL SPEAK OTHER LANGUAGES!
THEY'LL PRY MY BERLITZ TAPES FROM MY COLD, DEAD FINGERS!
ICH BIN EIN FREE-MAN!
AND ONCE THE LANGUAGE USED BY AMERICANS IN 99% OF THEIR DAILY TRANSACTIONS HAS BEEN ENSHRINED IN LAW, WILL CONGRESS WORK TO PASS OTHER, EQUALLY NECESSARY LEGISLATION?
I BELIEVE WE SHOULD DESIGNATE THE SUN OUR OFFICIAL LIFE-GIVING SOURCE OF HEAT & LIGHT!
NO PROBLEM! I'LL ATTACH A RIDER TO MY MANDATORY BREATHING BILL!
SURE BEATS TRYING TO PASS A BUDGET, DOESN'T IT?
TOM TOMORROW © 5-8-96

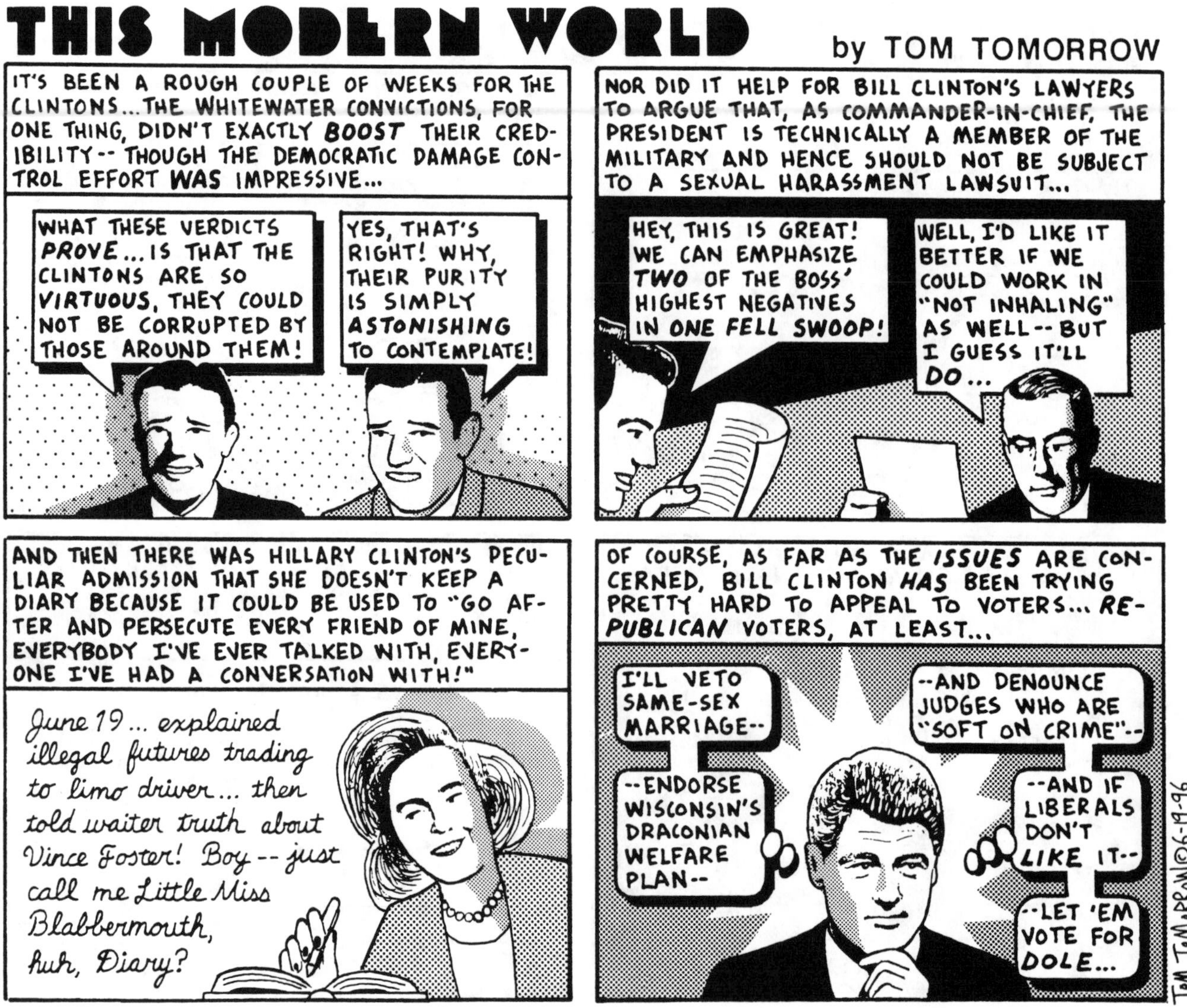
THIS MODERN WORLD
by TOM TOMORROW
IT'S BEEN A ROUGH COUPLE OF WEEKS FOR THE CLINTONS... THE WHITEWATER CONVICTIONS, FOR ONE THING, DIDN'T EXACTLY BOOST THEIR CREDIBILITY -- THOUGH THE DEMOCRATIC DAMAGE CONTROL EFFORT WAS IMPRESSIVE...
WHAT THESE VERDICTS PROVE... IS THAT THE CLINTONS ARE SO VIRTUOUS, THEY COULD NOT BE CORRUPTED BY THOSE AROUND THEM!
YES, THAT'S RIGHT! WHY, THEIR PURITY IS SIMPLY ASTONISHING TO CONTEMPLATE!
NOR DID IT HELP FOR BILL CLINTON'S LAWYERS TO ARGUE THAT, AS COMMANDER-IN-CHIEF, THE PRESIDENT IS TECHNICALLY A MEMBER OF THE MILITARY AND HENCE SHOULD NOT BE SUBJECT TO A SEXUAL HARASSMENT LAWSUIT...
HEY, THIS IS GREAT! WE CAN EMPHASIZE TWO OF THE BOSS' HIGHEST NEGATIVES IN ONE FELL SWOOP!
WELL, I'D LIKE IT BETTER IF WE COULD WORK IN "NOT INHALING" AS WELL -- BUT I GUESS IT'LL DO...
AND THEN THERE WAS HILLARY CLINTON'S PECULIAR ADMISSION THAT SHE DOESN'T KEEP A DIARY BECAUSE IT COULD BE USED TO "GO AFTER AND PERSECUTE EVERY FRIEND OF MINE, EVERYBODY I'VE EVER TALKED WITH, EVERYONE I'VE HAD A CONVERSATION WITH!"
June 19 ... explained illegal futures trading to limo driver ... then told waiter truth about Vince Foster! Boy -- just call me Little Miss Blabbermouth, huh, Diary?
OF COURSE, AS FAR AS THE ISSUES ARE CONCERNED, BILL CLINTON HAS BEEN TRYING PRETTY HARD TO APPEAL TO VOTERS... REPUBLICAN VOTERS, AT LEAST...
I'LL VETO SAME-SEX MARRIAGE--
--ENDORSE WISCONSIN'S DRACONIAN WELFARE PLAN--
--AND DENOUNCE JUDGES WHO ARE "SOFT ON CRIME"--
--AND IF LIBERALS DON'T LIKE IT--
--LET 'EM VOTE FOR DOLE...
TOM TOMORROW©6-19-96

THIS MODERN WORLD

by TOM TOMORROW

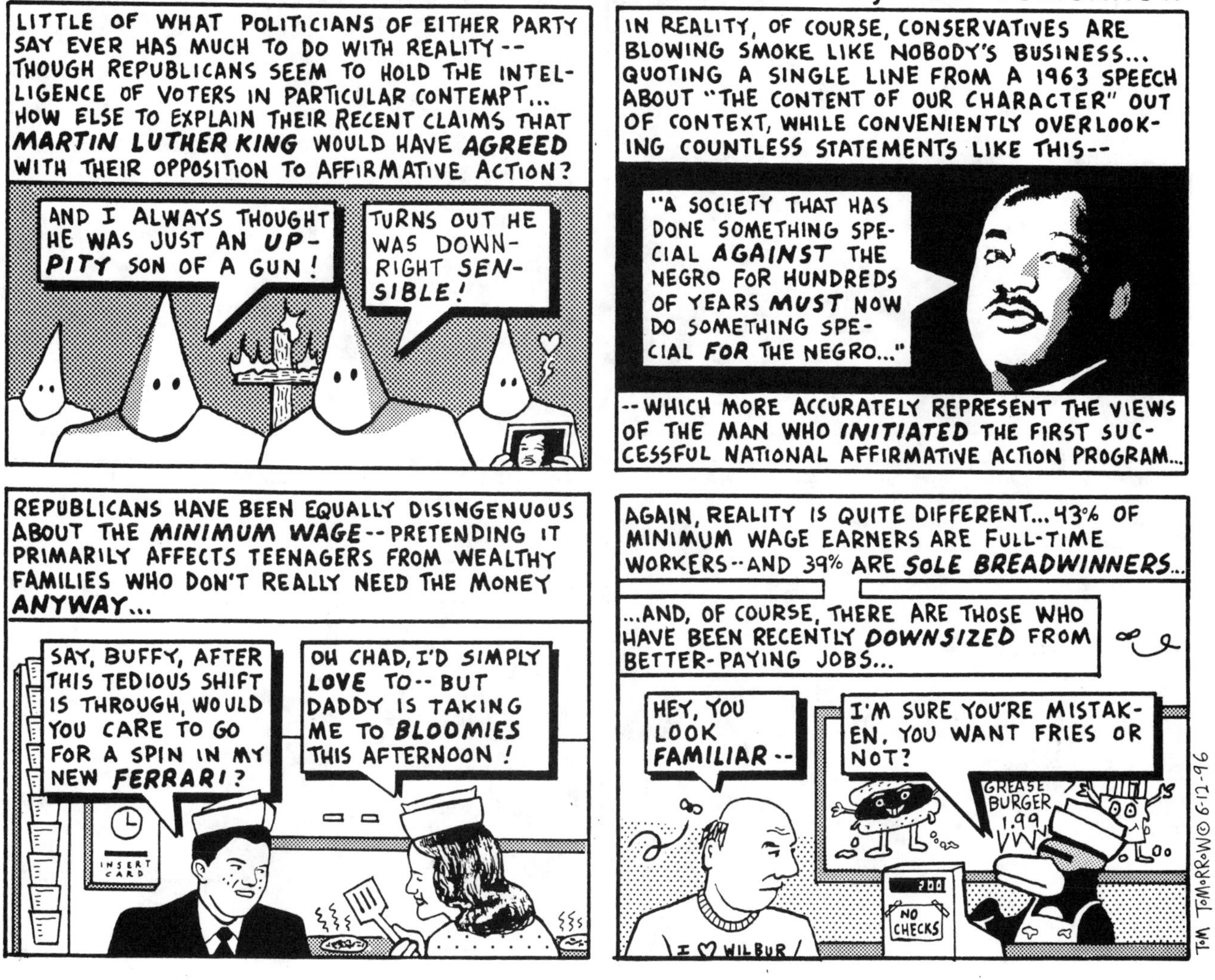
LITTLE OF WHAT POLITICIANS OF EITHER PARTY SAY EVER HAS MUCH TO DO WITH REALITY -- THOUGH REPUBLICANS SEEM TO HOLD THE INTELLIGENCE OF VOTERS IN PARTICULAR CONTEMPT... HOW ELSE TO EXPLAIN THEIR RECENT CLAIMS THAT MARTIN LUTHER KING WOULD HAVE AGREED WITH THEIR OPPOSITION TO AFFIRMATIVE ACTION?
AND I ALWAYS THOUGHT HE WAS JUST AN UPPITY SON OF A GUN!
TURNS OUT HE WAS DOWNRIGHT SENSIBLE!
IN REALITY, OF COURSE, CONSERVATIVES ARE BLOWING SMOKE LIKE NOBODY'S BUSINESS... QUOTING A SINGLE LINE FROM A 1963 SPEECH ABOUT "THE CONTENT OF OUR CHARACTER" OUT OF CONTEXT, WHILE CONVENIENTLY OVERLOOKING COUNTLESS STATEMENTS LIKE THIS--
"A SOCIETY THAT HAS DONE SOMETHING SPECIAL AGAINST THE NEGRO FOR HUNDREDS OF YEARS MUST NOW DO SOMETHING SPECIAL FOR THE NEGRO..."
--WHICH MORE ACCURATELY REPRESENT THE VIEWS OF THE MAN WHO INITIATED THE FIRST SUCCESSFUL NATIONAL AFFIRMATIVE ACTION PROGRAM...
REPUBLICANS HAVE BEEN EQUALLY DISINGENUOUS ABOUT THE MINIMUM WAGE -- PRETENDING IT PRIMARILY AFFECTS TEENAGERS FROM WEALTHY FAMILIES WHO DON'T REALLY NEED THE MONEY ANYWAY...
SAY, BUFFY, AFTER THIS TEDIOUS SHIFT IS THROUGH, WOULD YOU CARE TO GO FOR A SPIN IN MY NEW FERRARI?
OH CHAD, I'D SIMPLY LOVE TO -- BUT DADDY IS TAKING ME TO BLOOMIES THIS AFTERNOON!
INSERT CARD
AGAIN, REALITY IS QUITE DIFFERENT... 43% OF MINIMUM WAGE EARNERS ARE FULL-TIME WORKERS -- AND 39% ARE SOLE BREADWINNERS...
...AND, OF COURSE, THERE ARE THOSE WHO HAVE BEEN RECENTLY DOWNSIZED FROM BETTER-PAYING JOBS...
HEY, YOU LOOK FAMILIAR --
I'M SURE YOU'RE MISTAKEN. YOU WANT FRIES OR NOT?
GREASE BURGER 1.99
NO CHECKS
I ♡ WILBUR
TOM TOMORROW © 6-12-96

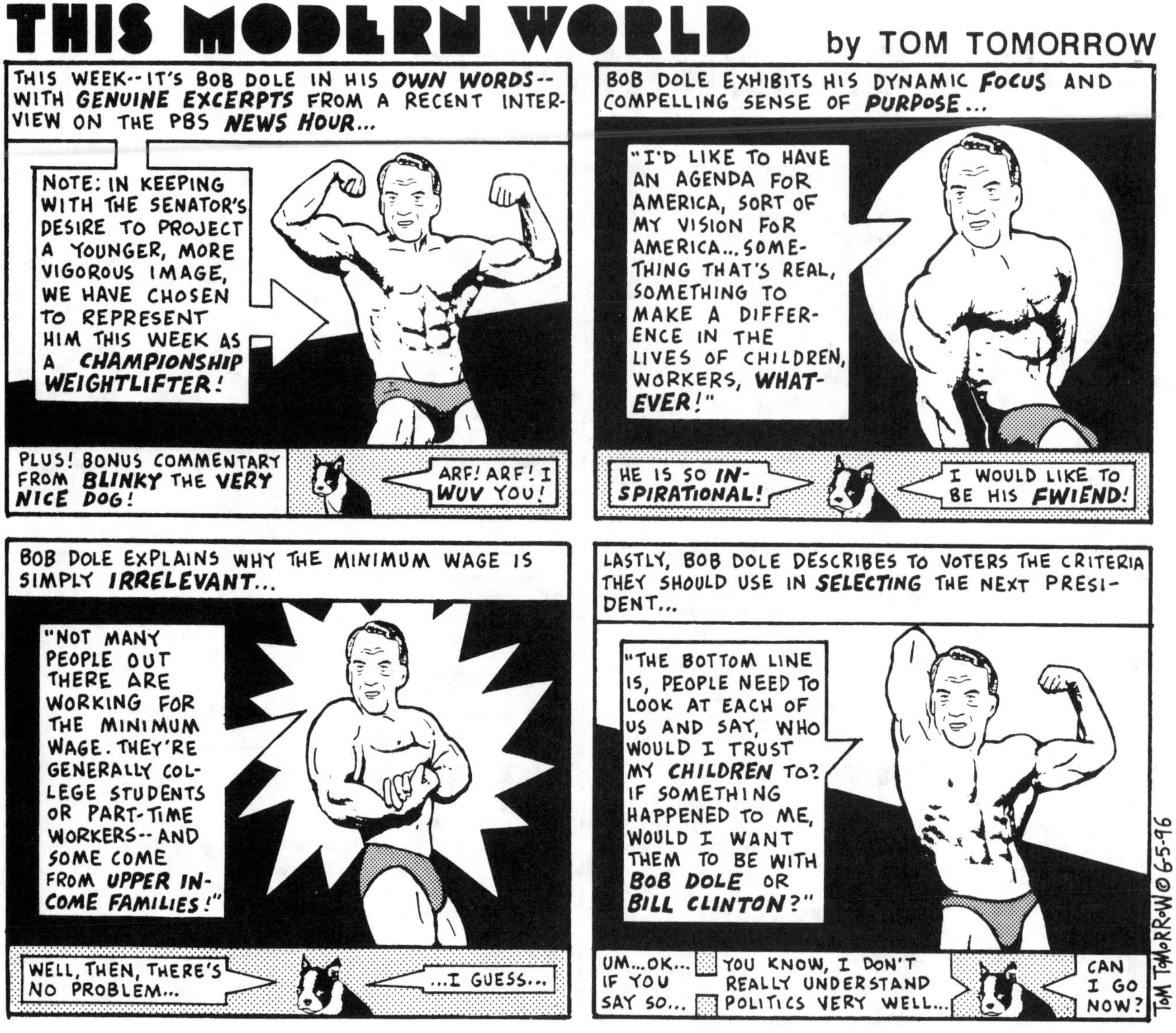
THIS MODERN WORLD
by TOM TOMORROW
THIS WEEK--IT'S BOB DOLE IN HIS OWN WORDS--WITH GENUINE EXCERPTS FROM A RECENT INTERVIEW ON THE PBS NEWS HOUR...
NOTE: IN KEEPING WITH THE SENATOR'S DESIRE TO PROJECT A YOUNGER, MORE VIGOROUS IMAGE, WE HAVE CHOSEN TO REPRESENT HIM THIS WEEK AS A CHAMPIONSHIP WEIGHTLIFTER!
PLUS! BONUS COMMENTARY FROM BLINKY THE VERY NICE DOG!
ARF! ARF! I WUV YOU!
BOB DOLE EXHIBITS HIS DYNAMIC FOCUS AND COMPELLING SENSE OF PURPOSE...
"I'D LIKE TO HAVE AN AGENDA FOR AMERICA, SORT OF MY VISION FOR AMERICA... SOMETHING THAT'S REAL, SOMETHING TO MAKE A DIFFERENCE IN THE LIVES OF CHILDREN, WORKERS, WHATEVER!"
HE IS SO INSPIRATIONAL!
I WOULD LIKE TO BE HIS FWIEND!
BOB DOLE EXPLAINS WHY THE MINIMUM WAGE IS SIMPLY IRRELEVANT...
"NOT MANY PEOPLE OUT THERE ARE WORKING FOR THE MINIMUM WAGE. THEY'RE GENERALLY COLLEGE STUDENTS OR PART-TIME WORKERS--AND SOME COME FROM UPPER INCOME FAMILIES!"
WELL, THEN, THERE'S NO PROBLEM...
...I GUESS...
LASTLY, BOB DOLE DESCRIBES TO VOTERS THE CRITERIA THEY SHOULD USE IN SELECTING THE NEXT PRESIDENT...
"THE BOTTOM LINE IS, PEOPLE NEED TO LOOK AT EACH OF US AND SAY, WHO WOULD I TRUST MY CHILDREN TO? IF SOMETHING HAPPENED TO ME, WOULD I WANT THEM TO BE WITH BOB DOLE OR BILL CLINTON?"
UM...OK... IF YOU SAY SO...
YOU KNOW, I DON'T REALLY UNDERSTAND POLITICS VERY WELL...
CAN I GO NOW?
TOM TOMORROW © 6-5-96

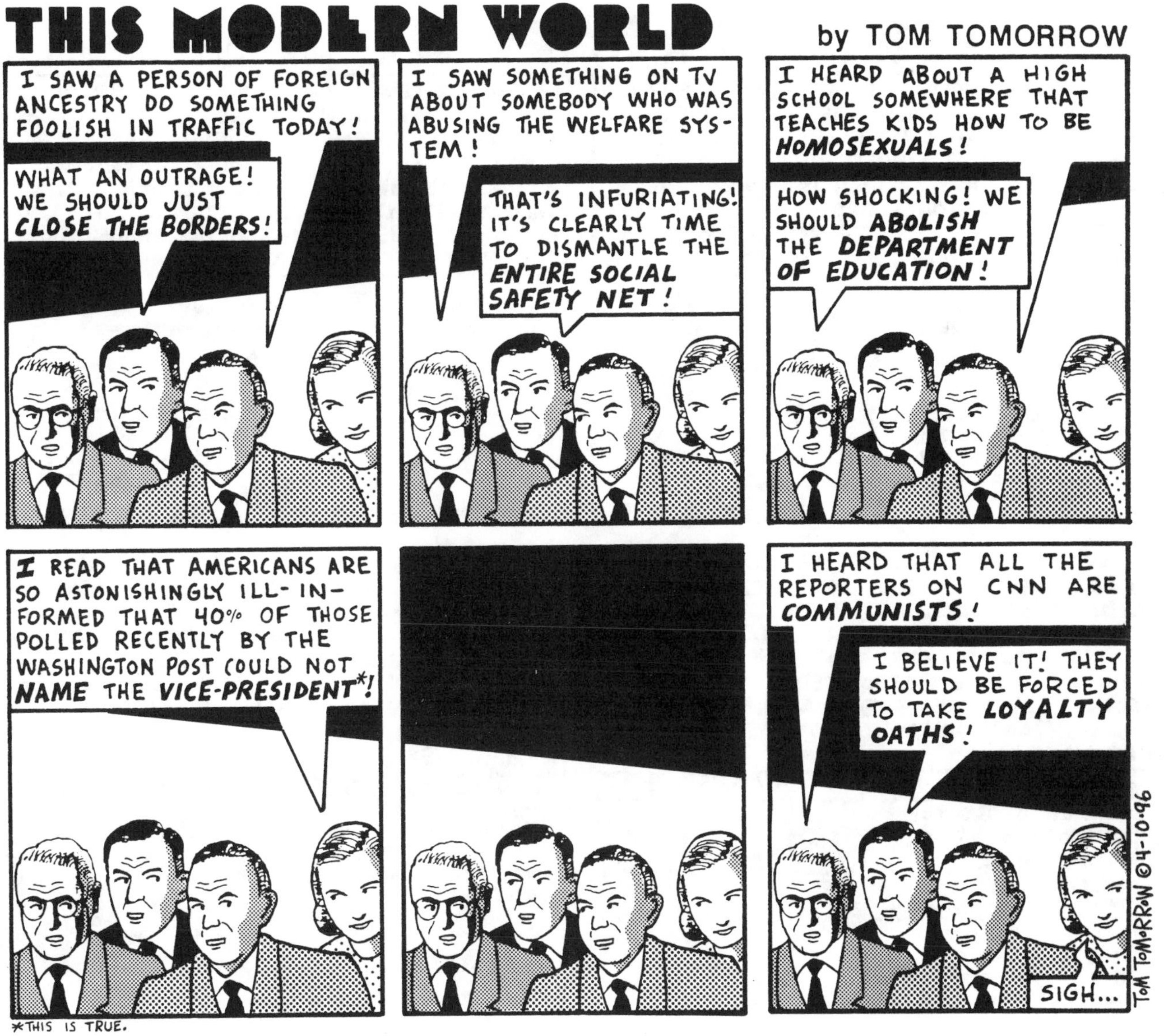
THIS MODERN WORLD
by TOM TOMORROW
I SAW A PERSON OF FOREIGN ANCESTRY DO SOMETHING FOOLISH IN TRAFFIC TODAY!
WHAT AN OUTRAGE! WE SHOULD JUST CLOSE THE BORDERS!
I SAW SOMETHING ON TV ABOUT SOMEBODY WHO WAS ABUSING THE WELFARE SYSTEM!
THAT'S INFURIATING! IT'S CLEARLY TIME TO DISMANTLE THE ENTIRE SOCIAL SAFETY NET!
I HEARD ABOUT A HIGH SCHOOL SOMEWHERE THAT TEACHES KIDS HOW TO BE HOMOSEXUALS!
HOW SHOCKING! WE SHOULD ABOLISH THE DEPARTMENT OF EDUCATION!
I READ THAT AMERICANS ARE SO ASTONISHINGLY ILL-INFORMED THAT 40% OF THOSE POLLED RECENTLY BY THE WASHINGTON POST COULD NOT NAME THE VICE-PRESIDENT*!
I HEARD THAT ALL THE REPORTERS ON CNN ARE COMMUNISTS!
I BELIEVE IT! THEY SHOULD BE FORCED TO TAKE LOYALTY OATHS!
SIGH...
TOM TOMORROW ©4-10-96
*THIS IS TRUE.

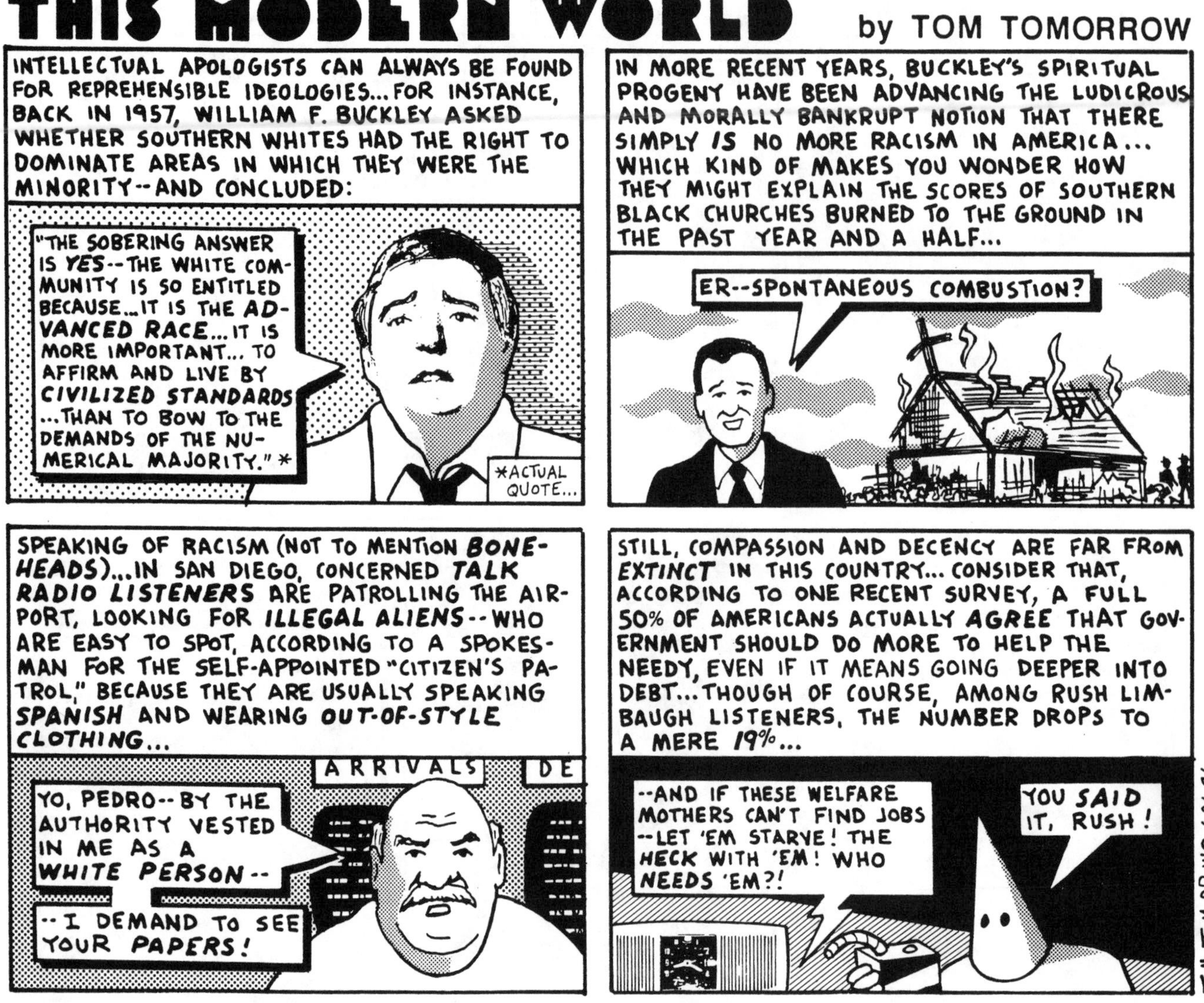
THIS MODERN WORLD by TOM TOMORROW
INTELLECTUAL APOLOGISTS CAN ALWAYS BE FOUND FOR REPREHENSIBLE IDEOLOGIES... FOR INSTANCE, BACK IN 1957, WILLIAM F. BUCKLEY ASKED WHETHER SOUTHERN WHITES HAD THE RIGHT TO DOMINATE AREAS IN WHICH THEY WERE THE MINORITY--AND CONCLUDED:
"THE SOBERING ANSWER IS YES--THE WHITE COMMUNITY IS SO ENTITLED BECAUSE...IT IS THE ADVANCED RACE... IT IS MORE IMPORTANT... TO AFFIRM AND LIVE BY CIVILIZED STANDARDS ...THAN TO BOW TO THE DEMANDS OF THE NUMERICAL MAJORITY." *
*ACTUAL QUOTE...
IN MORE RECENT YEARS, BUCKLEY'S SPIRITUAL PROGENY HAVE BEEN ADVANCING THE LUDICROUS AND MORALLY BANKRUPT NOTION THAT THERE SIMPLY IS NO MORE RACISM IN AMERICA... WHICH KIND OF MAKES YOU WONDER HOW THEY MIGHT EXPLAIN THE SCORES OF SOUTHERN BLACK CHURCHES BURNED TO THE GROUND IN THE PAST YEAR AND A HALF...
ER--SPONTANEOUS COMBUSTION?
SPEAKING OF RACISM (NOT TO MENTION BONEHEADS)...IN SAN DIEGO, CONCERNED TALK RADIO LISTENERS ARE PATROLLING THE AIRPORT, LOOKING FOR ILLEGAL ALIENS--WHO ARE EASY TO SPOT, ACCORDING TO A SPOKESMAN FOR THE SELF-APPOINTED "CITIZEN'S PATROL," BECAUSE THEY ARE USUALLY SPEAKING SPANISH AND WEARING OUT-OF-STYLE CLOTHING...
ARRIVALS
DE
YO, PEDRO--BY THE AUTHORITY VESTED IN ME AS A WHITE PERSON--
--I DEMAND TO SEE YOUR PAPERS!
STILL, COMPASSION AND DECENCY ARE FAR FROM EXTINCT IN THIS COUNTRY... CONSIDER THAT, ACCORDING TO ONE RECENT SURVEY, A FULL 50% OF AMERICANS ACTUALLY AGREE THAT GOVERNMENT SHOULD DO MORE TO HELP THE NEEDY, EVEN IF IT MEANS GOING DEEPER INTO DEBT... THOUGH OF COURSE, AMONG RUSH LIMBAUGH LISTENERS, THE NUMBER DROPS TO A MERE 19%...
--AND IF THESE WELFARE MOTHERS CAN'T FIND JOBS --LET 'EM STARVE! THE HECK WITH 'EM! WHO NEEDS 'EM?!
YOU SAID IT, RUSH!
TOM TOMORROW© 6-26-96

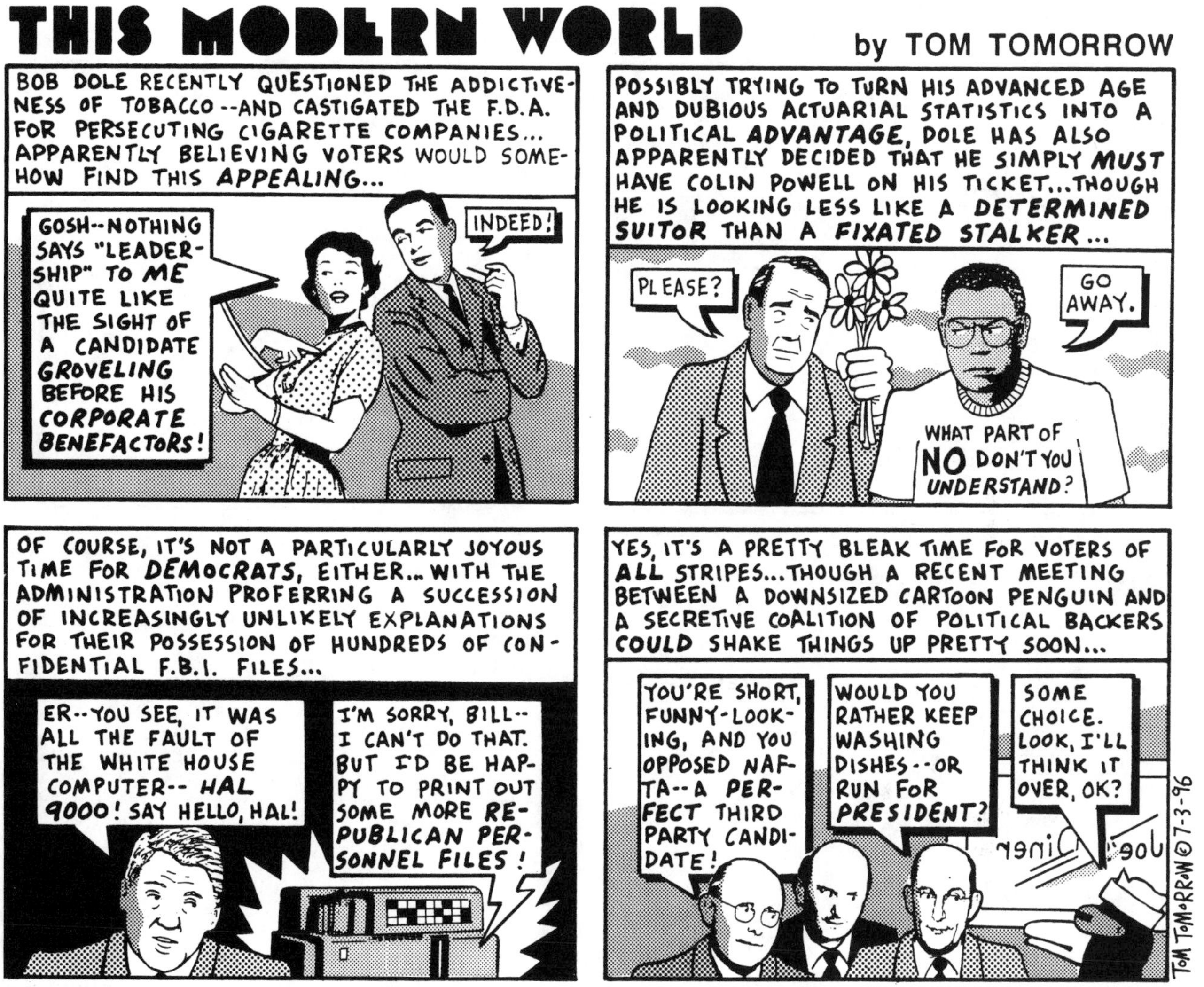
THIS MODERN WORLD
by TOM TOMORROW
BOB DOLE RECENTLY QUESTIONED THE ADDICTIVENESS OF TOBACCO--AND CASTIGATED THE F.D.A. FOR PERSECUTING CIGARETTE COMPANIES... APPARENTLY BELIEVING VOTERS WOULD SOMEHOW FIND THIS APPEALING...
GOSH--NOTHING SAYS "LEADERSHIP" TO ME QUITE LIKE THE SIGHT OF A CANDIDATE GROVELING BEFORE HIS CORPORATE BENEFACTORS!
INDEED!
POSSIBLY TRYING TO TURN HIS ADVANCED AGE AND DUBIOUS ACTUARIAL STATISTICS INTO A POLITICAL ADVANTAGE, DOLE HAS ALSO APPARENTLY DECIDED THAT HE SIMPLY MUST HAVE COLIN POWELL ON HIS TICKET...THOUGH HE IS LOOKING LESS LIKE A DETERMINED SUITOR THAN A FIXATED STALKER...
PLEASE?
GO AWAY.
WHAT PART OF NO DON'T YOU UNDERSTAND?
OF COURSE, IT'S NOT A PARTICULARLY JOYOUS TIME FOR DEMOCRATS, EITHER... WITH THE ADMINISTRATION PROFERRING A SUCCESSION OF INCREASINGLY UNLIKELY EXPLANATIONS FOR THEIR POSSESSION OF HUNDREDS OF CONFIDENTIAL F.B.I. FILES...
ER--YOU SEE, IT WAS ALL THE FAULT OF THE WHITE HOUSE COMPUTER-- HAL 9000! SAY HELLO, HAL!
I'M SORRY, BILL-- I CAN'T DO THAT. BUT I'D BE HAPPY TO PRINT OUT SOME MORE REPUBLICAN PERSONNEL FILES!
YES, IT'S A PRETTY BLEAK TIME FOR VOTERS OF ALL STRIPES...THOUGH A RECENT MEETING BETWEEN A DOWNSIZED CARTOON PENGUIN AND A SECRETIVE COALITION OF POLITICAL BACKERS COULD SHAKE THINGS UP PRETTY SOON...
YOU'RE SHORT, FUNNY-LOOKING, AND YOU OPPOSED NAFTA--A PERFECT THIRD PARTY CANDIDATE!
WOULD YOU RATHER KEEP WASHING DISHES--OR RUN FOR PRESIDENT?
SOME CHOICE. LOOK, I'LL THINK IT OVER, OK?
TOM TOMORROW © 7-3-96

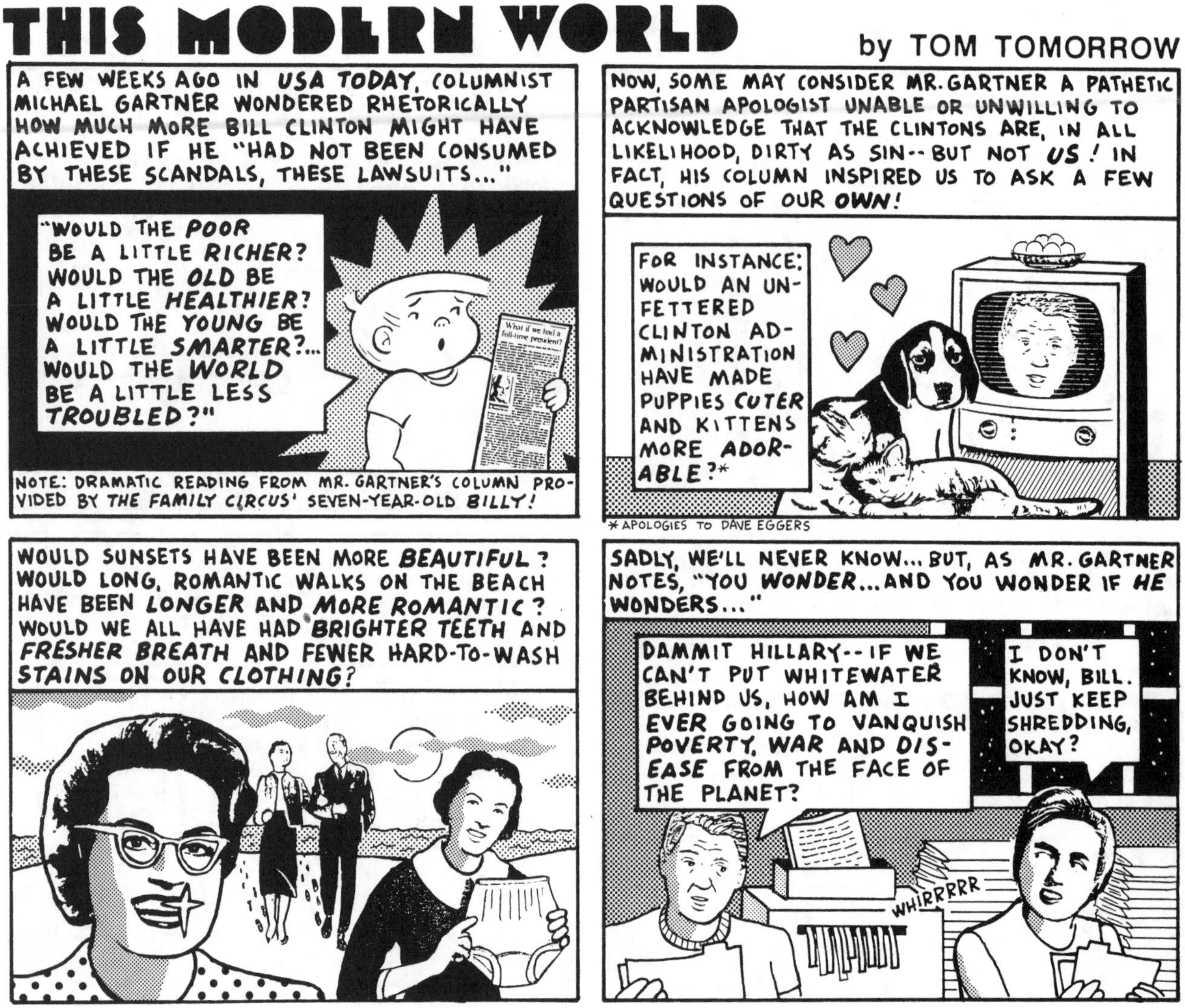

THIS MODERN WORLD
by TOM TOMORROW
A FEW WEEKS AGO IN USA TODAY, COLUMNIST MICHAEL GARTNER WONDERED RHETORICALLY HOW MUCH MORE BILL CLINTON MIGHT HAVE ACHIEVED IF HE "HAD NOT BEEN CONSUMED BY THESE SCANDALS, THESE LAWSUITS..."
"WOULD THE POOR BE A LITTLE RICHER? WOULD THE OLD BE A LITTLE HEALTHIER? WOULD THE YOUNG BE A LITTLE SMARTER?... WOULD THE WORLD BE A LITTLE LESS TROUBLED?"
What if we had a full-time president?
NOTE: DRAMATIC READING FROM MR. GARTNER'S COLUMN PROVIDED BY THE FAMILY CIRCUS' SEVEN-YEAR-OLD BILLY!
NOW, SOME MAY CONSIDER MR. GARTNER A PATHETIC PARTISAN APOLOGIST UNABLE OR UNWILLING TO ACKNOWLEDGE THAT THE CLINTONS ARE, IN ALL LIKELIHOOD, DIRTY AS SIN-- BUT NOT US! IN FACT, HIS COLUMN INSPIRED US TO ASK A FEW QUESTIONS OF OUR OWN!
FOR INSTANCE: WOULD AN UNFETTERED CLINTON ADMINISTRATION HAVE MADE PUPPIES CUTER AND KITTENS MORE ADORABLE?*
* APOLOGIES TO DAVE EGGERS
WOULD SUNSETS HAVE BEEN MORE BEAUTIFUL? WOULD LONG, ROMANTIC WALKS ON THE BEACH HAVE BEEN LONGER AND MORE ROMANTIC? WOULD WE ALL HAVE HAD BRIGHTER TEETH AND FRESHER BREATH AND FEWER HARD-TO-WASH STAINS ON OUR CLOTHING?
SADLY, WE'LL NEVER KNOW... BUT, AS MR. GARTNER NOTES, "YOU WONDER... AND YOU WONDER IF HE WONDERS..."
DAMMIT HILLARY-- IF WE CAN'T PUT WHITEWATER BEHIND US, HOW AM I EVER GOING TO VANQUISH POVERTY, WAR AND DISEASE FROM THE FACE OF THE PLANET?
I DON'T KNOW, BILL. JUST KEEP SHREDDING, OKAY?
WHIRRRRR

THIS MODERN WORLD

by TOM TOMORROW

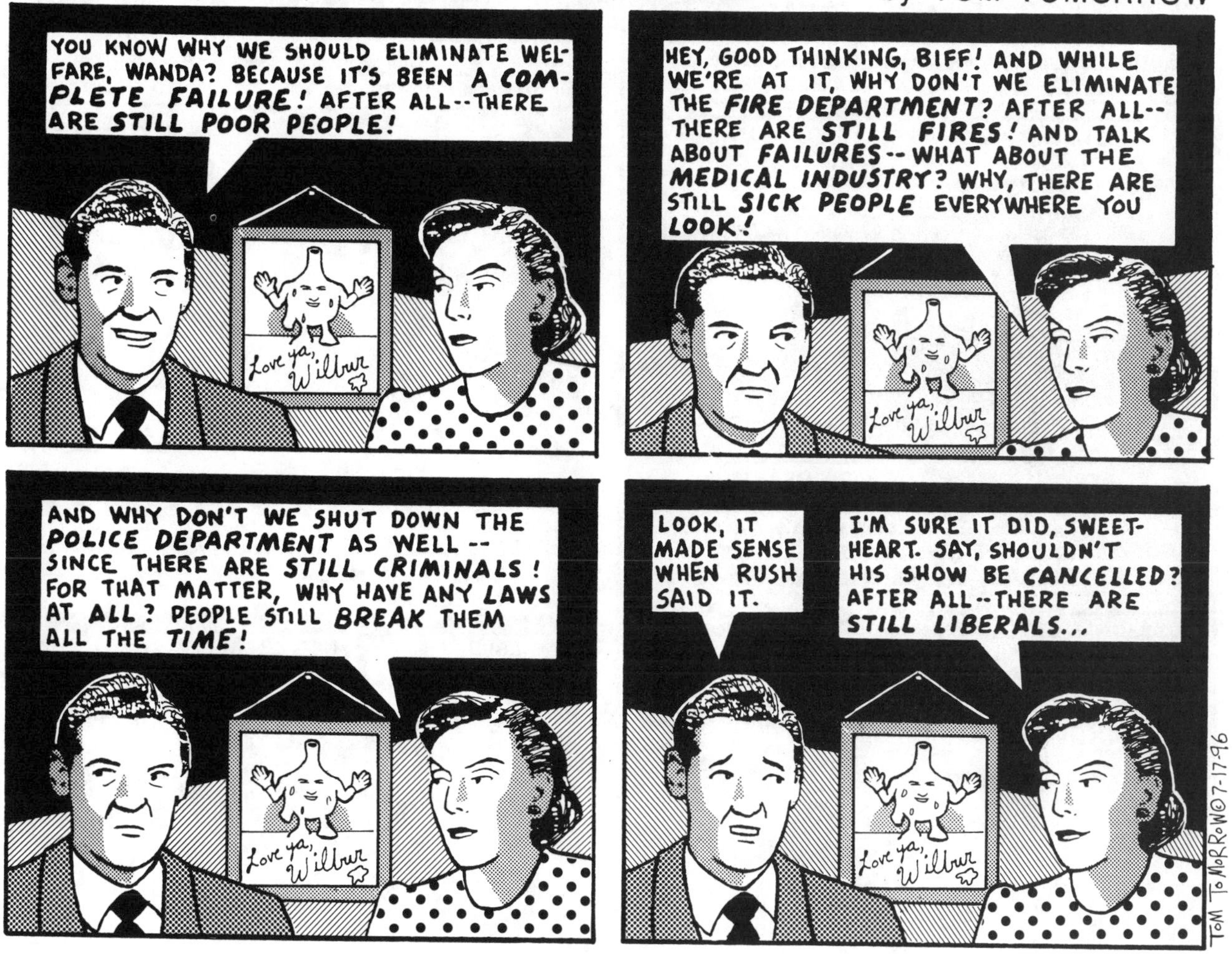
YOU KNOW WHY WE SHOULD ELIMINATE WELFARE, WANDA? BECAUSE IT'S BEEN A COMPLETE FAILURE! AFTER ALL--THERE ARE STILL POOR PEOPLE!
Love ya, Wilbur
HEY, GOOD THINKING, BIFF! AND WHILE WE'RE AT IT, WHY DON'T WE ELIMINATE THE FIRE DEPARTMENT? AFTER ALL--THERE ARE STILL FIRES! AND TALK ABOUT FAILURES--WHAT ABOUT THE MEDICAL INDUSTRY? WHY, THERE ARE STILL SICK PEOPLE EVERYWHERE YOU LOOK!
AND WHY DON'T WE SHUT DOWN THE POLICE DEPARTMENT AS WELL--SINCE THERE ARE STILL CRIMINALS! FOR THAT MATTER, WHY HAVE ANY LAWS AT ALL? PEOPLE STILL BREAK THEM ALL THE TIME!
LOOK, IT MADE SENSE WHEN RUSH SAID IT.
I'M SURE IT DID, SWEETHEART. SAY, SHOULDN'T HIS SHOW BE CANCELLED? AFTER ALL--THERE ARE STILL LIBERALS...
TOM TOMORROW©7-17-96

THIS MODERN WORLD

by TOM TOMORROW

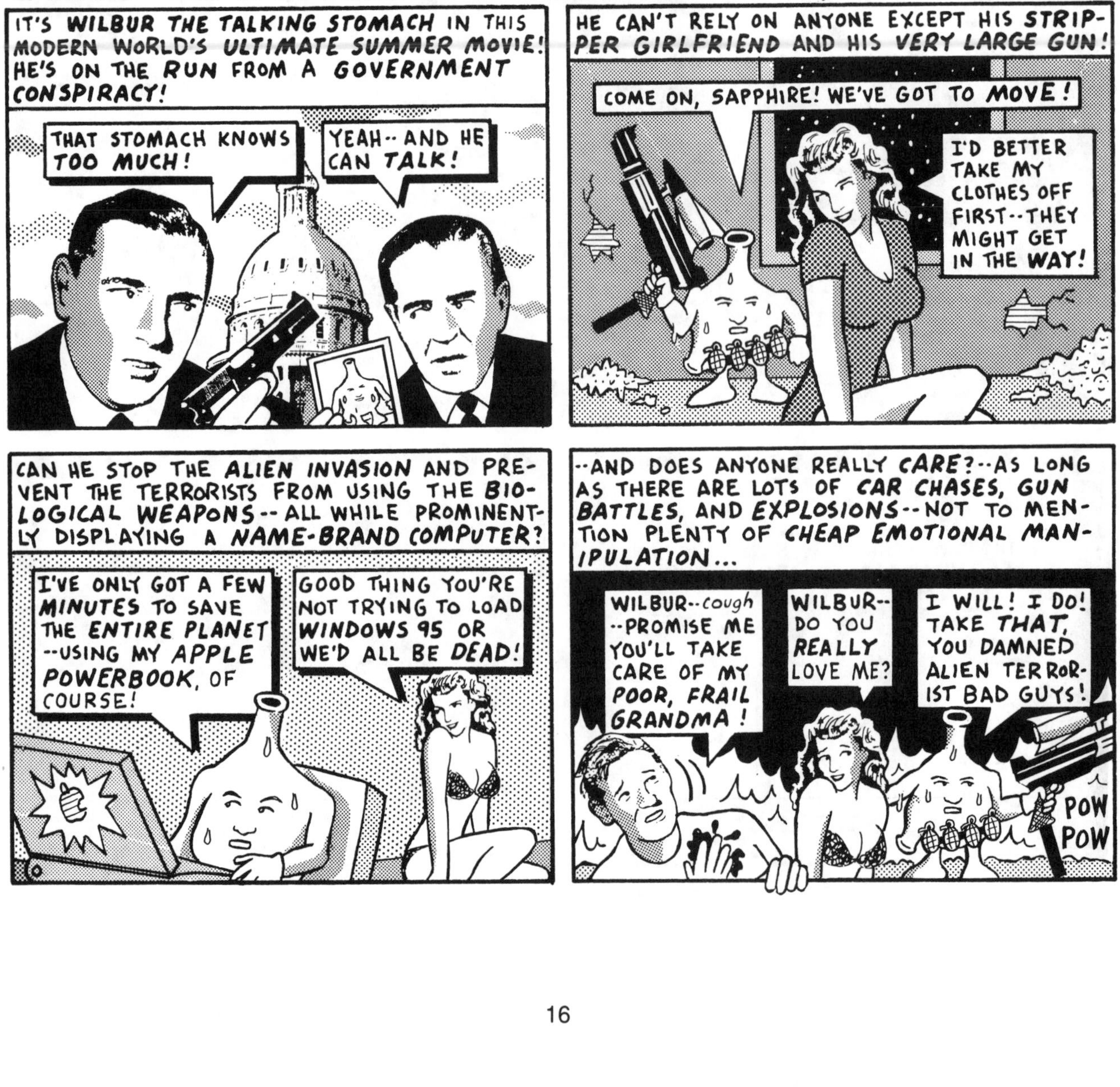
IT'S WILBUR THE TALKING STOMACH IN THIS MODERN WORLD'S ULTIMATE SUMMER MOVIE! HE'S ON THE RUN FROM A GOVERNMENT CONSPIRACY!
THAT STOMACH KNOWS TOO MUCH!
YEAH-- AND HE CAN TALK!
HE CAN'T RELY ON ANYONE EXCEPT HIS STRIPPER GIRLFRIEND AND HIS VERY LARGE GUN!
COME ON, SAPPHIRE! WE'VE GOT TO MOVE!
I'D BETTER TAKE MY CLOTHES OFF FIRST--THEY MIGHT GET IN THE WAY!
CAN HE STOP THE ALIEN INVASION AND PREVENT THE TERRORISTS FROM USING THE BIOLOGICAL WEAPONS-- ALL WHILE PROMINENTLY DISPLAYING A NAME-BRAND COMPUTER?
I'VE ONLY GOT A FEW MINUTES TO SAVE THE ENTIRE PLANET --USING MY APPLE POWERBOOK, OF COURSE!
GOOD THING YOU'RE NOT TRYING TO LOAD WINDOWS 95 OR WE'D ALL BE DEAD!
--AND DOES ANYONE REALLY CARE?--AS LONG AS THERE ARE LOTS OF CAR CHASES, GUN BATTLES, AND EXPLOSIONS--NOT TO MENTION PLENTY OF CHEAP EMOTIONAL MANIPULATION...
WILBUR--cough --PROMISE ME YOU'LL TAKE CARE OF MY POOR, FRAIL GRANDMA!
WILBUR-- DO YOU REALLY LOVE ME?
I WILL! I DO! TAKE THAT, YOU DAMNED ALIEN TERRORIST BAD GUYS!
POW POW
TOM TOMORROW © 7-24-96

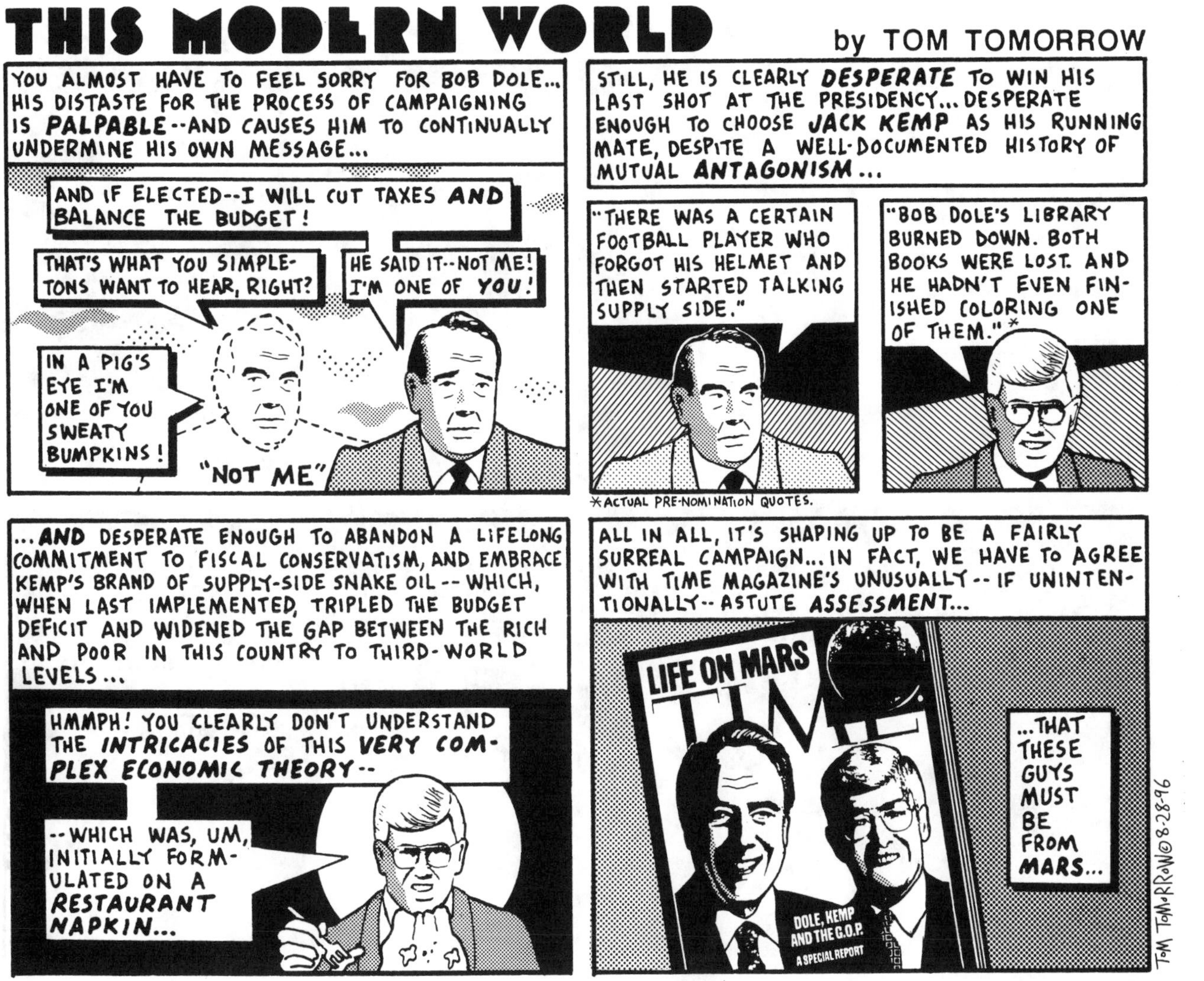
THIS MODERN WORLD
by TOM TOMORROW
YOU ALMOST HAVE TO FEEL SORRY FOR BOB DOLE... HIS DISTASTE FOR THE PROCESS OF CAMPAIGNING IS PALPABLE--AND CAUSES HIM TO CONTINUALLY UNDERMINE HIS OWN MESSAGE...
AND IF ELECTED--I WILL CUT TAXES AND BALANCE THE BUDGET!
THAT'S WHAT YOU SIMPLE-TONS WANT TO HEAR, RIGHT?
HE SAID IT--NOT ME! I'M ONE OF YOU!
IN A PIG'S EYE I'M ONE OF YOU SWEATY BUMPKINS!
"NOT ME"
STILL, HE IS CLEARLY DESPERATE TO WIN HIS LAST SHOT AT THE PRESIDENCY... DESPERATE ENOUGH TO CHOOSE JACK KEMP AS HIS RUNNING MATE, DESPITE A WELL-DOCUMENTED HISTORY OF MUTUAL ANTAGONISM...
"THERE WAS A CERTAIN FOOTBALL PLAYER WHO FORGOT HIS HELMET AND THEN STARTED TALKING SUPPLY SIDE."
"BOB DOLE'S LIBRARY BURNED DOWN. BOTH BOOKS WERE LOST. AND HE HADN'T EVEN FIN-ISHED COLORING ONE OF THEM."*
*ACTUAL PRE-NOMINATION QUOTES.
...AND DESPERATE ENOUGH TO ABANDON A LIFELONG COMMITMENT TO FISCAL CONSERVATISM, AND EMBRACE KEMP'S BRAND OF SUPPLY-SIDE SNAKE OIL -- WHICH, WHEN LAST IMPLEMENTED, TRIPLED THE BUDGET DEFICIT AND WIDENED THE GAP BETWEEN THE RICH AND POOR IN THIS COUNTRY TO THIRD-WORLD LEVELS...
HMMPH! YOU CLEARLY DON'T UNDERSTAND THE INTRICACIES OF THIS VERY COM-PLEX ECONOMIC THEORY--
--WHICH WAS, UM, INITIALLY FORM-ULATED ON A RESTAURANT NAPKIN...
ALL IN ALL, IT'S SHAPING UP TO BE A FAIRLY SURREAL CAMPAIGN... IN FACT, WE HAVE TO AGREE WITH TIME MAGAZINE'S UNUSUALLY -- IF UNINTEN-TIONALLY -- ASTUTE ASSESSMENT...
LIFE ON MARS
TIME
DOLE, KEMP AND THE G.O.P.
A SPECIAL REPORT
...THAT THESE GUYS MUST BE FROM MARS...
TOM TOMORROW©8-28-96

THIS MODERN WORLD

by TOM TOMORROW

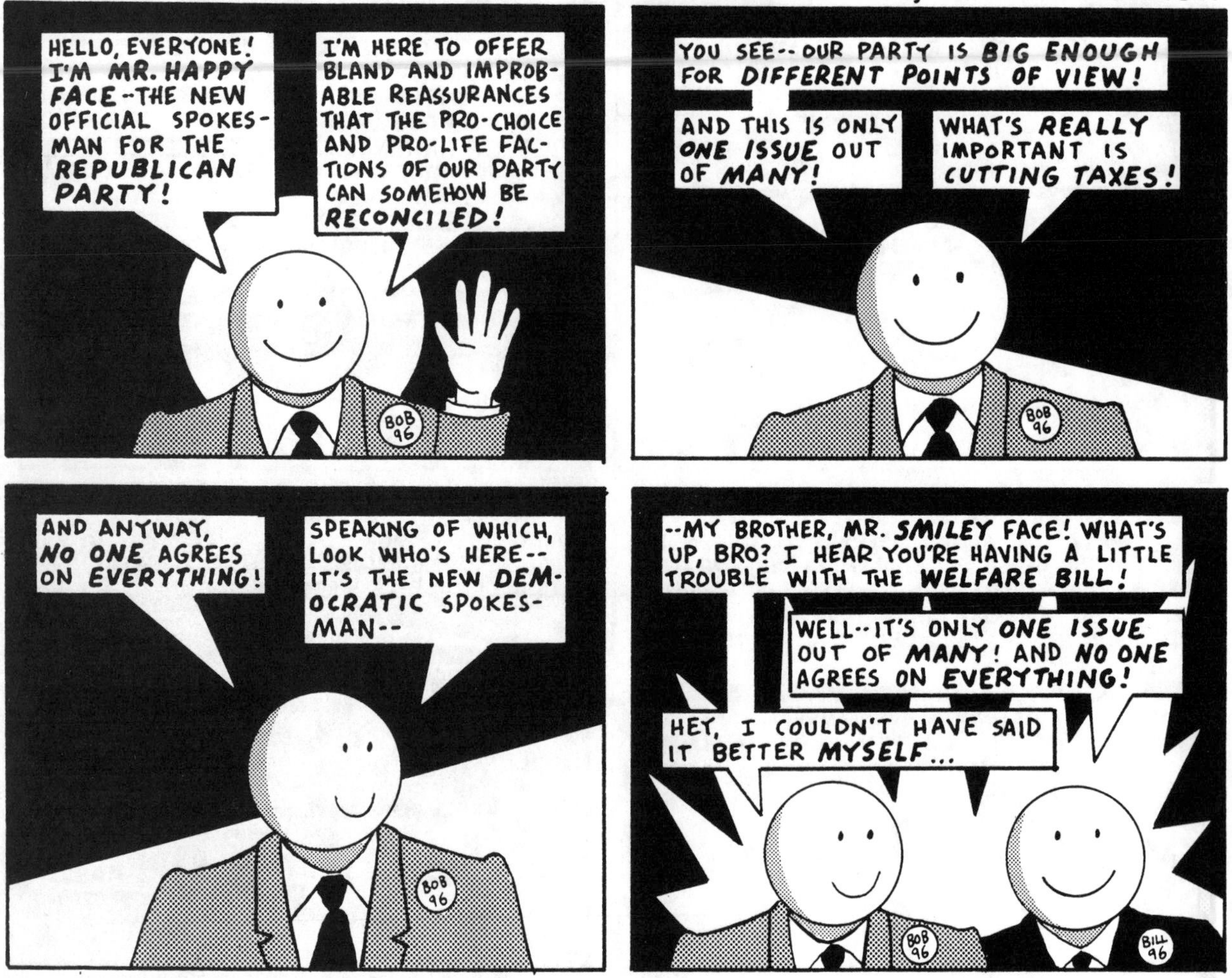
HELLO, EVERYONE! I'M MR. HAPPY FACE--THE NEW OFFICIAL SPOKESMAN FOR THE REPUBLICAN PARTY!
I'M HERE TO OFFER BLAND AND IMPROBABLE REASSURANCES THAT THE PRO-CHOICE AND PRO-LIFE FACTIONS OF OUR PARTY CAN SOMEHOW BE RECONCILED!
BOB 96
YOU SEE--OUR PARTY IS BIG ENOUGH FOR DIFFERENT POINTS OF VIEW!
AND THIS IS ONLY ONE ISSUE OUT OF MANY!
WHAT'S REALLY IMPORTANT IS CUTTING TAXES!
BOB 96
AND ANYWAY, NO ONE AGREES ON EVERYTHING!
SPEAKING OF WHICH, LOOK WHO'S HERE--IT'S THE NEW DEMOCRATIC SPOKESMAN--
BOB 96
--MY BROTHER, MR. SMILEY FACE! WHAT'S UP, BRO? I HEAR YOU'RE HAVING A LITTLE TROUBLE WITH THE WELFARE BILL!
WELL--IT'S ONLY ONE ISSUE OUT OF MANY! AND NO ONE AGREES ON EVERYTHING!
HEY, I COULDN'T HAVE SAID IT BETTER MYSELF...
BOB 96
BILL 96

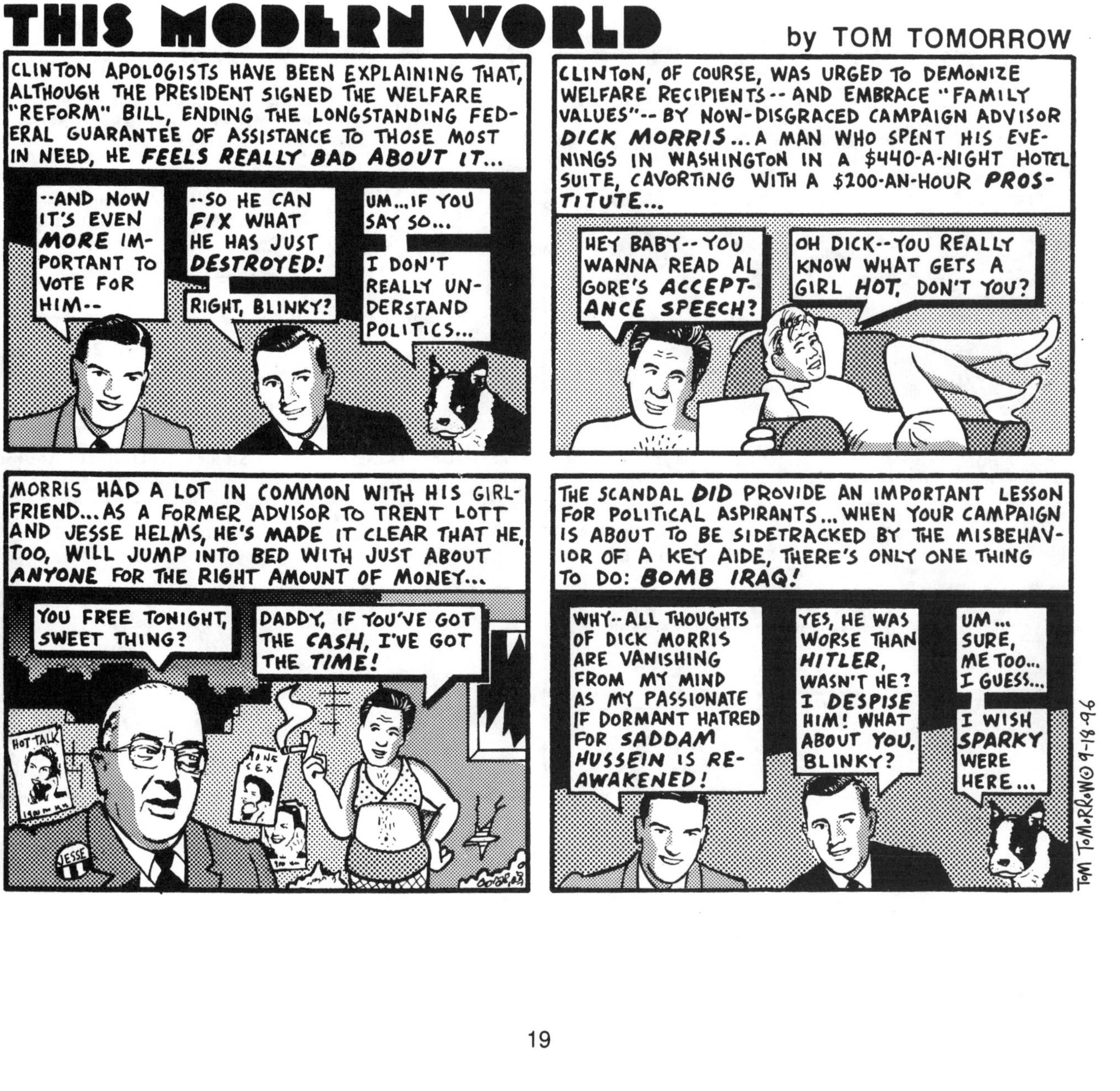
THIS MODERN WORLD
by TOM TOMORROW
CLINTON APOLOGISTS HAVE BEEN EXPLAINING THAT, ALTHOUGH THE PRESIDENT SIGNED THE WELFARE "REFORM" BILL, ENDING THE LONGSTANDING FEDERAL GUARANTEE OF ASSISTANCE TO THOSE MOST IN NEED, HE FEELS REALLY BAD ABOUT IT...
--AND NOW IT'S EVEN MORE IMPORTANT TO VOTE FOR HIM--
--SO HE CAN FIX WHAT HE HAS JUST DESTROYED!
RIGHT, BLINKY?
UM...IF YOU SAY SO...
I DON'T REALLY UNDERSTAND POLITICS...
CLINTON, OF COURSE, WAS URGED TO DEMONIZE WELFARE RECIPIENTS -- AND EMBRACE "FAMILY VALUES" -- BY NOW-DISGRACED CAMPAIGN ADVISOR DICK MORRIS... A MAN WHO SPENT HIS EVENINGS IN WASHINGTON IN A $440-A-NIGHT HOTEL SUITE, CAVORTING WITH A $200-AN-HOUR PROSTITUTE...
HEY BABY-- YOU WANNA READ AL GORE'S ACCEPTANCE SPEECH?
OH DICK--YOU REALLY KNOW WHAT GETS A GIRL HOT, DON'T YOU?
MORRIS HAD A LOT IN COMMON WITH HIS GIRLFRIEND... AS A FORMER ADVISOR TO TRENT LOTT AND JESSE HELMS, HE'S MADE IT CLEAR THAT HE, TOO, WILL JUMP INTO BED WITH JUST ABOUT ANYONE FOR THE RIGHT AMOUNT OF MONEY...
YOU FREE TONIGHT, SWEET THING?
DADDY, IF YOU'VE GOT THE CASH, I'VE GOT THE TIME!
HOT-TALK
JESSE
THE SCANDAL DID PROVIDE AN IMPORTANT LESSON FOR POLITICAL ASPIRANTS... WHEN YOUR CAMPAIGN IS ABOUT TO BE SIDETRACKED BY THE MISBEHAVIOR OF A KEY AIDE, THERE'S ONLY ONE THING TO DO: BOMB IRAQ!
WHY-- ALL THOUGHTS OF DICK MORRIS ARE VANISHING FROM MY MIND AS MY PASSIONATE IF DORMANT HATRED FOR SADDAM HUSSEIN IS REAWAKENED!
YES, HE WAS WORSE THAN HITLER, WASN'T HE? I DESPISE HIM! WHAT ABOUT YOU, BLINKY?
UM... SURE, ME TOO... I GUESS...
I WISH SPARKY WERE HERE...
TOM TOMORROW© 9-18-96

THIS MODERN WORLD

by TOM TOMORROW

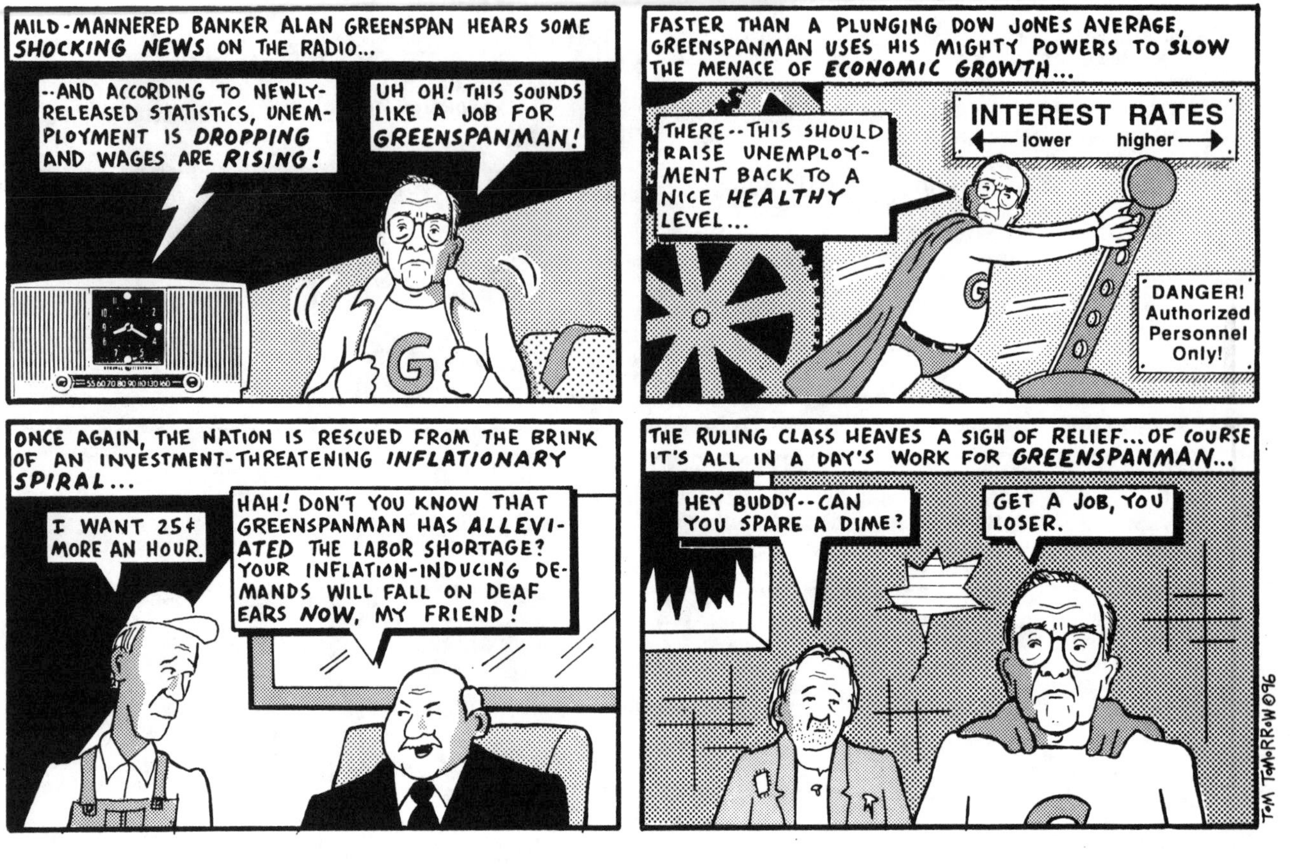

MILD-MANNERED BANKER ALAN GREENSPAN HEARS SOME SHOCKING NEWS ON THE RADIO...
--AND ACCORDING TO NEWLY-RELEASED STATISTICS, UNEMPLOYMENT IS DROPPING AND WAGES ARE RISING!
UH OH! THIS SOUNDS LIKE A JOB FOR GREENSPANMAN!
FASTER THAN A PLUNGING DOW JONES AVERAGE, GREENSPANMAN USES HIS MIGHTY POWERS TO SLOW THE MENACE OF ECONOMIC GROWTH...
THERE--THIS SHOULD RAISE UNEMPLOYMENT BACK TO A NICE HEALTHY LEVEL...
INTEREST RATES
lower higher
DANGER! Authorized Personnel Only!
ONCE AGAIN, THE NATION IS RESCUED FROM THE BRINK OF AN INVESTMENT-THREATENING INFLATIONARY SPIRAL...
I WANT 25¢ MORE AN HOUR.
HAH! DON'T YOU KNOW THAT GREENSPANMAN HAS ALLEVIATED THE LABOR SHORTAGE? YOUR INFLATION-INDUCING DEMANDS WILL FALL ON DEAF EARS NOW, MY FRIEND!
THE RULING CLASS HEAVES A SIGH OF RELIEF...OF COURSE IT'S ALL IN A DAY'S WORK FOR GREENSPANMAN...
HEY BUDDY--CAN YOU SPARE A DIME?
GET A JOB, YOU LOSER.
TOM TOMORROW ©96

THIS MODERN WORLD

by TOM TOMORROW

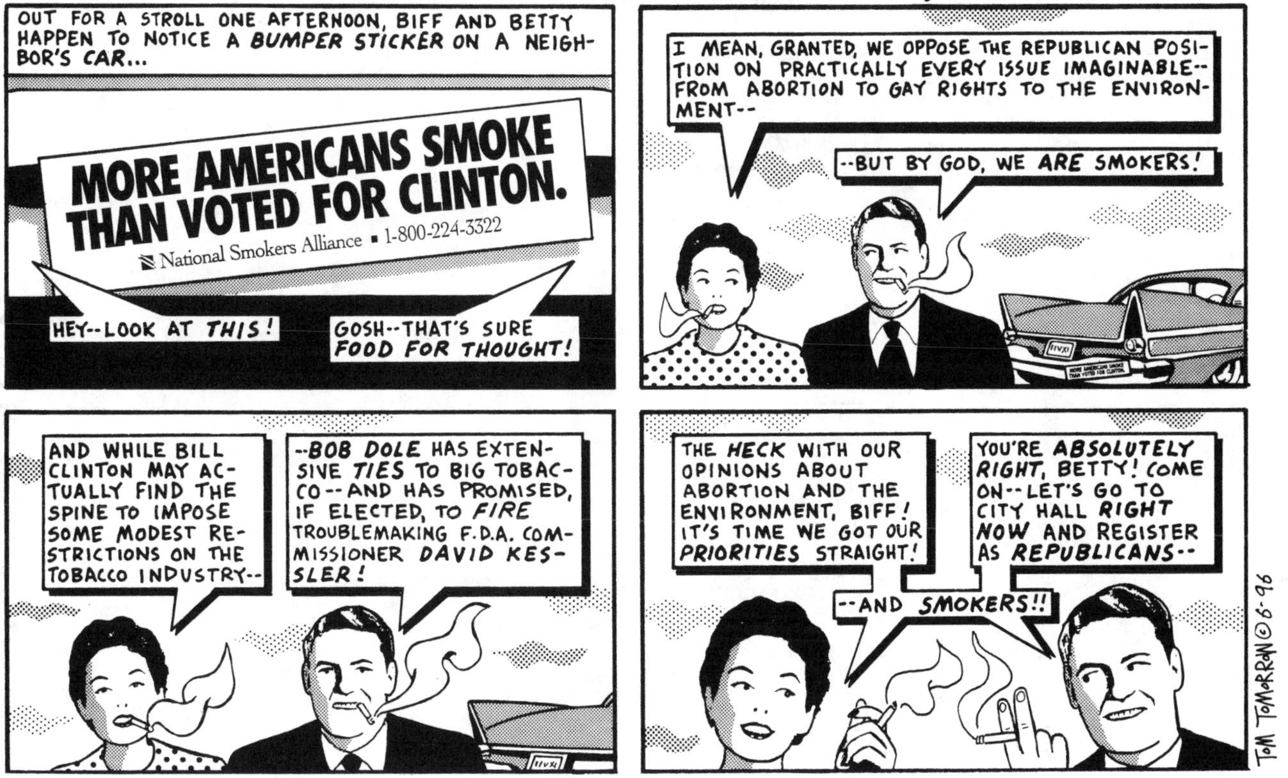
OUT FOR A STROLL ONE AFTERNOON, BIFF AND BETTY HAPPEN TO NOTICE A BUMPER STICKER ON A NEIGHBOR'S CAR...
MORE AMERICANS SMOKE THAN VOTED FOR CLINTON.
National Smokers Alliance ▪ 1-800-224-3322
HEY--LOOK AT THIS!
GOSH--THAT'S SURE FOOD FOR THOUGHT!
I MEAN, GRANTED, WE OPPOSE THE REPUBLICAN POSITION ON PRACTICALLY EVERY ISSUE IMAGINABLE-- FROM ABORTION TO GAY RIGHTS TO THE ENVIRONMENT--
--BUT BY GOD, WE ARE SMOKERS!
AND WHILE BILL CLINTON MAY ACTUALLY FIND THE SPINE TO IMPOSE SOME MODEST RESTRICTIONS ON THE TOBACCO INDUSTRY--
--BOB DOLE HAS EXTENSIVE TIES TO BIG TOBACCO--AND HAS PROMISED, IF ELECTED, TO FIRE TROUBLEMAKING F.D.A. COMMISSIONER DAVID KESSLER!
THE HECK WITH OUR OPINIONS ABOUT ABORTION AND THE ENVIRONMENT, BIFF! IT'S TIME WE GOT OUR PRIORITIES STRAIGHT!
YOU'RE ABSOLUTELY RIGHT, BETTY! COME ON--LET'S GO TO CITY HALL RIGHT NOW AND REGISTER AS REPUBLICANS--
--AND SMOKERS!!
TOM TOMORROW © 6-96

THIS MODERN WORLD

by TOM TOMORROW

A FEW LAST THOUGHTS ABOUT THE *CONVENTIONS*: THOUGH THEY WERE ESSENTIALLY *INFOMERCIALS*, THERE WERE STILL SOME TRULY ODD MOMENTS--SUCH AS NEWT GINGRICH'S INEXPLICABLE DECISION TO SING THE PRAISES OF *BEACH VOLLEYBALL*...

NO BUREAUCRAT COULD HAVE INVENTED *THIS* GAME!*

OR, ON THE DEMOCRATIC SIDE, MARIO CUOMO'S PECULIARLY PHRASED ASSERTION THAT REPUBLICANS --

--ARE THE REAL THREAT TO *OUR* WOMEN!*

"OUR" WOMEN..?

EMPLOYEE MUST WASH HANDS

TED KOPPEL LEFT SAN DIEGO MIDWAY THROUGH, DECLARING THAT THERE WAS NO NEWS TO BE FOUND THERE...IN OTHER WORDS, AS THE CHAMPIONS OF ANTI-IMMIGRANT FERVOR HELD THEIR CONVENTION A FEW MILES FROM ONE OF THE MOST HEAVILY-TRAFFICKED BORDER CROSSINGS IN THE WORLD, NO ONE WAS *SPOON FEEDING* TED ANY *INTERESTING STORIES*...

WELL, YOU CAN'T EXPECT MR. KOPPEL TO GO OUT *LOOKING* FOR NEWS!

HE'S A *BUSY MAN*!

JOURNALISTS DID MANAGE TO COVER THE NEWS A BIT MORE AGGRESSIVELY AT THE DEMOCRATIC CONVENTION...THOUGH--UNTIL THE MORRIS SCANDAL BROKE--MOST OF THE NEWS THEY COVERED WAS *28 YEARS OLD*...

--AND I'M STANDING HERE WITH AN ACTUAL *FORMER YOUNG PERSON*! TELL ME ABOUT CHICAGO IN 1968!

WELL TOM, I PERSONALLY WAS *SAFE AT HOME*--BUT FROM WHAT I SAW ON TV, IT LOOKED MIGHTY DANGEROUS!

GIVEN THAT THE CONVENTION CENTER IS A STONE'S THROW FROM SOME OF CHICAGO'S POOREST NEIGHBORHOODS, IT SEEMS TO *US* THAT REPORTERS *MIGHT* HAVE--FOR INSTANCE--TRIED TO PUT A HUMAN FACE ON THE NEW *WELFARE BILL*...BUT HECK, WHAT DO *WE* KNOW? WE JUST DRAW *FUNNY PICTURES*...

I KNOW! LET'S MAKE FUN OF DOLE'S *AGE*!

YES, THAT WILL BE MOST AMUSING! THEN WE CAN DRAW CLINTON AS A *BIG FAT GUY* EATING AT McDONALDS!

PULITZER PRIZE, HERE WE COME!

SIGH... I MISS *SPARKY*...

TMW STAFF MEETING

TOM TOMORROW © 9-11-96

* BOTH ACTUAL QUOTES.

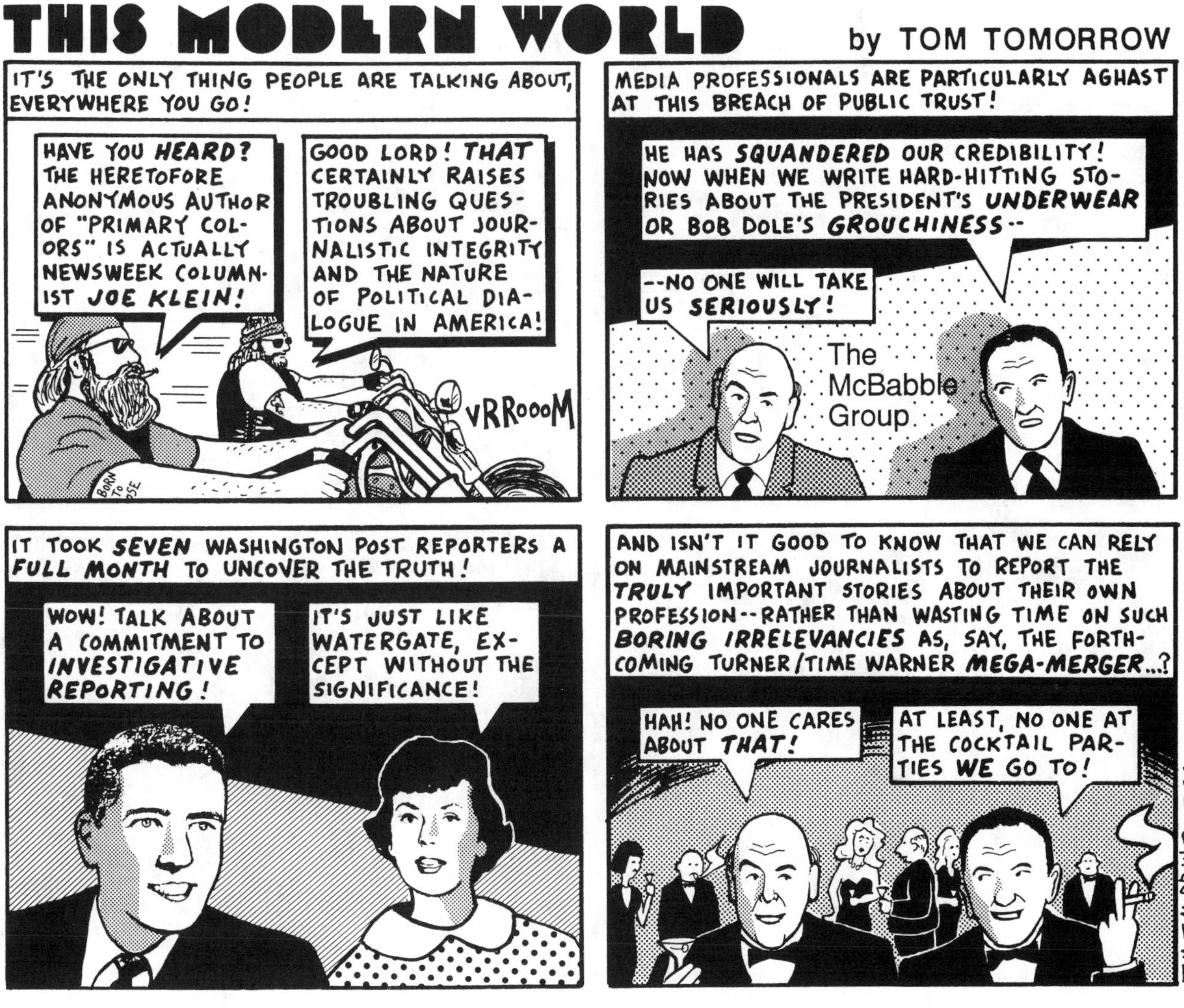

THIS MODERN WORLD
by TOM TOMORROW
IT'S THE ONLY THING PEOPLE ARE TALKING ABOUT, EVERYWHERE YOU GO!
HAVE YOU HEARD? THE HERETOFORE ANONYMOUS AUTHOR OF "PRIMARY COLORS" IS ACTUALLY NEWSWEEK COLUMNIST JOE KLEIN!
GOOD LORD! THAT CERTAINLY RAISES TROUBLING QUESTIONS ABOUT JOURNALISTIC INTEGRITY AND THE NATURE OF POLITICAL DIALOGUE IN AMERICA!
VRRoooM
MEDIA PROFESSIONALS ARE PARTICULARLY AGHAST AT THIS BREACH OF PUBLIC TRUST!
HE HAS SQUANDERED OUR CREDIBILITY! NOW WHEN WE WRITE HARD-HITTING STORIES ABOUT THE PRESIDENT'S UNDERWEAR OR BOB DOLE'S GROUCHINESS--
--NO ONE WILL TAKE US SERIOUSLY!
The McBabble Group
IT TOOK SEVEN WASHINGTON POST REPORTERS A FULL MONTH TO UNCOVER THE TRUTH!
WOW! TALK ABOUT A COMMITMENT TO INVESTIGATIVE REPORTING!
IT'S JUST LIKE WATERGATE, EXCEPT WITHOUT THE SIGNIFICANCE!
AND ISN'T IT GOOD TO KNOW THAT WE CAN RELY ON MAINSTREAM JOURNALISTS TO REPORT THE TRULY IMPORTANT STORIES ABOUT THEIR OWN PROFESSION--RATHER THAN WASTING TIME ON SUCH BORING IRRELEVANCIES AS, SAY, THE FORTHCOMING TURNER/TIME WARNER MEGA-MERGER...?
HAH! NO ONE CARES ABOUT THAT!
AT LEAST, NO ONE AT THE COCKTAIL PARTIES WE GO TO!
TOM TOMORROW © 8-7-96

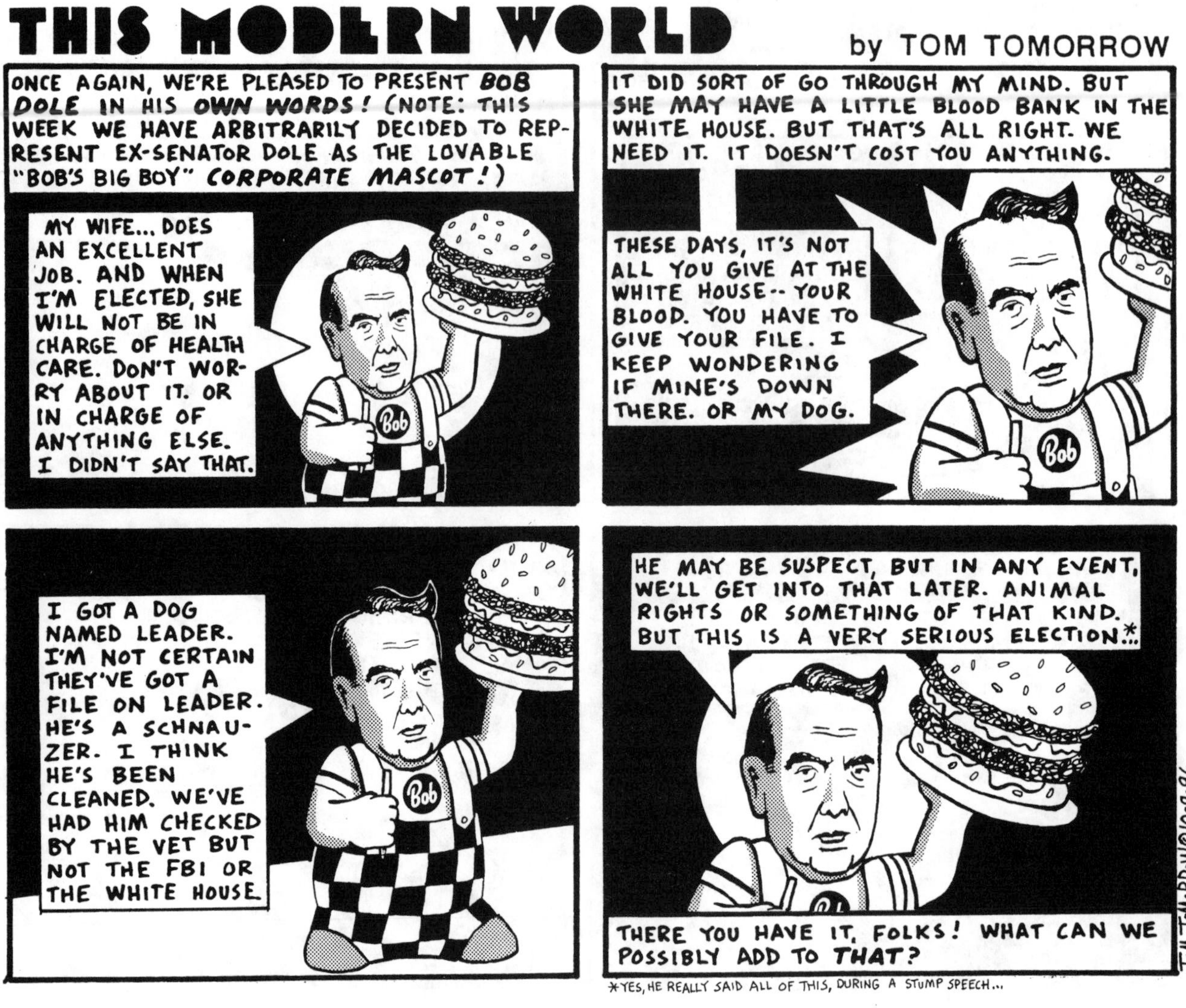
THIS MODERN WORLD
by TOM TOMORROW
ONCE AGAIN, WE'RE PLEASED TO PRESENT BOB DOLE IN HIS OWN WORDS! (NOTE: THIS WEEK WE HAVE ARBITRARILY DECIDED TO REPRESENT EX-SENATOR DOLE AS THE LOVABLE "BOB'S BIG BOY" CORPORATE MASCOT!)
MY WIFE... DOES AN EXCELLENT JOB. AND WHEN I'M ELECTED, SHE WILL NOT BE IN CHARGE OF HEALTH CARE. DON'T WORRY ABOUT IT. OR IN CHARGE OF ANYTHING ELSE. I DIDN'T SAY THAT.
Bob
IT DID SORT OF GO THROUGH MY MIND. BUT SHE MAY HAVE A LITTLE BLOOD BANK IN THE WHITE HOUSE. BUT THAT'S ALL RIGHT. WE NEED IT. IT DOESN'T COST YOU ANYTHING.
THESE DAYS, IT'S NOT ALL YOU GIVE AT THE WHITE HOUSE-- YOUR BLOOD. YOU HAVE TO GIVE YOUR FILE. I KEEP WONDERING IF MINE'S DOWN THERE. OR MY DOG.
Bob
I GOT A DOG NAMED LEADER. I'M NOT CERTAIN THEY'VE GOT A FILE ON LEADER. HE'S A SCHNAUZER. I THINK HE'S BEEN CLEANED. WE'VE HAD HIM CHECKED BY THE VET BUT NOT THE FBI OR THE WHITE HOUSE.
Bob
HE MAY BE SUSPECT, BUT IN ANY EVENT, WE'LL GET INTO THAT LATER. ANIMAL RIGHTS OR SOMETHING OF THAT KIND. BUT THIS IS A VERY SERIOUS ELECTION.*
THERE YOU HAVE IT, FOLKS! WHAT CAN WE POSSIBLY ADD TO THAT?
TOM TOMORROW©10-9-96
*YES, HE REALLY SAID ALL OF THIS, DURING A STUMP SPEECH...

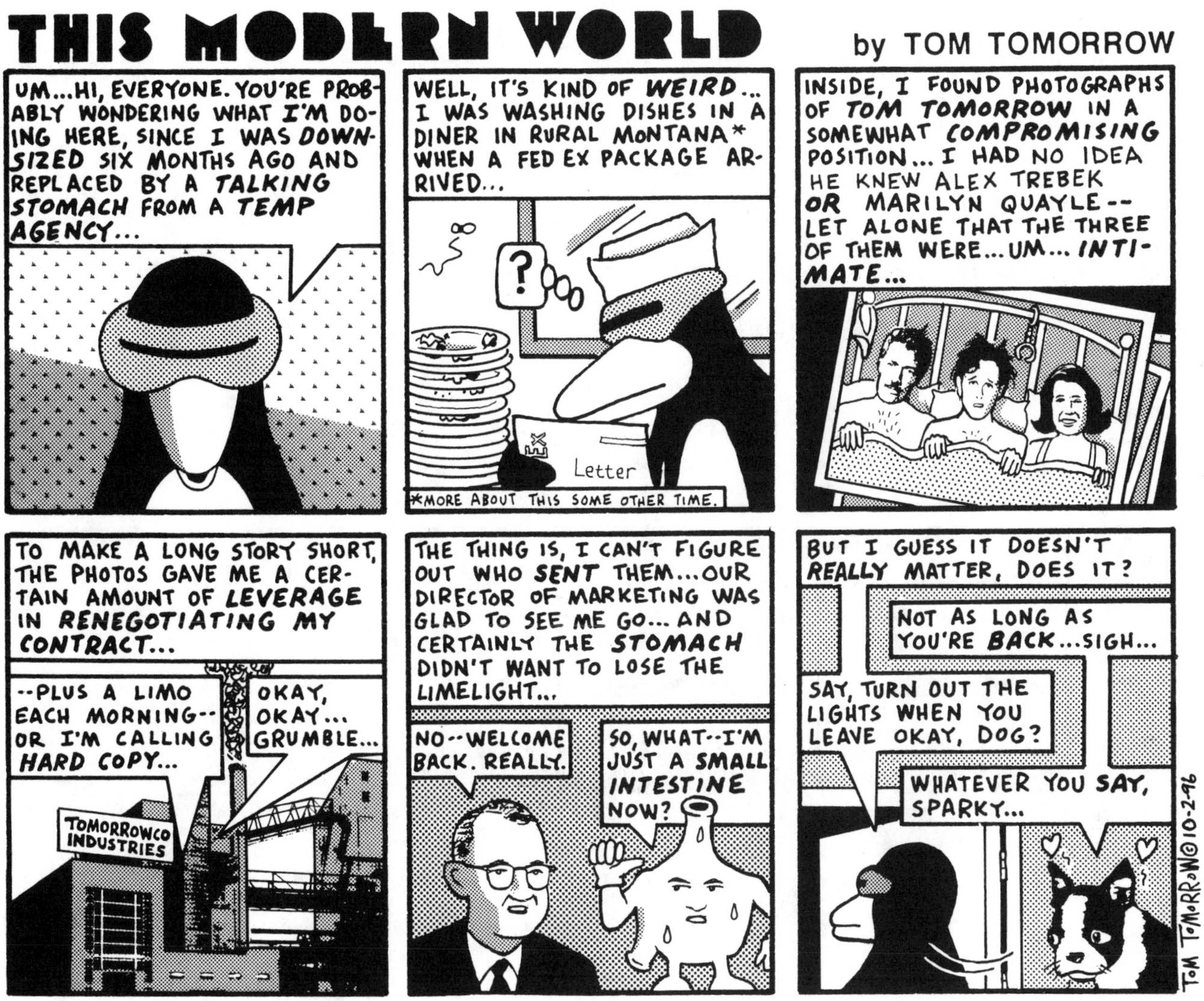
THIS MODERN WORLD
by TOM TOMORROW
UM...HI, EVERYONE. YOU'RE PROBABLY WONDERING WHAT I'M DOING HERE, SINCE I WAS DOWNSIZED SIX MONTHS AGO AND REPLACED BY A TALKING STOMACH FROM A TEMP AGENCY...
WELL, IT'S KIND OF WEIRD... I WAS WASHING DISHES IN A DINER IN RURAL MONTANA* WHEN A FED EX PACKAGE ARRIVED...
?
Letter
*MORE ABOUT THIS SOME OTHER TIME.
INSIDE, I FOUND PHOTOGRAPHS OF TOM TOMORROW IN A SOMEWHAT COMPROMISING POSITION... I HAD NO IDEA HE KNEW ALEX TREBEK OR MARILYN QUAYLE -- LET ALONE THAT THE THREE OF THEM WERE... UM... INTIMATE...
TO MAKE A LONG STORY SHORT, THE PHOTOS GAVE ME A CERTAIN AMOUNT OF LEVERAGE IN RENEGOTIATING MY CONTRACT...
--PLUS A LIMO EACH MORNING-- OR I'M CALLING HARD COPY...
OKAY, OKAY... GRUMBLE...
TOMORROWCO INDUSTRIES
THE THING IS, I CAN'T FIGURE OUT WHO SENT THEM... OUR DIRECTOR OF MARKETING WAS GLAD TO SEE ME GO... AND CERTAINLY THE STOMACH DIDN'T WANT TO LOSE THE LIMELIGHT...
NO--WELCOME BACK. REALLY.
SO, WHAT--I'M JUST A SMALL INTESTINE NOW?
BUT I GUESS IT DOESN'T REALLY MATTER, DOES IT?
NOT AS LONG AS YOU'RE BACK...SIGH...
SAY, TURN OUT THE LIGHTS WHEN YOU LEAVE OKAY, DOG?
WHATEVER YOU SAY, SPARKY...
TOM TOMORROW©10-2-96

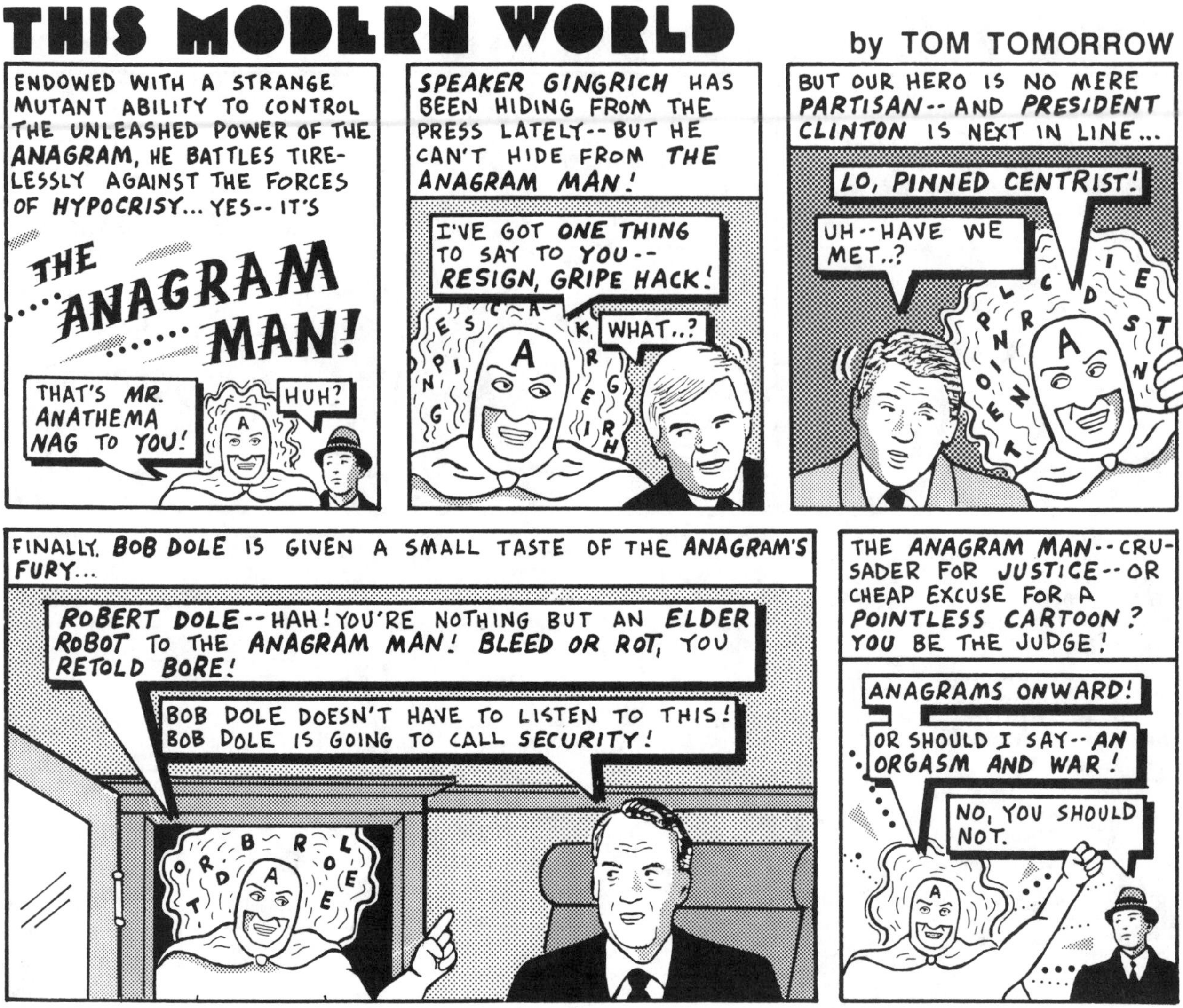
THIS MODERN WORLD
by TOM TOMORROW
ENDOWED WITH A STRANGE MUTANT ABILITY TO CONTROL THE UNLEASHED POWER OF THE ANAGRAM, HE BATTLES TIRELESSLY AGAINST THE FORCES OF HYPOCRISY... YES-- IT'S
THE ANAGRAM MAN!
THAT'S MR. ANATHEMA NAG TO YOU!
HUH?
SPEAKER GINGRICH HAS BEEN HIDING FROM THE PRESS LATELY-- BUT HE CAN'T HIDE FROM THE ANAGRAM MAN!
I'VE GOT ONE THING TO SAY TO YOU-- RESIGN, GRIPE HACK!
WHAT..?
BUT OUR HERO IS NO MERE PARTISAN-- AND PRESIDENT CLINTON IS NEXT IN LINE...
LO, PINNED CENTRIST!
UH--HAVE WE MET..?
FINALLY, BOB DOLE IS GIVEN A SMALL TASTE OF THE ANAGRAM'S FURY...
ROBERT DOLE--HAH! YOU'RE NOTHING BUT AN ELDER ROBOT TO THE ANAGRAM MAN! BLEED OR ROT, YOU RETOLD BORE!
BOB DOLE DOESN'T HAVE TO LISTEN TO THIS! BOB DOLE IS GOING TO CALL SECURITY!
THE ANAGRAM MAN--CRUSADER FOR JUSTICE--OR CHEAP EXCUSE FOR A POINTLESS CARTOON? YOU BE THE JUDGE!
ANAGRAMS ONWARD!
OR SHOULD I SAY--AN ORGASM AND WAR!
NO, YOU SHOULD NOT.

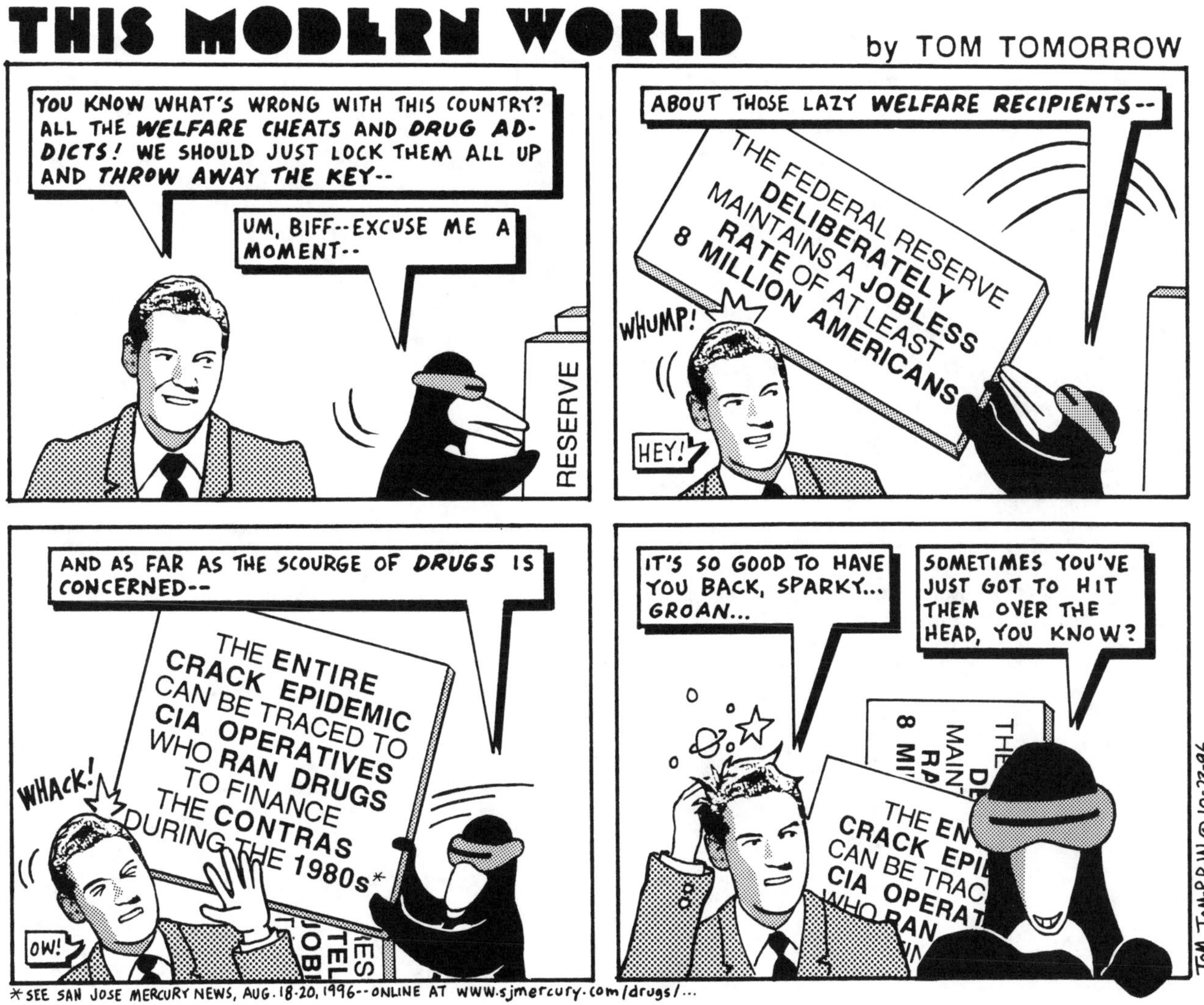
THIS MODERN WORLD
by TOM TOMORROW
YOU KNOW WHAT'S WRONG WITH THIS COUNTRY? ALL THE WELFARE CHEATS AND DRUG ADDICTS! WE SHOULD JUST LOCK THEM ALL UP AND THROW AWAY THE KEY--
UM, BIFF--EXCUSE ME A MOMENT--
RESERVE
ABOUT THOSE LAZY WELFARE RECIPIENTS--
THE FEDERAL RESERVE DELIBERATELY MAINTAINS A JOBLESS RATE OF AT LEAST 8 MILLION AMERICANS
WHUMP!
HEY!
AND AS FAR AS THE SCOURGE OF DRUGS IS CONCERNED--
THE ENTIRE CRACK EPIDEMIC CAN BE TRACED TO CIA OPERATIVES WHO RAN DRUGS TO FINANCE THE CONTRAS DURING THE 1980s*
WHACK!
OW!
IT'S SO GOOD TO HAVE YOU BACK, SPARKY... GROAN...
SOMETIMES YOU'VE JUST GOT TO HIT THEM OVER THE HEAD, YOU KNOW?
TOM TOMORROW © 10-23-96

*SEE SAN JOSE MERCURY NEWS, AUG. 18-20, 1996--ONLINE AT www.sjmercury.com/drugs/...

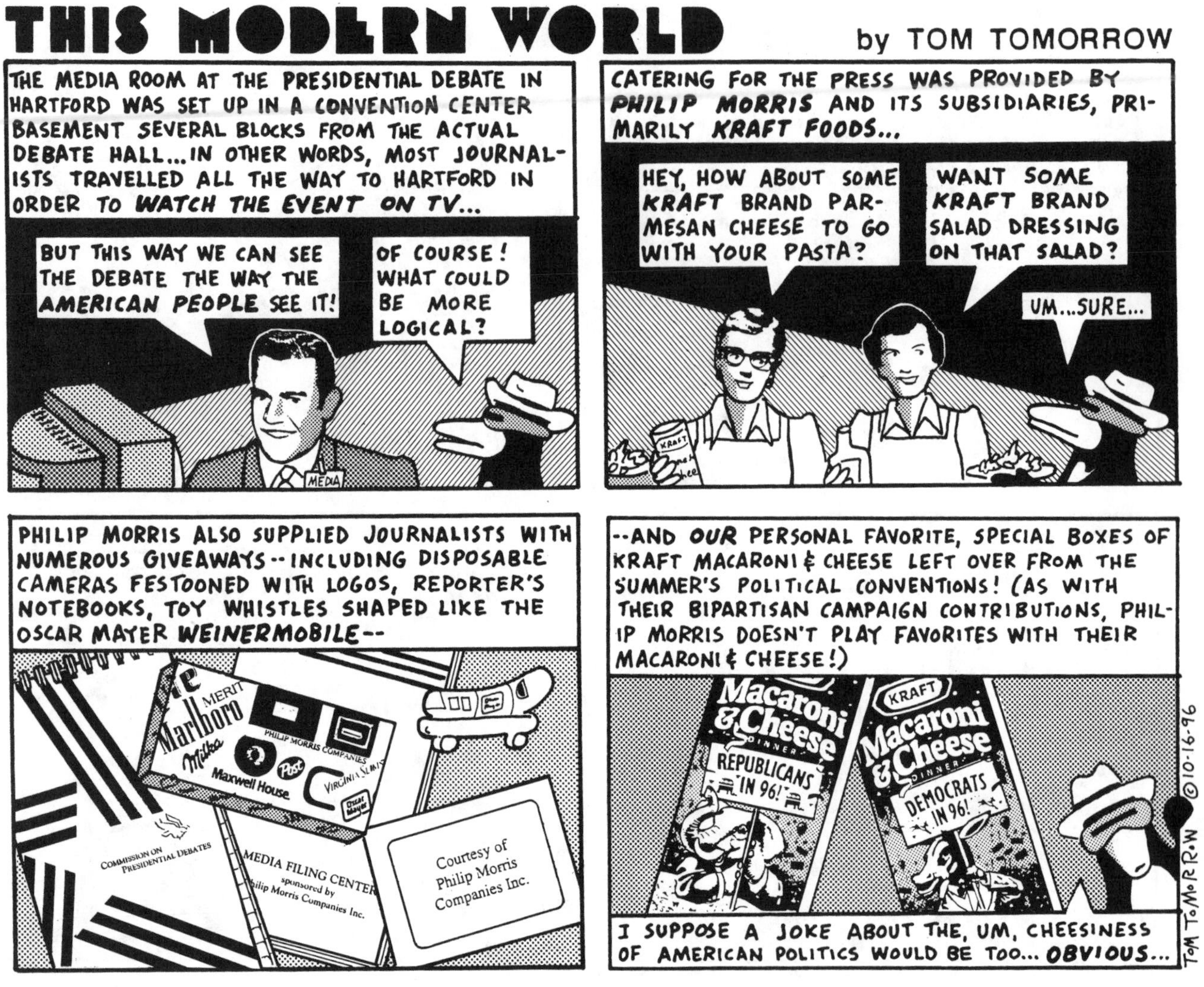
THIS MODERN WORLD
by TOM TOMORROW
THE MEDIA ROOM AT THE PRESIDENTIAL DEBATE IN HARTFORD WAS SET UP IN A CONVENTION CENTER BASEMENT SEVERAL BLOCKS FROM THE ACTUAL DEBATE HALL... IN OTHER WORDS, MOST JOURNALISTS TRAVELLED ALL THE WAY TO HARTFORD IN ORDER TO WATCH THE EVENT ON TV...
BUT THIS WAY WE CAN SEE THE DEBATE THE WAY THE AMERICAN PEOPLE SEE IT!
OF COURSE! WHAT COULD BE MORE LOGICAL?
MEDIA
CATERING FOR THE PRESS WAS PROVIDED BY PHILIP MORRIS AND ITS SUBSIDIARIES, PRIMARILY KRAFT FOODS...
HEY, HOW ABOUT SOME KRAFT BRAND PARMESAN CHEESE TO GO WITH YOUR PASTA?
WANT SOME KRAFT BRAND SALAD DRESSING ON THAT SALAD?
UM...SURE...
KRAFT
PHILIP MORRIS ALSO SUPPLIED JOURNALISTS WITH NUMEROUS GIVEAWAYS--INCLUDING DISPOSABLE CAMERAS FESTOONED WITH LOGOS, REPORTER'S NOTEBOOKS, TOY WHISTLES SHAPED LIKE THE OSCAR MAYER WEINERMOBILE--
MERIT
Marlboro
Milka
PHILIP MORRIS COMPANIES
Post
Maxwell House
VIRGINIA SLIMS
Oscar Mayer
COMMISSION ON PRESIDENTIAL DEBATES
MEDIA FILING CENTER
sponsored by
Courtesy of Philip Morris Companies Inc.
--AND OUR PERSONAL FAVORITE, SPECIAL BOXES OF KRAFT MACARONI & CHEESE LEFT OVER FROM THE SUMMER'S POLITICAL CONVENTIONS! (AS WITH THEIR BIPARTISAN CAMPAIGN CONTRIBUTIONS, PHILIP MORRIS DOESN'T PLAY FAVORITES WITH THEIR MACARONI & CHEESE!)
Macaroni & Cheese DINNER
REPUBLICANS IN 96!
KRAFT
Macaroni & Cheese DINNER
DEMOCRATS IN 96!
I SUPPOSE A JOKE ABOUT THE, UM, CHEESINESS OF AMERICAN POLITICS WOULD BE TOO... OBVIOUS...
TOM TOMORROW ©10-16-96

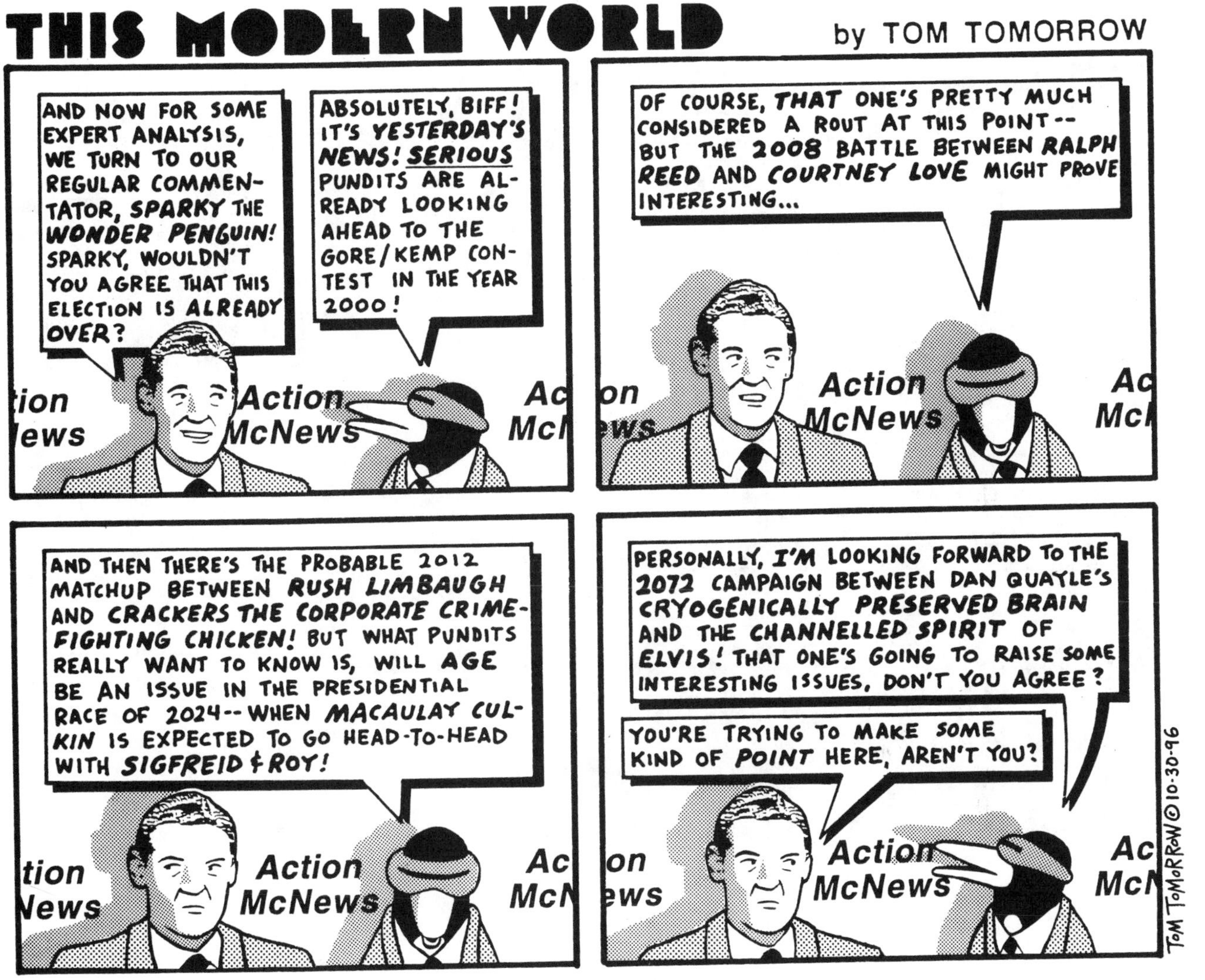
THIS MODERN WORLD
by TOM TOMORROW
AND NOW FOR SOME EXPERT ANALYSIS, WE TURN TO OUR REGULAR COMMENTATOR, SPARKY THE WONDER PENGUIN! SPARKY, WOULDN'T YOU AGREE THAT THIS ELECTION IS ALREADY OVER?
ABSOLUTELY, BIFF! IT'S YESTERDAY'S NEWS! SERIOUS PUNDITS ARE ALREADY LOOKING AHEAD TO THE GORE/KEMP CONTEST IN THE YEAR 2000!
Action McNews
OF COURSE, THAT ONE'S PRETTY MUCH CONSIDERED A ROUT AT THIS POINT-- BUT THE 2008 BATTLE BETWEEN RALPH REED AND COURTNEY LOVE MIGHT PROVE INTERESTING...
Action McNews
AND THEN THERE'S THE PROBABLE 2012 MATCHUP BETWEEN RUSH LIMBAUGH AND CRACKERS THE CORPORATE CRIME-FIGHTING CHICKEN! BUT WHAT PUNDITS REALLY WANT TO KNOW IS, WILL AGE BE AN ISSUE IN THE PRESIDENTIAL RACE OF 2024-- WHEN MACAULAY CULKIN IS EXPECTED TO GO HEAD-TO-HEAD WITH SIGFREID & ROY!
Action McNews
PERSONALLY, I'M LOOKING FORWARD TO THE 2072 CAMPAIGN BETWEEN DAN QUAYLE'S CRYOGENICALLY PRESERVED BRAIN AND THE CHANNELLED SPIRIT OF ELVIS! THAT ONE'S GOING TO RAISE SOME INTERESTING ISSUES, DON'T YOU AGREE?
YOU'RE TRYING TO MAKE SOME KIND OF POINT HERE, AREN'T YOU?
Action McNews
TOM TOMORROW © 10-30-96

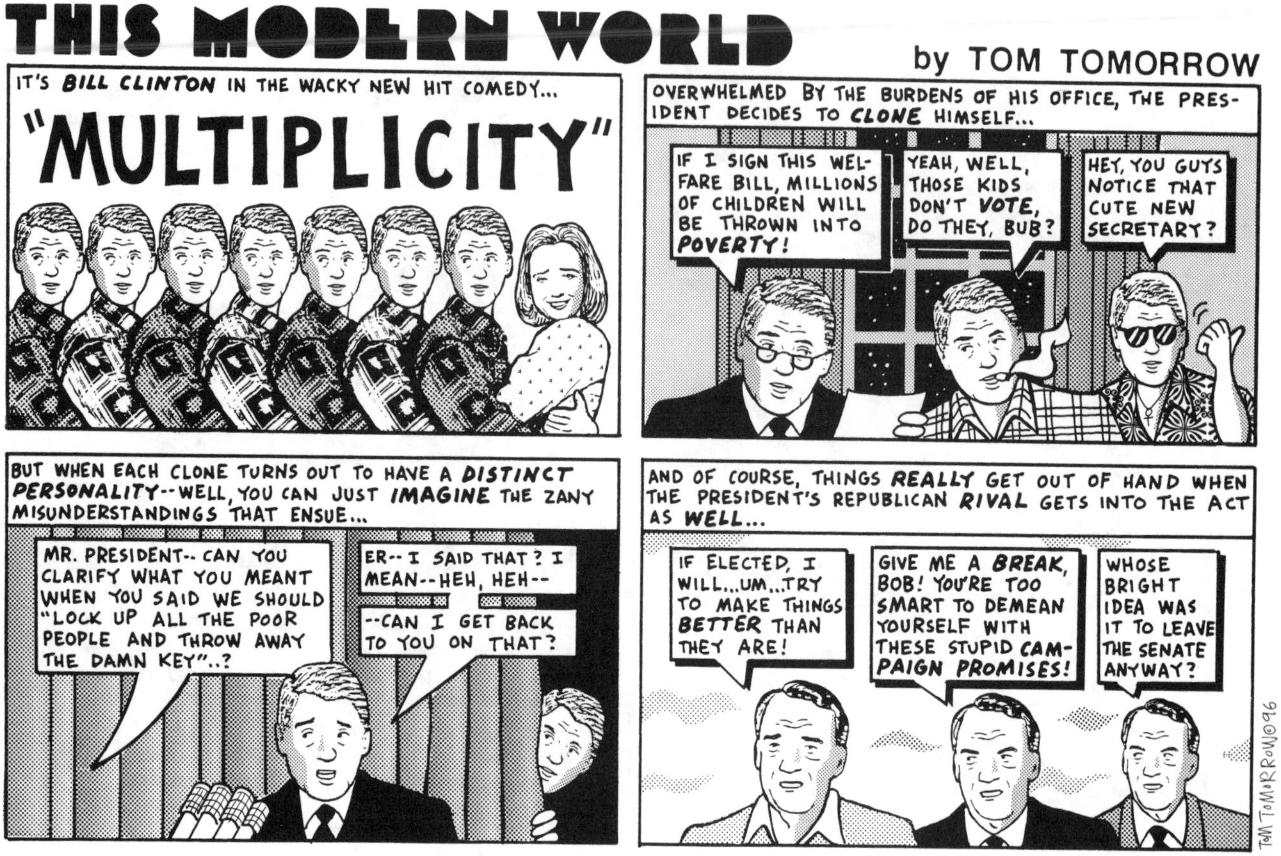
THIS MODERN WORLD
by TOM TOMORROW
IT'S BILL CLINTON IN THE WACKY NEW HIT COMEDY...
"MULTIPLICITY"
OVERWHELMED BY THE BURDENS OF HIS OFFICE, THE PRESIDENT DECIDES TO CLONE HIMSELF...
IF I SIGN THIS WELFARE BILL, MILLIONS OF CHILDREN WILL BE THROWN INTO POVERTY!
YEAH, WELL, THOSE KIDS DON'T VOTE, DO THEY, BUB?
HEY, YOU GUYS NOTICE THAT CUTE NEW SECRETARY?
BUT WHEN EACH CLONE TURNS OUT TO HAVE A DISTINCT PERSONALITY--WELL, YOU CAN JUST IMAGINE THE ZANY MISUNDERSTANDINGS THAT ENSUE...
MR. PRESIDENT-- CAN YOU CLARIFY WHAT YOU MEANT WHEN YOU SAID WE SHOULD "LOCK UP ALL THE POOR PEOPLE AND THROW AWAY THE DAMN KEY"..?
ER-- I SAID THAT? I MEAN--HEH, HEH--
--CAN I GET BACK TO YOU ON THAT?
AND OF COURSE, THINGS REALLY GET OUT OF HAND WHEN THE PRESIDENT'S REPUBLICAN RIVAL GETS INTO THE ACT AS WELL...
IF ELECTED, I WILL...UM...TRY TO MAKE THINGS BETTER THAN THEY ARE!
GIVE ME A BREAK, BOB! YOU'RE TOO SMART TO DEMEAN YOURSELF WITH THESE STUPID CAMPAIGN PROMISES!
WHOSE BRIGHT IDEA WAS IT TO LEAVE THE SENATE ANYWAY?
TOM TOMORROW©96

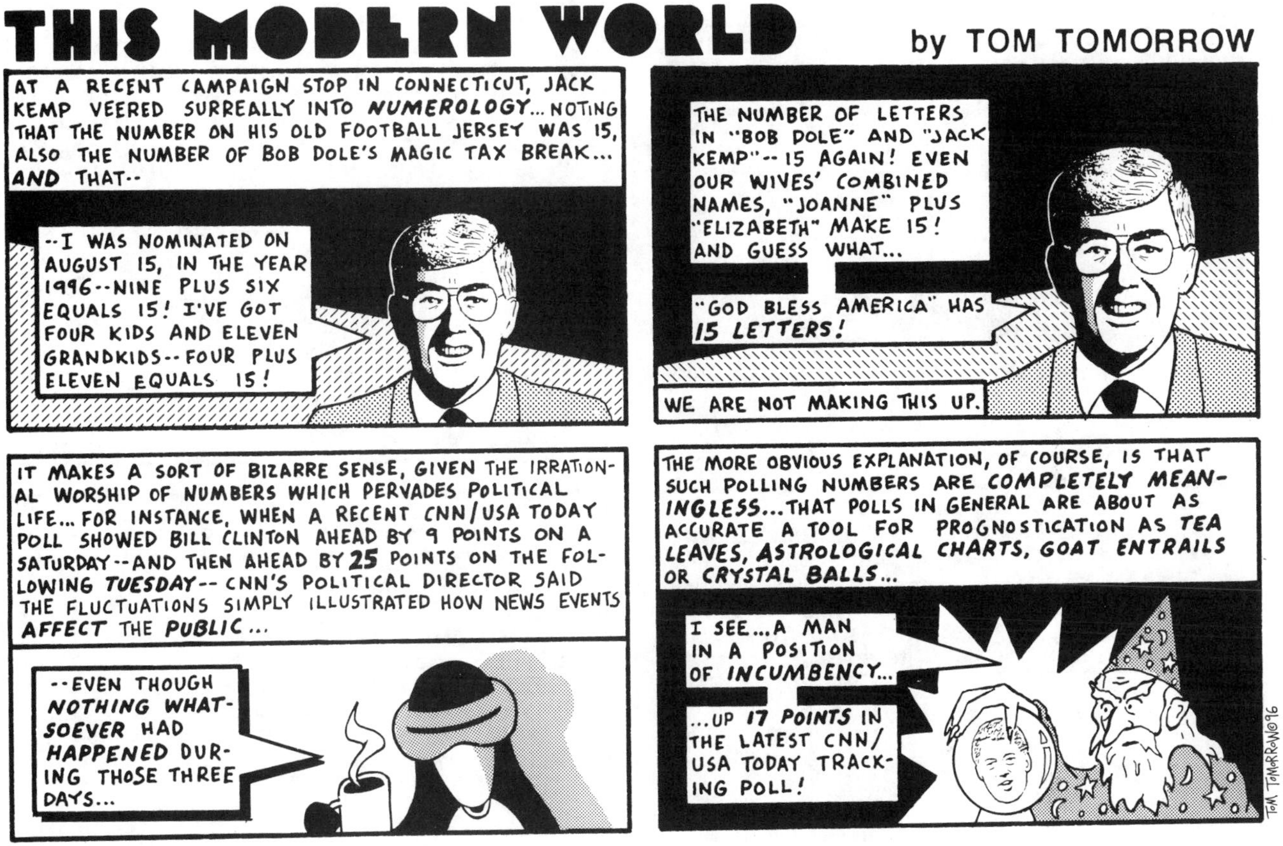
THIS MODERN WORLD
by TOM TOMORROW
AT A RECENT CAMPAIGN STOP IN CONNECTICUT, JACK KEMP VEERED SURREALLY INTO NUMEROLOGY... NOTING THAT THE NUMBER ON HIS OLD FOOTBALL JERSEY WAS 15, ALSO THE NUMBER OF BOB DOLE'S MAGIC TAX BREAK... AND THAT--
--I WAS NOMINATED ON AUGUST 15, IN THE YEAR 1996--NINE PLUS SIX EQUALS 15! I'VE GOT FOUR KIDS AND ELEVEN GRANDKIDS--FOUR PLUS ELEVEN EQUALS 15!
THE NUMBER OF LETTERS IN "BOB DOLE" AND "JACK KEMP"--15 AGAIN! EVEN OUR WIVES' COMBINED NAMES, "JOANNE" PLUS "ELIZABETH" MAKE 15! AND GUESS WHAT...
"GOD BLESS AMERICA" HAS 15 LETTERS!
WE ARE NOT MAKING THIS UP.
IT MAKES A SORT OF BIZARRE SENSE, GIVEN THE IRRATIONAL WORSHIP OF NUMBERS WHICH PERVADES POLITICAL LIFE... FOR INSTANCE, WHEN A RECENT CNN/USA TODAY POLL SHOWED BILL CLINTON AHEAD BY 9 POINTS ON A SATURDAY--AND THEN AHEAD BY 25 POINTS ON THE FOLLOWING TUESDAY--CNN'S POLITICAL DIRECTOR SAID THE FLUCTUATIONS SIMPLY ILLUSTRATED HOW NEWS EVENTS AFFECT THE PUBLIC...
--EVEN THOUGH NOTHING WHATSOEVER HAD HAPPENED DURING THOSE THREE DAYS...
THE MORE OBVIOUS EXPLANATION, OF COURSE, IS THAT SUCH POLLING NUMBERS ARE COMPLETELY MEANINGLESS... THAT POLLS IN GENERAL ARE ABOUT AS ACCURATE A TOOL FOR PROGNOSTICATION AS TEA LEAVES, ASTROLOGICAL CHARTS, GOAT ENTRAILS OR CRYSTAL BALLS...
I SEE... A MAN IN A POSITION OF INCUMBENCY...
...UP 17 POINTS IN THE LATEST CNN/USA TODAY TRACKING POLL!
TOM TOMORROW©96

THIS MODERN WORLD

by TOM TOMORROW

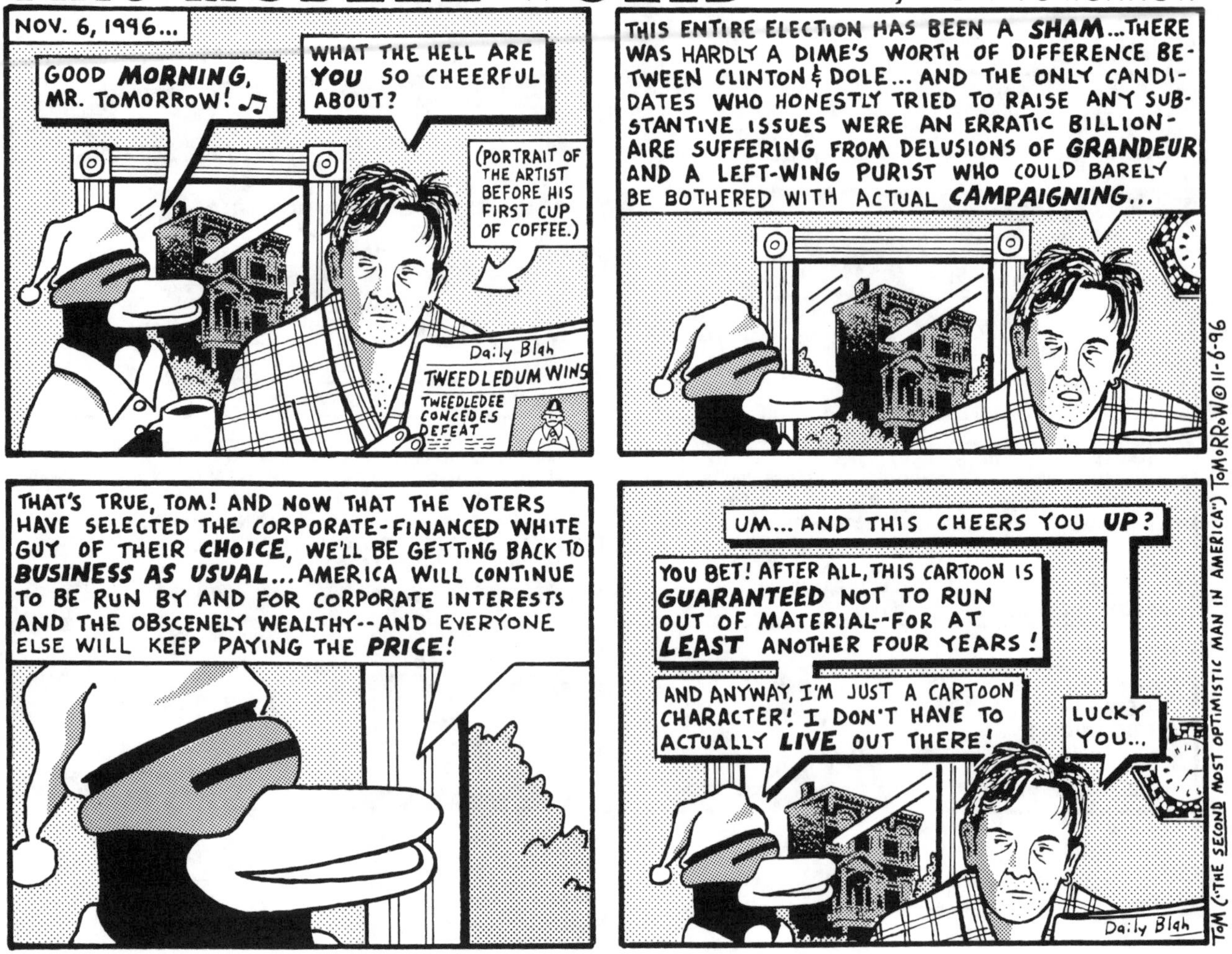

NOV. 6, 1996...
GOOD MORNING, MR. TOMORROW!
WHAT THE HELL ARE YOU SO CHEERFUL ABOUT?
(PORTRAIT OF THE ARTIST BEFORE HIS FIRST CUP OF COFFEE.)
Daily Blah
TWEEDLEDUM WINS
TWEEDLEDEE CONCEDES DEFEAT
THIS ENTIRE ELECTION HAS BEEN A SHAM...THERE WAS HARDLY A DIME'S WORTH OF DIFFERENCE BETWEEN CLINTON & DOLE... AND THE ONLY CANDIDATES WHO HONESTLY TRIED TO RAISE ANY SUBSTANTIVE ISSUES WERE AN ERRATIC BILLIONAIRE SUFFERING FROM DELUSIONS OF GRANDEUR AND A LEFT-WING PURIST WHO COULD BARELY BE BOTHERED WITH ACTUAL CAMPAIGNING...
THAT'S TRUE, TOM! AND NOW THAT THE VOTERS HAVE SELECTED THE CORPORATE-FINANCED WHITE GUY OF THEIR CHOICE, WE'LL BE GETTING BACK TO BUSINESS AS USUAL... AMERICA WILL CONTINUE TO BE RUN BY AND FOR CORPORATE INTERESTS AND THE OBSCENELY WEALTHY--AND EVERYONE ELSE WILL KEEP PAYING THE PRICE!
UM... AND THIS CHEERS YOU UP?
YOU BET! AFTER ALL, THIS CARTOON IS GUARANTEED NOT TO RUN OUT OF MATERIAL--FOR AT LEAST ANOTHER FOUR YEARS!
AND ANYWAY, I'M JUST A CARTOON CHARACTER! I DON'T HAVE TO ACTUALLY LIVE OUT THERE!
LUCKY YOU...
Daily Blah
TOMORROW©11-6-96
TOM ("THE SECOND MOST OPTIMISTIC MAN IN AMERICA")

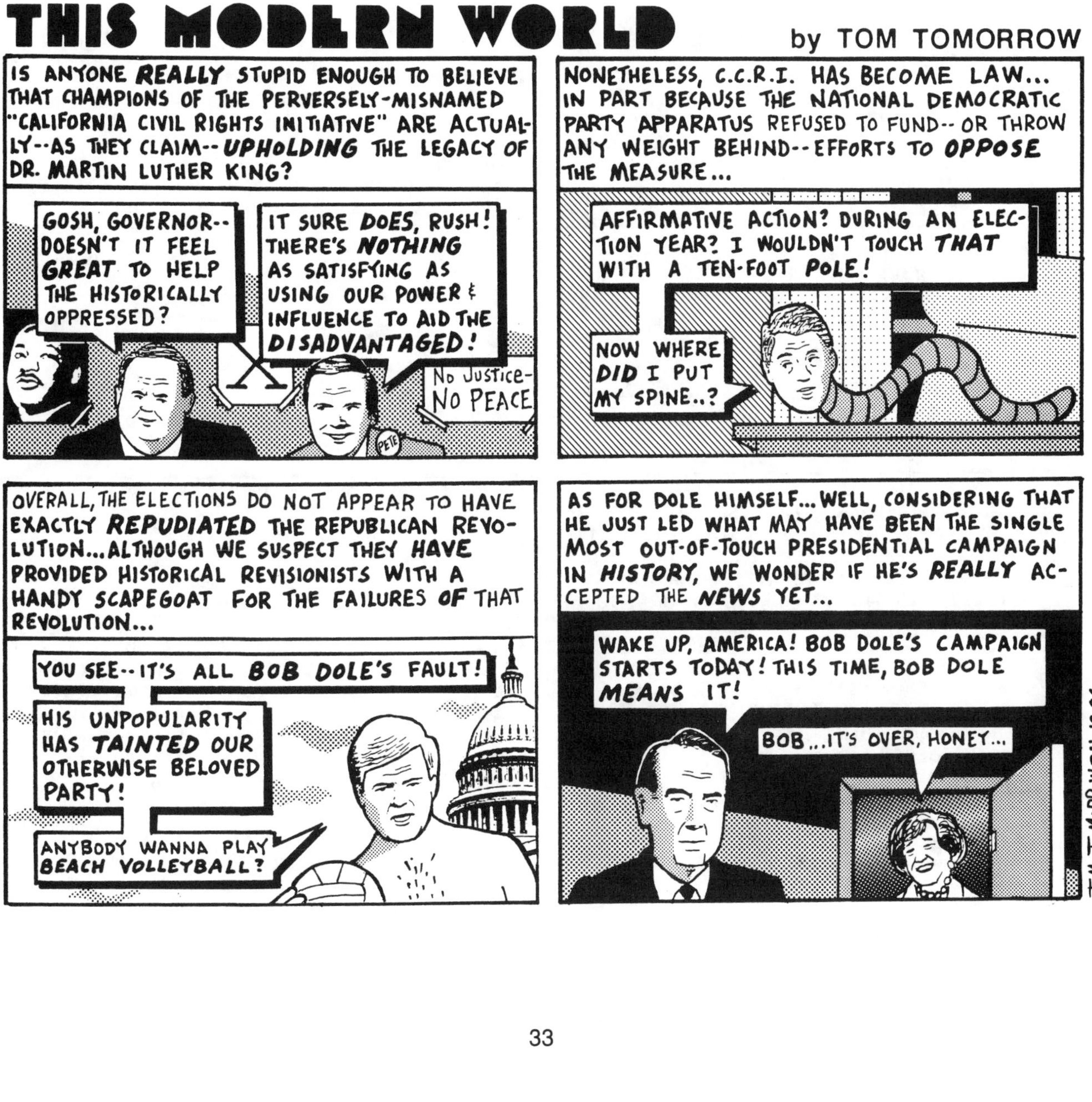
THIS MODERN WORLD
by TOM TOMORROW
IS ANYONE REALLY STUPID ENOUGH TO BELIEVE THAT CHAMPIONS OF THE PERVERSELY-MISNAMED "CALIFORNIA CIVIL RIGHTS INITIATIVE" ARE ACTUALLY--AS THEY CLAIM--UPHOLDING THE LEGACY OF DR. MARTIN LUTHER KING?
GOSH, GOVERNOR--DOESN'T IT FEEL GREAT TO HELP THE HISTORICALLY OPPRESSED?
IT SURE DOES, RUSH! THERE'S NOTHING AS SATISFYING AS USING OUR POWER & INFLUENCE TO AID THE DISADVANTAGED!
No Justice-No PEACE
PETE
NONETHELESS, C.C.R.I. HAS BECOME LAW... IN PART BECAUSE THE NATIONAL DEMOCRATIC PARTY APPARATUS REFUSED TO FUND--OR THROW ANY WEIGHT BEHIND--EFFORTS TO OPPOSE THE MEASURE...
AFFIRMATIVE ACTION? DURING AN ELECTION YEAR? I WOULDN'T TOUCH THAT WITH A TEN-FOOT POLE!
NOW WHERE DID I PUT MY SPINE..?
OVERALL, THE ELECTIONS DO NOT APPEAR TO HAVE EXACTLY REPUDIATED THE REPUBLICAN REVOLUTION...ALTHOUGH WE SUSPECT THEY HAVE PROVIDED HISTORICAL REVISIONISTS WITH A HANDY SCAPEGOAT FOR THE FAILURES OF THAT REVOLUTION...
YOU SEE--IT'S ALL BOB DOLE'S FAULT!
HIS UNPOPULARITY HAS TAINTED OUR OTHERWISE BELOVED PARTY!
ANYBODY WANNA PLAY BEACH VOLLEYBALL?
AS FOR DOLE HIMSELF...WELL, CONSIDERING THAT HE JUST LED WHAT MAY HAVE BEEN THE SINGLE MOST OUT-OF-TOUCH PRESIDENTIAL CAMPAIGN IN HISTORY, WE WONDER IF HE'S REALLY ACCEPTED THE NEWS YET...
WAKE UP, AMERICA! BOB DOLE'S CAMPAIGN STARTS TODAY! THIS TIME, BOB DOLE MEANS IT!
BOB...IT'S OVER, HONEY...
TOM TOMORROW©11-13-96

THIS MODERN WORLD

by TOM TOMORROW

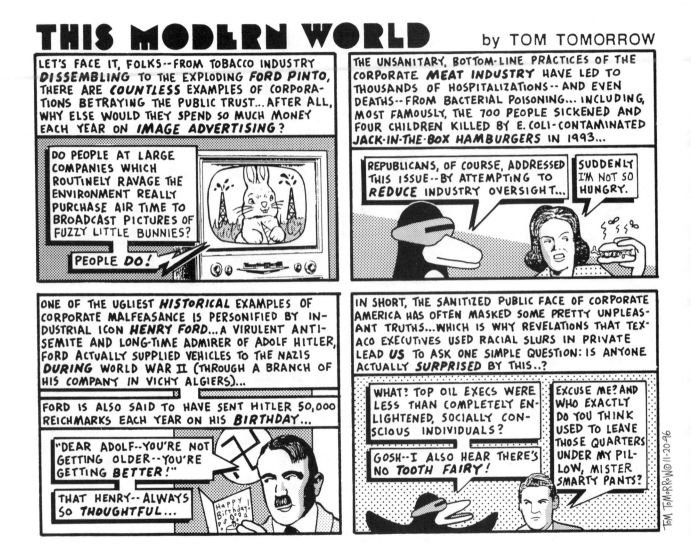

LET'S FACE IT, FOLKS--FROM TOBACCO INDUSTRY *DISSEMBLING* TO THE EXPLODING *FORD PINTO*, THERE ARE *COUNTLESS* EXAMPLES OF CORPORATIONS BETRAYING THE PUBLIC TRUST...AFTER ALL, WHY ELSE WOULD THEY SPEND SO MUCH MONEY EACH YEAR ON *IMAGE ADVERTISING*?

DO PEOPLE AT LARGE COMPANIES WHICH ROUTINELY RAVAGE THE ENVIRONMENT REALLY PURCHASE AIR TIME TO BROADCAST PICTURES OF FUZZY LITTLE BUNNIES?

PEOPLE *DO!*

THE UNSANITARY, BOTTOM-LINE PRACTICES OF THE CORPORATE *MEAT INDUSTRY* HAVE LED TO THOUSANDS OF HOSPITALIZATIONS--AND EVEN DEATHS--FROM BACTERIAL POISONING...INCLUDING, MOST FAMOUSLY, THE 700 PEOPLE SICKENED AND FOUR CHILDREN KILLED BY E. COLI-CONTAMINATED *JACK-IN-THE-BOX HAMBURGERS* IN 1993...

REPUBLICANS, OF COURSE, ADDRESSED THIS ISSUE--BY ATTEMPTING TO *REDUCE* INDUSTRY OVERSIGHT...

SUDDENLY I'M NOT SO HUNGRY.

ONE OF THE UGLIEST *HISTORICAL* EXAMPLES OF CORPORATE MALFEASANCE IS PERSONIFIED BY INDUSTRIAL ICON *HENRY FORD*...A VIRULENT ANTI-SEMITE AND LONG-TIME ADMIRER OF ADOLF HITLER, FORD ACTUALLY SUPPLIED VEHICLES TO THE NAZIS *DURING* WORLD WAR II (THROUGH A BRANCH OF HIS COMPANY IN VICHY ALGIERS)...

FORD IS ALSO SAID TO HAVE SENT HITLER 50,000 REICHMARKS EACH YEAR ON HIS *BIRTHDAY*...

"DEAR ADOLF--YOU'RE NOT GETTING OLDER--YOU'RE GETTING *BETTER!*"

THAT HENRY--ALWAYS SO *THOUGHTFUL*...

IN SHORT, THE SANITIZED PUBLIC FACE OF CORPORATE AMERICA HAS OFTEN MASKED SOME PRETTY UNPLEASANT TRUTHS...WHICH IS WHY REVELATIONS THAT TEXACO EXECUTIVES USED RACIAL SLURS IN PRIVATE LEAD *US* TO ASK ONE SIMPLE QUESTION: IS ANYONE ACTUALLY *SURPRISED* BY THIS..?

WHAT? TOP OIL EXECS WERE LESS THAN COMPLETELY ENLIGHTENED, SOCIALLY CONSCIOUS INDIVIDUALS?

GOSH--I ALSO HEAR THERE'S NO *TOOTH FAIRY!*

EXCUSE ME? AND WHO EXACTLY DO YOU THINK USED TO LEAVE THOSE QUARTERS UNDER MY PILLOW, MISTER SMARTY PANTS?

TOM TOMORROW © 11-20-96

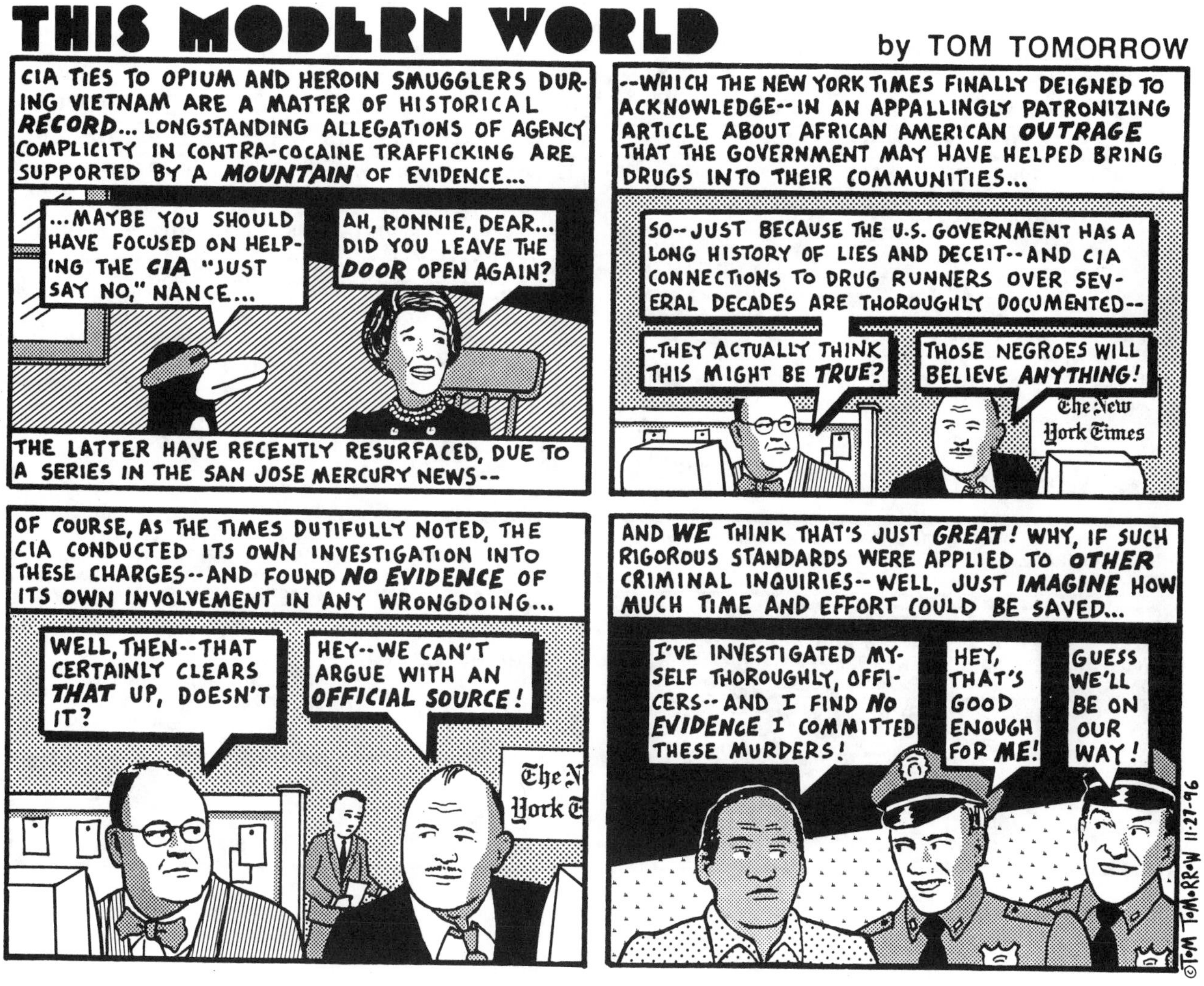
THIS MODERN WORLD
by TOM TOMORROW
CIA TIES TO OPIUM AND HEROIN SMUGGLERS DURING VIETNAM ARE A MATTER OF HISTORICAL RECORD... LONGSTANDING ALLEGATIONS OF AGENCY COMPLICITY IN CONTRA-COCAINE TRAFFICKING ARE SUPPORTED BY A MOUNTAIN OF EVIDENCE...
...MAYBE YOU SHOULD HAVE FOCUSED ON HELPING THE CIA "JUST SAY NO," NANCE...
AH, RONNIE, DEAR... DID YOU LEAVE THE DOOR OPEN AGAIN?
THE LATTER HAVE RECENTLY RESURFACED, DUE TO A SERIES IN THE SAN JOSE MERCURY NEWS--
--WHICH THE NEW YORK TIMES FINALLY DEIGNED TO ACKNOWLEDGE--IN AN APPALLINGLY PATRONIZING ARTICLE ABOUT AFRICAN AMERICAN OUTRAGE THAT THE GOVERNMENT MAY HAVE HELPED BRING DRUGS INTO THEIR COMMUNITIES...
SO--JUST BECAUSE THE U.S. GOVERNMENT HAS A LONG HISTORY OF LIES AND DECEIT--AND CIA CONNECTIONS TO DRUG RUNNERS OVER SEVERAL DECADES ARE THOROUGHLY DOCUMENTED--
--THEY ACTUALLY THINK THIS MIGHT BE TRUE?
THOSE NEGROES WILL BELIEVE ANYTHING!
The New York Times
OF COURSE, AS THE TIMES DUTIFULLY NOTED, THE CIA CONDUCTED ITS OWN INVESTIGATION INTO THESE CHARGES--AND FOUND NO EVIDENCE OF ITS OWN INVOLVEMENT IN ANY WRONGDOING...
WELL, THEN--THAT CERTAINLY CLEARS THAT UP, DOESN'T IT?
HEY--WE CAN'T ARGUE WITH AN OFFICIAL SOURCE!
AND WE THINK THAT'S JUST GREAT! WHY, IF SUCH RIGOROUS STANDARDS WERE APPLIED TO OTHER CRIMINAL INQUIRIES--WELL, JUST IMAGINE HOW MUCH TIME AND EFFORT COULD BE SAVED...
I'VE INVESTIGATED MYSELF THOROUGHLY, OFFICERS--AND I FIND NO EVIDENCE I COMMITTED THESE MURDERS!
HEY, THAT'S GOOD ENOUGH FOR ME!
GUESS WE'LL BE ON OUR WAY!
©TOM TOMORROW 11-27-96

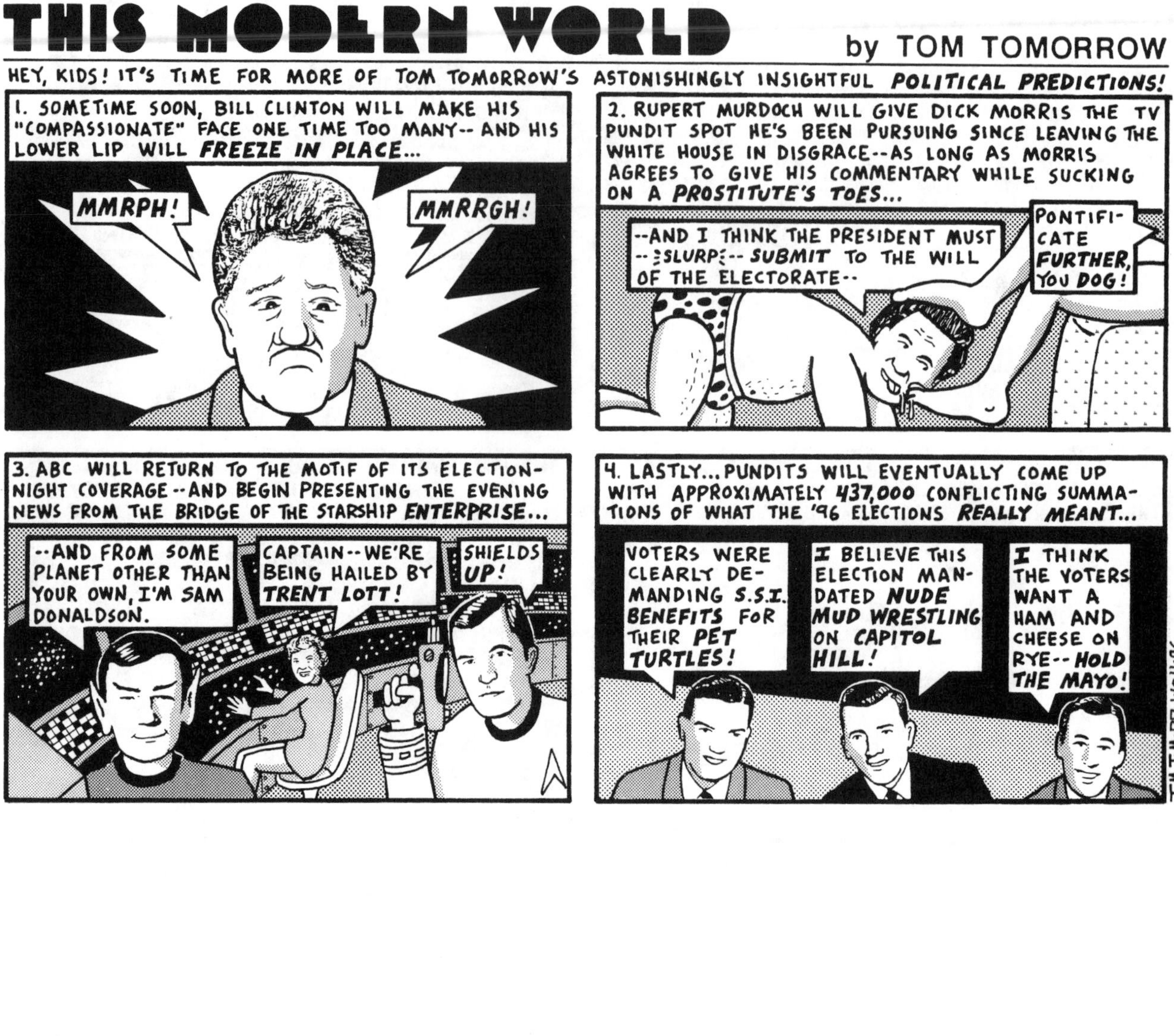
THIS MODERN WORLD
by TOM TOMORROW
HEY, KIDS! IT'S TIME FOR MORE OF TOM TOMORROW'S ASTONISHINGLY INSIGHTFUL POLITICAL PREDICTIONS!
1. SOMETIME SOON, BILL CLINTON WILL MAKE HIS "COMPASSIONATE" FACE ONE TIME TOO MANY-- AND HIS LOWER LIP WILL FREEZE IN PLACE...
MMRPH!
MMRRGH!
2. RUPERT MURDOCH WILL GIVE DICK MORRIS THE TV PUNDIT SPOT HE'S BEEN PURSUING SINCE LEAVING THE WHITE HOUSE IN DISGRACE--AS LONG AS MORRIS AGREES TO GIVE HIS COMMENTARY WHILE SUCKING ON A PROSTITUTE'S TOES...
--AND I THINK THE PRESIDENT MUST --SLURP-- SUBMIT TO THE WILL OF THE ELECTORATE--
PONTIFICATE FURTHER, YOU DOG!
3. ABC WILL RETURN TO THE MOTIF OF ITS ELECTION-NIGHT COVERAGE--AND BEGIN PRESENTING THE EVENING NEWS FROM THE BRIDGE OF THE STARSHIP ENTERPRISE...
--AND FROM SOME PLANET OTHER THAN YOUR OWN, I'M SAM DONALDSON.
CAPTAIN--WE'RE BEING HAILED BY TRENT LOTT!
SHIELDS UP!
4. LASTLY...PUNDITS WILL EVENTUALLY COME UP WITH APPROXIMATELY 437,000 CONFLICTING SUMMATIONS OF WHAT THE '96 ELECTIONS REALLY MEANT...
VOTERS WERE CLEARLY DEMANDING S.S.I. BENEFITS FOR THEIR PET TURTLES!
I BELIEVE THIS ELECTION MANDATED NUDE MUD WRESTLING ON CAPITOL HILL!
I THINK THE VOTERS WANT A HAM AND CHEESE ON RYE--HOLD THE MAYO!
TOM TOMORROW©11-96

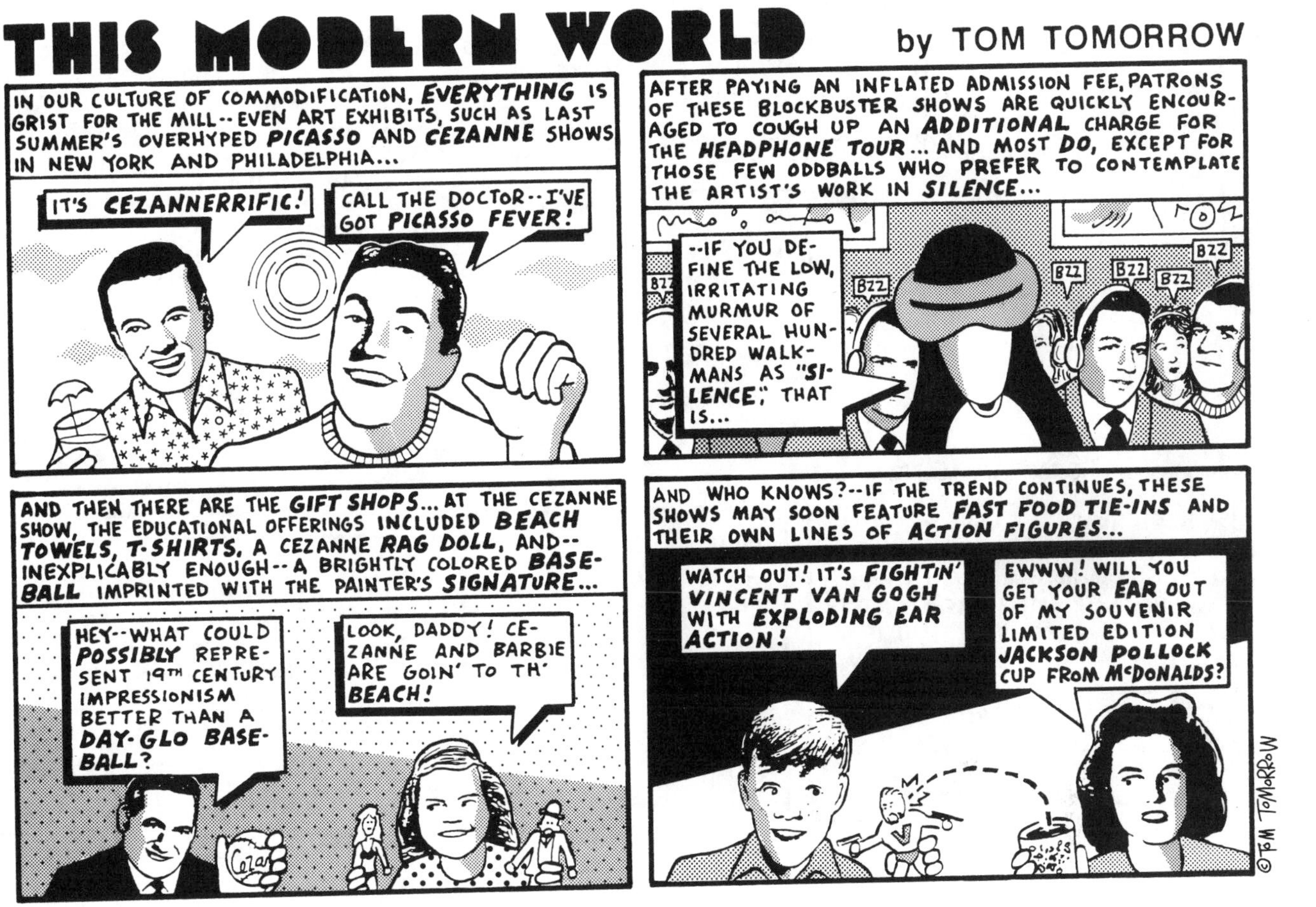
THIS MODERN WORLD
by TOM TOMORROW
IN OUR CULTURE OF COMMODIFICATION, EVERYTHING IS GRIST FOR THE MILL--EVEN ART EXHIBITS, SUCH AS LAST SUMMER'S OVERHYPED PICASSO AND CEZANNE SHOWS IN NEW YORK AND PHILADELPHIA...
IT'S CEZANNERRIFIC!
CALL THE DOCTOR--I'VE GOT PICASSO FEVER!
AFTER PAYING AN INFLATED ADMISSION FEE, PATRONS OF THESE BLOCKBUSTER SHOWS ARE QUICKLY ENCOURAGED TO COUGH UP AN ADDITIONAL CHARGE FOR THE HEADPHONE TOUR... AND MOST DO, EXCEPT FOR THOSE FEW ODDBALLS WHO PREFER TO CONTEMPLATE THE ARTIST'S WORK IN SILENCE...
--IF YOU DEFINE THE LOW, IRRITATING MURMUR OF SEVERAL HUNDRED WALKMANS AS "SILENCE," THAT IS...
BZZ
AND THEN THERE ARE THE GIFT SHOPS... AT THE CEZANNE SHOW, THE EDUCATIONAL OFFERINGS INCLUDED BEACH TOWELS, T-SHIRTS, A CEZANNE RAG DOLL, AND--INEXPLICABLY ENOUGH--A BRIGHTLY COLORED BASEBALL IMPRINTED WITH THE PAINTER'S SIGNATURE...
HEY--WHAT COULD POSSIBLY REPRESENT 19TH CENTURY IMPRESSIONISM BETTER THAN A DAY-GLO BASEBALL?
LOOK, DADDY! CEZANNE AND BARBIE ARE GOIN' TO TH' BEACH!
AND WHO KNOWS?--IF THE TREND CONTINUES, THESE SHOWS MAY SOON FEATURE FAST FOOD TIE-INS AND THEIR OWN LINES OF ACTION FIGURES...
WATCH OUT! IT'S FIGHTIN' VINCENT VAN GOGH WITH EXPLODING EAR ACTION!
EWWW! WILL YOU GET YOUR EAR OUT OF MY SOUVENIR LIMITED EDITION JACKSON POLLOCK CUP FROM McDONALDS?
© TOM TOMORROW

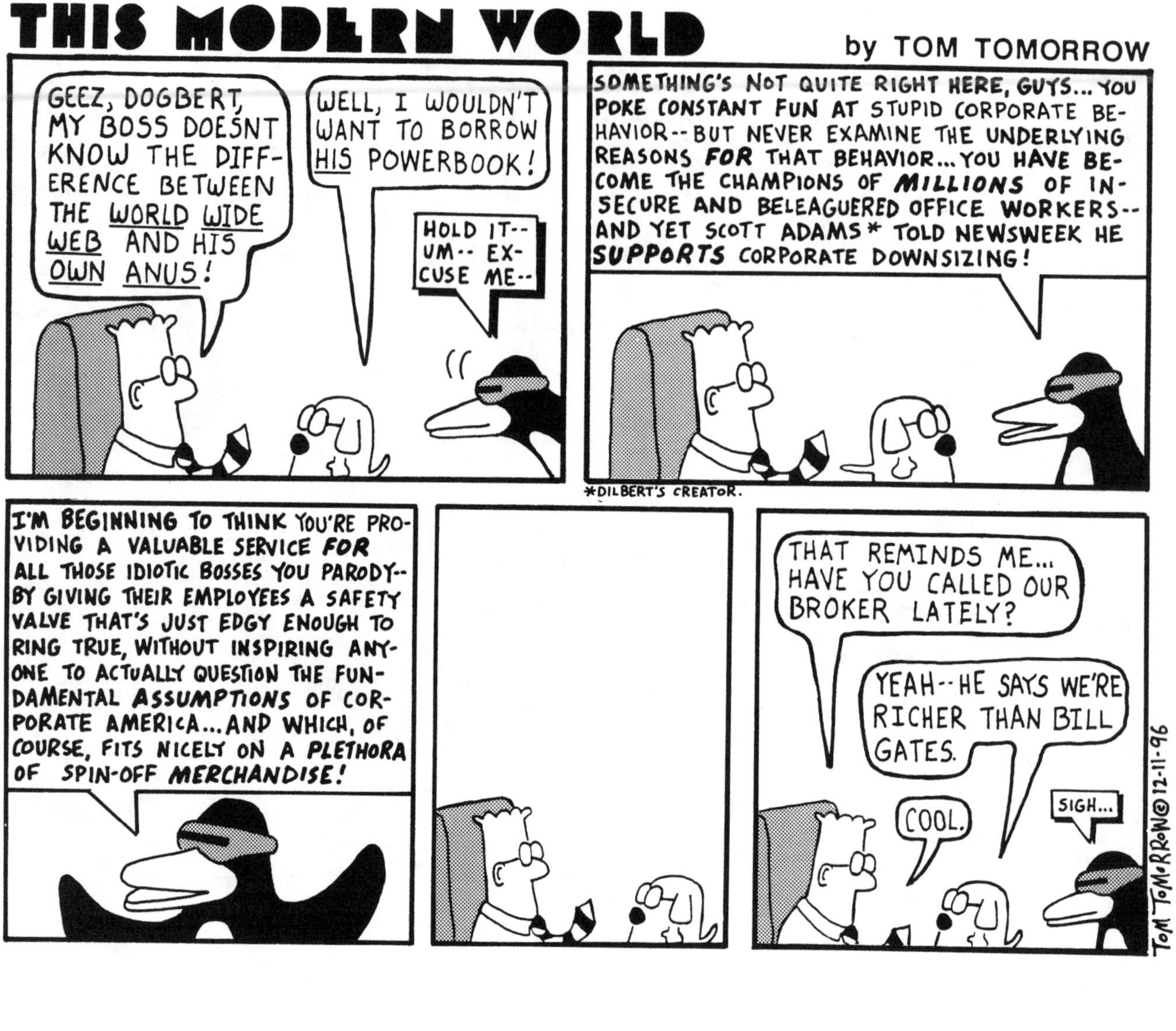
THIS MODERN WORLD
by TOM TOMORROW
GEEZ, DOGBERT, MY BOSS DOESNT KNOW THE DIFFERENCE BETWEEN THE WORLD WIDE WEB AND HIS OWN ANUS!
WELL, I WOULDN'T WANT TO BORROW HIS POWERBOOK!
HOLD IT-- UM-- EXCUSE ME--
SOMETHING'S NOT QUITE RIGHT HERE, GUYS... YOU POKE CONSTANT FUN AT STUPID CORPORATE BEHAVIOR--BUT NEVER EXAMINE THE UNDERLYING REASONS FOR THAT BEHAVIOR... YOU HAVE BECOME THE CHAMPIONS OF MILLIONS OF INSECURE AND BELEAGUERED OFFICE WORKERS--AND YET SCOTT ADAMS* TOLD NEWSWEEK HE SUPPORTS CORPORATE DOWNSIZING!
*DILBERT'S CREATOR.
I'M BEGINNING TO THINK YOU'RE PROVIDING A VALUABLE SERVICE FOR ALL THOSE IDIOTIC BOSSES YOU PARODY--BY GIVING THEIR EMPLOYEES A SAFETY VALVE THAT'S JUST EDGY ENOUGH TO RING TRUE, WITHOUT INSPIRING ANYONE TO ACTUALLY QUESTION THE FUNDAMENTAL ASSUMPTIONS OF CORPORATE AMERICA... AND WHICH, OF COURSE, FITS NICELY ON A PLETHORA OF SPIN-OFF MERCHANDISE!
THAT REMINDS ME... HAVE YOU CALLED OUR BROKER LATELY?
YEAH--HE SAYS WE'RE RICHER THAN BILL GATES.
COOL.
SIGH...
TOM TOMORROW © 12-11-96

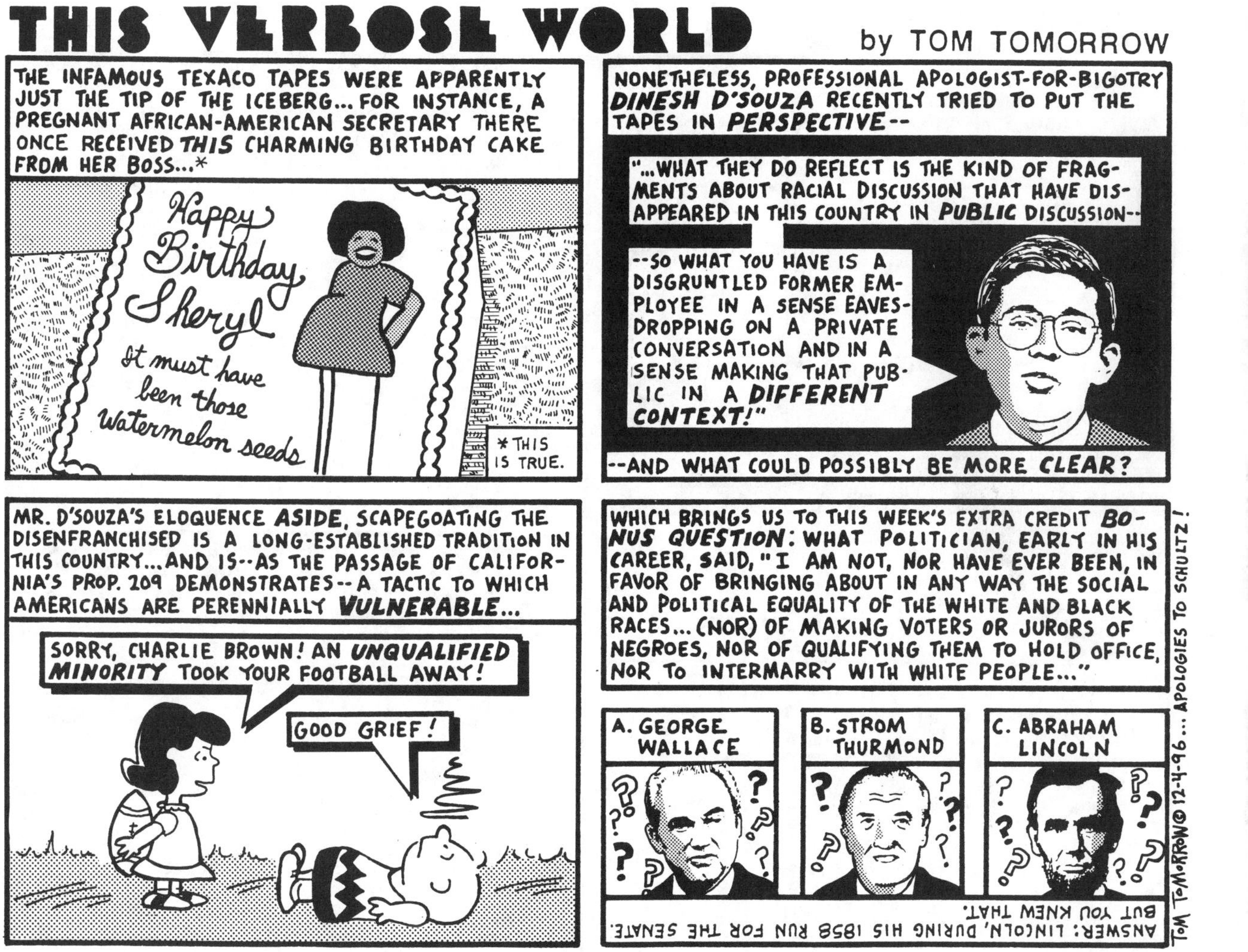
THIS VERBOSE WORLD
by TOM TOMORROW
THE INFAMOUS TEXACO TAPES WERE APPARENTLY JUST THE TIP OF THE ICEBERG... FOR INSTANCE, A PREGNANT AFRICAN-AMERICAN SECRETARY THERE ONCE RECEIVED THIS CHARMING BIRTHDAY CAKE FROM HER BOSS...*
Happy Birthday Sheryl
It must have been those Watermelon seeds
*THIS IS TRUE.
NONETHELESS, PROFESSIONAL APOLOGIST-FOR-BIGOTRY DINESH D'SOUZA RECENTLY TRIED TO PUT THE TAPES IN PERSPECTIVE--
"...WHAT THEY DO REFLECT IS THE KIND OF FRAGMENTS ABOUT RACIAL DISCUSSION THAT HAVE DISAPPEARED IN THIS COUNTRY IN PUBLIC DISCUSSION--
--SO WHAT YOU HAVE IS A DISGRUNTLED FORMER EMPLOYEE IN A SENSE EAVESDROPPING ON A PRIVATE CONVERSATION AND IN A SENSE MAKING THAT PUBLIC IN A DIFFERENT CONTEXT!"
--AND WHAT COULD POSSIBLY BE MORE CLEAR?
MR. D'SOUZA'S ELOQUENCE ASIDE, SCAPEGOATING THE DISENFRANCHISED IS A LONG-ESTABLISHED TRADITION IN THIS COUNTRY... AND IS--AS THE PASSAGE OF CALIFORNIA'S PROP. 209 DEMONSTRATES--A TACTIC TO WHICH AMERICANS ARE PERENNIALLY VULNERABLE...
SORRY, CHARLIE BROWN! AN UNQUALIFIED MINORITY TOOK YOUR FOOTBALL AWAY!
GOOD GRIEF!
WHICH BRINGS US TO THIS WEEK'S EXTRA CREDIT BONUS QUESTION: WHAT POLITICIAN, EARLY IN HIS CAREER, SAID, "I AM NOT, NOR HAVE EVER BEEN, IN FAVOR OF BRINGING ABOUT IN ANY WAY THE SOCIAL AND POLITICAL EQUALITY OF THE WHITE AND BLACK RACES... (NOR) OF MAKING VOTERS OR JURORS OF NEGROES, NOR OF QUALIFYING THEM TO HOLD OFFICE, NOR TO INTERMARRY WITH WHITE PEOPLE..."
A. GEORGE WALLACE
B. STROM THURMOND
C. ABRAHAM LINCOLN
ANSWER: LINCOLN, DURING HIS 1858 RUN FOR THE SENATE. BUT YOU KNEW THAT.
TOM TOMORROW© 12-4-96... APOLOGIES TO SCHULTZ!

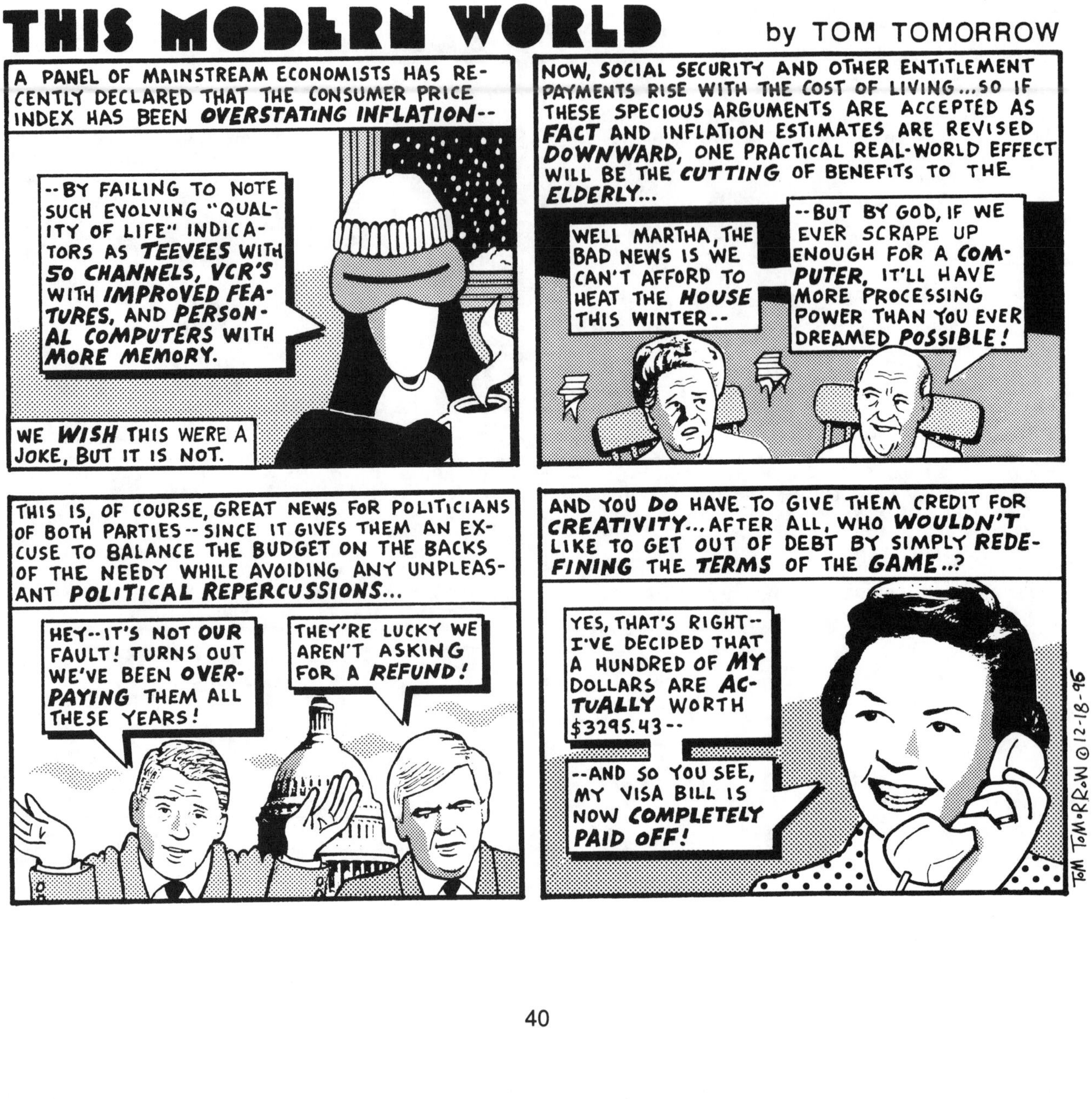
THIS MODERN WORLD
by TOM TOMORROW
A PANEL OF MAINSTREAM ECONOMISTS HAS RECENTLY DECLARED THAT THE CONSUMER PRICE INDEX HAS BEEN OVERSTATING INFLATION--
--BY FAILING TO NOTE SUCH EVOLVING "QUALITY OF LIFE" INDICATORS AS TEEVEES WITH 50 CHANNELS, VCR'S WITH IMPROVED FEATURES, AND PERSONAL COMPUTERS WITH MORE MEMORY.
WE WISH THIS WERE A JOKE, BUT IT IS NOT.
NOW, SOCIAL SECURITY AND OTHER ENTITLEMENT PAYMENTS RISE WITH THE COST OF LIVING...SO IF THESE SPECIOUS ARGUMENTS ARE ACCEPTED AS FACT AND INFLATION ESTIMATES ARE REVISED DOWNWARD, ONE PRACTICAL REAL-WORLD EFFECT WILL BE THE CUTTING OF BENEFITS TO THE ELDERLY...
WELL MARTHA, THE BAD NEWS IS WE CAN'T AFFORD TO HEAT THE HOUSE THIS WINTER--
--BUT BY GOD, IF WE EVER SCRAPE UP ENOUGH FOR A COMPUTER, IT'LL HAVE MORE PROCESSING POWER THAN YOU EVER DREAMED POSSIBLE!
THIS IS, OF COURSE, GREAT NEWS FOR POLITICIANS OF BOTH PARTIES--SINCE IT GIVES THEM AN EXCUSE TO BALANCE THE BUDGET ON THE BACKS OF THE NEEDY WHILE AVOIDING ANY UNPLEASANT POLITICAL REPERCUSSIONS...
HEY--IT'S NOT OUR FAULT! TURNS OUT WE'VE BEEN OVERPAYING THEM ALL THESE YEARS!
THEY'RE LUCKY WE AREN'T ASKING FOR A REFUND!
AND YOU DO HAVE TO GIVE THEM CREDIT FOR CREATIVITY...AFTER ALL, WHO WOULDN'T LIKE TO GET OUT OF DEBT BY SIMPLY REDEFINING THE TERMS OF THE GAME..?
YES, THAT'S RIGHT--I'VE DECIDED THAT A HUNDRED OF MY DOLLARS ARE ACTUALLY WORTH $3295.43--
--AND SO YOU SEE, MY VISA BILL IS NOW COMPLETELY PAID OFF!
TOM TOMORROW ©12-18-96

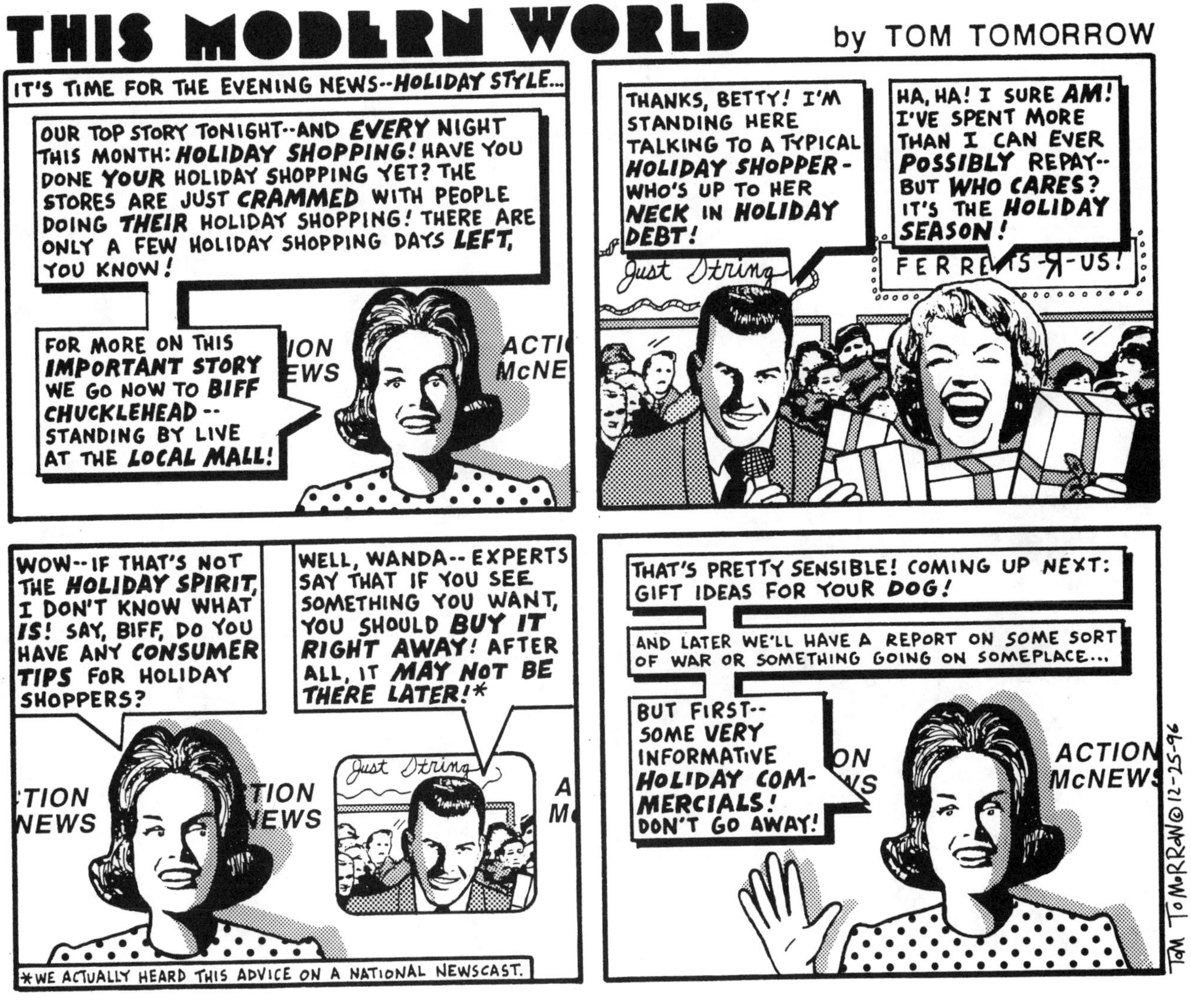
THIS MODERN WORLD
by TOM TOMORROW
IT'S TIME FOR THE EVENING NEWS--HOLIDAY STYLE...
OUR TOP STORY TONIGHT--AND EVERY NIGHT THIS MONTH: HOLIDAY SHOPPING! HAVE YOU DONE YOUR HOLIDAY SHOPPING YET? THE STORES ARE JUST CRAMMED WITH PEOPLE DOING THEIR HOLIDAY SHOPPING! THERE ARE ONLY A FEW HOLIDAY SHOPPING DAYS LEFT, YOU KNOW!
FOR MORE ON THIS IMPORTANT STORY WE GO NOW TO BIFF CHUCKLEHEAD -- STANDING BY LIVE AT THE LOCAL MALL!
THANKS, BETTY! I'M STANDING HERE TALKING TO A TYPICAL HOLIDAY SHOPPER - WHO'S UP TO HER NECK IN HOLIDAY DEBT!
HA, HA! I SURE AM! I'VE SPENT MORE THAN I CAN EVER POSSIBLY REPAY-- BUT WHO CARES? IT'S THE HOLIDAY SEASON!
Just String
WOW--IF THAT'S NOT THE HOLIDAY SPIRIT, I DON'T KNOW WHAT IS! SAY, BIFF, DO YOU HAVE ANY CONSUMER TIPS FOR HOLIDAY SHOPPERS?
WELL, WANDA-- EXPERTS SAY THAT IF YOU SEE SOMETHING YOU WANT, YOU SHOULD BUY IT RIGHT AWAY! AFTER ALL, IT MAY NOT BE THERE LATER!*
*WE ACTUALLY HEARD THIS ADVICE ON A NATIONAL NEWSCAST.
THAT'S PRETTY SENSIBLE! COMING UP NEXT: GIFT IDEAS FOR YOUR DOG!
AND LATER WE'LL HAVE A REPORT ON SOME SORT OF WAR OR SOMETHING GOING ON SOMEPLACE...
BUT FIRST-- SOME VERY INFORMATIVE HOLIDAY COMMERCIALS! DON'T GO AWAY!
ACTION McNEWS
TOM TOMORROW © 12-25-96

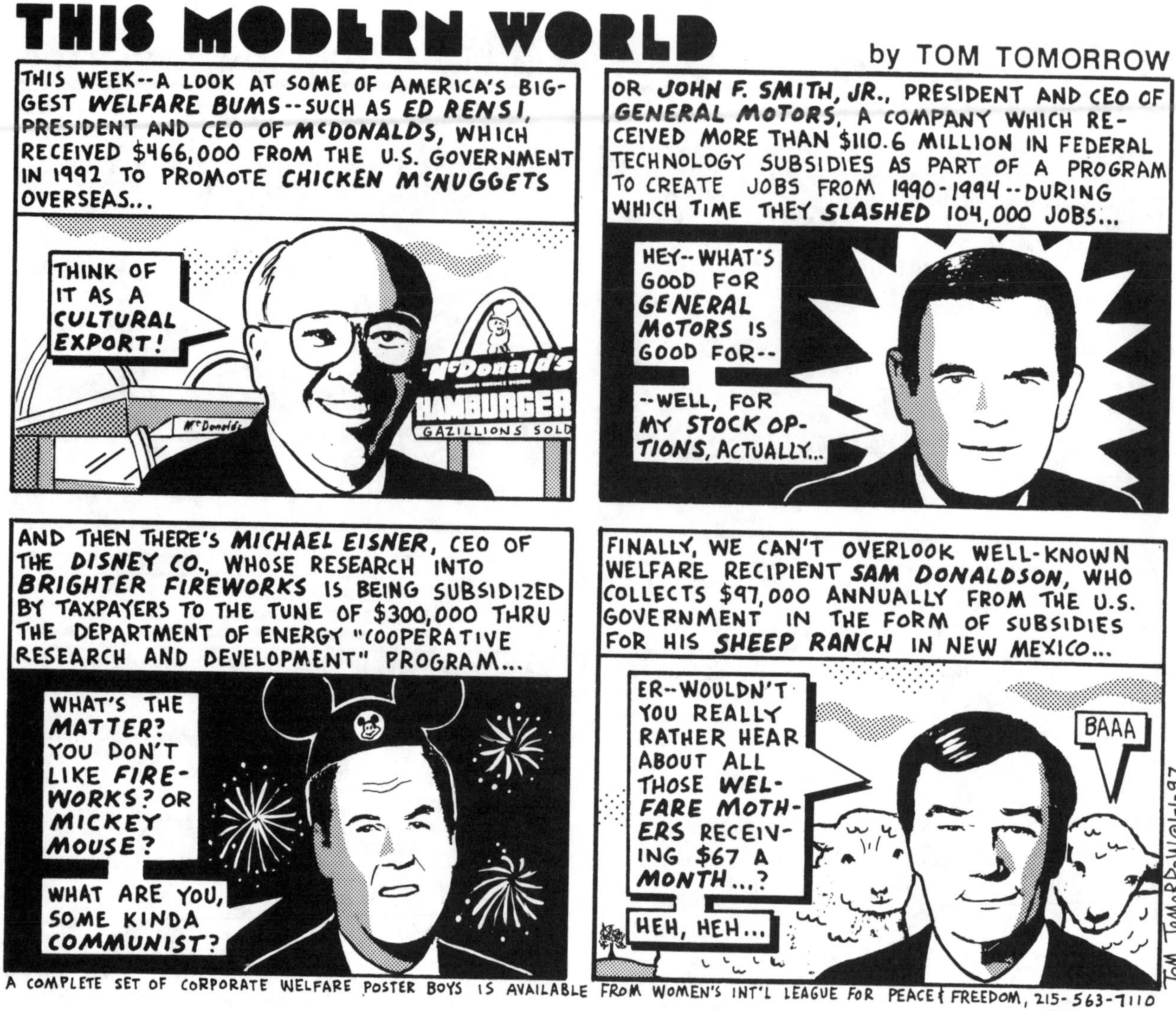
THIS MODERN WORLD
by TOM TOMORROW
THIS WEEK--A LOOK AT SOME OF AMERICA'S BIGGEST WELFARE BUMS--SUCH AS ED RENSI, PRESIDENT AND CEO OF McDONALDS, WHICH RECEIVED $466,000 FROM THE U.S. GOVERNMENT IN 1992 TO PROMOTE CHICKEN McNUGGETS OVERSEAS...
THINK OF IT AS A CULTURAL EXPORT!
McDonald's
HAMBURGER
GAZILLIONS SOLD
OR JOHN F. SMITH, JR., PRESIDENT AND CEO OF GENERAL MOTORS, A COMPANY WHICH RECEIVED MORE THAN $110.6 MILLION IN FEDERAL TECHNOLOGY SUBSIDIES AS PART OF A PROGRAM TO CREATE JOBS FROM 1990-1994--DURING WHICH TIME THEY SLASHED 104,000 JOBS...
HEY--WHAT'S GOOD FOR GENERAL MOTORS IS GOOD FOR--
--WELL, FOR MY STOCK OPTIONS, ACTUALLY...
AND THEN THERE'S MICHAEL EISNER, CEO OF THE DISNEY CO., WHOSE RESEARCH INTO BRIGHTER FIREWORKS IS BEING SUBSIDIZED BY TAXPAYERS TO THE TUNE OF $300,000 THRU THE DEPARTMENT OF ENERGY "COOPERATIVE RESEARCH AND DEVELOPMENT" PROGRAM...
WHAT'S THE MATTER? YOU DON'T LIKE FIREWORKS? OR MICKEY MOUSE?
WHAT ARE YOU, SOME KINDA COMMUNIST?
FINALLY, WE CAN'T OVERLOOK WELL-KNOWN WELFARE RECIPIENT SAM DONALDSON, WHO COLLECTS $97,000 ANNUALLY FROM THE U.S. GOVERNMENT IN THE FORM OF SUBSIDIES FOR HIS SHEEP RANCH IN NEW MEXICO...
ER--WOULDN'T YOU REALLY RATHER HEAR ABOUT ALL THOSE WELFARE MOTHERS RECEIVING $67 A MONTH...?
HEH, HEH...
BAAA
TOM TOMORROW©1-1-97
A COMPLETE SET OF CORPORATE WELFARE POSTER BOYS IS AVAILABLE FROM WOMEN'S INT'L LEAGUE FOR PEACE & FREEDOM, 215-563-7110

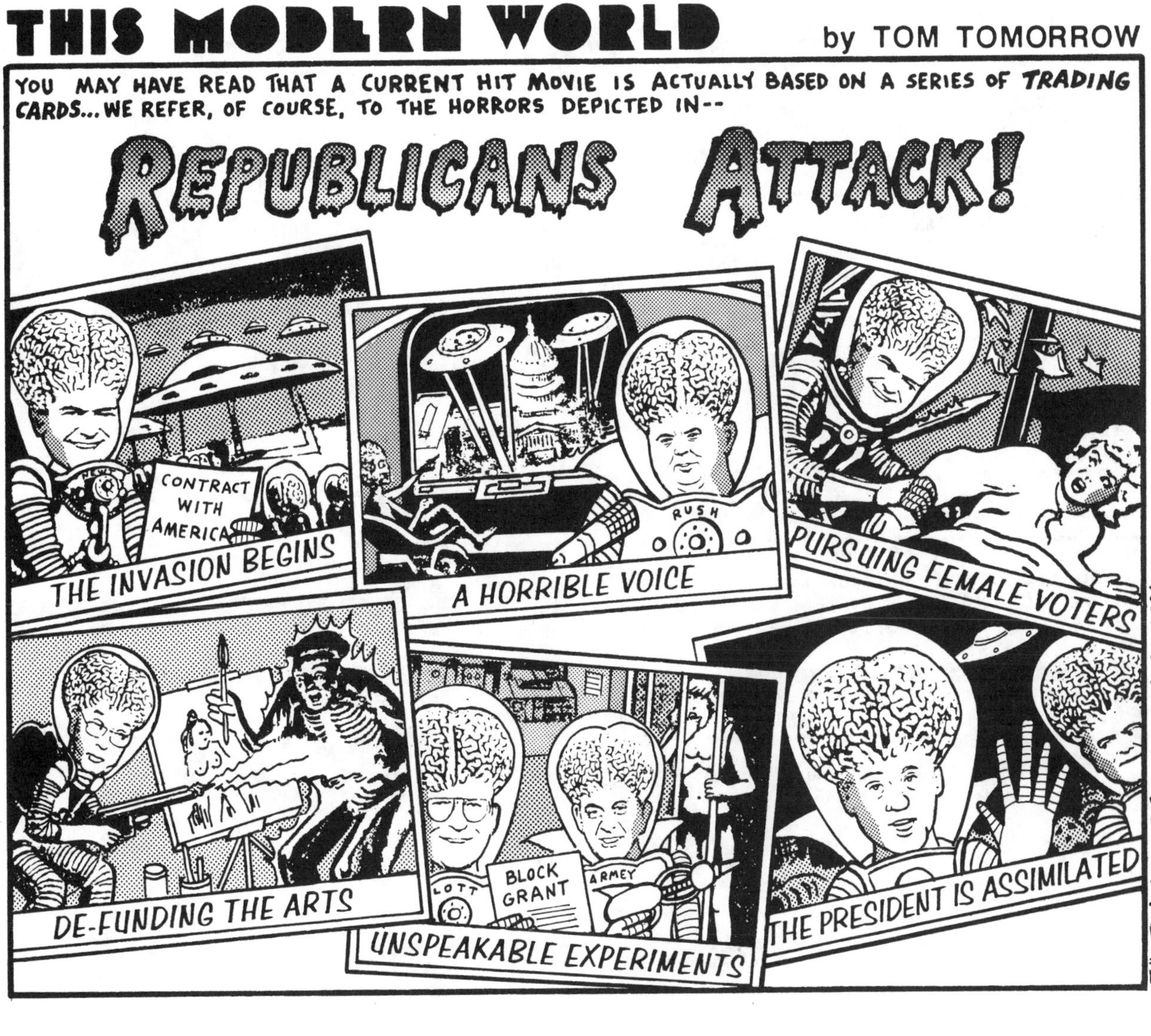
THIS MODERN WORLD
by TOM TOMORROW
YOU MAY HAVE READ THAT A CURRENT HIT MOVIE IS ACTUALLY BASED ON A SERIES OF TRADING CARDS... WE REFER, OF COURSE, TO THE HORRORS DEPICTED IN--
REPUBLICANS ATTACK!
CONTRACT WITH AMERICA
THE INVASION BEGINS
RUSH
A HORRIBLE VOICE
PURSUING FEMALE VOTERS
DE-FUNDING THE ARTS
LOTT
BLOCK GRANT
ARMEY
UNSPEAKABLE EXPERIMENTS
THE PRESIDENT IS ASSIMILATED
TOM TOMORROW ©1-15-97 · APOLOGIES TO TOPPS

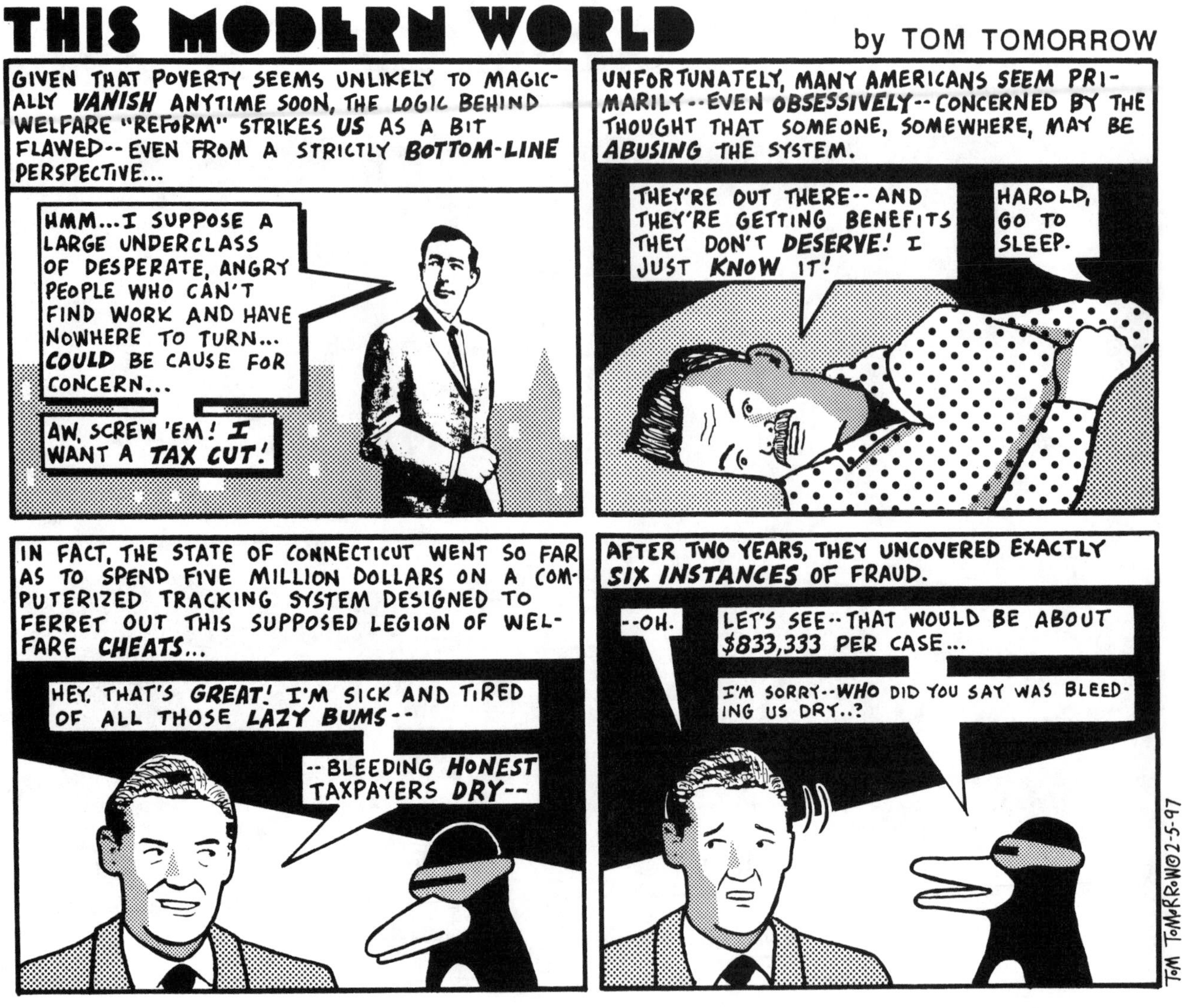
THIS MODERN WORLD
by TOM TOMORROW
GIVEN THAT POVERTY SEEMS UNLIKELY TO MAGICALLY VANISH ANYTIME SOON, THE LOGIC BEHIND WELFARE "REFORM" STRIKES US AS A BIT FLAWED--EVEN FROM A STRICTLY BOTTOM-LINE PERSPECTIVE...
HMM...I SUPPOSE A LARGE UNDERCLASS OF DESPERATE, ANGRY PEOPLE WHO CAN'T FIND WORK AND HAVE NOWHERE TO TURN... COULD BE CAUSE FOR CONCERN...
AW, SCREW 'EM! I WANT A TAX CUT!
UNFORTUNATELY, MANY AMERICANS SEEM PRIMARILY--EVEN OBSESSIVELY--CONCERNED BY THE THOUGHT THAT SOMEONE, SOMEWHERE, MAY BE ABUSING THE SYSTEM.
THEY'RE OUT THERE--AND THEY'RE GETTING BENEFITS THEY DON'T DESERVE! I JUST KNOW IT!
HAROLD, GO TO SLEEP.
IN FACT, THE STATE OF CONNECTICUT WENT SO FAR AS TO SPEND FIVE MILLION DOLLARS ON A COMPUTERIZED TRACKING SYSTEM DESIGNED TO FERRET OUT THIS SUPPOSED LEGION OF WELFARE CHEATS...
HEY, THAT'S GREAT! I'M SICK AND TIRED OF ALL THOSE LAZY BUMS--
--BLEEDING HONEST TAXPAYERS DRY--
AFTER TWO YEARS, THEY UNCOVERED EXACTLY SIX INSTANCES OF FRAUD.
--OH.
LET'S SEE--THAT WOULD BE ABOUT $833,333 PER CASE...
I'M SORRY--WHO DID YOU SAY WAS BLEEDING US DRY..?
TOM TOMORROW©2-5-97

THIS MODERN WORLD
by TOM TOMORROW

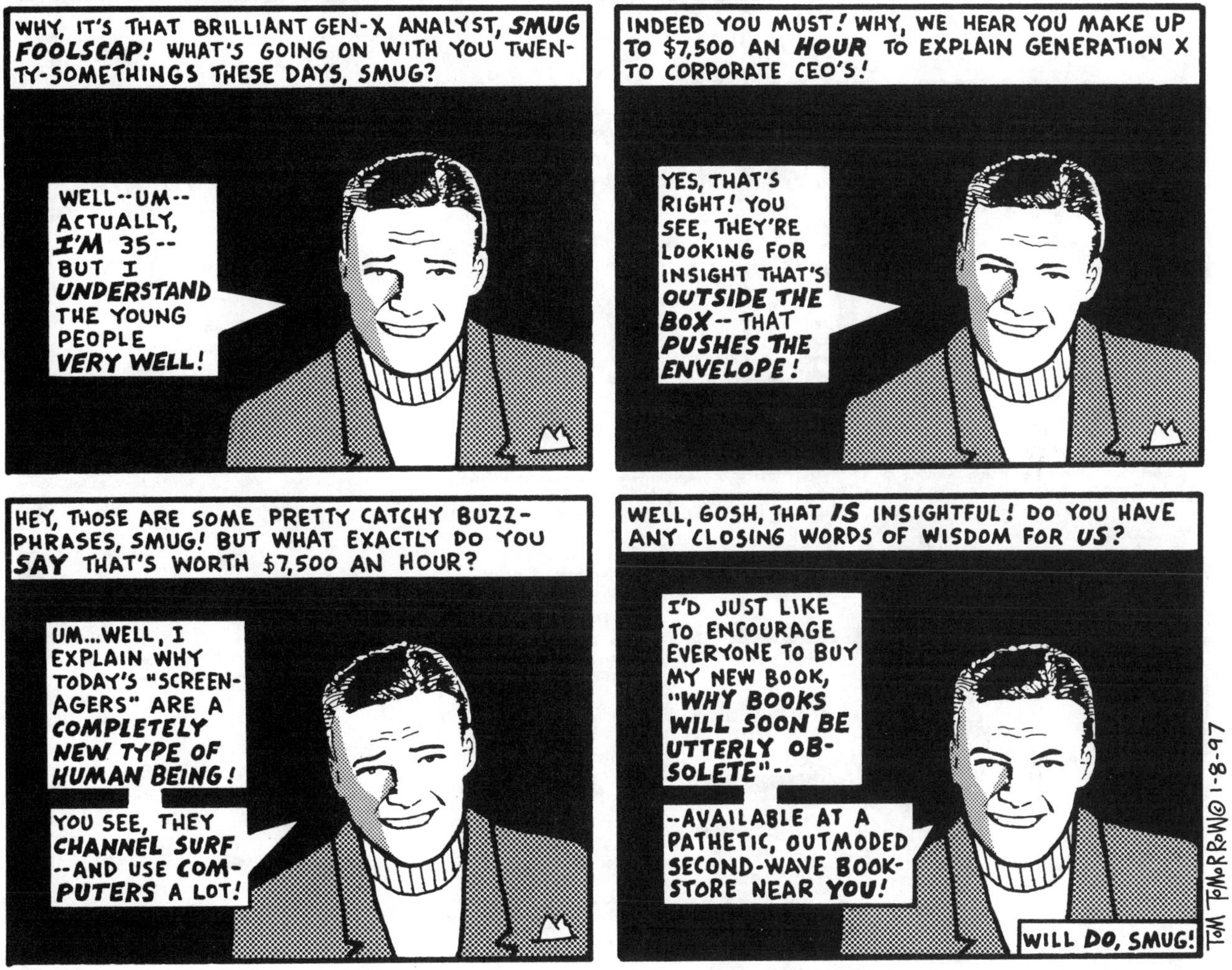
WHY, IT'S THAT BRILLIANT GEN-X ANALYST, SMUG FOOLSCAP! WHAT'S GOING ON WITH YOU TWENTY-SOMETHINGS THESE DAYS, SMUG?
WELL--UM--ACTUALLY, I'M 35--BUT I UNDERSTAND THE YOUNG PEOPLE VERY WELL!
INDEED YOU MUST! WHY, WE HEAR YOU MAKE UP TO $7,500 AN HOUR TO EXPLAIN GENERATION X TO CORPORATE CEO'S!
YES, THAT'S RIGHT! YOU SEE, THEY'RE LOOKING FOR INSIGHT THAT'S OUTSIDE THE BOX--THAT PUSHES THE ENVELOPE!
HEY, THOSE ARE SOME PRETTY CATCHY BUZZ-PHRASES, SMUG! BUT WHAT EXACTLY DO YOU SAY THAT'S WORTH $7,500 AN HOUR?
UM...WELL, I EXPLAIN WHY TODAY'S "SCREEN-AGERS" ARE A COMPLETELY NEW TYPE OF HUMAN BEING!
YOU SEE, THEY CHANNEL SURF--AND USE COMPUTERS A LOT!
WELL, GOSH, THAT IS INSIGHTFUL! DO YOU HAVE ANY CLOSING WORDS OF WISDOM FOR US?
I'D JUST LIKE TO ENCOURAGE EVERYONE TO BUY MY NEW BOOK, "WHY BOOKS WILL SOON BE UTTERLY OBSOLETE"--
--AVAILABLE AT A PATHETIC, OUTMODED SECOND-WAVE BOOKSTORE NEAR YOU!
WILL DO, SMUG!
TOM TOMORROW © 1-8-97

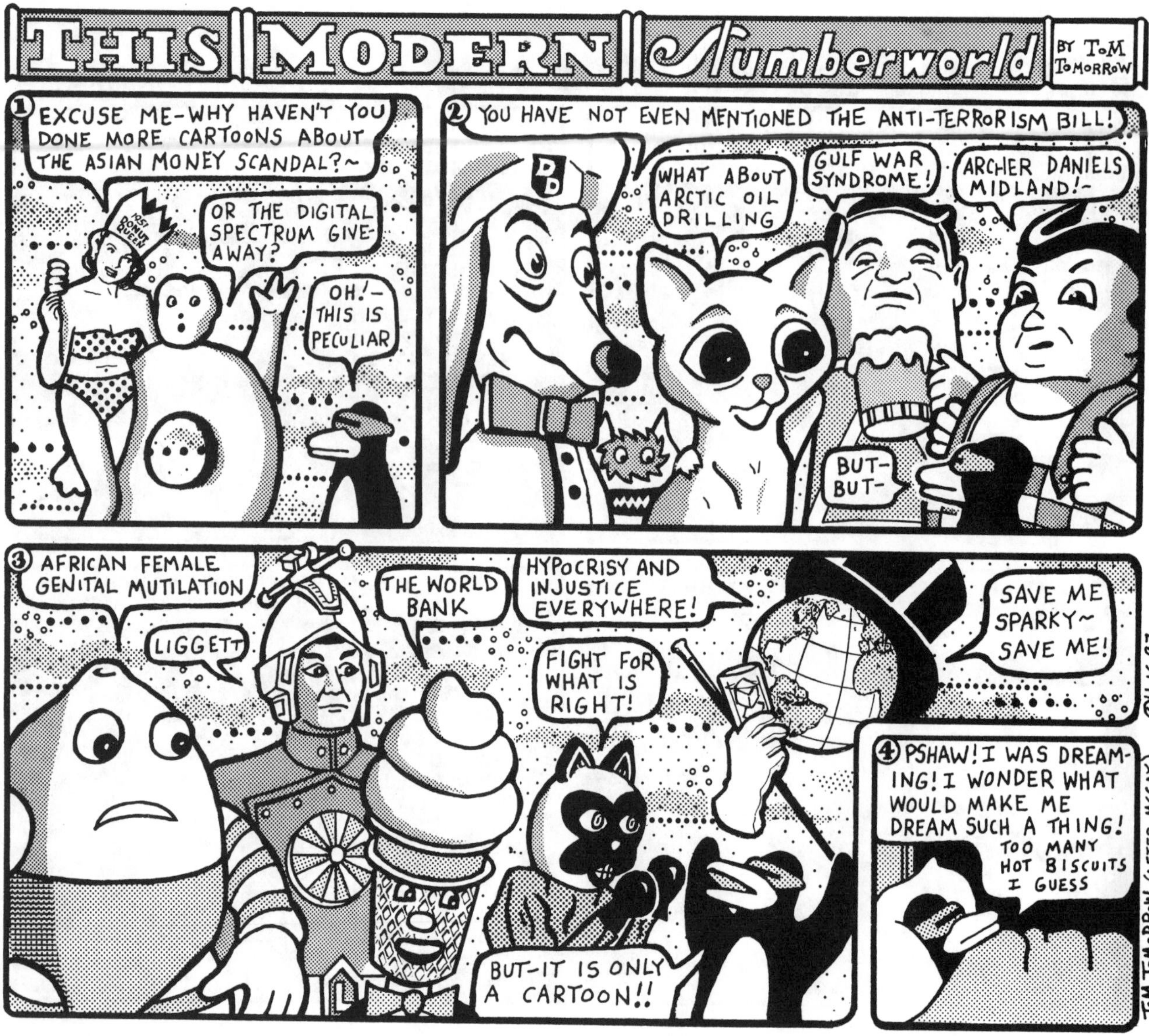
THIS MODERN Slumberworld
BY TOM TOMORROW
EXCUSE ME-WHY HAVEN'T YOU DONE MORE CARTOONS ABOUT THE ASIAN MONEY SCANDAL?~
1951 DONUT QUEEN
OR THE DIGITAL SPECTRUM GIVE-AWAY?
OH!- THIS IS PECULIAR
YOU HAVE NOT EVEN MENTIONED THE ANTI-TERRORISM BILL!
WHAT ABOUT ARCTIC OIL DRILLING
GULF WAR SYNDROME!
ARCHER DANIELS MIDLAND!~
BUT- BUT-
AFRICAN FEMALE GENITAL MUTILATION
LIGGETT
THE WORLD BANK
HYPOCRISY AND INJUSTICE EVERYWHERE!
FIGHT FOR WHAT IS RIGHT!
SAVE ME SPARKY~ SAVE ME!
BUT-IT IS ONLY A CARTOON!!
©4-16-97
PSHAW! I WAS DREAMING! I WONDER WHAT WOULD MAKE ME DREAM SUCH A THING!
TOO MANY HOT BISCUITS I GUESS
TOM TOMORROW (AFTER McCAY)

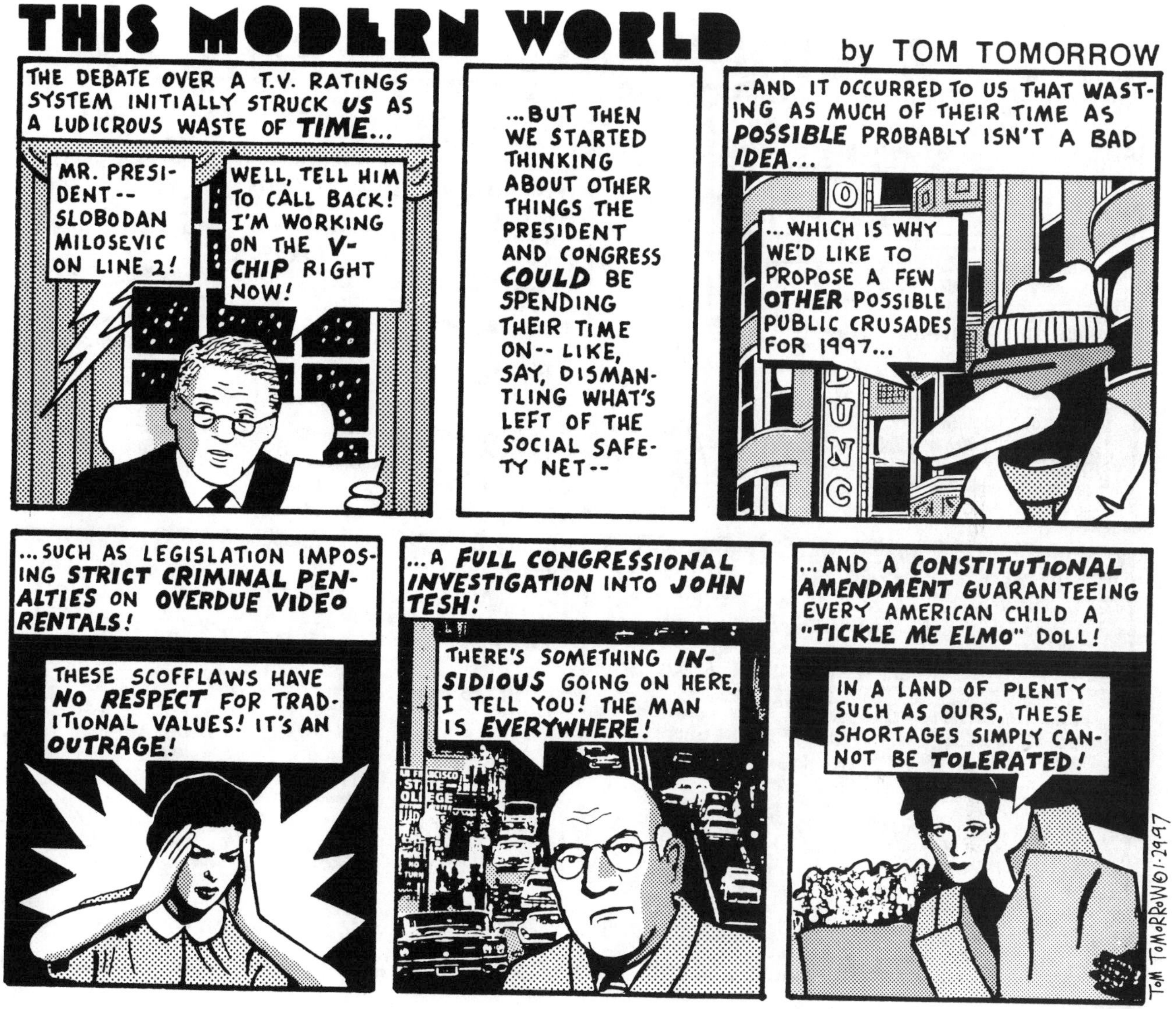
THIS MODERN WORLD
by TOM TOMORROW
THE DEBATE OVER A T.V. RATINGS SYSTEM INITIALLY STRUCK **US** AS A LUDICROUS WASTE OF **TIME**...
MR. PRESIDENT -- SLOBODAN MILOSEVIC ON LINE 2!
WELL, TELL HIM TO CALL BACK! I'M WORKING ON THE **V-CHIP** RIGHT NOW!
...BUT THEN WE STARTED THINKING ABOUT OTHER THINGS THE PRESIDENT AND CONGRESS **COULD** BE SPENDING THEIR TIME ON-- LIKE, SAY, DISMANTLING WHAT'S LEFT OF THE SOCIAL SAFETY NET--
--AND IT OCCURRED TO US THAT WASTING AS MUCH OF THEIR TIME AS **POSSIBLE** PROBABLY ISN'T A BAD **IDEA**...
...WHICH IS WHY WE'D LIKE TO PROPOSE A FEW **OTHER** POSSIBLE PUBLIC CRUSADES FOR 1997...
...SUCH AS LEGISLATION IMPOSING **STRICT CRIMINAL PENALTIES** ON **OVERDUE VIDEO RENTALS**!
THESE SCOFFLAWS HAVE **NO RESPECT** FOR TRADITIONAL VALUES! IT'S AN **OUTRAGE**!
...A **FULL CONGRESSIONAL INVESTIGATION** INTO **JOHN TESH**!
THERE'S SOMETHING **INSIDIOUS** GOING ON HERE, I TELL YOU! THE MAN IS **EVERYWHERE**!
...AND A **CONSTITUTIONAL AMENDMENT** GUARANTEEING EVERY AMERICAN CHILD A **"TICKLE ME ELMO"** DOLL!
IN A LAND OF PLENTY SUCH AS OURS, THESE SHORTAGES SIMPLY CANNOT BE **TOLERATED**!
TOM TOMORROW©1-29-97

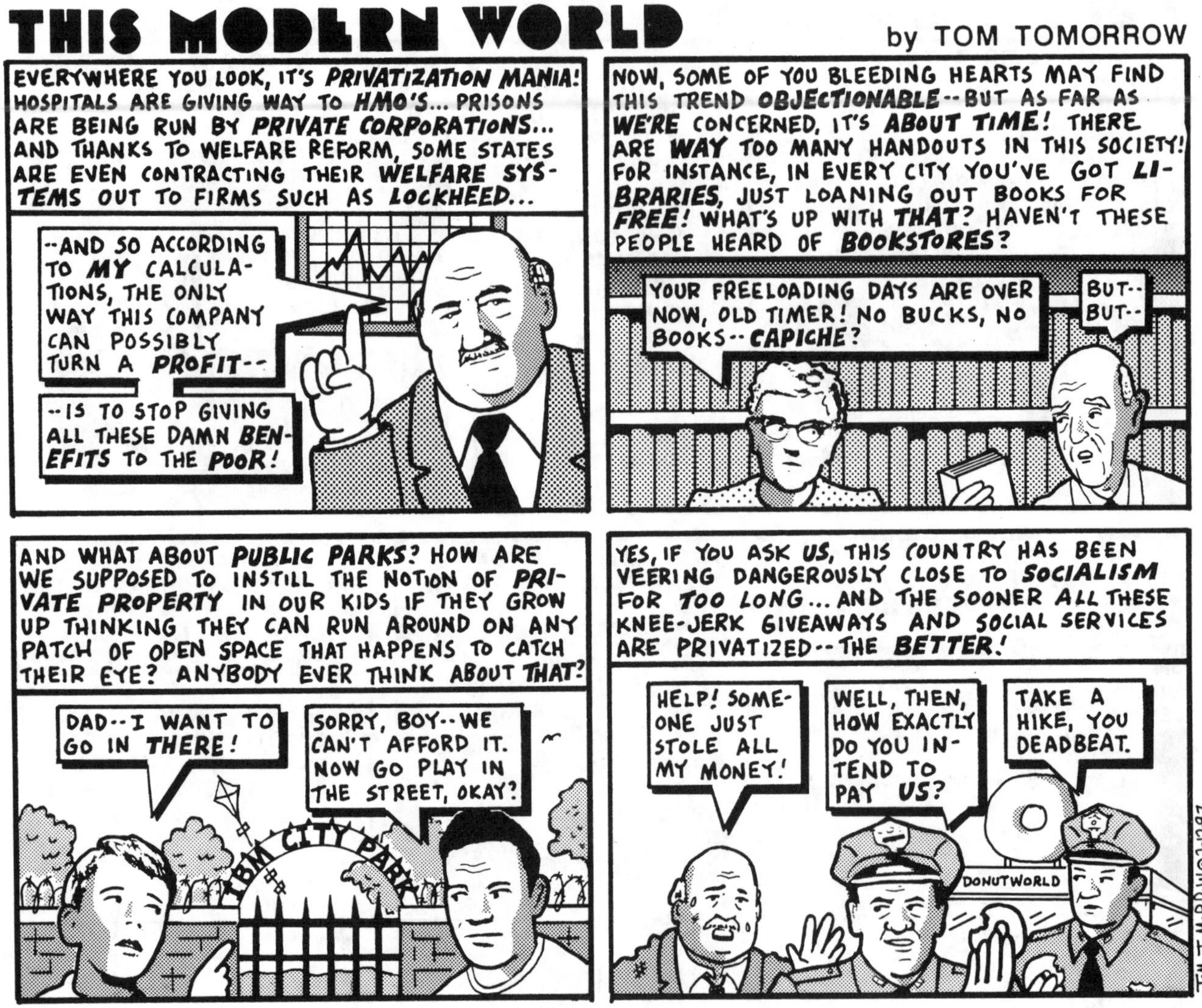
THIS MODERN WORLD
by TOM TOMORROW
EVERYWHERE YOU LOOK, IT'S PRIVATIZATION MANIA! HOSPITALS ARE GIVING WAY TO HMO'S... PRISONS ARE BEING RUN BY PRIVATE CORPORATIONS... AND THANKS TO WELFARE REFORM, SOME STATES ARE EVEN CONTRACTING THEIR WELFARE SYSTEMS OUT TO FIRMS SUCH AS LOCKHEED...
--AND SO ACCORDING TO MY CALCULATIONS, THE ONLY WAY THIS COMPANY CAN POSSIBLY TURN A PROFIT--
--IS TO STOP GIVING ALL THESE DAMN BENEFITS TO THE POOR!
NOW, SOME OF YOU BLEEDING HEARTS MAY FIND THIS TREND OBJECTIONABLE--BUT AS FAR AS WE'RE CONCERNED, IT'S ABOUT TIME! THERE ARE WAY TOO MANY HANDOUTS IN THIS SOCIETY! FOR INSTANCE, IN EVERY CITY YOU'VE GOT LIBRARIES, JUST LOANING OUT BOOKS FOR FREE! WHAT'S UP WITH THAT? HAVEN'T THESE PEOPLE HEARD OF BOOKSTORES?
YOUR FREELOADING DAYS ARE OVER NOW, OLD TIMER! NO BUCKS, NO BOOKS--CAPICHE?
BUT--BUT--
AND WHAT ABOUT PUBLIC PARKS? HOW ARE WE SUPPOSED TO INSTILL THE NOTION OF PRIVATE PROPERTY IN OUR KIDS IF THEY GROW UP THINKING THEY CAN RUN AROUND ON ANY PATCH OF OPEN SPACE THAT HAPPENS TO CATCH THEIR EYE? ANYBODY EVER THINK ABOUT THAT?
DAD--I WANT TO GO IN THERE!
SORRY, BOY--WE CAN'T AFFORD IT. NOW GO PLAY IN THE STREET, OKAY?
IBM CITY PARK
YES, IF YOU ASK US, THIS COUNTRY HAS BEEN VEERING DANGEROUSLY CLOSE TO SOCIALISM FOR TOO LONG... AND THE SOONER ALL THESE KNEE-JERK GIVEAWAYS AND SOCIAL SERVICES ARE PRIVATIZED--THE BETTER!
HELP! SOMEONE JUST STOLE ALL MY MONEY!
WELL, THEN, HOW EXACTLY DO YOU INTEND TO PAY US?
TAKE A HIKE, YOU DEADBEAT.
DONUTWORLD
TOM TOMORROW©2-12-97

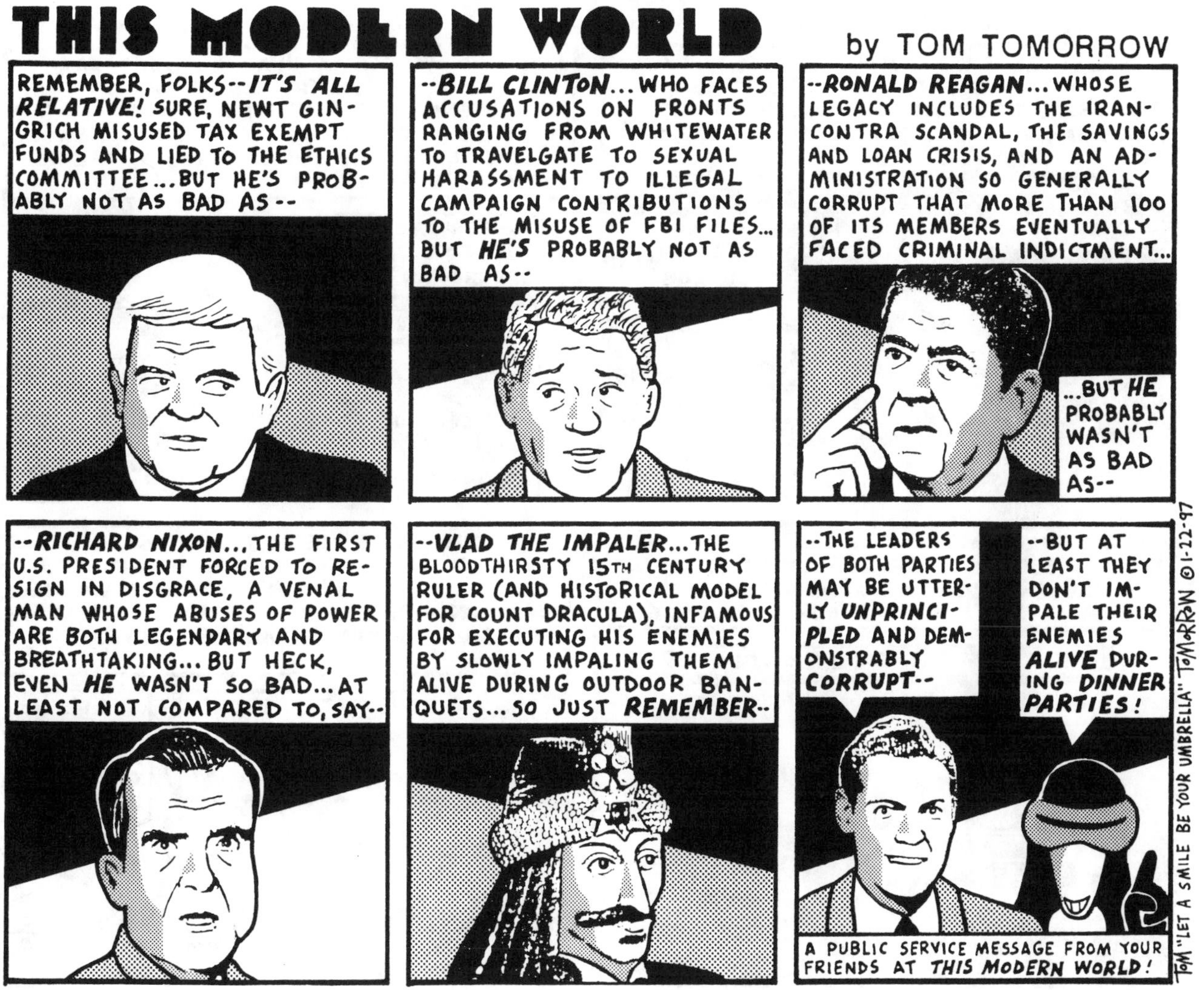
THIS MODERN WORLD
by TOM TOMORROW
REMEMBER, FOLKS--IT'S ALL RELATIVE! SURE, NEWT GINGRICH MISUSED TAX EXEMPT FUNDS AND LIED TO THE ETHICS COMMITTEE... BUT HE'S PROBABLY NOT AS BAD AS--
--BILL CLINTON... WHO FACES ACCUSATIONS ON FRONTS RANGING FROM WHITEWATER TO TRAVELGATE TO SEXUAL HARASSMENT TO ILLEGAL CAMPAIGN CONTRIBUTIONS TO THE MISUSE OF FBI FILES... BUT HE'S PROBABLY NOT AS BAD AS--
--RONALD REAGAN... WHOSE LEGACY INCLUDES THE IRAN-CONTRA SCANDAL, THE SAVINGS AND LOAN CRISIS, AND AN ADMINISTRATION SO GENERALLY CORRUPT THAT MORE THAN 100 OF ITS MEMBERS EVENTUALLY FACED CRIMINAL INDICTMENT...
...BUT HE PROBABLY WASN'T AS BAD AS--
--RICHARD NIXON... THE FIRST U.S. PRESIDENT FORCED TO RESIGN IN DISGRACE, A VENAL MAN WHOSE ABUSES OF POWER ARE BOTH LEGENDARY AND BREATHTAKING... BUT HECK, EVEN HE WASN'T SO BAD... AT LEAST NOT COMPARED TO, SAY--
--VLAD THE IMPALER... THE BLOODTHIRSTY 15TH CENTURY RULER (AND HISTORICAL MODEL FOR COUNT DRACULA), INFAMOUS FOR EXECUTING HIS ENEMIES BY SLOWLY IMPALING THEM ALIVE DURING OUTDOOR BANQUETS... SO JUST REMEMBER--
--THE LEADERS OF BOTH PARTIES MAY BE UTTERLY UNPRINCIPLED AND DEMONSTRABLY CORRUPT--
--BUT AT LEAST THEY DON'T IMPALE THEIR ENEMIES ALIVE DURING DINNER PARTIES!
A PUBLIC SERVICE MESSAGE FROM YOUR FRIENDS AT THIS MODERN WORLD!
TOM "LET A SMILE BE YOUR UMBRELLA" TOMORROW ©1-22-97

THIS MODERN WORLD

by TOM TOMORROW

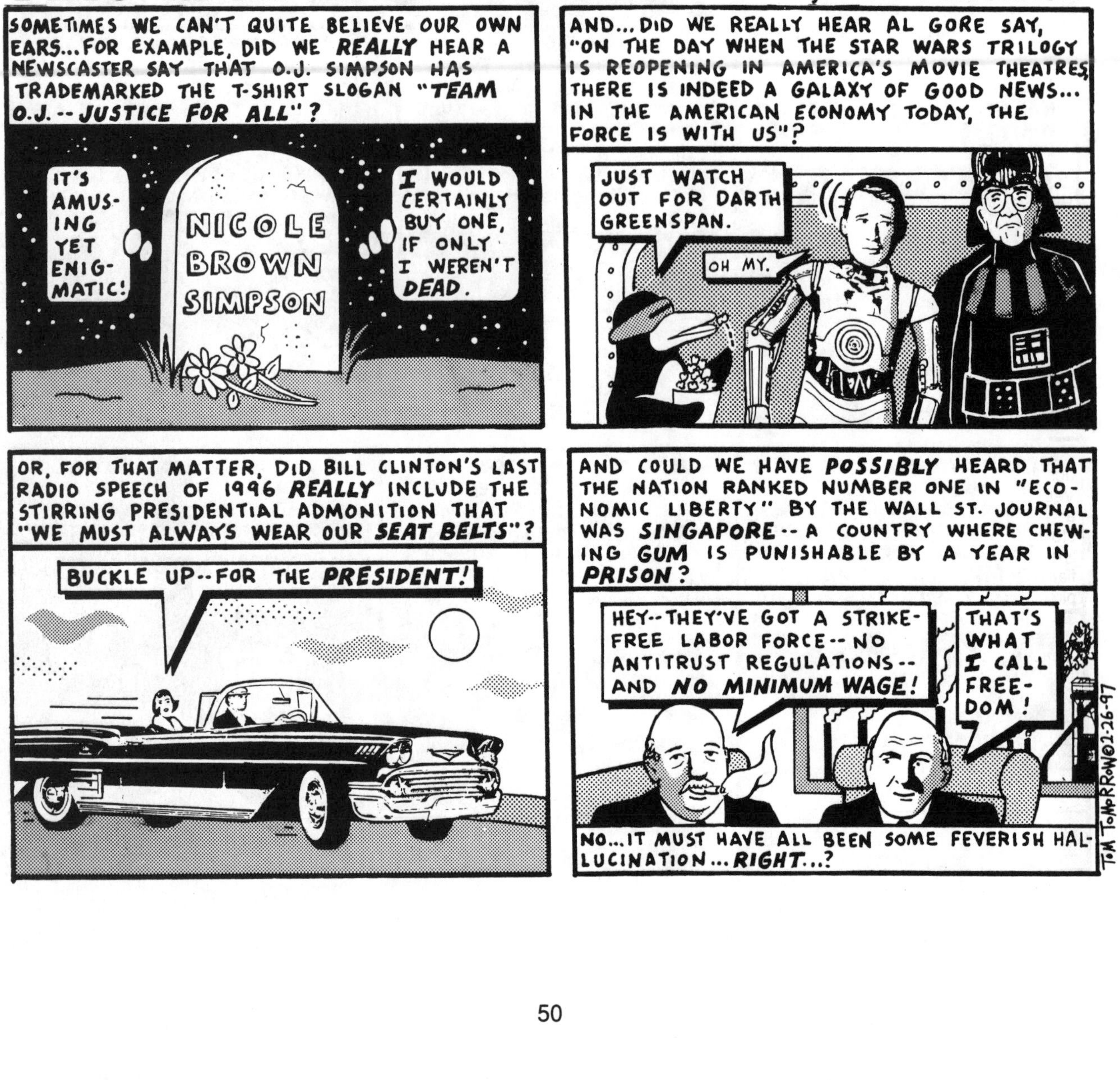
SOMETIMES WE CAN'T QUITE BELIEVE OUR OWN EARS... FOR EXAMPLE, DID WE REALLY HEAR A NEWSCASTER SAY THAT O.J. SIMPSON HAS TRADEMARKED THE T-SHIRT SLOGAN "TEAM O.J. -- JUSTICE FOR ALL"?
IT'S AMUSING YET ENIGMATIC!
NICOLE BROWN SIMPSON
I WOULD CERTAINLY BUY ONE, IF ONLY I WEREN'T DEAD.
AND... DID WE REALLY HEAR AL GORE SAY, "ON THE DAY WHEN THE STAR WARS TRILOGY IS REOPENING IN AMERICA'S MOVIE THEATRES, THERE IS INDEED A GALAXY OF GOOD NEWS... IN THE AMERICAN ECONOMY TODAY, THE FORCE IS WITH US"?
JUST WATCH OUT FOR DARTH GREENSPAN.
OH MY.
OR, FOR THAT MATTER, DID BILL CLINTON'S LAST RADIO SPEECH OF 1996 REALLY INCLUDE THE STIRRING PRESIDENTIAL ADMONITION THAT "WE MUST ALWAYS WEAR OUR SEAT BELTS"?
BUCKLE UP--FOR THE PRESIDENT!
AND COULD WE HAVE POSSIBLY HEARD THAT THE NATION RANKED NUMBER ONE IN "ECONOMIC LIBERTY" BY THE WALL ST. JOURNAL WAS SINGAPORE -- A COUNTRY WHERE CHEWING GUM IS PUNISHABLE BY A YEAR IN PRISON?
HEY--THEY'VE GOT A STRIKE-FREE LABOR FORCE--NO ANTITRUST REGULATIONS--AND NO MINIMUM WAGE!
THAT'S WHAT I CALL FREEDOM!
NO... IT MUST HAVE ALL BEEN SOME FEVERISH HALLUCINATION... RIGHT...?
TOM TOMORROW©2-26-97

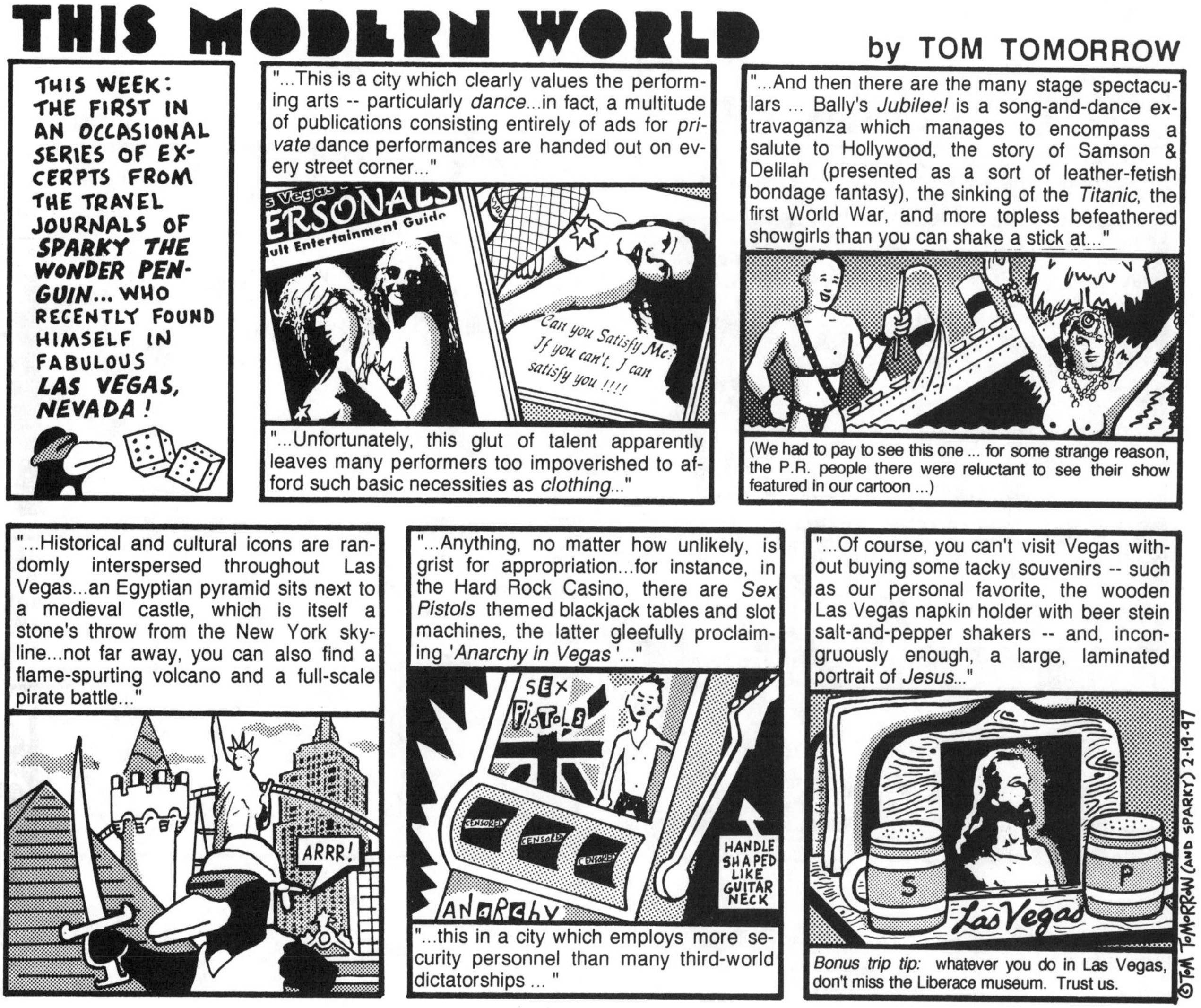
THIS MODERN WORLD
by TOM TOMORROW
THIS WEEK: THE FIRST IN AN OCCASIONAL SERIES OF EXCERPTS FROM THE TRAVEL JOURNALS OF SPARKY THE WONDER PENGUIN... WHO RECENTLY FOUND HIMSELF IN FABULOUS LAS VEGAS, NEVADA!
"...This is a city which clearly values the performing arts -- particularly dance...in fact, a multitude of publications consisting entirely of ads for private dance performances are handed out on every street corner..."
ERSONALS
ult Entertainment Guide
Can you Satisfy Me? If you can't, I can satisfy you !!!!
"...Unfortunately, this glut of talent apparently leaves many performers too impoverished to afford such basic necessities as clothing..."
"...And then there are the many stage spectaculars ... Bally's Jubilee! is a song-and-dance extravaganza which manages to encompass a salute to Hollywood, the story of Samson & Delilah (presented as a sort of leather-fetish bondage fantasy), the sinking of the Titanic, the first World War, and more topless befeathered showgirls than you can shake a stick at..."
(We had to pay to see this one ... for some strange reason, the P.R. people there were reluctant to see their show featured in our cartoon ...)
"...Historical and cultural icons are randomly interspersed throughout Las Vegas...an Egyptian pyramid sits next to a medieval castle, which is itself a stone's throw from the New York skyline...not far away, you can also find a flame-spurting volcano and a full-scale pirate battle..."
ARRR!
"...Anything, no matter how unlikely, is grist for appropriation...for instance, in the Hard Rock Casino, there are Sex Pistols themed blackjack tables and slot machines, the latter gleefully proclaiming 'Anarchy in Vegas'..."
SEX PISTOLS
CENSORED
CENSORED
CENSORED
ANARCHY
HANDLE SHAPED LIKE GUITAR NECK
"...this in a city which employs more security personnel than many third-world dictatorships ... "
"...Of course, you can't visit Vegas without buying some tacky souvenirs -- such as our personal favorite, the wooden Las Vegas napkin holder with beer stein salt-and-pepper shakers -- and, incongruously enough, a large, laminated portrait of Jesus..."
S
P
Las Vegas
Bonus trip tip: whatever you do in Las Vegas, don't miss the Liberace museum. Trust us.
©TOM TOMORROW (AND SPARKY) 2-19-97

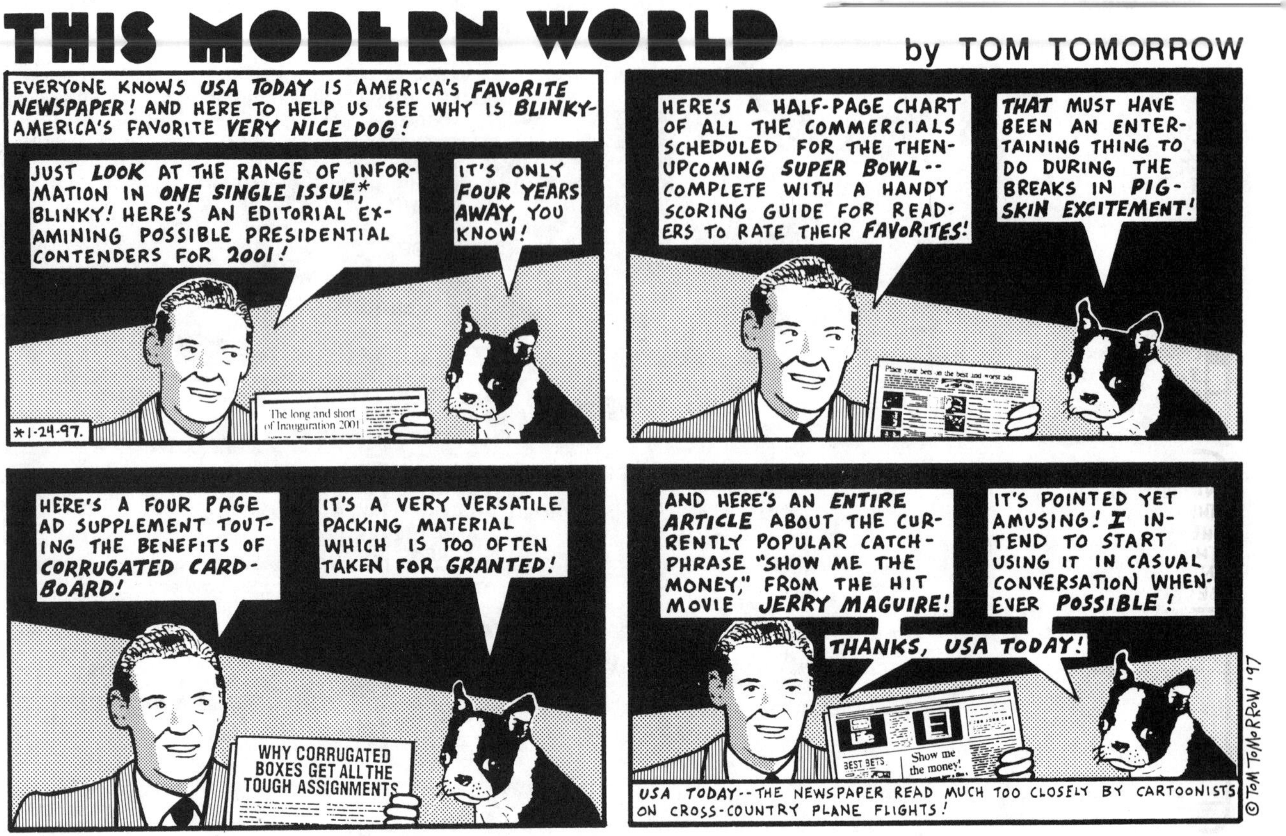
THIS MODERN WORLD
by TOM TOMORROW
EVERYONE KNOWS USA TODAY IS AMERICA'S FAVORITE NEWSPAPER! AND HERE TO HELP US SEE WHY IS BLINKY-AMERICA'S FAVORITE VERY NICE DOG!
JUST LOOK AT THE RANGE OF INFORMATION IN ONE SINGLE ISSUE,* BLINKY! HERE'S AN EDITORIAL EXAMINING POSSIBLE PRESIDENTIAL CONTENDERS FOR 2001!
IT'S ONLY FOUR YEARS AWAY, YOU KNOW!
The long and short of Inauguration 2001
*1-24-97.
HERE'S A HALF-PAGE CHART OF ALL THE COMMERCIALS SCHEDULED FOR THE THEN-UPCOMING SUPER BOWL-- COMPLETE WITH A HANDY SCORING GUIDE FOR READERS TO RATE THEIR FAVORITES!
THAT MUST HAVE BEEN AN ENTERTAINING THING TO DO DURING THE BREAKS IN PIGSKIN EXCITEMENT!
Place your bets on the best and worst ads
HERE'S A FOUR PAGE AD SUPPLEMENT TOUTING THE BENEFITS OF CORRUGATED CARDBOARD!
IT'S A VERY VERSATILE PACKING MATERIAL WHICH IS TOO OFTEN TAKEN FOR GRANTED!
WHY CORRUGATED BOXES GET ALL THE TOUGH ASSIGNMENTS
AND HERE'S AN ENTIRE ARTICLE ABOUT THE CURRENTLY POPULAR CATCH-PHRASE "SHOW ME THE MONEY," FROM THE HIT MOVIE JERRY MAGUIRE!
IT'S POINTED YET AMUSING! I INTEND TO START USING IT IN CASUAL CONVERSATION WHENEVER POSSIBLE!
THANKS, USA TODAY!
BEST BETS
Show me the money!
USA TODAY--THE NEWSPAPER READ MUCH TOO CLOSELY BY CARTOONISTS ON CROSS-COUNTRY PLANE FLIGHTS!
© TOM TOMORROW '97

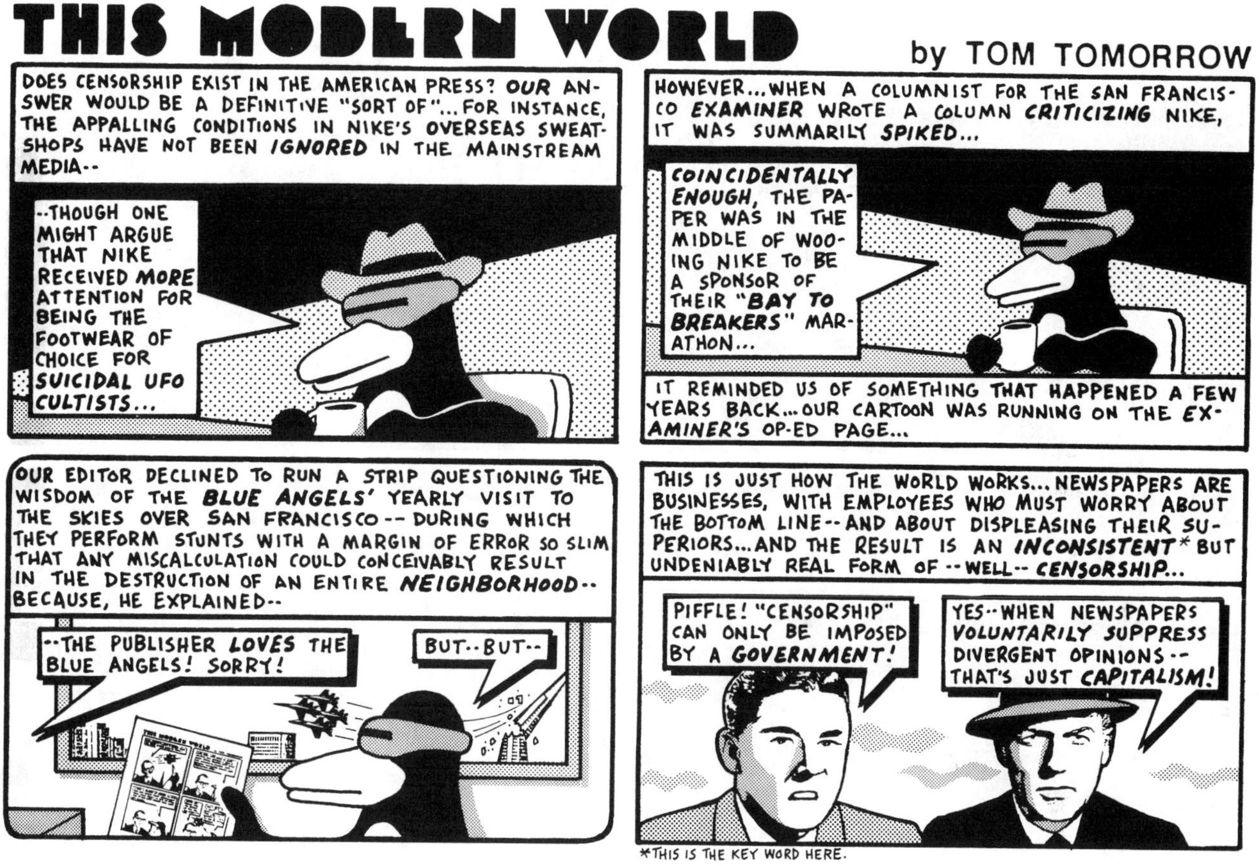
THIS MODERN WORLD
by TOM TOMORROW
DOES CENSORSHIP EXIST IN THE AMERICAN PRESS? OUR ANSWER WOULD BE A DEFINITIVE "SORT OF"... FOR INSTANCE, THE APPALLING CONDITIONS IN NIKE'S OVERSEAS SWEATSHOPS HAVE NOT BEEN IGNORED IN THE MAINSTREAM MEDIA--
--THOUGH ONE MIGHT ARGUE THAT NIKE RECEIVED MORE ATTENTION FOR BEING THE FOOTWEAR OF CHOICE FOR SUICIDAL UFO CULTISTS...
HOWEVER... WHEN A COLUMNIST FOR THE SAN FRANCISCO EXAMINER WROTE A COLUMN CRITICIZING NIKE, IT WAS SUMMARILY SPIKED...
COINCIDENTALLY ENOUGH, THE PAPER WAS IN THE MIDDLE OF WOOING NIKE TO BE A SPONSOR OF THEIR "BAY TO BREAKERS" MARATHON...
IT REMINDED US OF SOMETHING THAT HAPPENED A FEW YEARS BACK... OUR CARTOON WAS RUNNING ON THE EXAMINER'S OP-ED PAGE...
OUR EDITOR DECLINED TO RUN A STRIP QUESTIONING THE WISDOM OF THE BLUE ANGELS' YEARLY VISIT TO THE SKIES OVER SAN FRANCISCO -- DURING WHICH THEY PERFORM STUNTS WITH A MARGIN OF ERROR SO SLIM THAT ANY MISCALCULATION COULD CONCEIVABLY RESULT IN THE DESTRUCTION OF AN ENTIRE NEIGHBORHOOD-- BECAUSE, HE EXPLAINED--
--THE PUBLISHER LOVES THE BLUE ANGELS! SORRY!
BUT--BUT--
THIS IS JUST HOW THE WORLD WORKS... NEWSPAPERS ARE BUSINESSES, WITH EMPLOYEES WHO MUST WORRY ABOUT THE BOTTOM LINE -- AND ABOUT DISPLEASING THEIR SUPERIORS... AND THE RESULT IS AN INCONSISTENT* BUT UNDENIABLY REAL FORM OF -- WELL -- CENSORSHIP...
PIFFLE! "CENSORSHIP" CAN ONLY BE IMPOSED BY A GOVERNMENT!
YES--WHEN NEWSPAPERS VOLUNTARILY SUPPRESS DIVERGENT OPINIONS -- THAT'S JUST CAPITALISM!
*THIS IS THE KEY WORD HERE.

THIS MODERN WORLD

by TOM TOMORROW

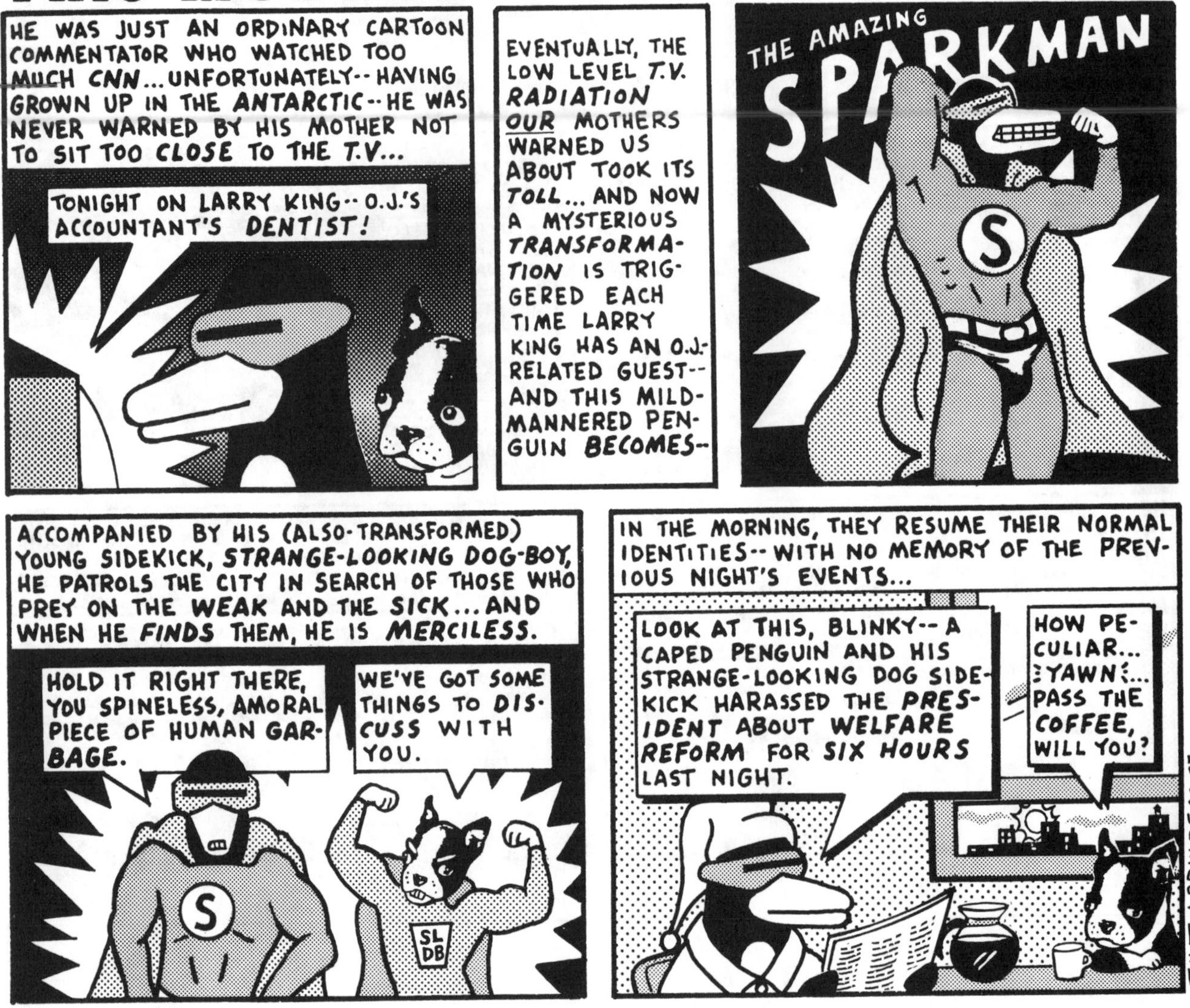
HE WAS JUST AN ORDINARY CARTOON COMMENTATOR WHO WATCHED TOO MUCH CNN... UNFORTUNATELY-- HAVING GROWN UP IN THE ANTARCTIC-- HE WAS NEVER WARNED BY HIS MOTHER NOT TO SIT TOO CLOSE TO THE T.V...
TONIGHT ON LARRY KING-- O.J.'S ACCOUNTANT'S DENTIST!
EVENTUALLY, THE LOW LEVEL T.V. RADIATION OUR MOTHERS WARNED US ABOUT TOOK ITS TOLL... AND NOW A MYSTERIOUS TRANSFORMATION IS TRIGGERED EACH TIME LARRY KING HAS AN O.J.-RELATED GUEST-- AND THIS MILD-MANNERED PENGUIN BECOMES--
THE AMAZING SPARKMAN
S
ACCOMPANIED BY HIS (ALSO-TRANSFORMED) YOUNG SIDEKICK, STRANGE-LOOKING DOG-BOY, HE PATROLS THE CITY IN SEARCH OF THOSE WHO PREY ON THE WEAK AND THE SICK... AND WHEN HE FINDS THEM, HE IS MERCILESS.
HOLD IT RIGHT THERE, YOU SPINELESS, AMORAL PIECE OF HUMAN GARBAGE.
WE'VE GOT SOME THINGS TO DISCUSS WITH YOU.
S
SL DB
IN THE MORNING, THEY RESUME THEIR NORMAL IDENTITIES-- WITH NO MEMORY OF THE PREVIOUS NIGHT'S EVENTS...
LOOK AT THIS, BLINKY-- A CAPED PENGUIN AND HIS STRANGE-LOOKING DOG SIDEKICK HARASSED THE PRESIDENT ABOUT WELFARE REFORM FOR SIX HOURS LAST NIGHT.
HOW PECULIAR... :YAWN:... PASS THE COFFEE, WILL YOU?
TOM TOMORROW©5-28-97

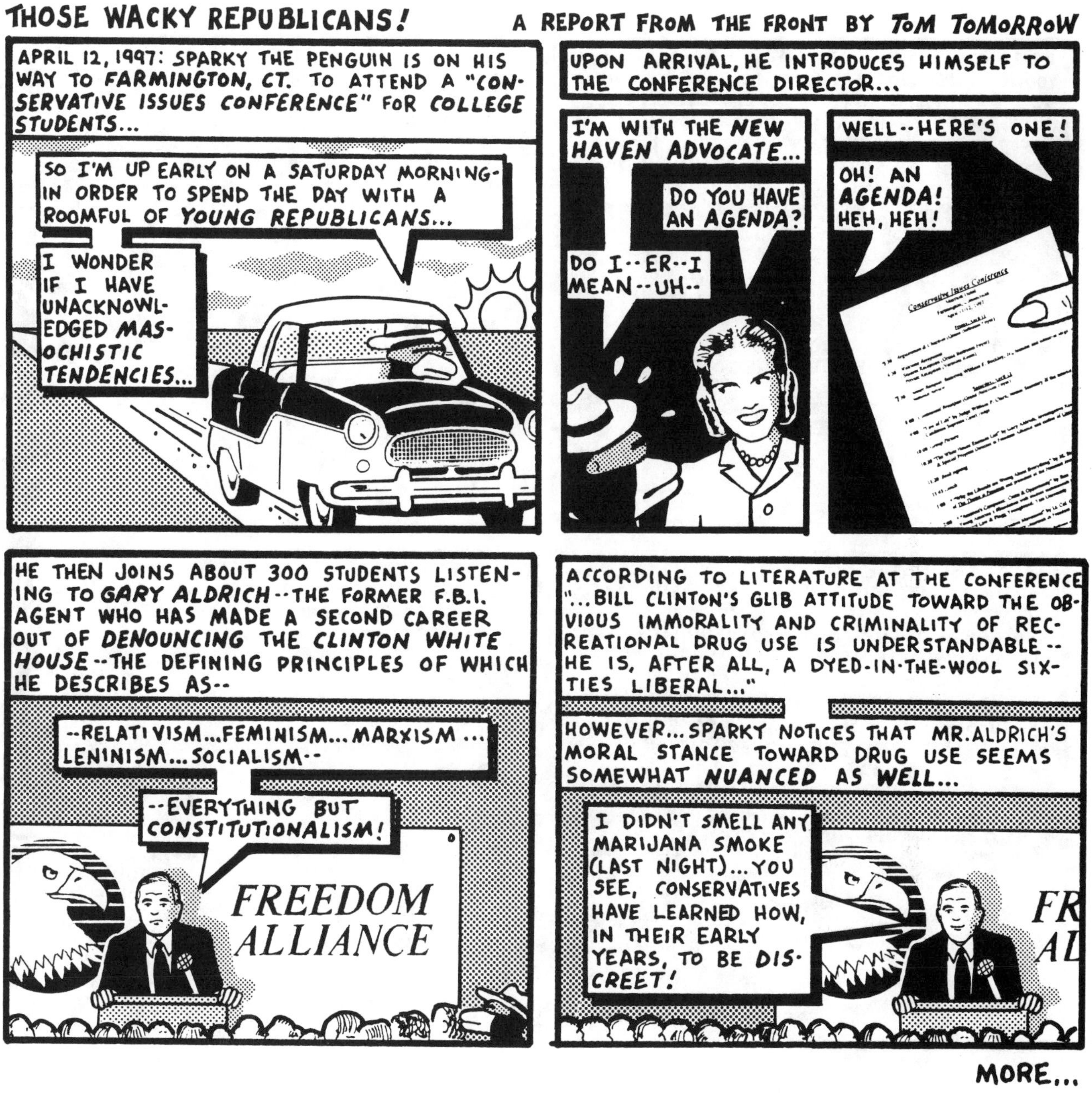
THOSE WACKY REPUBLICANS!
A REPORT FROM THE FRONT BY TOM TOMORROW
APRIL 12, 1997: SPARKY THE PENGUIN IS ON HIS WAY TO FARMINGTON, CT. TO ATTEND A "CONSERVATIVE ISSUES CONFERENCE" FOR COLLEGE STUDENTS...
SO I'M UP EARLY ON A SATURDAY MORNING-IN ORDER TO SPEND THE DAY WITH A ROOMFUL OF YOUNG REPUBLICANS...
I WONDER IF I HAVE UNACKNOWLEDGED MASOCHISTIC TENDENCIES...
UPON ARRIVAL, HE INTRODUCES HIMSELF TO THE CONFERENCE DIRECTOR...
I'M WITH THE NEW HAVEN ADVOCATE...
DO YOU HAVE AN AGENDA?
DO I--ER--I MEAN--UH--
WELL--HERE'S ONE!
OH! AN AGENDA! HEH, HEH!
Conservative Issues Conference
HE THEN JOINS ABOUT 300 STUDENTS LISTENING TO GARY ALDRICH--THE FORMER F.B.I. AGENT WHO HAS MADE A SECOND CAREER OUT OF DENOUNCING THE CLINTON WHITE HOUSE--THE DEFINING PRINCIPLES OF WHICH HE DESCRIBES AS--
--RELATIVISM...FEMINISM...MARXISM... LENINISM...SOCIALISM--
--EVERYTHING BUT CONSTITUTIONALISM!
FREEDOM ALLIANCE
ACCORDING TO LITERATURE AT THE CONFERENCE "...BILL CLINTON'S GLIB ATTITUDE TOWARD THE OBVIOUS IMMORALITY AND CRIMINALITY OF RECREATIONAL DRUG USE IS UNDERSTANDABLE--HE IS, AFTER ALL, A DYED-IN-THE-WOOL SIXTIES LIBERAL..."
HOWEVER...SPARKY NOTICES THAT MR. ALDRICH'S MORAL STANCE TOWARD DRUG USE SEEMS SOMEWHAT NUANCED AS WELL...
I DIDN'T SMELL ANY MARIJANA SMOKE (LAST NIGHT)...YOU SEE, CONSERVATIVES HAVE LEARNED HOW, IN THEIR EARLY YEARS, TO BE DISCREET!
MORE...

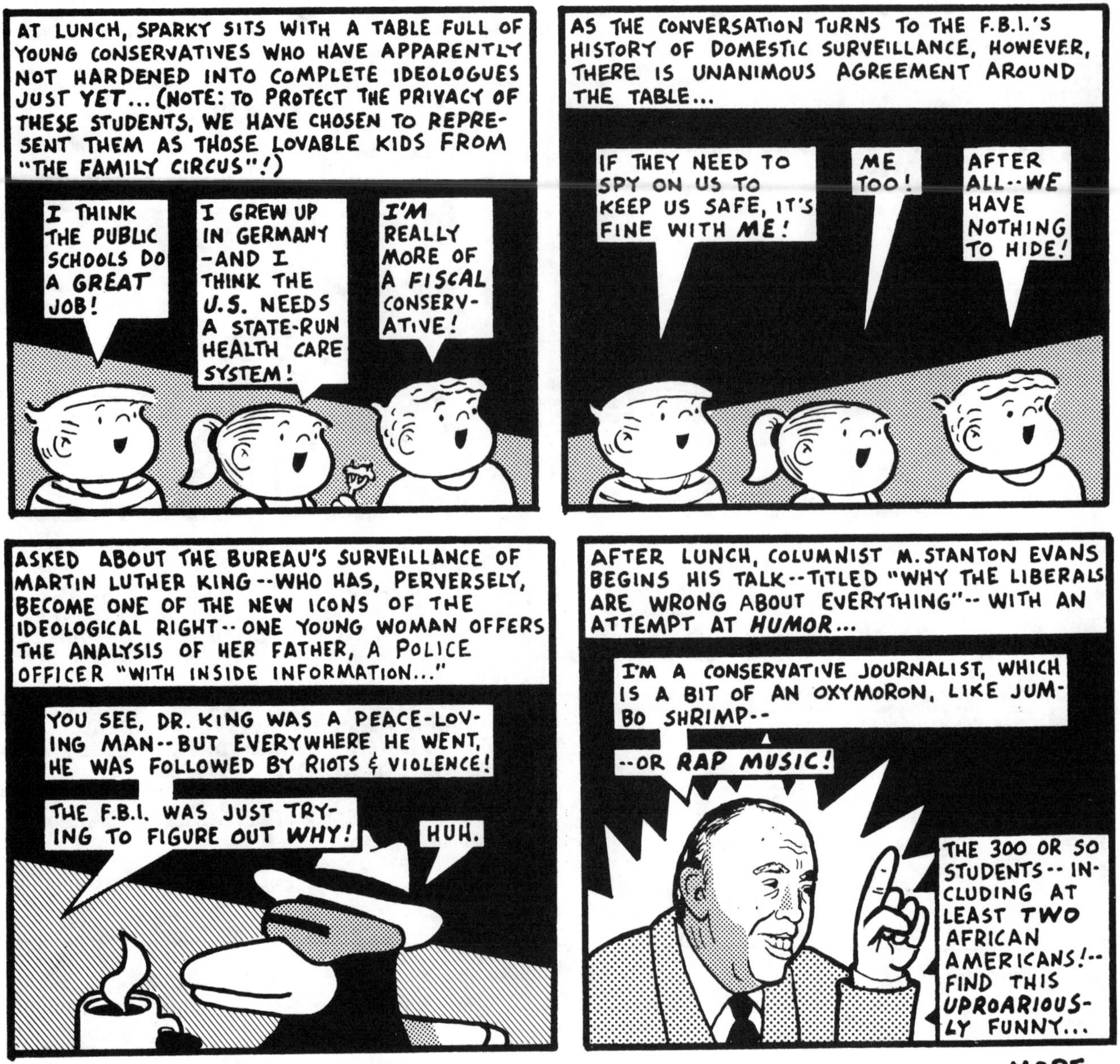
AT LUNCH, SPARKY SITS WITH A TABLE FULL OF YOUNG CONSERVATIVES WHO HAVE APPARENTLY NOT HARDENED INTO COMPLETE IDEOLOGUES JUST YET... (NOTE: TO PROTECT THE PRIVACY OF THESE STUDENTS, WE HAVE CHOSEN TO REPRESENT THEM AS THOSE LOVABLE KIDS FROM "THE FAMILY CIRCUS"!)
I THINK THE PUBLIC SCHOOLS DO A GREAT JOB!
I GREW UP IN GERMANY -AND I THINK THE U.S. NEEDS A STATE-RUN HEALTH CARE SYSTEM!
I'M REALLY MORE OF A FISCAL CONSERVATIVE!
AS THE CONVERSATION TURNS TO THE F.B.I.'S HISTORY OF DOMESTIC SURVEILLANCE, HOWEVER, THERE IS UNANIMOUS AGREEMENT AROUND THE TABLE...
IF THEY NEED TO SPY ON US TO KEEP US SAFE, IT'S FINE WITH ME!
ME TOO!
AFTER ALL--WE HAVE NOTHING TO HIDE!
ASKED ABOUT THE BUREAU'S SURVEILLANCE OF MARTIN LUTHER KING--WHO HAS, PERVERSELY, BECOME ONE OF THE NEW ICONS OF THE IDEOLOGICAL RIGHT--ONE YOUNG WOMAN OFFERS THE ANALYSIS OF HER FATHER, A POLICE OFFICER "WITH INSIDE INFORMATION..."
YOU SEE, DR. KING WAS A PEACE-LOVING MAN--BUT EVERYWHERE HE WENT, HE WAS FOLLOWED BY RIOTS & VIOLENCE!
THE F.B.I. WAS JUST TRYING TO FIGURE OUT WHY!
HUH.
AFTER LUNCH, COLUMNIST M. STANTON EVANS BEGINS HIS TALK--TITLED "WHY THE LIBERALS ARE WRONG ABOUT EVERYTHING"--WITH AN ATTEMPT AT HUMOR...
I'M A CONSERVATIVE JOURNALIST, WHICH IS A BIT OF AN OXYMORON, LIKE JUMBO SHRIMP--
--OR RAP MUSIC!
THE 300 OR SO STUDENTS--INCLUDING AT LEAST TWO AFRICAN AMERICANS!--FIND THIS UPROARIOUSLY FUNNY...

MORE...

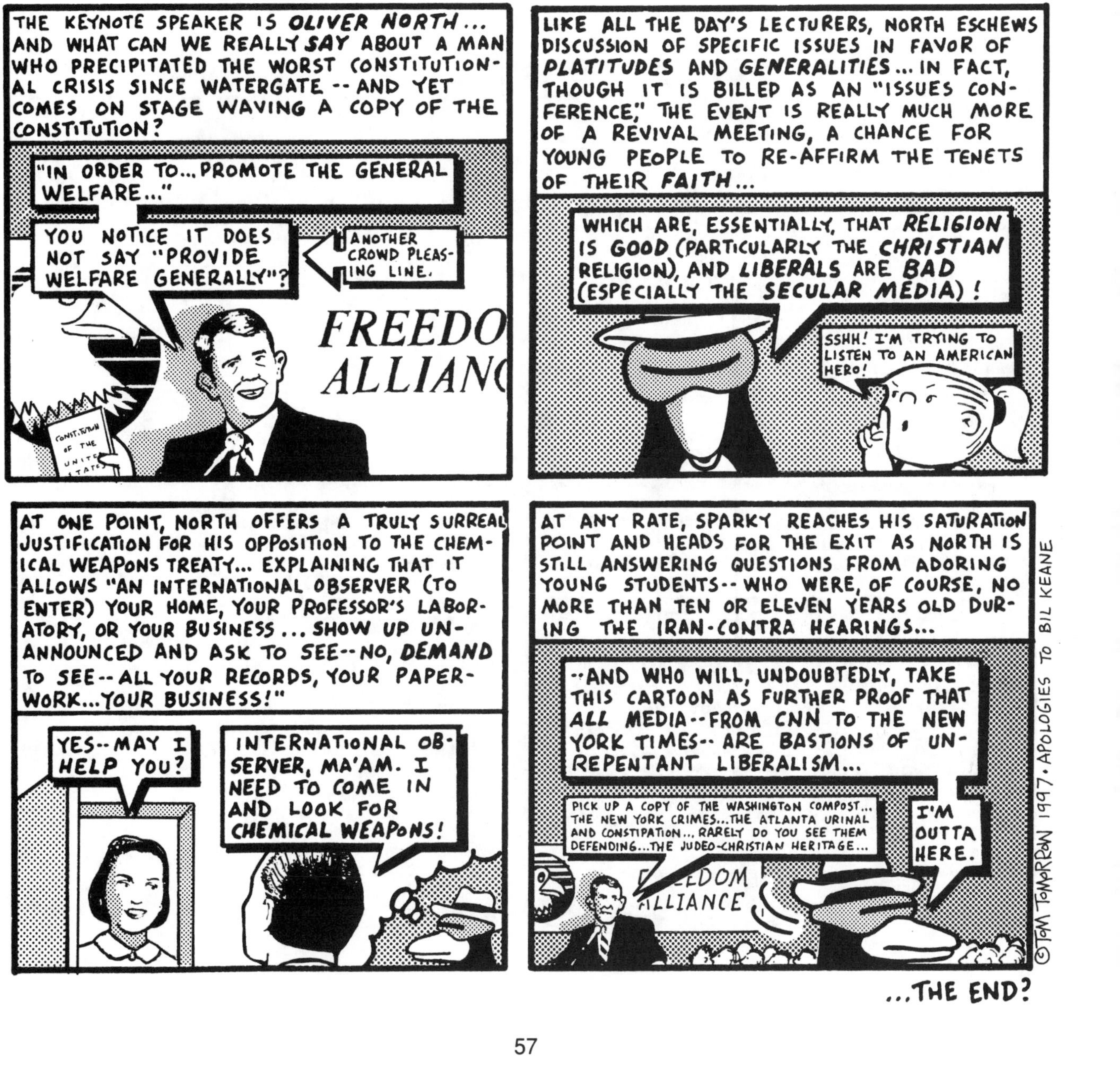
THE KEYNOTE SPEAKER IS OLIVER NORTH... AND WHAT CAN WE REALLY SAY ABOUT A MAN WHO PRECIPITATED THE WORST CONSTITUTIONAL CRISIS SINCE WATERGATE -- AND YET COMES ON STAGE WAVING A COPY OF THE CONSTITUTION?
"IN ORDER TO... PROMOTE THE GENERAL WELFARE..."
YOU NOTICE IT DOES NOT SAY "PROVIDE WELFARE GENERALLY"?
ANOTHER CROWD PLEASING LINE.
FREEDO
ALLIANC
CONSTITUTION OF THE UNITED STATES
LIKE ALL THE DAY'S LECTURERS, NORTH ESCHEWS DISCUSSION OF SPECIFIC ISSUES IN FAVOR OF PLATITUDES AND GENERALITIES... IN FACT, THOUGH IT IS BILLED AS AN "ISSUES CONFERENCE," THE EVENT IS REALLY MUCH MORE OF A REVIVAL MEETING, A CHANCE FOR YOUNG PEOPLE TO RE-AFFIRM THE TENETS OF THEIR FAITH...
WHICH ARE, ESSENTIALLY, THAT RELIGION IS GOOD (PARTICULARLY THE CHRISTIAN RELIGION), AND LIBERALS ARE BAD (ESPECIALLY THE SECULAR MEDIA)!
SSHH! I'M TRYING TO LISTEN TO AN AMERICAN HERO!
AT ONE POINT, NORTH OFFERS A TRULY SURREAL JUSTIFICATION FOR HIS OPPOSITION TO THE CHEMICAL WEAPONS TREATY... EXPLAINING THAT IT ALLOWS "AN INTERNATIONAL OBSERVER (TO ENTER) YOUR HOME, YOUR PROFESSOR'S LABORATORY, OR YOUR BUSINESS... SHOW UP UNANNOUNCED AND ASK TO SEE-- NO, DEMAND TO SEE-- ALL YOUR RECORDS, YOUR PAPERWORK... YOUR BUSINESS!"
YES-- MAY I HELP YOU?
INTERNATIONAL OBSERVER, MA'AM. I NEED TO COME IN AND LOOK FOR CHEMICAL WEAPONS!
AT ANY RATE, SPARKY REACHES HIS SATURATION POINT AND HEADS FOR THE EXIT AS NORTH IS STILL ANSWERING QUESTIONS FROM ADORING YOUNG STUDENTS-- WHO WERE, OF COURSE, NO MORE THAN TEN OR ELEVEN YEARS OLD DURING THE IRAN-CONTRA HEARINGS...
--AND WHO WILL, UNDOUBTEDLY, TAKE THIS CARTOON AS FURTHER PROOF THAT ALL MEDIA-- FROM CNN TO THE NEW YORK TIMES-- ARE BASTIONS OF UNREPENTANT LIBERALISM...
PICK UP A COPY OF THE WASHINGTON COMPOST... THE NEW YORK CRIMES... THE ATLANTA URINAL AND CONSTIPATION... RARELY DO YOU SEE THEM DEFENDING... THE JUDEO-CHRISTIAN HERITAGE...
I'M OUTTA HERE.
EDOM
ALLIANCE
©TOM TOMORROW 1997 · APOLOGIES TO BIL KEANE
...THE END?

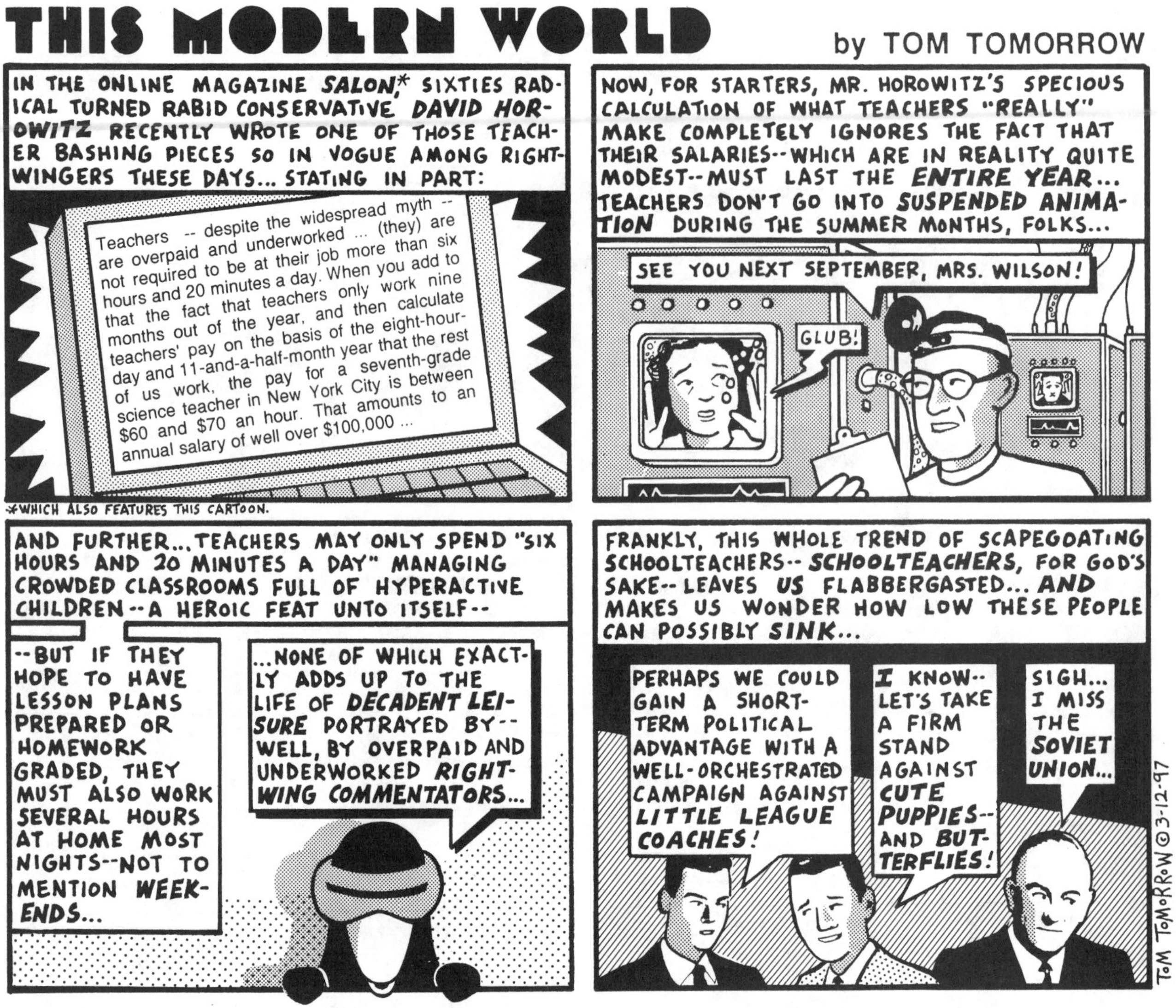
THIS MODERN WORLD
by TOM TOMORROW
IN THE ONLINE MAGAZINE SALON,* SIXTIES RADICAL TURNED RABID CONSERVATIVE DAVID HOROWITZ RECENTLY WROTE ONE OF THOSE TEACHER BASHING PIECES SO IN VOGUE AMONG RIGHT-WINGERS THESE DAYS... STATING IN PART:
Teachers -- despite the widespread myth -- are overpaid and underworked ... (they) are not required to be at their job more than six hours and 20 minutes a day. When you add to that the fact that teachers only work nine months out of the year, and then calculate teachers' pay on the basis of the eight-hour-day and 11-and-a-half-month year that the rest of us work, the pay for a seventh-grade science teacher in New York City is between $60 and $70 an hour. That amounts to an annual salary of well over $100,000 ...
*WHICH ALSO FEATURES THIS CARTOON.
NOW, FOR STARTERS, MR. HOROWITZ'S SPECIOUS CALCULATION OF WHAT TEACHERS "REALLY" MAKE COMPLETELY IGNORES THE FACT THAT THEIR SALARIES--WHICH ARE IN REALITY QUITE MODEST--MUST LAST THE ENTIRE YEAR... TEACHERS DON'T GO INTO SUSPENDED ANIMATION DURING THE SUMMER MONTHS, FOLKS...
SEE YOU NEXT SEPTEMBER, MRS. WILSON!
GLUB!
AND FURTHER... TEACHERS MAY ONLY SPEND "SIX HOURS AND 20 MINUTES A DAY" MANAGING CROWDED CLASSROOMS FULL OF HYPERACTIVE CHILDREN--A HEROIC FEAT UNTO ITSELF--
--BUT IF THEY HOPE TO HAVE LESSON PLANS PREPARED OR HOMEWORK GRADED, THEY MUST ALSO WORK SEVERAL HOURS AT HOME MOST NIGHTS--NOT TO MENTION WEEKENDS...
...NONE OF WHICH EXACTLY ADDS UP TO THE LIFE OF DECADENT LEISURE PORTRAYED BY--WELL, BY OVERPAID AND UNDERWORKED RIGHT-WING COMMENTATORS...
FRANKLY, THIS WHOLE TREND OF SCAPEGOATING SCHOOLTEACHERS--SCHOOLTEACHERS, FOR GOD'S SAKE--LEAVES US FLABBERGASTED... AND MAKES US WONDER HOW LOW THESE PEOPLE CAN POSSIBLY SINK...
PERHAPS WE COULD GAIN A SHORT-TERM POLITICAL ADVANTAGE WITH A WELL-ORCHESTRATED CAMPAIGN AGAINST LITTLE LEAGUE COACHES!
I KNOW--LET'S TAKE A FIRM STAND AGAINST CUTE PUPPIES--AND BUTTERFLIES!
SIGH... I MISS THE SOVIET UNION...
TOM TOMORROW ©3-12-97

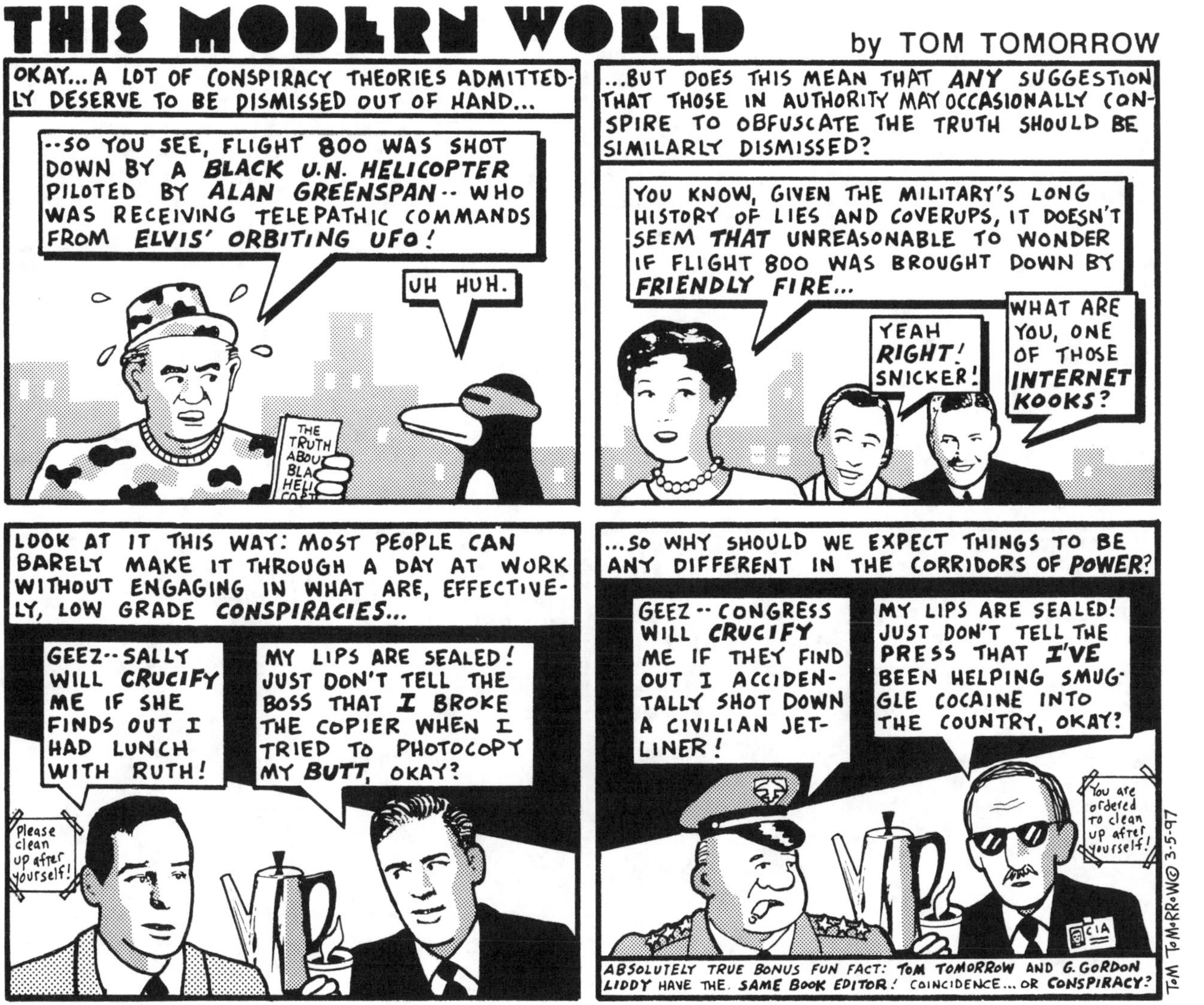
THIS MODERN WORLD
by TOM TOMORROW
OKAY... A LOT OF CONSPIRACY THEORIES ADMITTEDLY DESERVE TO BE DISMISSED OUT OF HAND...
--SO YOU SEE, FLIGHT 800 WAS SHOT DOWN BY A BLACK U.N. HELICOPTER PILOTED BY ALAN GREENSPAN-- WHO WAS RECEIVING TELEPATHIC COMMANDS FROM ELVIS' ORBITING UFO!
UH HUH.
...BUT DOES THIS MEAN THAT ANY SUGGESTION THAT THOSE IN AUTHORITY MAY OCCASIONALLY CONSPIRE TO OBFUSCATE THE TRUTH SHOULD BE SIMILARLY DISMISSED?
YOU KNOW, GIVEN THE MILITARY'S LONG HISTORY OF LIES AND COVERUPS, IT DOESN'T SEEM THAT UNREASONABLE TO WONDER IF FLIGHT 800 WAS BROUGHT DOWN BY FRIENDLY FIRE...
YEAH RIGHT! SNICKER!
WHAT ARE YOU, ONE OF THOSE INTERNET KOOKS?
LOOK AT IT THIS WAY: MOST PEOPLE CAN BARELY MAKE IT THROUGH A DAY AT WORK WITHOUT ENGAGING IN WHAT ARE, EFFECTIVELY, LOW GRADE CONSPIRACIES...
GEEZ-- SALLY WILL CRUCIFY ME IF SHE FINDS OUT I HAD LUNCH WITH RUTH!
MY LIPS ARE SEALED! JUST DON'T TELL THE BOSS THAT I BROKE THE COPIER WHEN I TRIED TO PHOTOCOPY MY BUTT, OKAY?
Please clean up after yourself!
...SO WHY SHOULD WE EXPECT THINGS TO BE ANY DIFFERENT IN THE CORRIDORS OF POWER?
GEEZ-- CONGRESS WILL CRUCIFY ME IF THEY FIND OUT I ACCIDENTALLY SHOT DOWN A CIVILIAN JETLINER!
MY LIPS ARE SEALED! JUST DON'T TELL THE PRESS THAT I'VE BEEN HELPING SMUGGLE COCAINE INTO THE COUNTRY, OKAY?
You are ordered to clean up after yourself!
CIA
ABSOLUTELY TRUE BONUS FUN FACT: TOM TOMORROW AND G. GORDON LIDDY HAVE THE SAME BOOK EDITOR! COINCIDENCE... OR CONSPIRACY?
TOM TOMORROW© 3-5-97

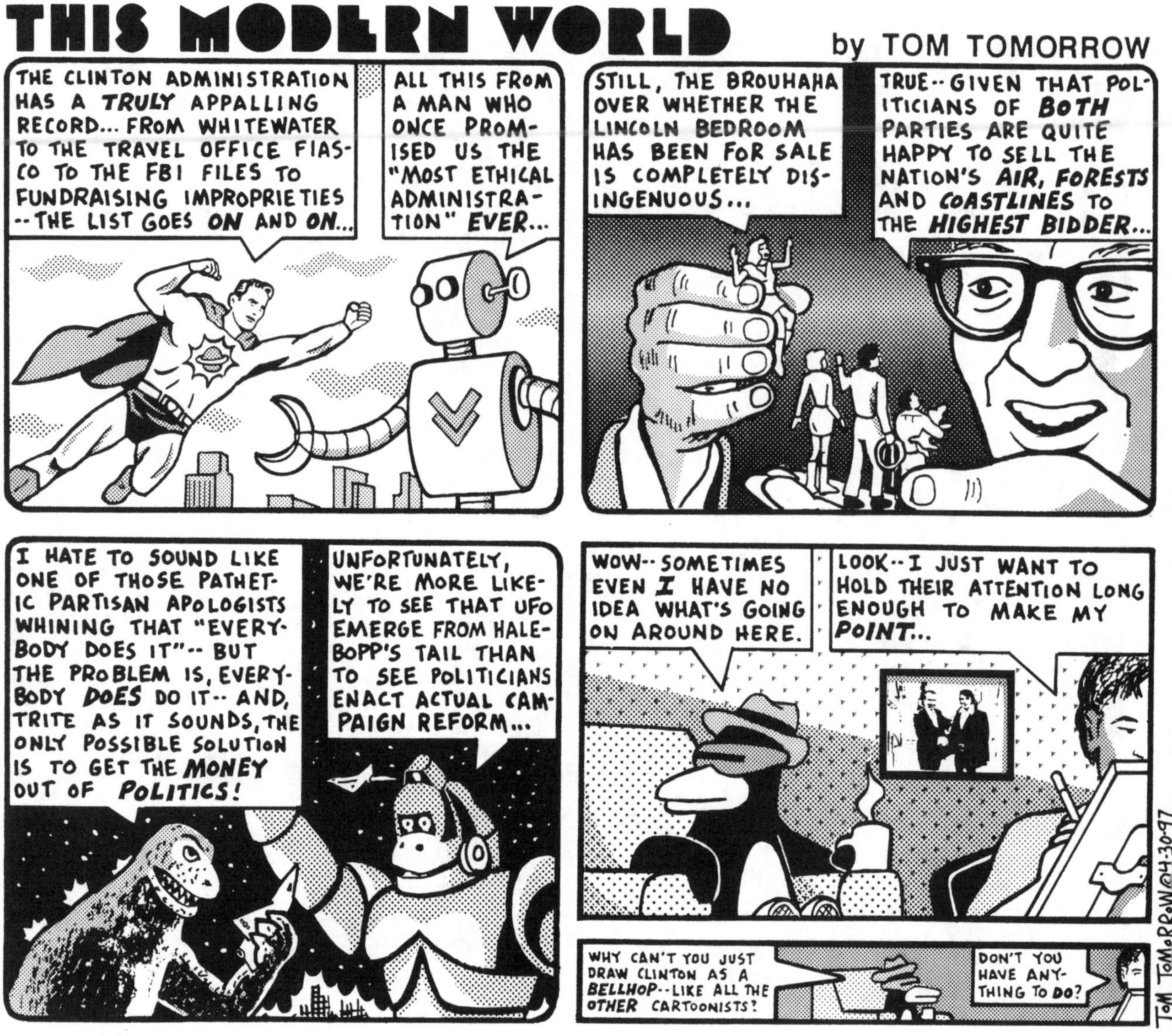
THIS MODERN WORLD
by TOM TOMORROW
THE CLINTON ADMINISTRATION HAS A TRULY APPALLING RECORD... FROM WHITEWATER TO THE TRAVEL OFFICE FIASCO TO THE FBI FILES TO FUNDRAISING IMPROPRIETIES --THE LIST GOES ON AND ON...
ALL THIS FROM A MAN WHO ONCE PROMISED US THE "MOST ETHICAL ADMINISTRATION" EVER...
STILL, THE BROUHAHA OVER WHETHER THE LINCOLN BEDROOM HAS BEEN FOR SALE IS COMPLETELY DISINGENUOUS...
TRUE--GIVEN THAT POLITICIANS OF BOTH PARTIES ARE QUITE HAPPY TO SELL THE NATION'S AIR, FORESTS AND COASTLINES TO THE HIGHEST BIDDER...
I HATE TO SOUND LIKE ONE OF THOSE PATHETIC PARTISAN APOLOGISTS WHINING THAT "EVERYBODY DOES IT"-- BUT THE PROBLEM IS, EVERYBODY DOES DO IT-- AND, TRITE AS IT SOUNDS, THE ONLY POSSIBLE SOLUTION IS TO GET THE MONEY OUT OF POLITICS!
UNFORTUNATELY, WE'RE MORE LIKELY TO SEE THAT UFO EMERGE FROM HALE-BOPP'S TAIL THAN TO SEE POLITICIANS ENACT ACTUAL CAMPAIGN REFORM...
WOW-- SOMETIMES EVEN I HAVE NO IDEA WHAT'S GOING ON AROUND HERE.
LOOK-- I JUST WANT TO HOLD THEIR ATTENTION LONG ENOUGH TO MAKE MY POINT...
WHY CAN'T YOU JUST DRAW CLINTON AS A BELLHOP--LIKE ALL THE OTHER CARTOONISTS?
DON'T YOU HAVE ANYTHING TO DO?
TOM TOMORROW©4-30-97

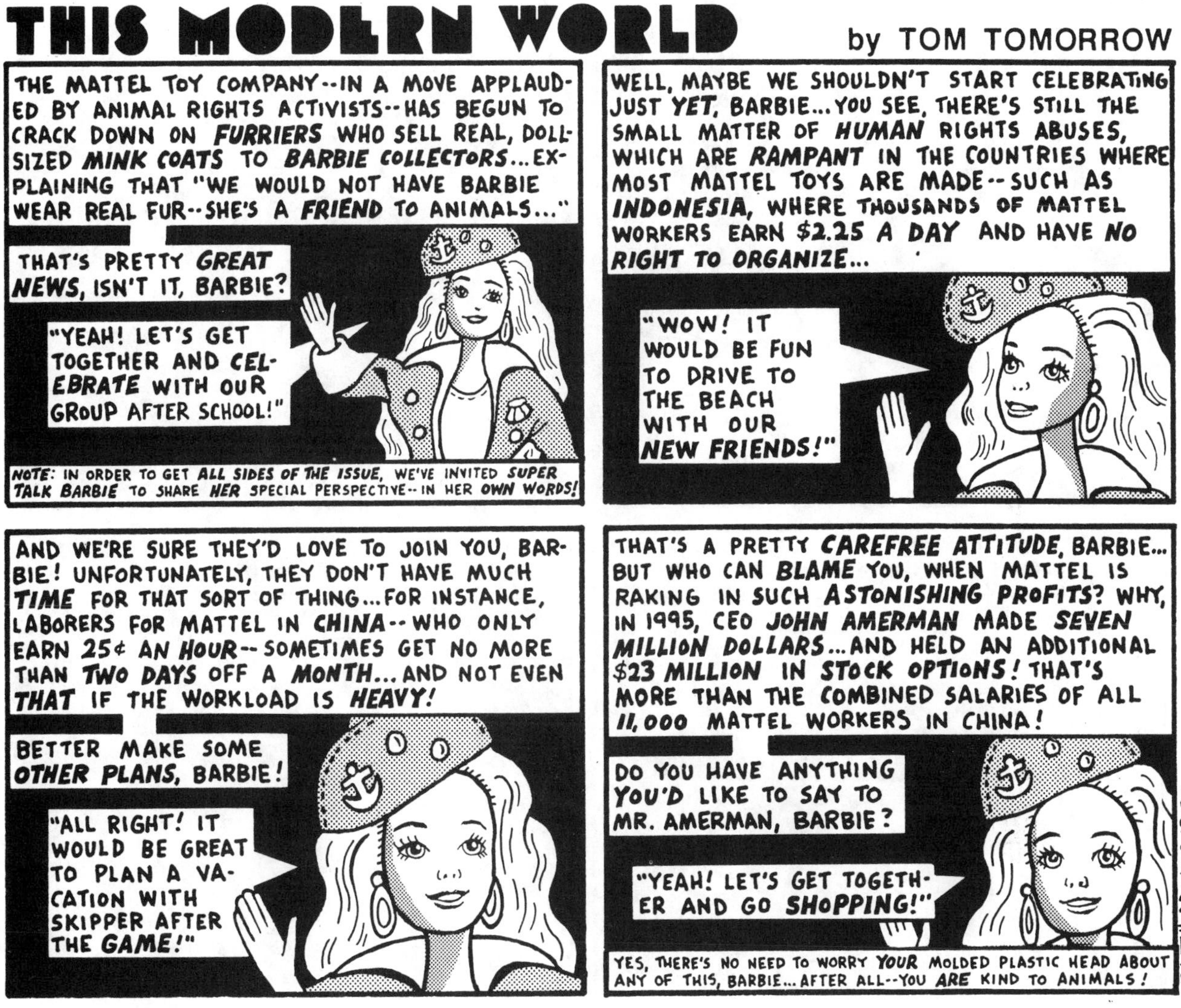
THIS MODERN WORLD
by TOM TOMORROW
THE MATTEL TOY COMPANY--IN A MOVE APPLAUDED BY ANIMAL RIGHTS ACTIVISTS--HAS BEGUN TO CRACK DOWN ON FURRIERS WHO SELL REAL, DOLL-SIZED MINK COATS TO BARBIE COLLECTORS...EXPLAINING THAT "WE WOULD NOT HAVE BARBIE WEAR REAL FUR--SHE'S A FRIEND TO ANIMALS..."
THAT'S PRETTY GREAT NEWS, ISN'T IT, BARBIE?
"YEAH! LET'S GET TOGETHER AND CELEBRATE WITH OUR GROUP AFTER SCHOOL!"
NOTE: IN ORDER TO GET ALL SIDES OF THE ISSUE, WE'VE INVITED SUPER TALK BARBIE TO SHARE HER SPECIAL PERSPECTIVE--IN HER OWN WORDS!
WELL, MAYBE WE SHOULDN'T START CELEBRATING JUST YET, BARBIE...YOU SEE, THERE'S STILL THE SMALL MATTER OF HUMAN RIGHTS ABUSES, WHICH ARE RAMPANT IN THE COUNTRIES WHERE MOST MATTEL TOYS ARE MADE--SUCH AS INDONESIA, WHERE THOUSANDS OF MATTEL WORKERS EARN $2.25 A DAY AND HAVE NO RIGHT TO ORGANIZE...
"WOW! IT WOULD BE FUN TO DRIVE TO THE BEACH WITH OUR NEW FRIENDS!"
AND WE'RE SURE THEY'D LOVE TO JOIN YOU, BARBIE! UNFORTUNATELY, THEY DON'T HAVE MUCH TIME FOR THAT SORT OF THING...FOR INSTANCE, LABORERS FOR MATTEL IN CHINA--WHO ONLY EARN 25¢ AN HOUR--SOMETIMES GET NO MORE THAN TWO DAYS OFF A MONTH...AND NOT EVEN THAT IF THE WORKLOAD IS HEAVY!
BETTER MAKE SOME OTHER PLANS, BARBIE!
"ALL RIGHT! IT WOULD BE GREAT TO PLAN A VACATION WITH SKIPPER AFTER THE GAME!"
THAT'S A PRETTY CAREFREE ATTITUDE, BARBIE... BUT WHO CAN BLAME YOU, WHEN MATTEL IS RAKING IN SUCH ASTONISHING PROFITS? WHY, IN 1995, CEO JOHN AMERMAN MADE SEVEN MILLION DOLLARS...AND HELD AN ADDITIONAL $23 MILLION IN STOCK OPTIONS! THAT'S MORE THAN THE COMBINED SALARIES OF ALL 11,000 MATTEL WORKERS IN CHINA!
DO YOU HAVE ANYTHING YOU'D LIKE TO SAY TO MR. AMERMAN, BARBIE?
"YEAH! LET'S GET TOGETHER AND GO SHOPPING!"
YES, THERE'S NO NEED TO WORRY YOUR MOLDED PLASTIC HEAD ABOUT ANY OF THIS, BARBIE... AFTER ALL--YOU ARE KIND TO ANIMALS!
TOM TOMORROW © 3-19-97

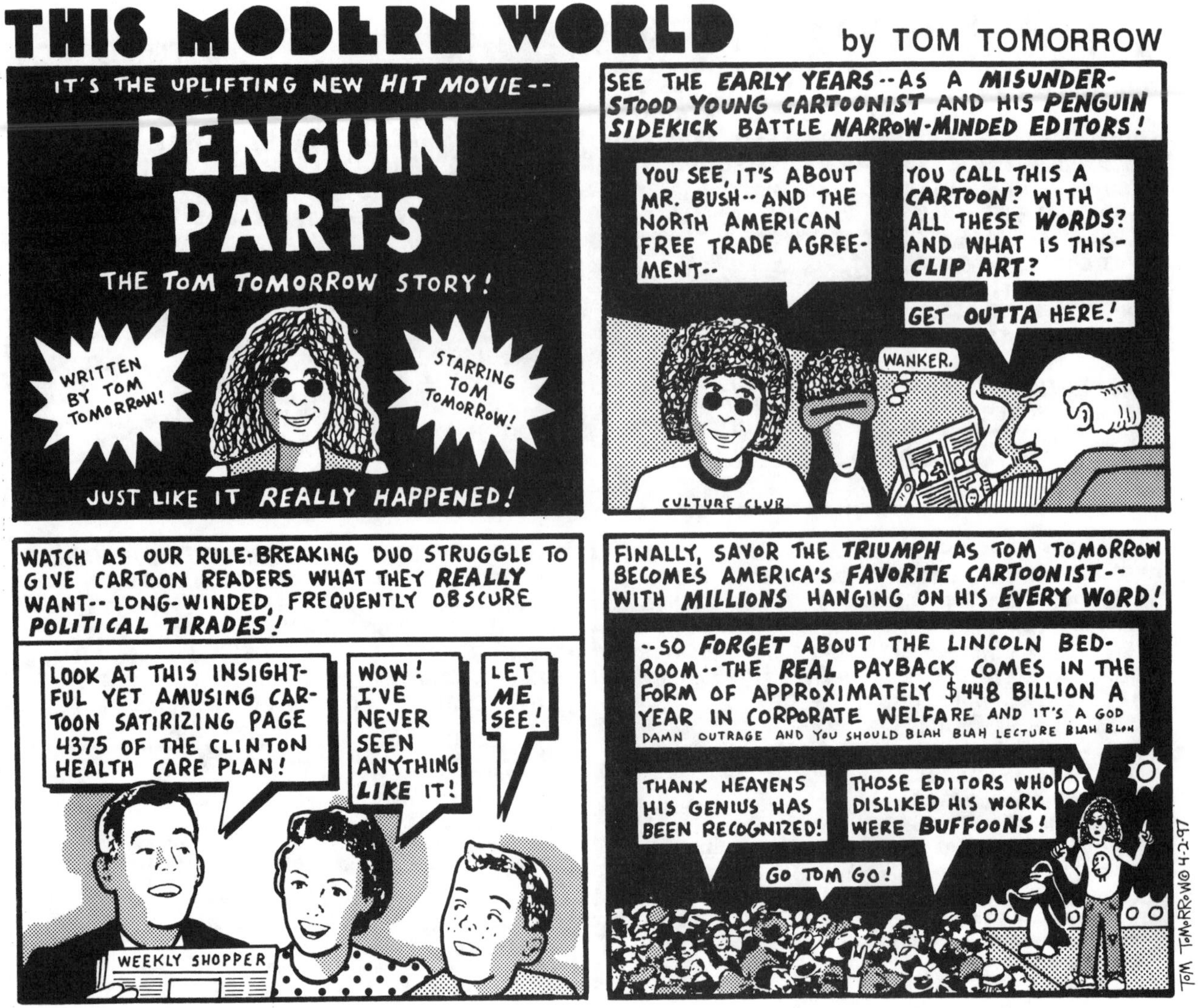
THIS MODERN WORLD
by TOM TOMORROW
IT'S THE UPLIFTING NEW HIT MOVIE--
PENGUIN PARTS
THE TOM TOMORROW STORY!
WRITTEN BY TOM TOMORROW!
STARRING TOM TOMORROW!
JUST LIKE IT REALLY HAPPENED!
SEE THE EARLY YEARS--AS A MISUNDERSTOOD YOUNG CARTOONIST AND HIS PENGUIN SIDEKICK BATTLE NARROW-MINDED EDITORS!
YOU SEE, IT'S ABOUT MR. BUSH--AND THE NORTH AMERICAN FREE TRADE AGREEMENT--
YOU CALL THIS A CARTOON? WITH ALL THESE WORDS? AND WHAT IS THIS-- CLIP ART?
GET OUTTA HERE!
WANKER.
CULTURE CLUB
WATCH AS OUR RULE-BREAKING DUO STRUGGLE TO GIVE CARTOON READERS WHAT THEY REALLY WANT--LONG-WINDED, FREQUENTLY OBSCURE POLITICAL TIRADES!
LOOK AT THIS INSIGHTFUL YET AMUSING CARTOON SATIRIZING PAGE 4375 OF THE CLINTON HEALTH CARE PLAN!
WOW! I'VE NEVER SEEN ANYTHING LIKE IT!
LET ME SEE!
WEEKLY SHOPPER
FINALLY, SAVOR THE TRIUMPH AS TOM TOMORROW BECOMES AMERICA'S FAVORITE CARTOONIST--WITH MILLIONS HANGING ON HIS EVERY WORD!
--SO FORGET ABOUT THE LINCOLN BEDROOM--THE REAL PAYBACK COMES IN THE FORM OF APPROXIMATELY $448 BILLION A YEAR IN CORPORATE WELFARE AND IT'S A GOD DAMN OUTRAGE AND YOU SHOULD BLAH BLAH LECTURE BLAH BLAH
THANK HEAVENS HIS GENIUS HAS BEEN RECOGNIZED!
THOSE EDITORS WHO DISLIKED HIS WORK WERE BUFFOONS!
GO TOM GO!
TOM TOMORROW © 4-2-97

THIS MODERN WORLD

by TOM TOMORROW

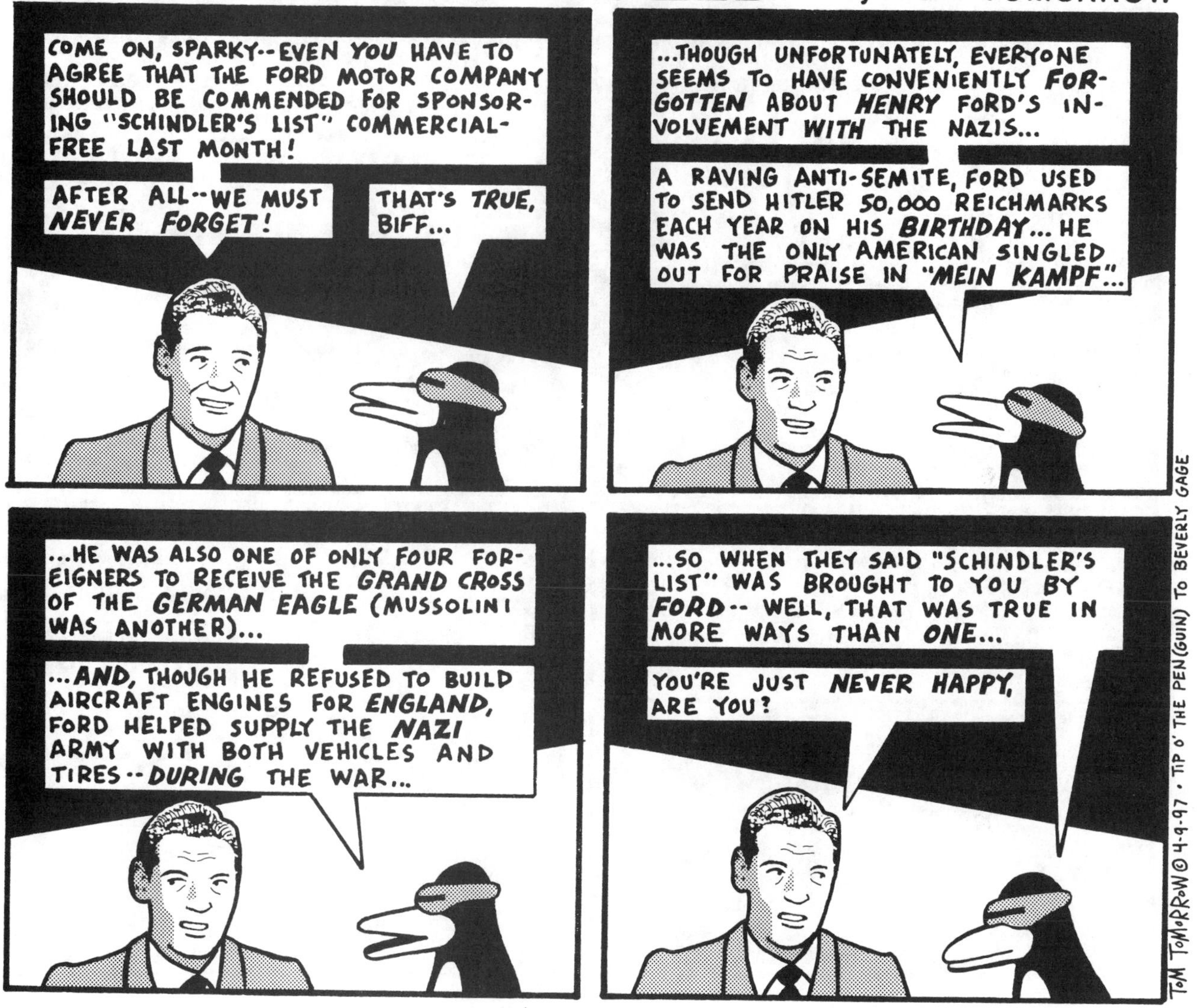
COME ON, SPARKY--EVEN *YOU* HAVE TO AGREE THAT THE FORD MOTOR COMPANY SHOULD BE COMMENDED FOR SPONSORING "SCHINDLER'S LIST" COMMERCIAL-FREE LAST MONTH!
AFTER ALL--WE MUST *NEVER FORGET*!
THAT'S *TRUE*, BIFF...
...THOUGH UNFORTUNATELY, EVERYONE SEEMS TO HAVE CONVENIENTLY *FORGOTTEN* ABOUT *HENRY* FORD'S INVOLVEMENT *WITH* THE NAZIS...
A RAVING ANTI-SEMITE, FORD USED TO SEND HITLER 50,000 REICHMARKS EACH YEAR ON HIS *BIRTHDAY*... HE WAS THE ONLY AMERICAN SINGLED OUT FOR PRAISE IN *"MEIN KAMPF"*...
...HE WAS ALSO ONE OF ONLY FOUR FOREIGNERS TO RECEIVE THE *GRAND CROSS* OF THE *GERMAN EAGLE* (MUSSOLINI WAS ANOTHER)...
...*AND*, THOUGH HE REFUSED TO BUILD AIRCRAFT ENGINES FOR *ENGLAND*, FORD HELPED SUPPLY THE *NAZI* ARMY WITH BOTH VEHICLES AND TIRES--*DURING* THE WAR...
...SO WHEN THEY SAID "SCHINDLER'S LIST" WAS BROUGHT TO YOU *BY FORD*-- WELL, THAT WAS TRUE IN MORE WAYS THAN *ONE*...
YOU'RE JUST *NEVER HAPPY*, ARE YOU?
TOM TOMORROW © 4-9-97 • TIP O' THE PEN(GUIN) TO BEVERLY GAGE

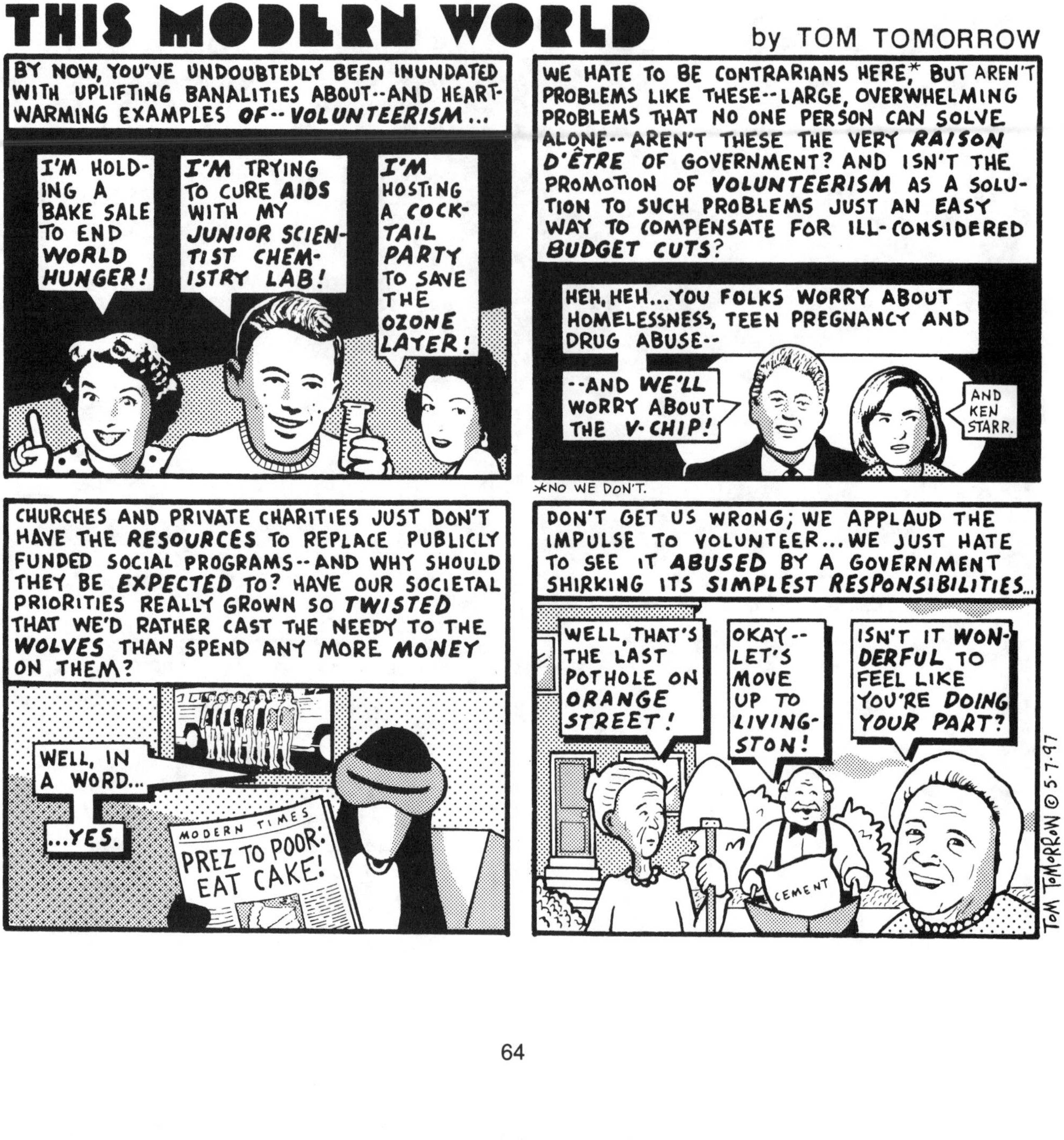
THIS MODERN WORLD
by TOM TOMORROW
BY NOW, YOU'VE UNDOUBTEDLY BEEN INUNDATED WITH UPLIFTING BANALITIES ABOUT--AND HEART-WARMING EXAMPLES OF--VOLUNTEERISM...
I'M HOLDING A BAKE SALE TO END WORLD HUNGER!
I'M TRYING TO CURE AIDS WITH MY JUNIOR SCIENTIST CHEMISTRY LAB!
I'M HOSTING A COCKTAIL PARTY TO SAVE THE OZONE LAYER!
WE HATE TO BE CONTRARIANS HERE,* BUT AREN'T PROBLEMS LIKE THESE--LARGE, OVERWHELMING PROBLEMS THAT NO ONE PERSON CAN SOLVE ALONE--AREN'T THESE THE VERY RAISON D'ÊTRE OF GOVERNMENT? AND ISN'T THE PROMOTION OF VOLUNTEERISM AS A SOLUTION TO SUCH PROBLEMS JUST AN EASY WAY TO COMPENSATE FOR ILL-CONSIDERED BUDGET CUTS?
HEH, HEH... YOU FOLKS WORRY ABOUT HOMELESSNESS, TEEN PREGNANCY AND DRUG ABUSE--
--AND WE'LL WORRY ABOUT THE V-CHIP!
AND KEN STARR.
*NO WE DON'T.
CHURCHES AND PRIVATE CHARITIES JUST DON'T HAVE THE RESOURCES TO REPLACE PUBLICLY FUNDED SOCIAL PROGRAMS--AND WHY SHOULD THEY BE EXPECTED TO? HAVE OUR SOCIETAL PRIORITIES REALLY GROWN SO TWISTED THAT WE'D RATHER CAST THE NEEDY TO THE WOLVES THAN SPEND ANY MORE MONEY ON THEM?
WELL, IN A WORD...
...YES.
MODERN TIMES
PREZ TO POOR: EAT CAKE!
DON'T GET US WRONG; WE APPLAUD THE IMPULSE TO VOLUNTEER... WE JUST HATE TO SEE IT ABUSED BY A GOVERNMENT SHIRKING ITS SIMPLEST RESPONSIBILITIES...
WELL, THAT'S THE LAST POTHOLE ON ORANGE STREET!
OKAY--LET'S MOVE UP TO LIVINGSTON!
ISN'T IT WONDERFUL TO FEEL LIKE YOU'RE DOING YOUR PART?
CEMENT
TOM TOMORROW © 5·7·97

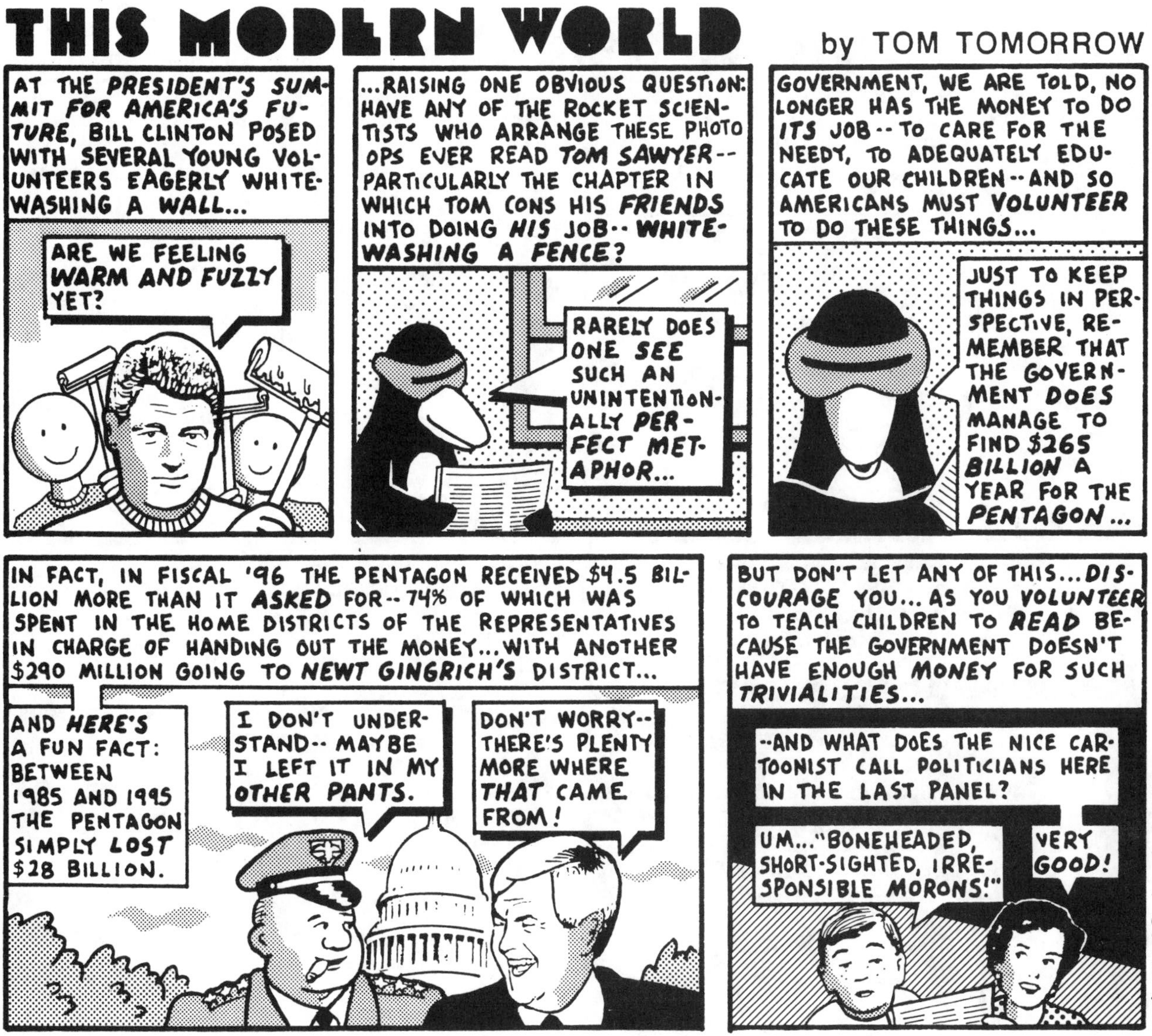
THIS MODERN WORLD
by TOM TOMORROW
AT THE PRESIDENT'S SUMMIT FOR AMERICA'S FUTURE, BILL CLINTON POSED WITH SEVERAL YOUNG VOLUNTEERS EAGERLY WHITE-WASHING A WALL...
ARE WE FEELING WARM AND FUZZY YET?
...RAISING ONE OBVIOUS QUESTION: HAVE ANY OF THE ROCKET SCIENTISTS WHO ARRANGE THESE PHOTO OPS EVER READ TOM SAWYER-- PARTICULARLY THE CHAPTER IN WHICH TOM CONS HIS FRIENDS INTO DOING HIS JOB-- WHITE-WASHING A FENCE?
RARELY DOES ONE SEE SUCH AN UNINTENTIONALLY PERFECT METAPHOR...
GOVERNMENT, WE ARE TOLD, NO LONGER HAS THE MONEY TO DO ITS JOB-- TO CARE FOR THE NEEDY, TO ADEQUATELY EDUCATE OUR CHILDREN--AND SO AMERICANS MUST VOLUNTEER TO DO THESE THINGS...
JUST TO KEEP THINGS IN PERSPECTIVE, REMEMBER THAT THE GOVERNMENT DOES MANAGE TO FIND $265 BILLION A YEAR FOR THE PENTAGON...
IN FACT, IN FISCAL '96 THE PENTAGON RECEIVED $4.5 BILLION MORE THAN IT ASKED FOR--74% OF WHICH WAS SPENT IN THE HOME DISTRICTS OF THE REPRESENTATIVES IN CHARGE OF HANDING OUT THE MONEY...WITH ANOTHER $290 MILLION GOING TO NEWT GINGRICH'S DISTRICT...
AND HERE'S A FUN FACT: BETWEEN 1985 AND 1995 THE PENTAGON SIMPLY LOST $28 BILLION.
I DON'T UNDERSTAND-- MAYBE I LEFT IT IN MY OTHER PANTS.
DON'T WORRY-- THERE'S PLENTY MORE WHERE THAT CAME FROM!
BUT DON'T LET ANY OF THIS...DISCOURAGE YOU...AS YOU VOLUNTEER TO TEACH CHILDREN TO READ BECAUSE THE GOVERNMENT DOESN'T HAVE ENOUGH MONEY FOR SUCH TRIVIALITIES...
--AND WHAT DOES THE NICE CARTOONIST CALL POLITICIANS HERE IN THE LAST PANEL?
UM..."BONEHEADED, SHORT-SIGHTED, IRRESPONSIBLE MORONS!"
VERY GOOD!
TOM TOMORROW © 5-14-97

THIS MODERN WORLD

by TOM TOMORROW

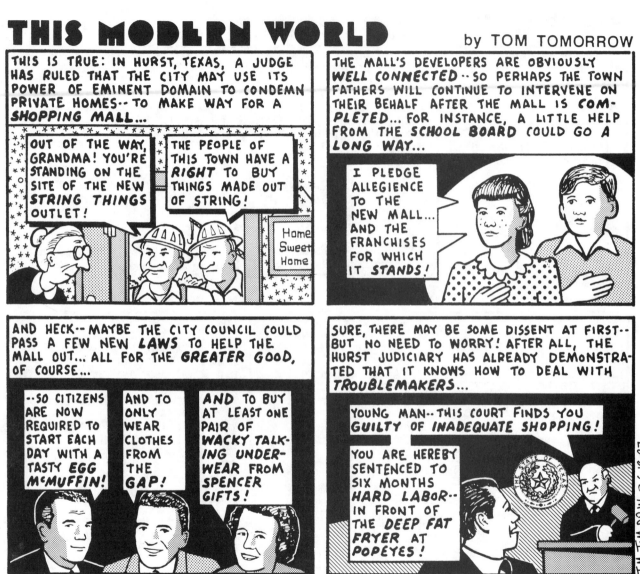

THIS IS TRUE: IN HURST, TEXAS, A JUDGE HAS RULED THAT THE CITY MAY USE ITS POWER OF EMINENT DOMAIN TO CONDEMN PRIVATE HOMES--TO MAKE WAY FOR A SHOPPING MALL...

OUT OF THE WAY, GRANDMA! YOU'RE STANDING ON THE SITE OF THE NEW STRING THINGS OUTLET!

THE PEOPLE OF THIS TOWN HAVE A RIGHT TO BUY THINGS MADE OUT OF STRING!

Home Sweet Home

THE MALL'S DEVELOPERS ARE OBVIOUSLY WELL CONNECTED--SO PERHAPS THE TOWN FATHERS WILL CONTINUE TO INTERVENE ON THEIR BEHALF AFTER THE MALL IS COMPLETED... FOR INSTANCE, A LITTLE HELP FROM THE SCHOOL BOARD COULD GO A LONG WAY...

I PLEDGE ALLEGIENCE TO THE NEW MALL... AND THE FRANCHISES FOR WHICH IT STANDS!

AND HECK--MAYBE THE CITY COUNCIL COULD PASS A FEW NEW LAWS TO HELP THE MALL OUT... ALL FOR THE GREATER GOOD, OF COURSE...

--SO CITIZENS ARE NOW REQUIRED TO START EACH DAY WITH A TASTY EGG McMUFFIN!

AND TO ONLY WEAR CLOTHES FROM THE GAP!

AND TO BUY AT LEAST ONE PAIR OF WACKY TALKING UNDERWEAR FROM SPENCER GIFTS!

SURE, THERE MAY BE SOME DISSENT AT FIRST-- BUT NO NEED TO WORRY! AFTER ALL, THE HURST JUDICIARY HAS ALREADY DEMONSTRATED THAT IT KNOWS HOW TO DEAL WITH TROUBLEMAKERS...

YOUNG MAN--THIS COURT FINDS YOU GUILTY OF INADEQUATE SHOPPING!

YOU ARE HEREBY SENTENCED TO SIX MONTHS HARD LABOR-- IN FRONT OF THE DEEP FAT FRYER AT POPEYES!

THE STATE OF TEXAS

TOM TOMORROW ©6-18-97

66

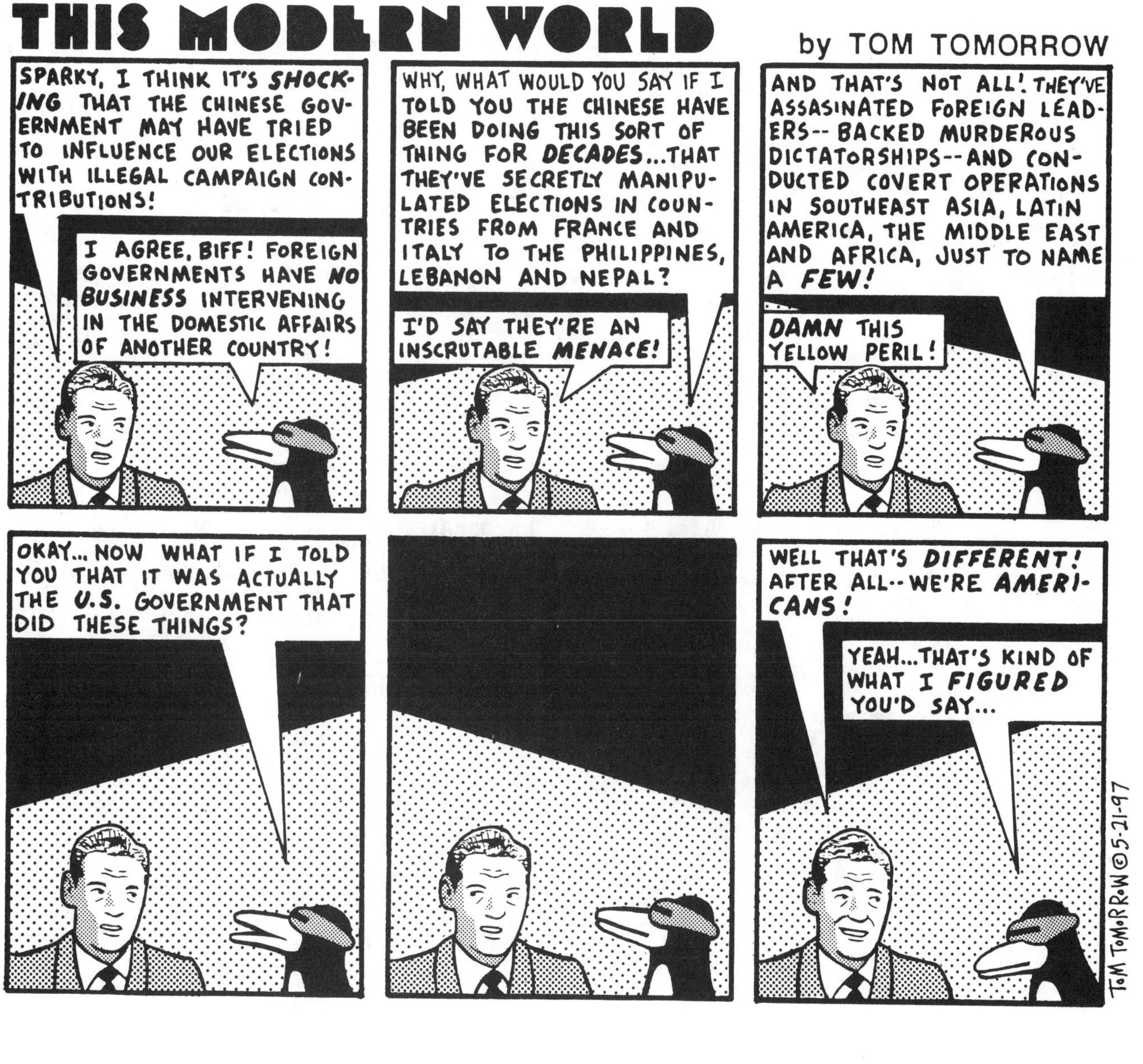
THIS MODERN WORLD
by TOM TOMORROW
SPARKY, I THINK IT'S SHOCKING THAT THE CHINESE GOVERNMENT MAY HAVE TRIED TO INFLUENCE OUR ELECTIONS WITH ILLEGAL CAMPAIGN CONTRIBUTIONS!
I AGREE, BIFF! FOREIGN GOVERNMENTS HAVE NO BUSINESS INTERVENING IN THE DOMESTIC AFFAIRS OF ANOTHER COUNTRY!
WHY, WHAT WOULD YOU SAY IF I TOLD YOU THE CHINESE HAVE BEEN DOING THIS SORT OF THING FOR DECADES...THAT THEY'VE SECRETLY MANIPULATED ELECTIONS IN COUNTRIES FROM FRANCE AND ITALY TO THE PHILIPPINES, LEBANON AND NEPAL?
I'D SAY THEY'RE AN INSCRUTABLE MENACE!
AND THAT'S NOT ALL! THEY'VE ASSASINATED FOREIGN LEADERS-- BACKED MURDEROUS DICTATORSHIPS--AND CONDUCTED COVERT OPERATIONS IN SOUTHEAST ASIA, LATIN AMERICA, THE MIDDLE EAST AND AFRICA, JUST TO NAME A FEW!
DAMN THIS YELLOW PERIL!
OKAY... NOW WHAT IF I TOLD YOU THAT IT WAS ACTUALLY THE U.S. GOVERNMENT THAT DID THESE THINGS?
WELL THAT'S DIFFERENT! AFTER ALL--WE'RE AMERICANS!
YEAH...THAT'S KIND OF WHAT I FIGURED YOU'D SAY...
TOM TOMORROW©5-21-97

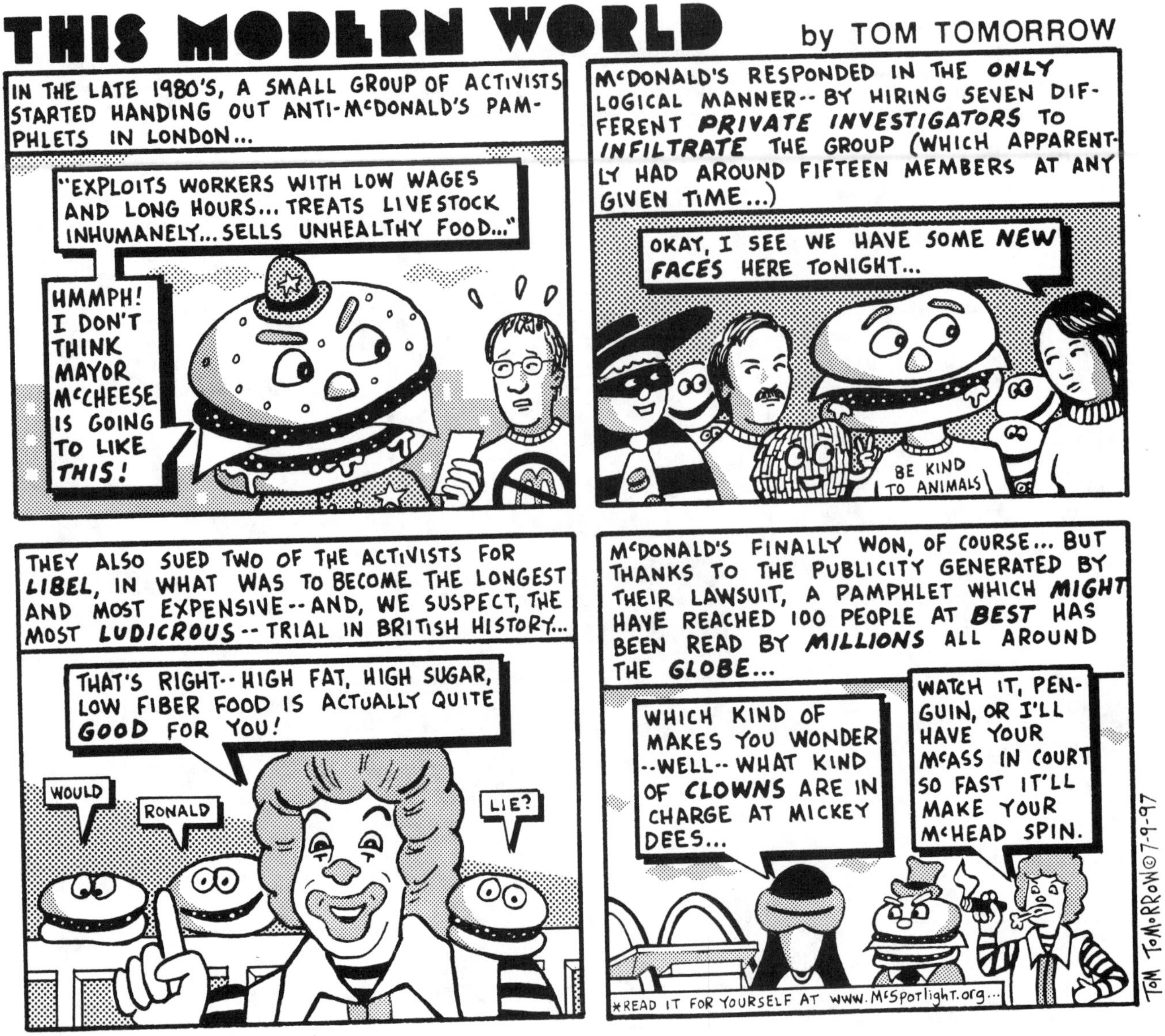
THIS MODERN WORLD
by TOM TOMORROW
IN THE LATE 1980'S, A SMALL GROUP OF ACTIVISTS STARTED HANDING OUT ANTI-McDONALD'S PAMPHLETS IN LONDON...
"EXPLOITS WORKERS WITH LOW WAGES AND LONG HOURS... TREATS LIVESTOCK INHUMANELY... SELLS UNHEALTHY FOOD..."
HMMPH! I DON'T THINK MAYOR McCHEESE IS GOING TO LIKE THIS!
McDONALD'S RESPONDED IN THE ONLY LOGICAL MANNER-- BY HIRING SEVEN DIFFERENT PRIVATE INVESTIGATORS TO INFILTRATE THE GROUP (WHICH APPARENTLY HAD AROUND FIFTEEN MEMBERS AT ANY GIVEN TIME...)
OKAY, I SEE WE HAVE SOME NEW FACES HERE TONIGHT...
BE KIND TO ANIMALS
THEY ALSO SUED TWO OF THE ACTIVISTS FOR LIBEL, IN WHAT WAS TO BECOME THE LONGEST AND MOST EXPENSIVE--AND, WE SUSPECT, THE MOST LUDICROUS-- TRIAL IN BRITISH HISTORY...
THAT'S RIGHT-- HIGH FAT, HIGH SUGAR, LOW FIBER FOOD IS ACTUALLY QUITE GOOD FOR YOU!
WOULD
RONALD
LIE?
McDONALD'S FINALLY WON, OF COURSE... BUT THANKS TO THE PUBLICITY GENERATED BY THEIR LAWSUIT, A PAMPHLET WHICH MIGHT HAVE REACHED 100 PEOPLE AT BEST HAS BEEN READ BY MILLIONS ALL AROUND THE GLOBE...
WHICH KIND OF MAKES YOU WONDER --WELL-- WHAT KIND OF CLOWNS ARE IN CHARGE AT MICKEY DEES...
WATCH IT, PENGUIN, OR I'LL HAVE YOUR McASS IN COURT SO FAST IT'LL MAKE YOUR McHEAD SPIN.
*READ IT FOR YOURSELF AT www.McSpotlight.org...
TOM TOMORROW©7-9-97

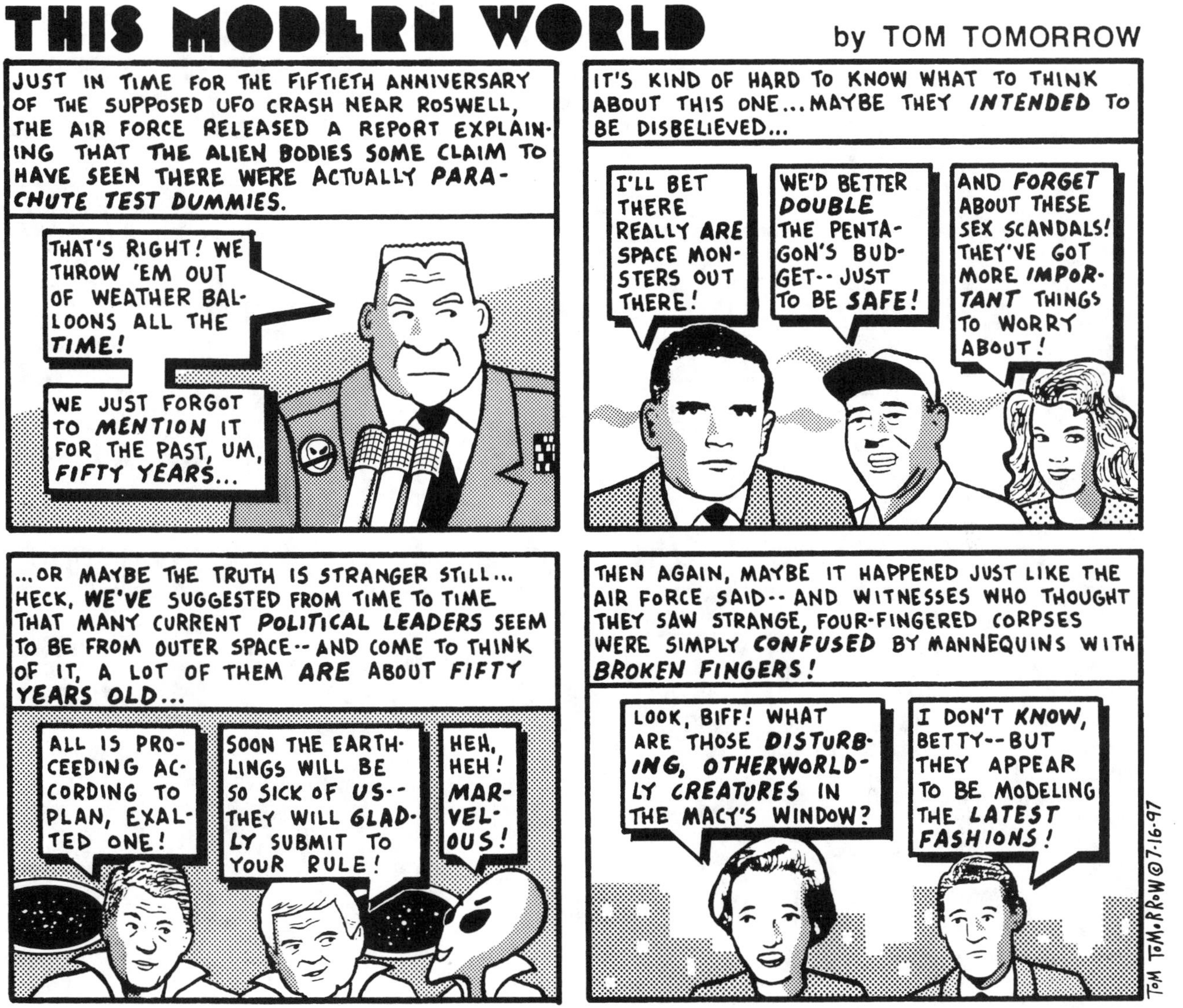
THIS MODERN WORLD
by TOM TOMORROW
JUST IN TIME FOR THE FIFTIETH ANNIVERSARY OF THE SUPPOSED UFO CRASH NEAR ROSWELL, THE AIR FORCE RELEASED A REPORT EXPLAINING THAT THE ALIEN BODIES SOME CLAIM TO HAVE SEEN THERE WERE ACTUALLY PARACHUTE TEST DUMMIES.
THAT'S RIGHT! WE THROW 'EM OUT OF WEATHER BALLOONS ALL THE TIME!
WE JUST FORGOT TO MENTION IT FOR THE PAST, UM, FIFTY YEARS...
IT'S KIND OF HARD TO KNOW WHAT TO THINK ABOUT THIS ONE... MAYBE THEY INTENDED TO BE DISBELIEVED...
I'LL BET THERE REALLY ARE SPACE MONSTERS OUT THERE!
WE'D BETTER DOUBLE THE PENTAGON'S BUDGET-- JUST TO BE SAFE!
AND FORGET ABOUT THESE SEX SCANDALS! THEY'VE GOT MORE IMPORTANT THINGS TO WORRY ABOUT!
...OR MAYBE THE TRUTH IS STRANGER STILL... HECK, WE'VE SUGGESTED FROM TIME TO TIME THAT MANY CURRENT POLITICAL LEADERS SEEM TO BE FROM OUTER SPACE-- AND COME TO THINK OF IT, A LOT OF THEM ARE ABOUT FIFTY YEARS OLD...
ALL IS PROCEEDING ACCORDING TO PLAN, EXALTED ONE!
SOON THE EARTHLINGS WILL BE SO SICK OF US-- THEY WILL GLADLY SUBMIT TO YOUR RULE!
HEH, HEH! MARVELOUS!
THEN AGAIN, MAYBE IT HAPPENED JUST LIKE THE AIR FORCE SAID-- AND WITNESSES WHO THOUGHT THEY SAW STRANGE, FOUR-FINGERED CORPSES WERE SIMPLY CONFUSED BY MANNEQUINS WITH BROKEN FINGERS!
LOOK, BIFF! WHAT ARE THOSE DISTURBING, OTHERWORLDLY CREATURES IN THE MACY'S WINDOW?
I DON'T KNOW, BETTY-- BUT THEY APPEAR TO BE MODELING THE LATEST FASHIONS!
TOM TOMORROW©7-16-97

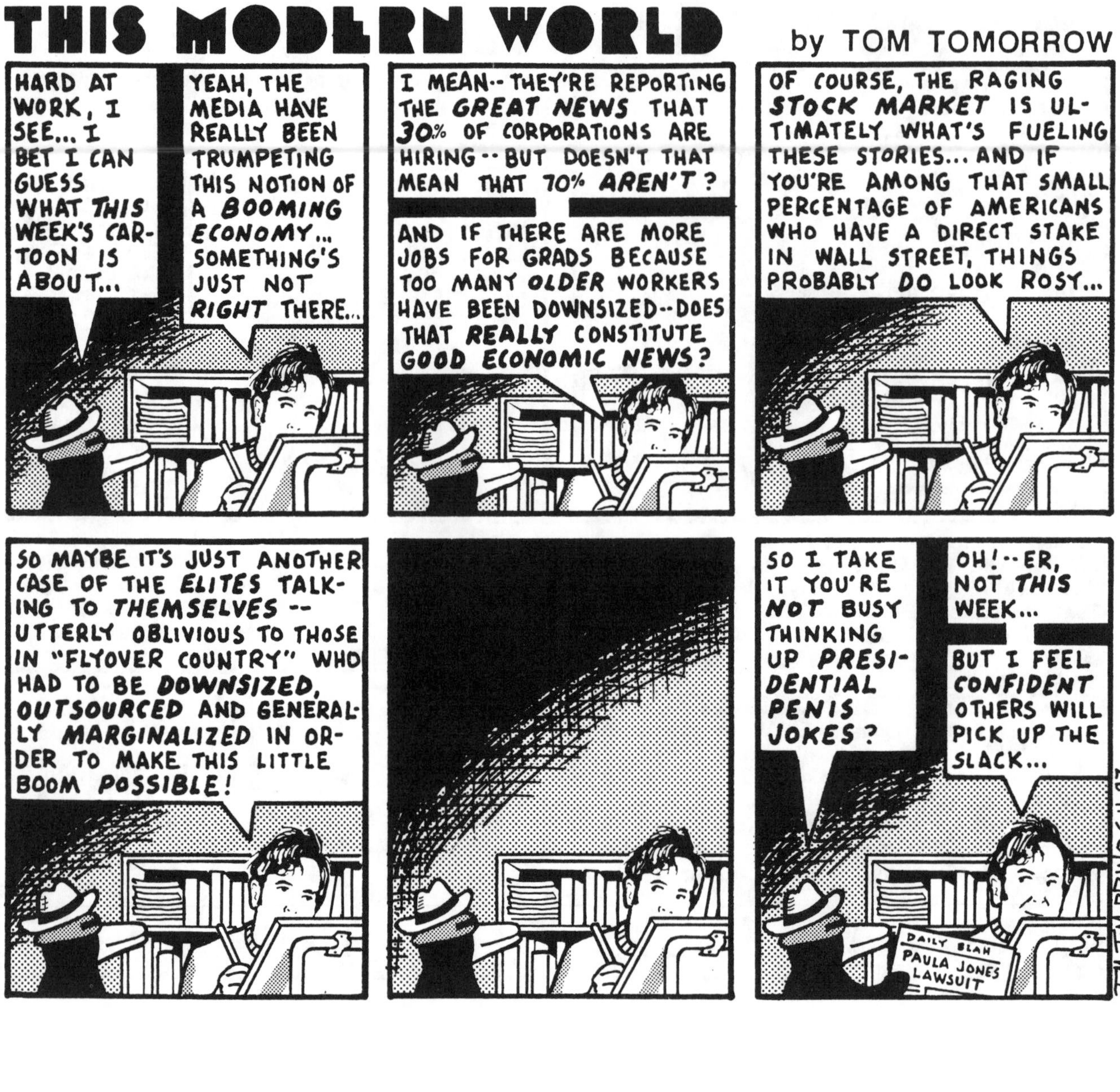

THIS MODERN WORLD
by TOM TOMORROW
HARD AT WORK, I SEE... I BET I CAN GUESS WHAT THIS WEEK'S CARTOON IS ABOUT...
YEAH, THE MEDIA HAVE REALLY BEEN TRUMPETING THIS NOTION OF A BOOMING ECONOMY... SOMETHING'S JUST NOT RIGHT THERE...
I MEAN -- THEY'RE REPORTING THE GREAT NEWS THAT 30% OF CORPORATIONS ARE HIRING -- BUT DOESN'T THAT MEAN THAT 70% AREN'T?
AND IF THERE ARE MORE JOBS FOR GRADS BECAUSE TOO MANY OLDER WORKERS HAVE BEEN DOWNSIZED -- DOES THAT REALLY CONSTITUTE GOOD ECONOMIC NEWS?
OF COURSE, THE RAGING STOCK MARKET IS ULTIMATELY WHAT'S FUELING THESE STORIES... AND IF YOU'RE AMONG THAT SMALL PERCENTAGE OF AMERICANS WHO HAVE A DIRECT STAKE IN WALL STREET, THINGS PROBABLY DO LOOK ROSY...
SO MAYBE IT'S JUST ANOTHER CASE OF THE ELITES TALKING TO THEMSELVES -- UTTERLY OBLIVIOUS TO THOSE IN "FLYOVER COUNTRY" WHO HAD TO BE DOWNSIZED, OUTSOURCED AND GENERALLY MARGINALIZED IN ORDER TO MAKE THIS LITTLE BOOM POSSIBLE!
SO I TAKE IT YOU'RE NOT BUSY THINKING UP PRESIDENTIAL PENIS JOKES?
OH! -- ER, NOT THIS WEEK...
BUT I FEEL CONFIDENT OTHERS WILL PICK UP THE SLACK...
DAILY BLAH
PAULA JONES LAWSUIT
TOM TOMORROW © 6-11-97

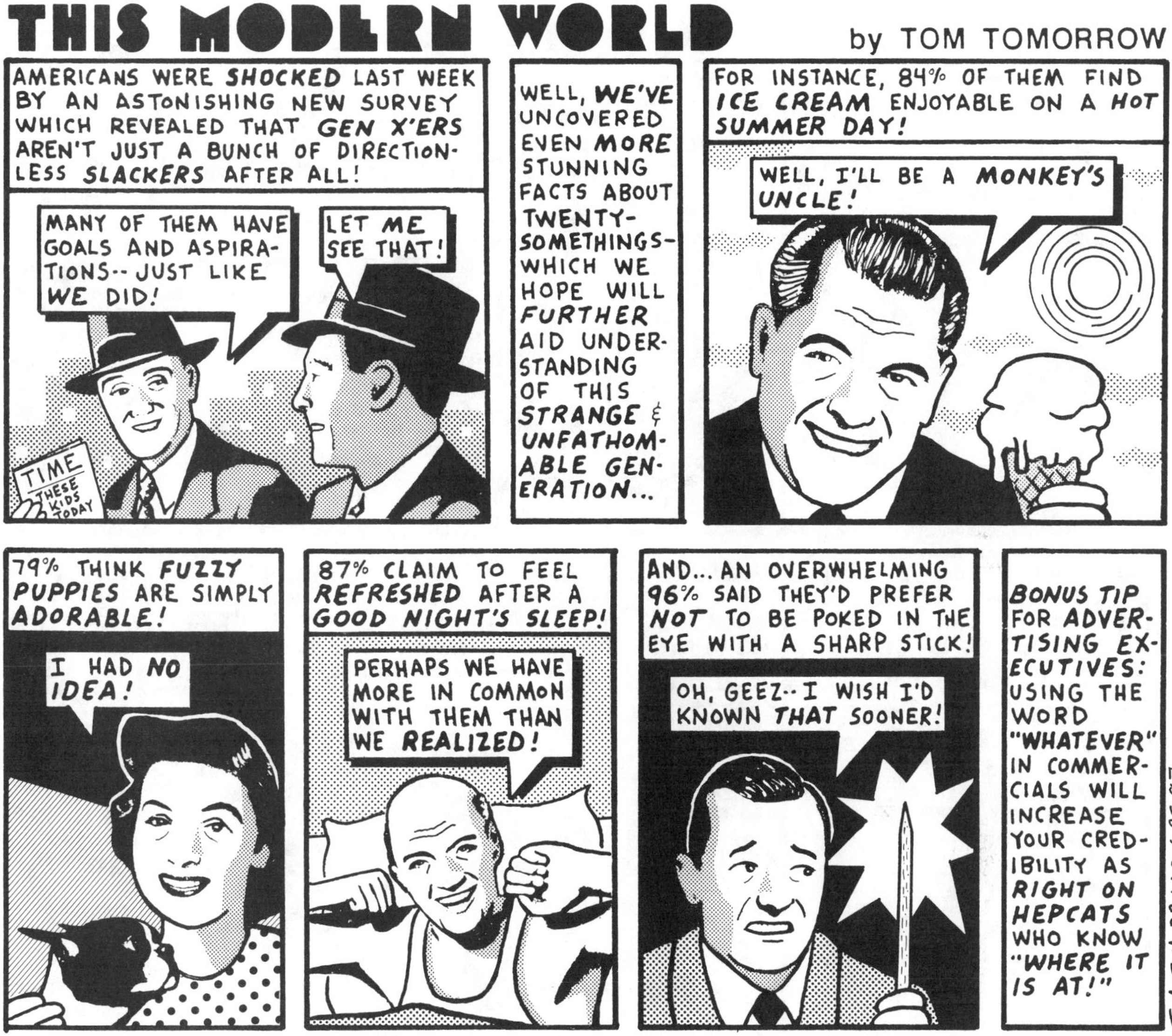
THIS MODERN WORLD
by TOM TOMORROW
AMERICANS WERE SHOCKED LAST WEEK BY AN ASTONISHING NEW SURVEY WHICH REVEALED THAT GEN X'ERS AREN'T JUST A BUNCH OF DIRECTIONLESS SLACKERS AFTER ALL!
MANY OF THEM HAVE GOALS AND ASPIRATIONS-- JUST LIKE WE DID!
LET ME SEE THAT!
TIME
THESE KIDS TODAY
WELL, WE'VE UNCOVERED EVEN MORE STUNNING FACTS ABOUT TWENTY-SOMETHINGS- WHICH WE HOPE WILL FURTHER AID UNDERSTANDING OF THIS STRANGE & UNFATHOMABLE GENERATION...
FOR INSTANCE, 84% OF THEM FIND ICE CREAM ENJOYABLE ON A HOT SUMMER DAY!
WELL, I'LL BE A MONKEY'S UNCLE!
79% THINK FUZZY PUPPIES ARE SIMPLY ADORABLE!
I HAD NO IDEA!
87% CLAIM TO FEEL REFRESHED AFTER A GOOD NIGHT'S SLEEP!
PERHAPS WE HAVE MORE IN COMMON WITH THEM THAN WE REALIZED!
AND... AN OVERWHELMING 96% SAID THEY'D PREFER NOT TO BE POKED IN THE EYE WITH A SHARP STICK!
OH, GEEZ-- I WISH I'D KNOWN THAT SOONER!
BONUS TIP FOR ADVERTISING EXECUTIVES: USING THE WORD "WHATEVER" IN COMMERCIALS WILL INCREASE YOUR CREDIBILITY AS RIGHT ON HEPCATS WHO KNOW "WHERE IT IS AT!"
TOM TOMORROW© 6-25-97

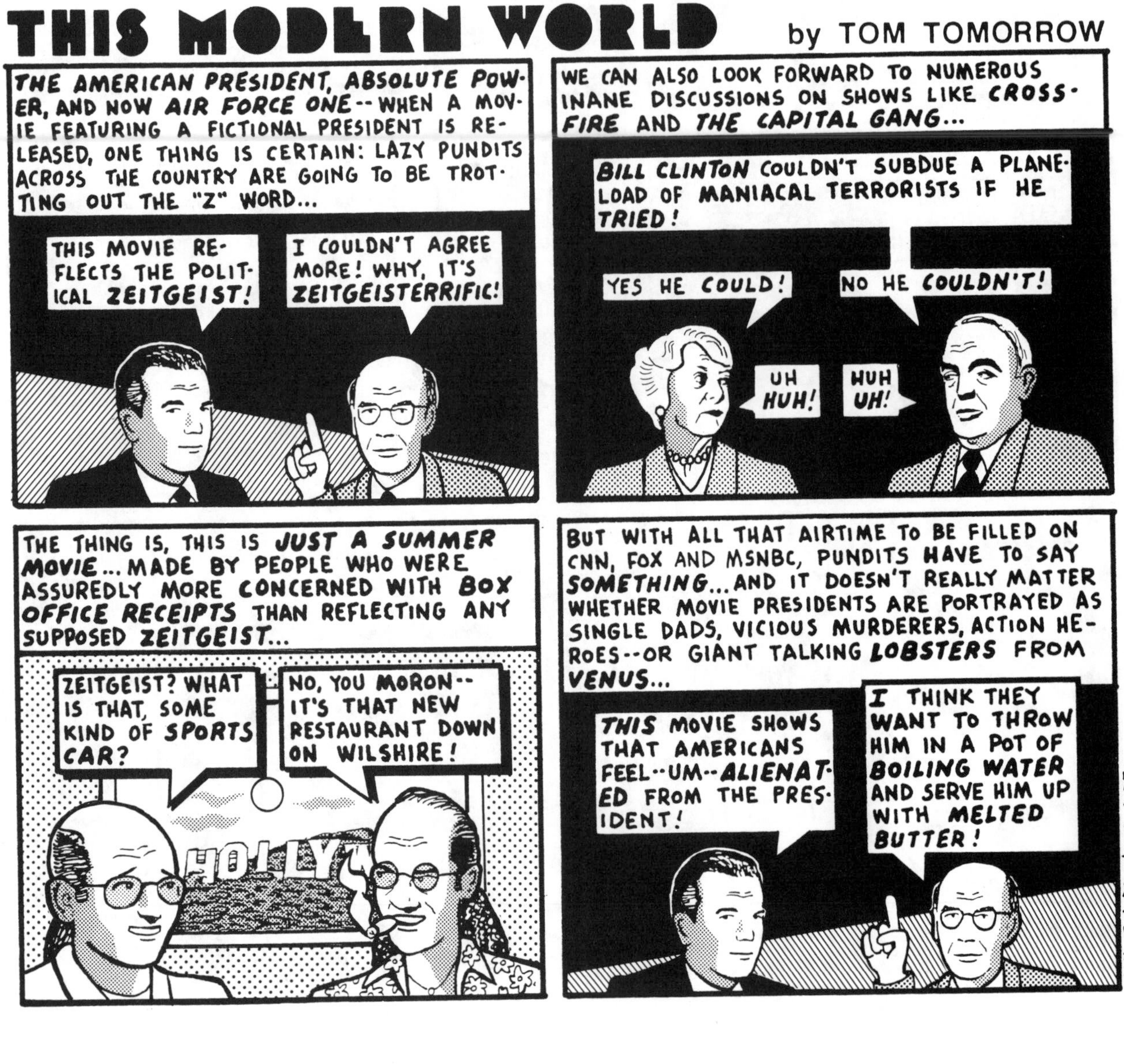
THIS MODERN WORLD
by TOM TOMORROW
THE AMERICAN PRESIDENT, ABSOLUTE POWER, AND NOW AIR FORCE ONE--WHEN A MOVIE FEATURING A FICTIONAL PRESIDENT IS RELEASED, ONE THING IS CERTAIN: LAZY PUNDITS ACROSS THE COUNTRY ARE GOING TO BE TROTTING OUT THE "Z" WORD...
THIS MOVIE REFLECTS THE POLITICAL ZEITGEIST!
I COULDN'T AGREE MORE! WHY, IT'S ZEITGEISTERRIFIC!
WE CAN ALSO LOOK FORWARD TO NUMEROUS INANE DISCUSSIONS ON SHOWS LIKE CROSSFIRE AND THE CAPITAL GANG...
BILL CLINTON COULDN'T SUBDUE A PLANELOAD OF MANIACAL TERRORISTS IF HE TRIED!
YES HE COULD!
NO HE COULDN'T!
UH HUH!
HUH UH!
THE THING IS, THIS IS JUST A SUMMER MOVIE... MADE BY PEOPLE WHO WERE ASSUREDLY MORE CONCERNED WITH BOX OFFICE RECEIPTS THAN REFLECTING ANY SUPPOSED ZEITGEIST...
ZEITGEIST? WHAT IS THAT, SOME KIND OF SPORTS CAR?
NO, YOU MORON--IT'S THAT NEW RESTAURANT DOWN ON WILSHIRE!
BUT WITH ALL THAT AIRTIME TO BE FILLED ON CNN, FOX AND MSNBC, PUNDITS HAVE TO SAY SOMETHING... AND IT DOESN'T REALLY MATTER WHETHER MOVIE PRESIDENTS ARE PORTRAYED AS SINGLE DADS, VICIOUS MURDERERS, ACTION HEROES--OR GIANT TALKING LOBSTERS FROM VENUS...
THIS MOVIE SHOWS THAT AMERICANS FEEL--UM--ALIENATED FROM THE PRESIDENT!
I THINK THEY WANT TO THROW HIM IN A POT OF BOILING WATER AND SERVE HIM UP WITH MELTED BUTTER!
TOM TOMORROW © 8-6-97

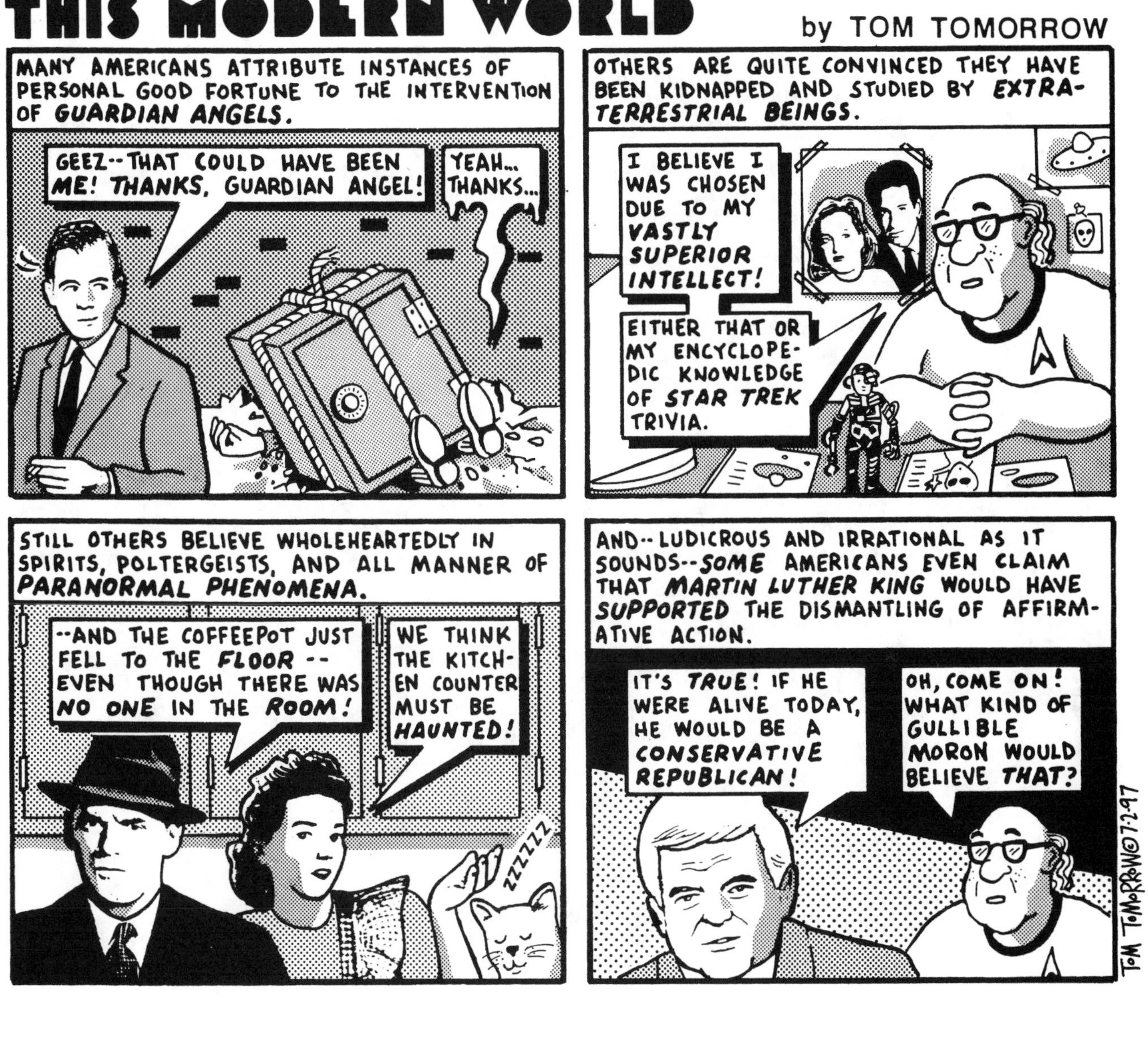
THIS MODERN WORLD
by TOM TOMORROW
MANY AMERICANS ATTRIBUTE INSTANCES OF PERSONAL GOOD FORTUNE TO THE INTERVENTION OF GUARDIAN ANGELS.
GEEZ--THAT COULD HAVE BEEN ME! THANKS, GUARDIAN ANGEL!
YEAH... THANKS...
OTHERS ARE QUITE CONVINCED THEY HAVE BEEN KIDNAPPED AND STUDIED BY EXTRA-TERRESTRIAL BEINGS.
I BELIEVE I WAS CHOSEN DUE TO MY VASTLY SUPERIOR INTELLECT!
EITHER THAT OR MY ENCYCLOPE-DIC KNOWLEDGE OF STAR TREK TRIVIA.
STILL OTHERS BELIEVE WHOLEHEARTEDLY IN SPIRITS, POLTERGEISTS, AND ALL MANNER OF PARANORMAL PHENOMENA.
--AND THE COFFEEPOT JUST FELL TO THE FLOOR -- EVEN THOUGH THERE WAS NO ONE IN THE ROOM!
WE THINK THE KITCH-EN COUNTER MUST BE HAUNTED!
ZZZZZZ
AND--LUDICROUS AND IRRATIONAL AS IT SOUNDS--SOME AMERICANS EVEN CLAIM THAT MARTIN LUTHER KING WOULD HAVE SUPPORTED THE DISMANTLING OF AFFIRM-ATIVE ACTION.
IT'S TRUE! IF HE WERE ALIVE TODAY, HE WOULD BE A CONSERVATIVE REPUBLICAN!
OH, COME ON! WHAT KIND OF GULLIBLE MORON WOULD BELIEVE THAT?
TOM TOMORROW©7-2-97

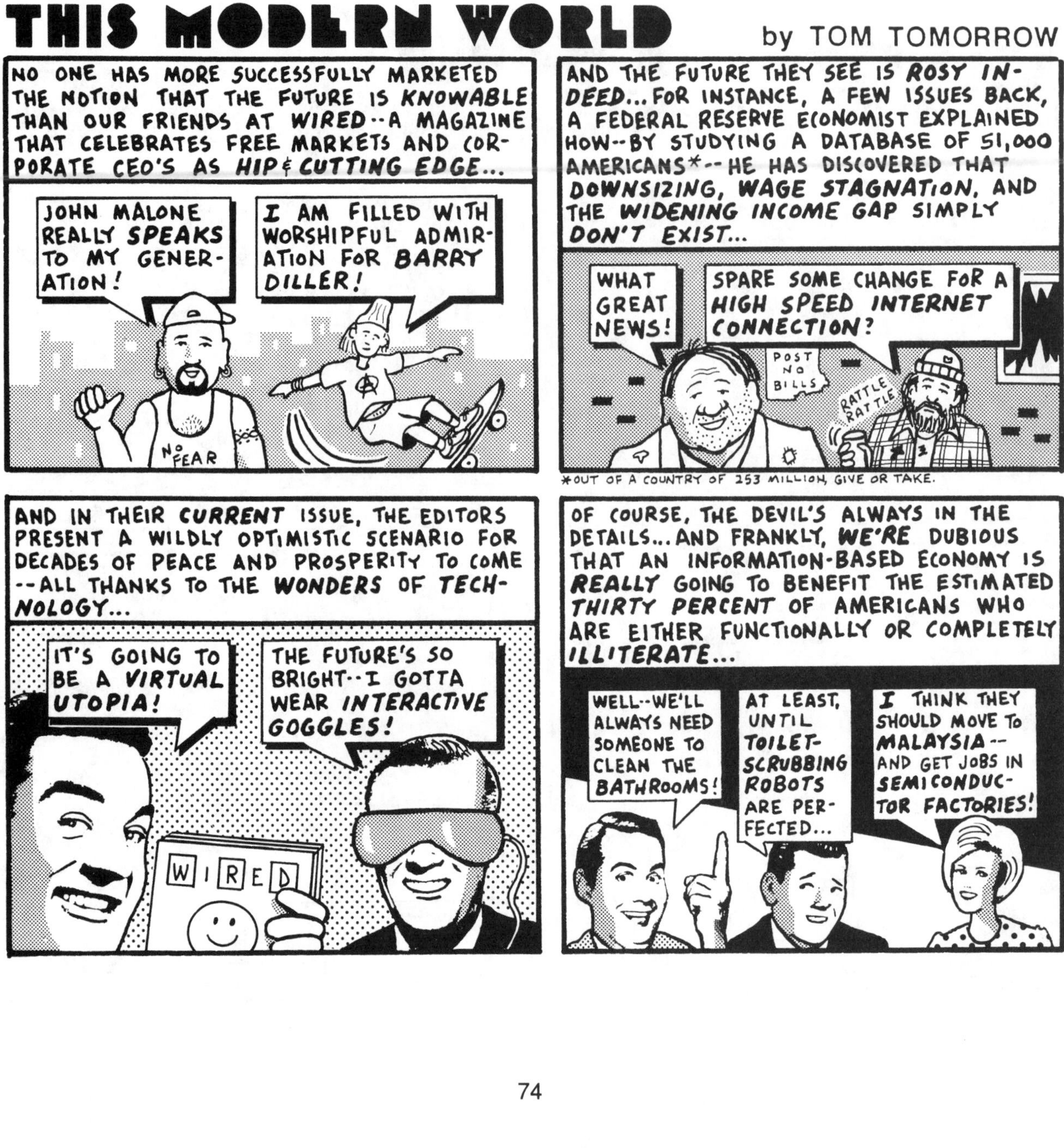
THIS MODERN WORLD
by TOM TOMORROW
NO ONE HAS MORE SUCCESSFULLY MARKETED THE NOTION THAT THE FUTURE IS KNOWABLE THAN OUR FRIENDS AT WIRED--A MAGAZINE THAT CELEBRATES FREE MARKETS AND CORPORATE CEO'S AS HIP & CUTTING EDGE...
JOHN MALONE REALLY SPEAKS TO MY GENERATION!
I AM FILLED WITH WORSHIPFUL ADMIRATION FOR BARRY DILLER!
NO FEAR
AND THE FUTURE THEY SEE IS ROSY INDEED... FOR INSTANCE, A FEW ISSUES BACK, A FEDERAL RESERVE ECONOMIST EXPLAINED HOW--BY STUDYING A DATABASE OF 51,000 AMERICANS*--HE HAS DISCOVERED THAT DOWNSIZING, WAGE STAGNATION, AND THE WIDENING INCOME GAP SIMPLY DON'T EXIST...
WHAT GREAT NEWS!
SPARE SOME CHANGE FOR A HIGH SPEED INTERNET CONNECTION?
POST NO BILLS
RATTLE RATTLE
*OUT OF A COUNTRY OF 253 MILLION, GIVE OR TAKE.
AND IN THEIR CURRENT ISSUE, THE EDITORS PRESENT A WILDLY OPTIMISTIC SCENARIO FOR DECADES OF PEACE AND PROSPERITY TO COME--ALL THANKS TO THE WONDERS OF TECHNOLOGY...
IT'S GOING TO BE A VIRTUAL UTOPIA!
THE FUTURE'S SO BRIGHT--I GOTTA WEAR INTERACTIVE GOGGLES!
WIRED
OF COURSE, THE DEVIL'S ALWAYS IN THE DETAILS... AND FRANKLY, WE'RE DUBIOUS THAT AN INFORMATION-BASED ECONOMY IS REALLY GOING TO BENEFIT THE ESTIMATED THIRTY PERCENT OF AMERICANS WHO ARE EITHER FUNCTIONALLY OR COMPLETELY ILLITERATE...
WELL--WE'LL ALWAYS NEED SOMEONE TO CLEAN THE BATHROOMS!
AT LEAST, UNTIL TOILET-SCRUBBING ROBOTS ARE PERFECTED...
I THINK THEY SHOULD MOVE TO MALAYSIA--AND GET JOBS IN SEMICONDUCTOR FACTORIES!
TOM TOMORROW©7.23.97

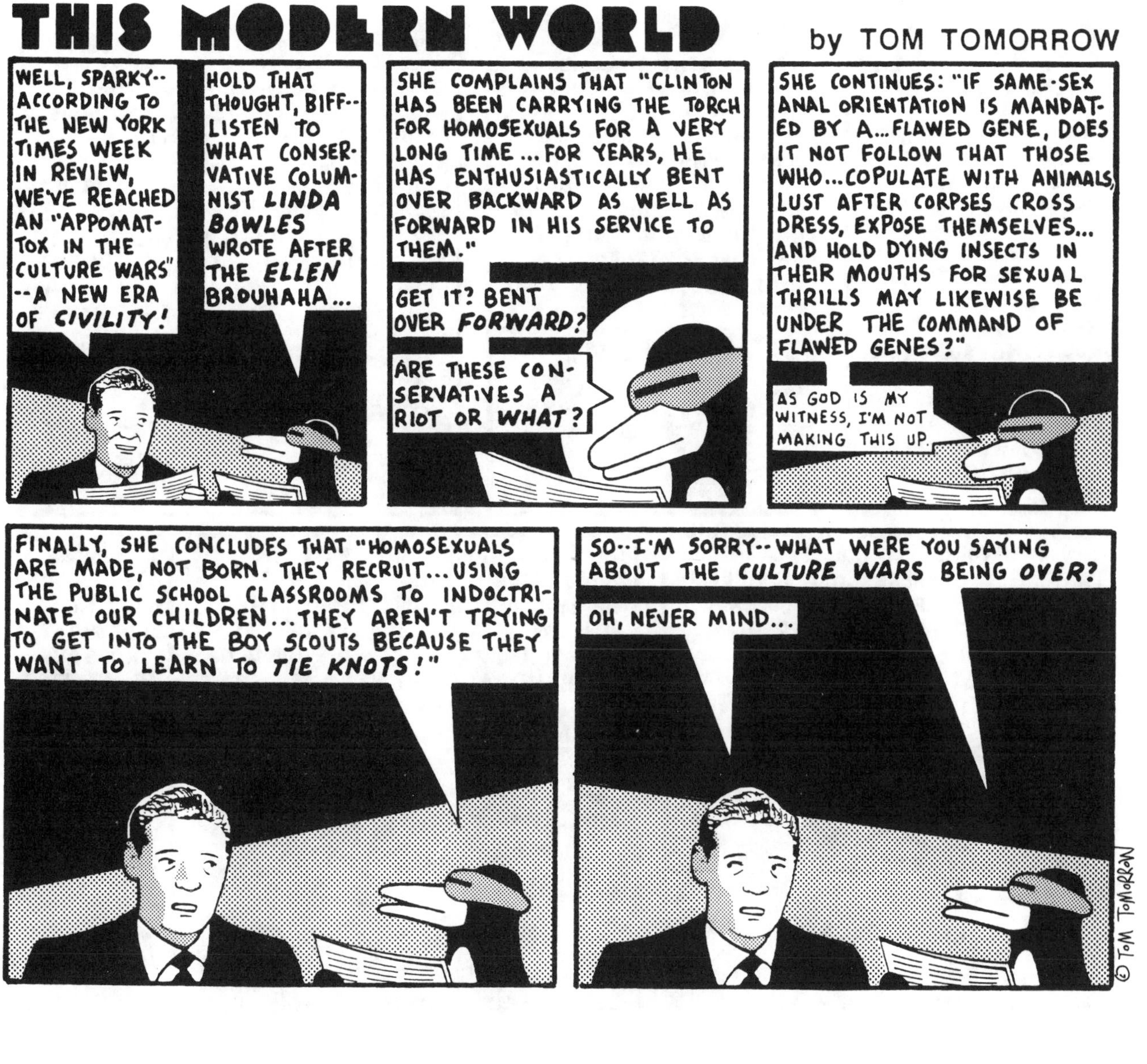
THIS MODERN WORLD
by TOM TOMORROW
WELL, SPARKY-- ACCORDING TO THE NEW YORK TIMES WEEK IN REVIEW, WE'VE REACHED AN "APPOMATTOX IN THE CULTURE WARS" --A NEW ERA OF CIVILITY!
HOLD THAT THOUGHT, BIFF-- LISTEN TO WHAT CONSERVATIVE COLUMNIST LINDA BOWLES WROTE AFTER THE ELLEN BROUHAHA...
SHE COMPLAINS THAT "CLINTON HAS BEEN CARRYING THE TORCH FOR HOMOSEXUALS FOR A VERY LONG TIME... FOR YEARS, HE HAS ENTHUSIASTICALLY BENT OVER BACKWARD AS WELL AS FORWARD IN HIS SERVICE TO THEM."
GET IT? BENT OVER FORWARD?
ARE THESE CONSERVATIVES A RIOT OR WHAT?
SHE CONTINUES: "IF SAME-SEX ANAL ORIENTATION IS MANDATED BY A...FLAWED GENE, DOES IT NOT FOLLOW THAT THOSE WHO...COPULATE WITH ANIMALS, LUST AFTER CORPSES CROSS DRESS, EXPOSE THEMSELVES... AND HOLD DYING INSECTS IN THEIR MOUTHS FOR SEXUAL THRILLS MAY LIKEWISE BE UNDER THE COMMAND OF FLAWED GENES?"
AS GOD IS MY WITNESS, I'M NOT MAKING THIS UP.
FINALLY, SHE CONCLUDES THAT "HOMOSEXUALS ARE MADE, NOT BORN. THEY RECRUIT... USING THE PUBLIC SCHOOL CLASSROOMS TO INDOCTRINATE OUR CHILDREN... THEY AREN'T TRYING TO GET INTO THE BOY SCOUTS BECAUSE THEY WANT TO LEARN TO TIE KNOTS!"
SO--I'M SORRY--WHAT WERE YOU SAYING ABOUT THE CULTURE WARS BEING OVER?
OH, NEVER MIND...
© TOM TOMORROW

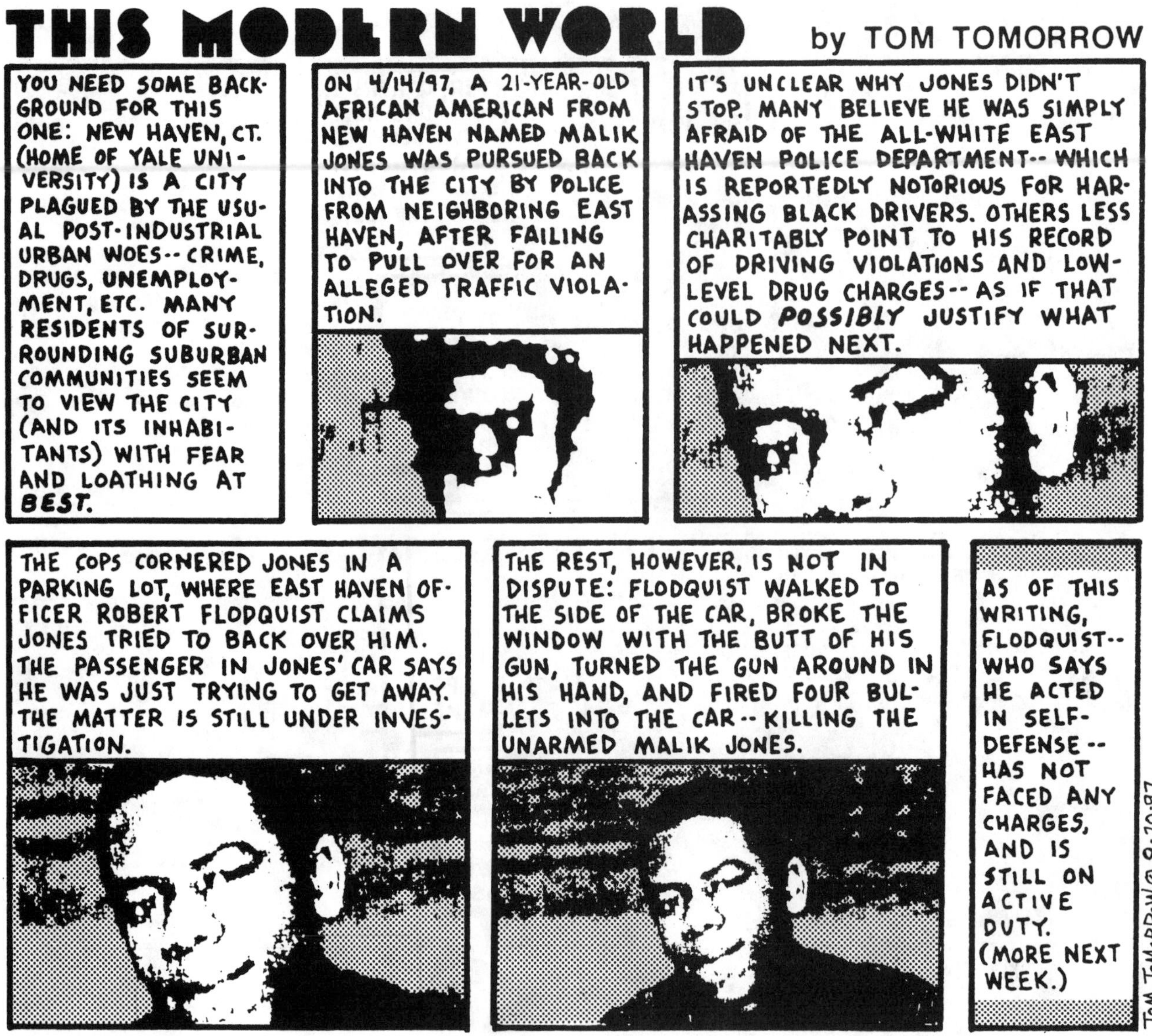

THIS MODERN WORLD

by TOM TOMORROW

YOU NEED SOME BACK-GROUND FOR THIS ONE: NEW HAVEN, CT. (HOME OF YALE UNI-VERSITY) IS A CITY PLAGUED BY THE USU-AL POST-INDUSTRIAL URBAN WOES-- CRIME, DRUGS, UNEMPLOY-MENT, ETC. MANY RESIDENTS OF SUR-ROUNDING SUBURBAN COMMUNITIES SEEM TO VIEW THE CITY (AND ITS INHABI-TANTS) WITH FEAR AND LOATHING AT **BEST.**

ON 4/14/97, A 21-YEAR-OLD AFRICAN AMERICAN FROM NEW HAVEN NAMED MALIK JONES WAS PURSUED BACK INTO THE CITY BY POLICE FROM NEIGHBORING EAST HAVEN, AFTER FAILING TO PULL OVER FOR AN ALLEGED TRAFFIC VIOLA-TION.

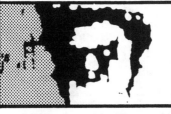

IT'S UNCLEAR WHY JONES DIDN'T STOP. MANY BELIEVE HE WAS SIMPLY AFRAID OF THE ALL-WHITE EAST HAVEN POLICE DEPARTMENT-- WHICH IS REPORTEDLY NOTORIOUS FOR HAR-ASSING BLACK DRIVERS. OTHERS LESS CHARITABLY POINT TO HIS RECORD OF DRIVING VIOLATIONS AND LOW-LEVEL DRUG CHARGES-- AS IF THAT COULD **POSSIBLY** JUSTIFY WHAT HAPPENED NEXT.

THE COPS CORNERED JONES IN A PARKING LOT, WHERE EAST HAVEN OF-FICER ROBERT FLODQUIST CLAIMS JONES TRIED TO BACK OVER HIM. THE PASSENGER IN JONES' CAR SAYS HE WAS JUST TRYING TO GET AWAY. THE MATTER IS STILL UNDER INVES-TIGATION.

THE REST, HOWEVER, IS NOT IN DISPUTE: FLODQUIST WALKED TO THE SIDE OF THE CAR, BROKE THE WINDOW WITH THE BUTT OF HIS GUN, TURNED THE GUN AROUND IN HIS HAND, AND FIRED FOUR BUL-LETS INTO THE CAR-- KILLING THE UNARMED MALIK JONES.

AS OF THIS WRITING, FLODQUIST-- WHO SAYS HE ACTED IN SELF-DEFENSE -- HAS NOT FACED ANY CHARGES, AND IS STILL ON ACTIVE DUTY. (MORE NEXT WEEK.)

TOM TOMORROW © 8-20-97

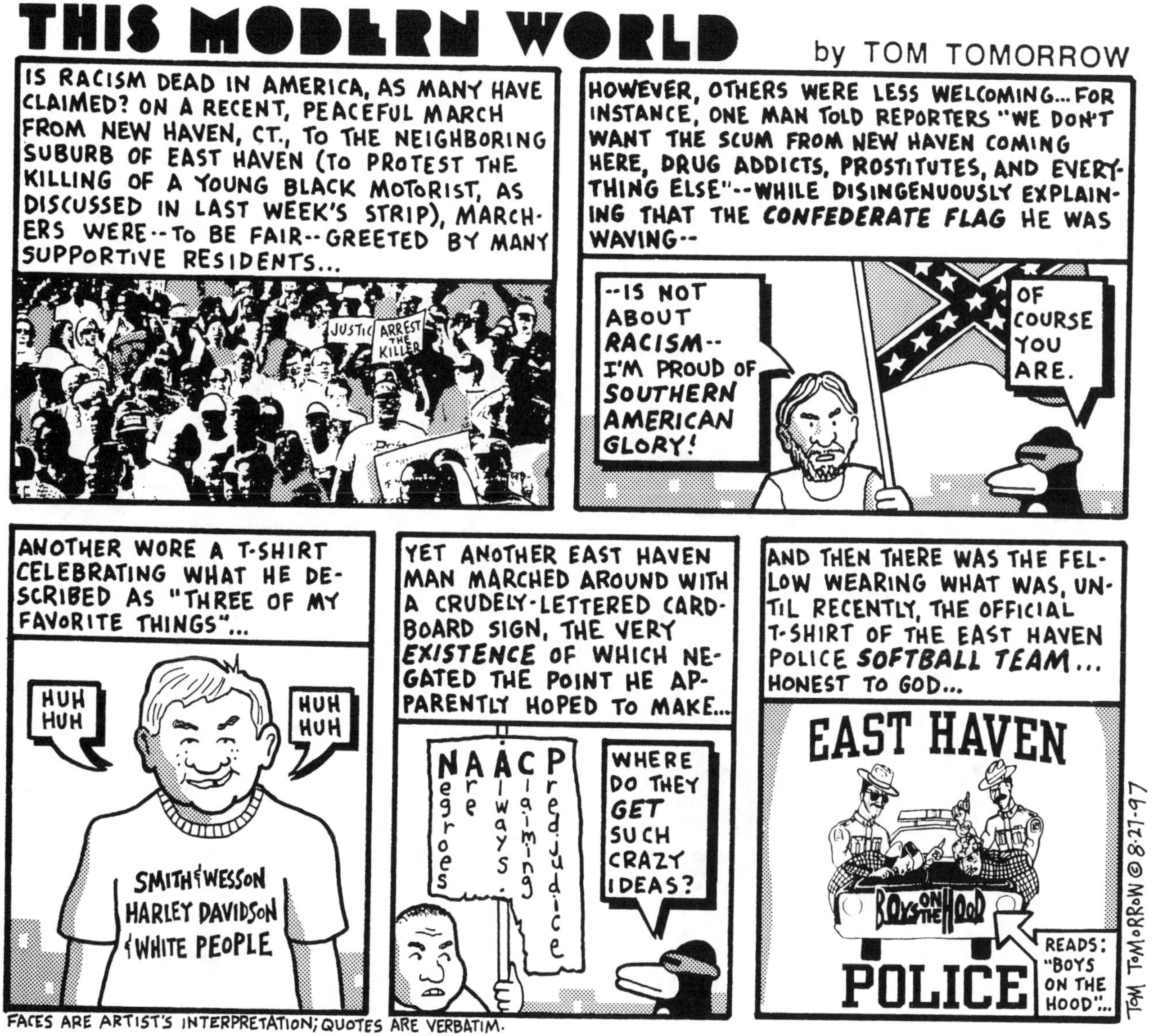

THIS MODERN WORLD
by TOM TOMORROW
IS RACISM DEAD IN AMERICA, AS MANY HAVE CLAIMED? ON A RECENT, PEACEFUL MARCH FROM NEW HAVEN, CT., TO THE NEIGHBORING SUBURB OF EAST HAVEN (TO PROTEST THE KILLING OF A YOUNG BLACK MOTORIST, AS DISCUSSED IN LAST WEEK'S STRIP), MARCHERS WERE--TO BE FAIR--GREETED BY MANY SUPPORTIVE RESIDENTS...
JUSTIC
ARREST THE KILLER
HOWEVER, OTHERS WERE LESS WELCOMING... FOR INSTANCE, ONE MAN TOLD REPORTERS "WE DON'T WANT THE SCUM FROM NEW HAVEN COMING HERE, DRUG ADDICTS, PROSTITUTES, AND EVERYTHING ELSE"--WHILE DISINGENUOUSLY EXPLAINING THAT THE CONFEDERATE FLAG HE WAS WAVING--
--IS NOT ABOUT RACISM-- I'M PROUD OF SOUTHERN AMERICAN GLORY!
OF COURSE YOU ARE.
ANOTHER WORE A T-SHIRT CELEBRATING WHAT HE DESCRIBED AS "THREE OF MY FAVORITE THINGS"...
HUH HUH
HUH HUH
SMITH & WESSON
HARLEY DAVIDSON
& WHITE PEOPLE
YET ANOTHER EAST HAVEN MAN MARCHED AROUND WITH A CRUDELY-LETTERED CARDBOARD SIGN, THE VERY EXISTENCE OF WHICH NEGATED THE POINT HE APPARENTLY HOPED TO MAKE...
N A A C P
Negroes Are Always. Claiming Predjudice
WHERE DO THEY GET SUCH CRAZY IDEAS?
AND THEN THERE WAS THE FELLOW WEARING WHAT WAS, UNTIL RECENTLY, THE OFFICIAL T-SHIRT OF THE EAST HAVEN POLICE SOFTBALL TEAM... HONEST TO GOD...
EAST HAVEN
BOYS ON THE HOOD
POLICE
READS: "BOYS ON THE HOOD"...
TOM TOMORROW © 8-27-97
FACES ARE ARTIST'S INTERPRETATION; QUOTES ARE VERBATIM.

THIS MODERN WORLD

by TOM TOMORROW

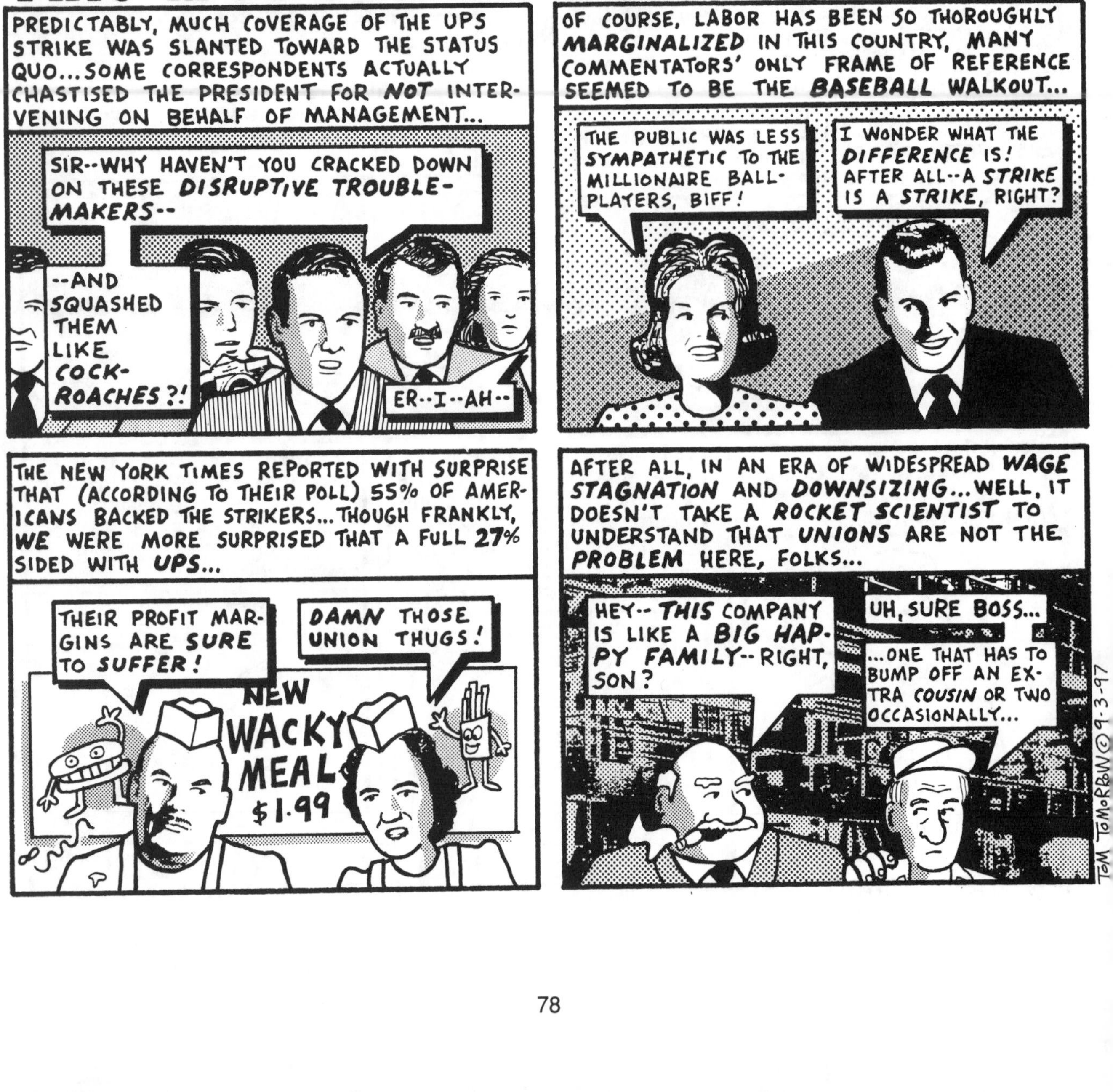
PREDICTABLY, MUCH COVERAGE OF THE UPS STRIKE WAS SLANTED TOWARD THE STATUS QUO...SOME CORRESPONDENTS ACTUALLY CHASTISED THE PRESIDENT FOR NOT INTERVENING ON BEHALF OF MANAGEMENT...
SIR--WHY HAVEN'T YOU CRACKED DOWN ON THESE DISRUPTIVE TROUBLEMAKERS--
--AND SQUASHED THEM LIKE COCKROACHES?!
ER--I--AH--
OF COURSE, LABOR HAS BEEN SO THOROUGHLY MARGINALIZED IN THIS COUNTRY, MANY COMMENTATORS' ONLY FRAME OF REFERENCE SEEMED TO BE THE BASEBALL WALKOUT...
THE PUBLIC WAS LESS SYMPATHETIC TO THE MILLIONAIRE BALLPLAYERS, BIFF!
I WONDER WHAT THE DIFFERENCE IS! AFTER ALL--A STRIKE IS A STRIKE, RIGHT?
THE NEW YORK TIMES REPORTED WITH SURPRISE THAT (ACCORDING TO THEIR POLL) 55% OF AMERICANS BACKED THE STRIKERS...THOUGH FRANKLY, WE WERE MORE SURPRISED THAT A FULL 27% SIDED WITH UPS...
THEIR PROFIT MARGINS ARE SURE TO SUFFER!
DAMN THOSE UNION THUGS!
NEW WACKY MEAL $1.99
AFTER ALL, IN AN ERA OF WIDESPREAD WAGE STAGNATION AND DOWNSIZING...WELL, IT DOESN'T TAKE A ROCKET SCIENTIST TO UNDERSTAND THAT UNIONS ARE NOT THE PROBLEM HERE, FOLKS...
HEY--THIS COMPANY IS LIKE A BIG HAPPY FAMILY--RIGHT, SON?
UH, SURE BOSS...
...ONE THAT HAS TO BUMP OFF AN EXTRA COUSIN OR TWO OCCASIONALLY...
TOM TOMORROW©9-3-97

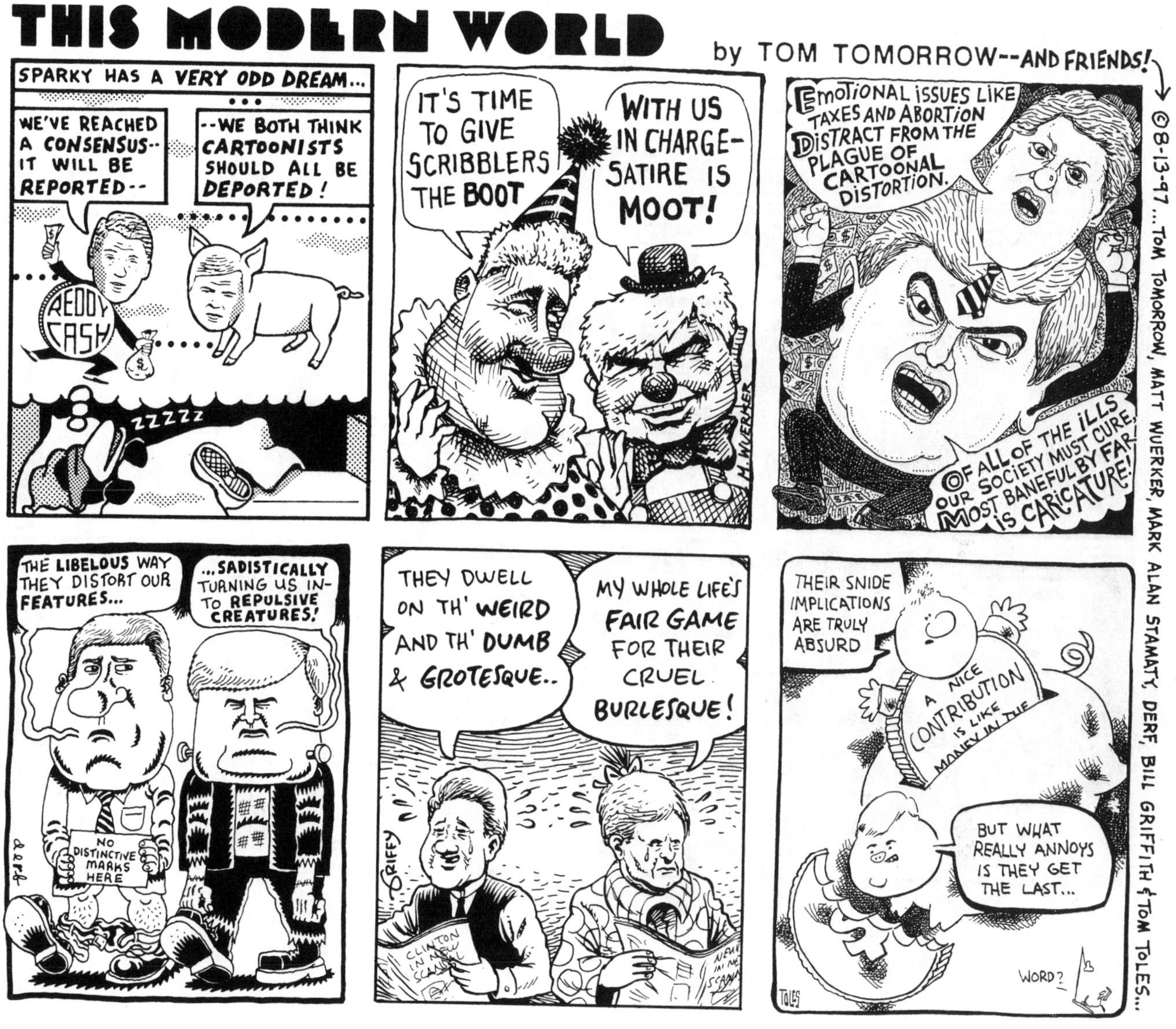
THIS MODERN WORLD
by TOM TOMORROW--AND FRIENDS!
SPARKY HAS A VERY ODD DREAM...
WE'VE REACHED A CONSENSUS-- IT WILL BE REPORTED--
--WE BOTH THINK CARTOONISTS SHOULD ALL BE DEPORTED!
REDDY CASH
ZZZZZ
IT'S TIME TO GIVE SCRIBBLERS THE BOOT
WITH US IN CHARGE-SATIRE IS MOOT!
EMOTIONAL ISSUES LIKE TAXES AND ABORTION DISTRACT FROM THE PLAGUE OF CARTOONAL DISTORTION.
OF ALL OF THE ILLS OUR SOCIETY MUST CURE, MOST BANEFUL BY FAR IS CARICATURE!
THE LIBELOUS WAY THEY DISTORT OUR FEATURES...
...SADISTICALLY TURNING US INTO REPULSIVE CREATURES!
NO DISTINCTIVE MARKS HERE
THEY DWELL ON TH' WEIRD AND TH' DUMB & GROTESQUE..
MY WHOLE LIFE'S FAIR GAME FOR THEIR CRUEL BURLESQUE!
THEIR SNIDE IMPLICATIONS ARE TRULY ABSURD
A NICE CONTRIBUTION IS LIKE
BUT WHAT REALLY ANNOYS IS THEY GET THE LAST...
WORD?
©8-13-97...TOM TOMORROW, MATT WUERKER, MARK ALAN STAMATY, DERF, BILL GRIFFITH & TOM TOLES...

THIS MODERN WORLD

by TOM TOMORROW

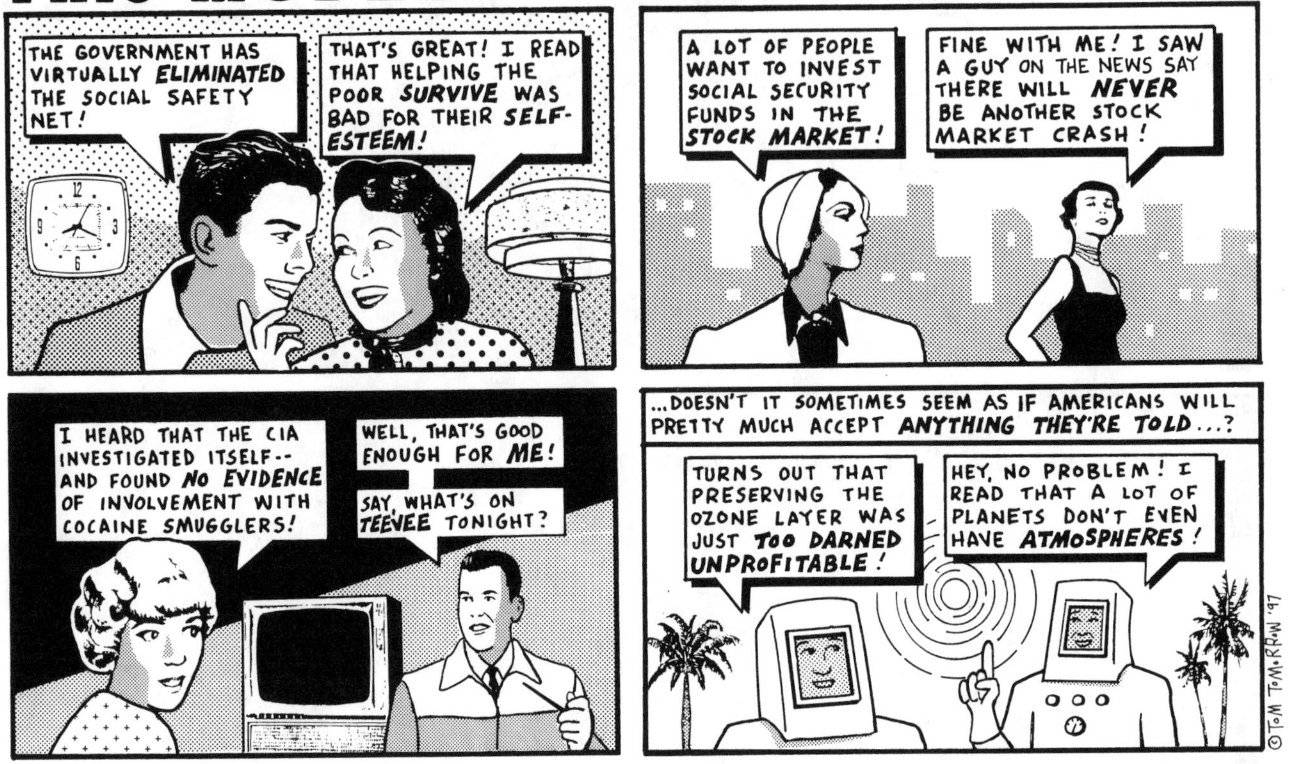
THE GOVERNMENT HAS VIRTUALLY ELIMINATED THE SOCIAL SAFETY NET!
THAT'S GREAT! I READ THAT HELPING THE POOR SURVIVE WAS BAD FOR THEIR SELF-ESTEEM!
A LOT OF PEOPLE WANT TO INVEST SOCIAL SECURITY FUNDS IN THE STOCK MARKET!
FINE WITH ME! I SAW A GUY ON THE NEWS SAY THERE WILL NEVER BE ANOTHER STOCK MARKET CRASH!
I HEARD THAT THE CIA INVESTIGATED ITSELF-- AND FOUND NO EVIDENCE OF INVOLVEMENT WITH COCAINE SMUGGLERS!
WELL, THAT'S GOOD ENOUGH FOR ME!
SAY, WHAT'S ON TEEVEE TONIGHT?
...DOESN'T IT SOMETIMES SEEM AS IF AMERICANS WILL PRETTY MUCH ACCEPT ANYTHING THEY'RE TOLD...?
TURNS OUT THAT PRESERVING THE OZONE LAYER WAS JUST TOO DARNED UNPROFITABLE!
HEY, NO PROBLEM! I READ THAT A LOT OF PLANETS DON'T EVEN HAVE ATMOSPHERES!
©TOM TOMORROW '97

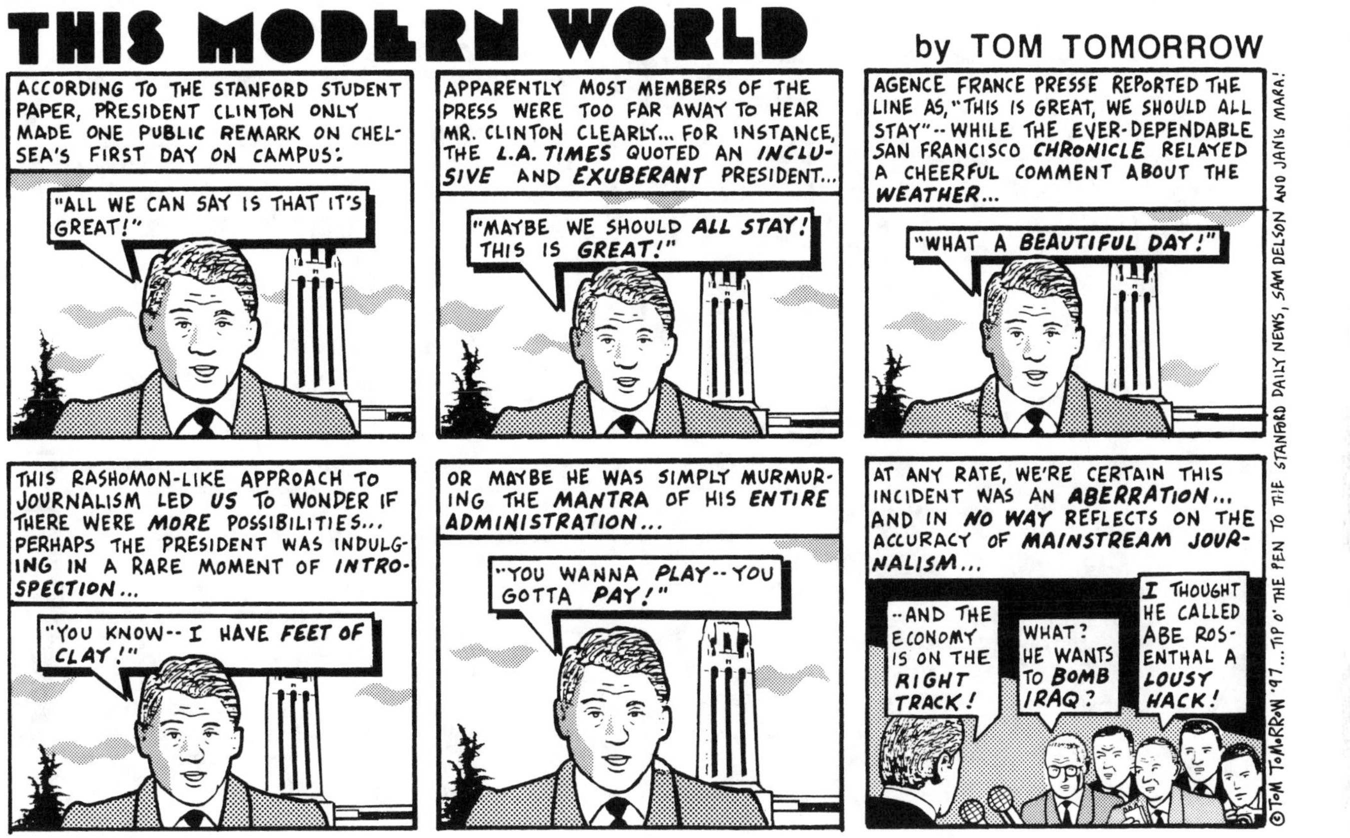
THIS MODERN WORLD
by TOM TOMORROW
ACCORDING TO THE STANFORD STUDENT PAPER, PRESIDENT CLINTON ONLY MADE ONE PUBLIC REMARK ON CHELSEA'S FIRST DAY ON CAMPUS:
"ALL WE CAN SAY IS THAT IT'S GREAT!"
APPARENTLY MOST MEMBERS OF THE PRESS WERE TOO FAR AWAY TO HEAR MR. CLINTON CLEARLY... FOR INSTANCE, THE L.A. TIMES QUOTED AN INCLUSIVE AND EXUBERANT PRESIDENT...
"MAYBE WE SHOULD ALL STAY! THIS IS GREAT!"
AGENCE FRANCE PRESSE REPORTED THE LINE AS, "THIS IS GREAT, WE SHOULD ALL STAY"--WHILE THE EVER-DEPENDABLE SAN FRANCISCO CHRONICLE RELAYED A CHEERFUL COMMENT ABOUT THE WEATHER...
"WHAT A BEAUTIFUL DAY!"
THIS RASHOMON-LIKE APPROACH TO JOURNALISM LED US TO WONDER IF THERE WERE MORE POSSIBILITIES... PERHAPS THE PRESIDENT WAS INDULGING IN A RARE MOMENT OF INTROSPECTION...
"YOU KNOW--I HAVE FEET OF CLAY!"
OR MAYBE HE WAS SIMPLY MURMURING THE MANTRA OF HIS ENTIRE ADMINISTRATION...
"YOU WANNA PLAY--YOU GOTTA PAY!"
AT ANY RATE, WE'RE CERTAIN THIS INCIDENT WAS AN ABERRATION... AND IN NO WAY REFLECTS ON THE ACCURACY OF MAINSTREAM JOURNALISM...
--AND THE ECONOMY IS ON THE RIGHT TRACK!
WHAT? HE WANTS TO BOMB IRAQ?
I THOUGHT HE CALLED ABE ROSENTHAL A LOUSY HACK!
©TOM TOMORROW '97... TIP O' THE PEN TO THE STANFORD DAILY NEWS, SAM DELSON AND JANIS MARA!

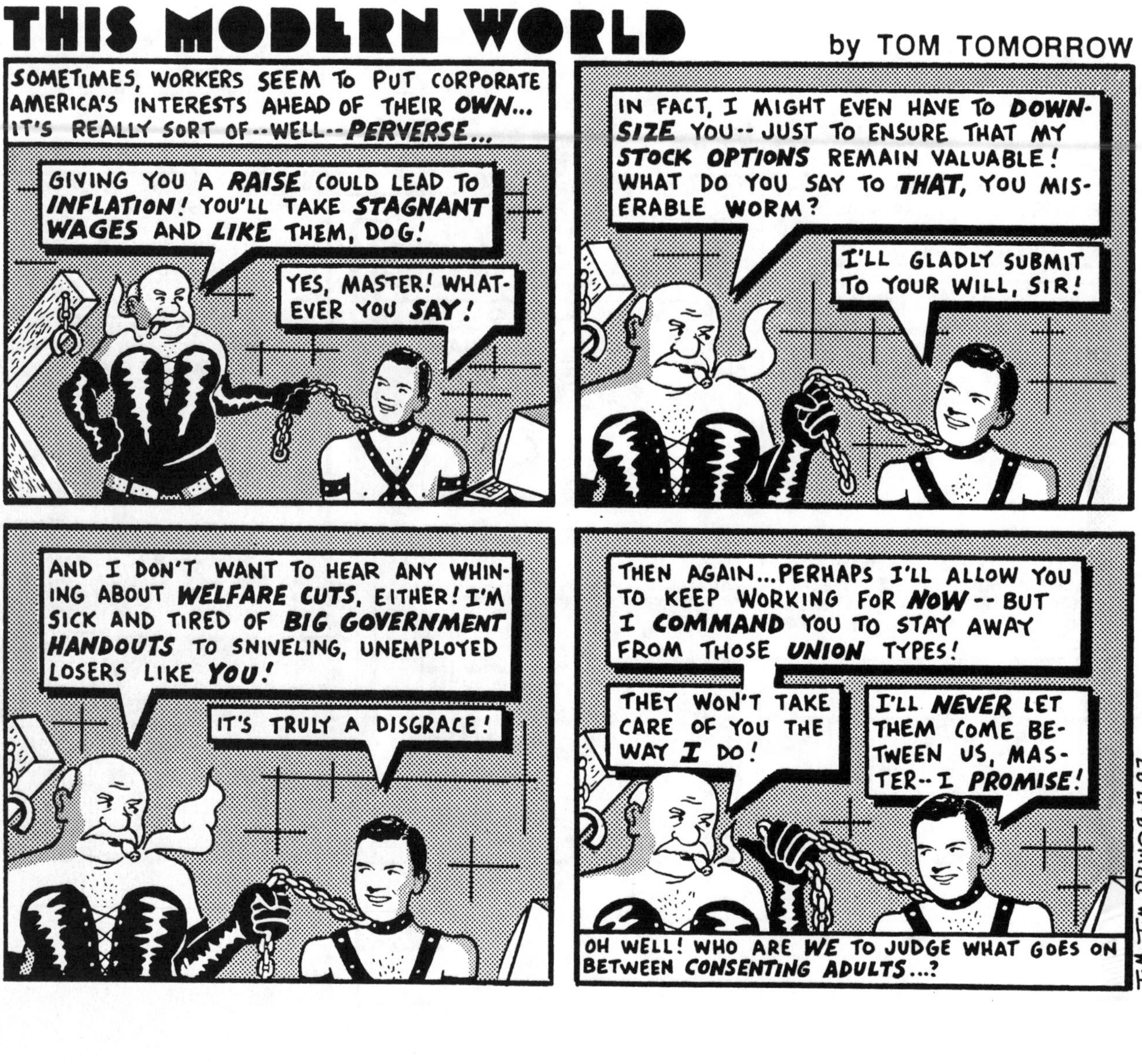
THIS MODERN WORLD
by TOM TOMORROW
SOMETIMES, WORKERS SEEM TO PUT CORPORATE AMERICA'S INTERESTS AHEAD OF THEIR OWN... IT'S REALLY SORT OF--WELL--PERVERSE...
GIVING YOU A RAISE COULD LEAD TO INFLATION! YOU'LL TAKE STAGNANT WAGES AND LIKE THEM, DOG!
YES, MASTER! WHATEVER YOU SAY!
IN FACT, I MIGHT EVEN HAVE TO DOWNSIZE YOU-- JUST TO ENSURE THAT MY STOCK OPTIONS REMAIN VALUABLE! WHAT DO YOU SAY TO THAT, YOU MISERABLE WORM?
I'LL GLADLY SUBMIT TO YOUR WILL, SIR!
AND I DON'T WANT TO HEAR ANY WHINING ABOUT WELFARE CUTS, EITHER! I'M SICK AND TIRED OF BIG GOVERNMENT HANDOUTS TO SNIVELING, UNEMPLOYED LOSERS LIKE YOU!
IT'S TRULY A DISGRACE!
THEN AGAIN...PERHAPS I'LL ALLOW YOU TO KEEP WORKING FOR NOW -- BUT I COMMAND YOU TO STAY AWAY FROM THOSE UNION TYPES!
THEY WON'T TAKE CARE OF YOU THE WAY I DO!
I'LL NEVER LET THEM COME BETWEEN US, MASTER-- I PROMISE!
OH WELL! WHO ARE WE TO JUDGE WHAT GOES ON BETWEEN CONSENTING ADULTS...?
TOM TOMORROW©9-17-97

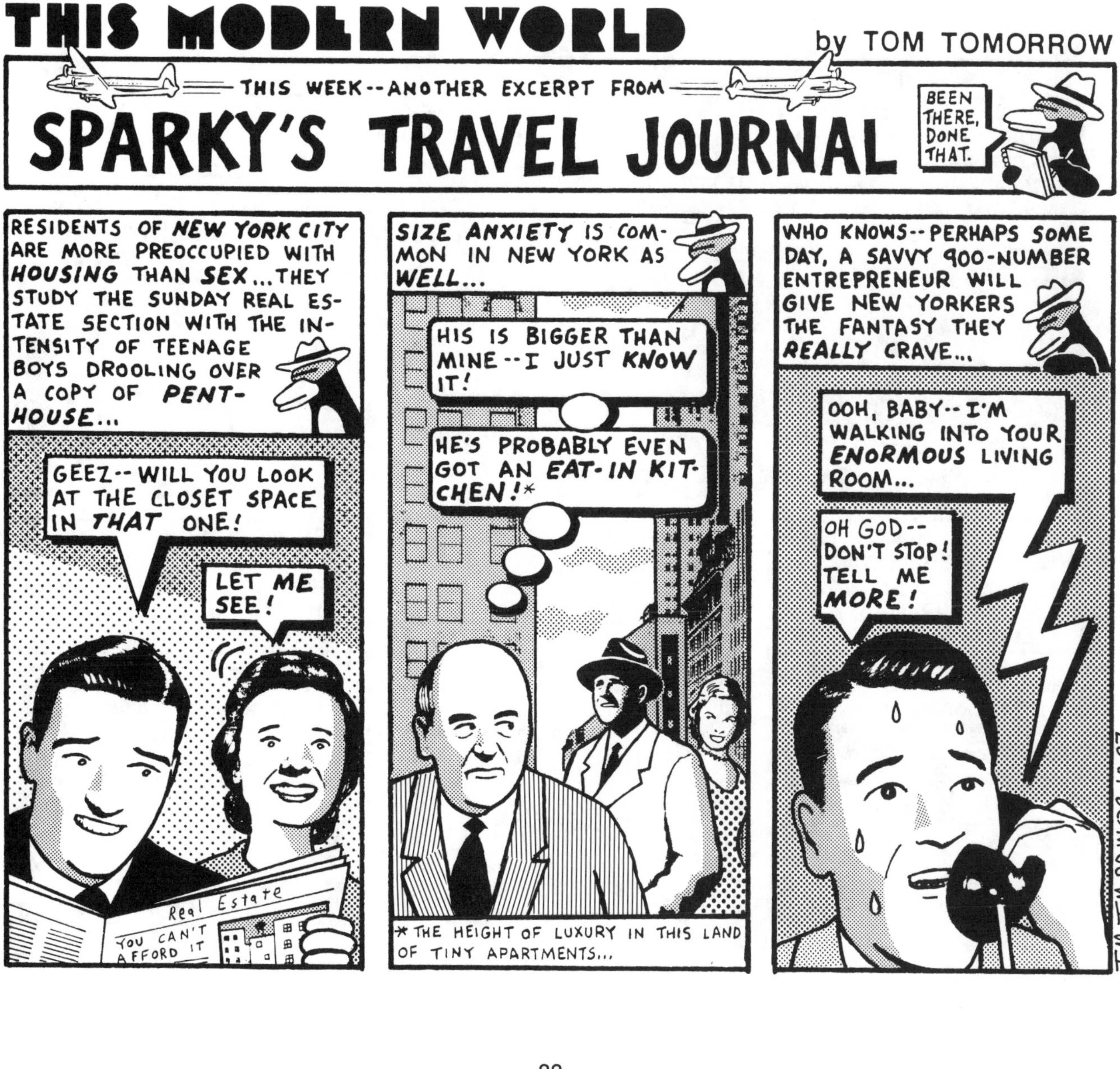
THIS MODERN WORLD
by TOM TOMORROW
THIS WEEK--ANOTHER EXCERPT FROM
SPARKY'S TRAVEL JOURNAL
BEEN THERE, DONE THAT.
RESIDENTS OF NEW YORK CITY ARE MORE PREOCCUPIED WITH HOUSING THAN SEX...THEY STUDY THE SUNDAY REAL ESTATE SECTION WITH THE INTENSITY OF TEENAGE BOYS DROOLING OVER A COPY OF PENTHOUSE...
GEEZ--WILL YOU LOOK AT THE CLOSET SPACE IN THAT ONE!
LET ME SEE!
Real Estate
YOU CAN'T AFFORD IT
SIZE ANXIETY IS COMMON IN NEW YORK AS WELL...
HIS IS BIGGER THAN MINE--I JUST KNOW IT!
HE'S PROBABLY EVEN GOT AN EAT-IN KITCHEN!*
* THE HEIGHT OF LUXURY IN THIS LAND OF TINY APARTMENTS...
WHO KNOWS--PERHAPS SOME DAY, A SAVVY 900-NUMBER ENTREPRENEUR WILL GIVE NEW YORKERS THE FANTASY THEY REALLY CRAVE...
OOH, BABY--I'M WALKING INTO YOUR ENORMOUS LIVING ROOM...
OH GOD--DON'T STOP! TELL ME MORE!
TOM TOMORROW ©9-10-97

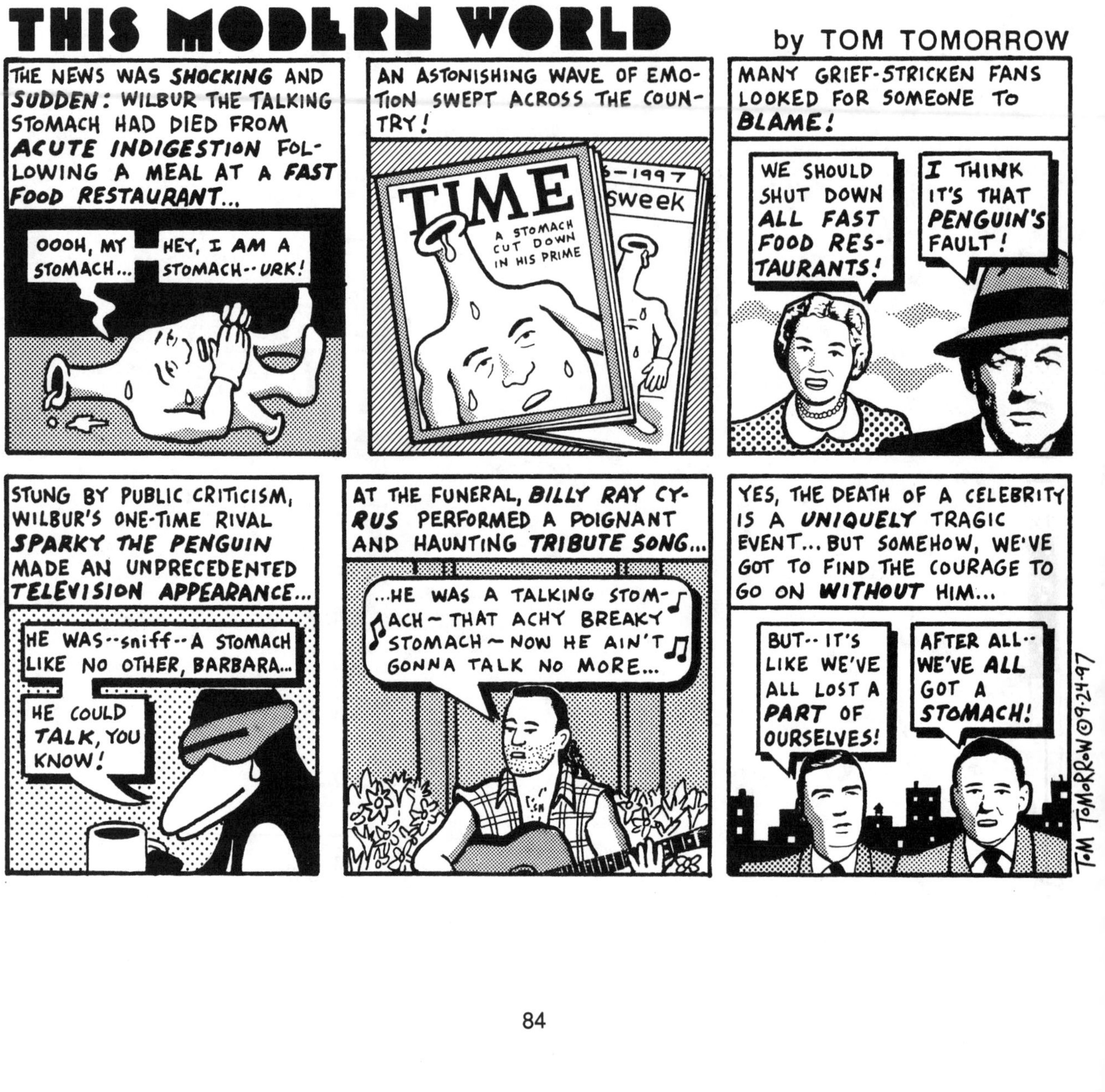
THIS MODERN WORLD
by TOM TOMORROW
THE NEWS WAS SHOCKING AND SUDDEN: WILBUR THE TALKING STOMACH HAD DIED FROM ACUTE INDIGESTION FOLLOWING A MEAL AT A FAST FOOD RESTAURANT...
OOOH, MY STOMACH...
HEY, I AM A STOMACH--URK!
AN ASTONISHING WAVE OF EMOTION SWEPT ACROSS THE COUNTRY!
TIME
A STOMACH CUT DOWN IN HIS PRIME
-1997
sweek
MANY GRIEF-STRICKEN FANS LOOKED FOR SOMEONE TO BLAME!
WE SHOULD SHUT DOWN ALL FAST FOOD RESTAURANTS!
I THINK IT'S THAT PENGUIN'S FAULT!
STUNG BY PUBLIC CRITICISM, WILBUR'S ONE-TIME RIVAL SPARKY THE PENGUIN MADE AN UNPRECEDENTED TELEVISION APPEARANCE...
HE WAS--sniff--A STOMACH LIKE NO OTHER, BARBARA...
HE COULD TALK, YOU KNOW!
AT THE FUNERAL, BILLY RAY CYRUS PERFORMED A POIGNANT AND HAUNTING TRIBUTE SONG...
...HE WAS A TALKING STOMACH~THAT ACHY BREAKY STOMACH~NOW HE AIN'T GONNA TALK NO MORE...
YES, THE DEATH OF A CELEBRITY IS A UNIQUELY TRAGIC EVENT... BUT SOMEHOW, WE'VE GOT TO FIND THE COURAGE TO GO ON WITHOUT HIM...
BUT--IT'S LIKE WE'VE ALL LOST A PART OF OURSELVES!
AFTER ALL--WE'VE ALL GOT A STOMACH!
TOM TOMORROW©9-24-97

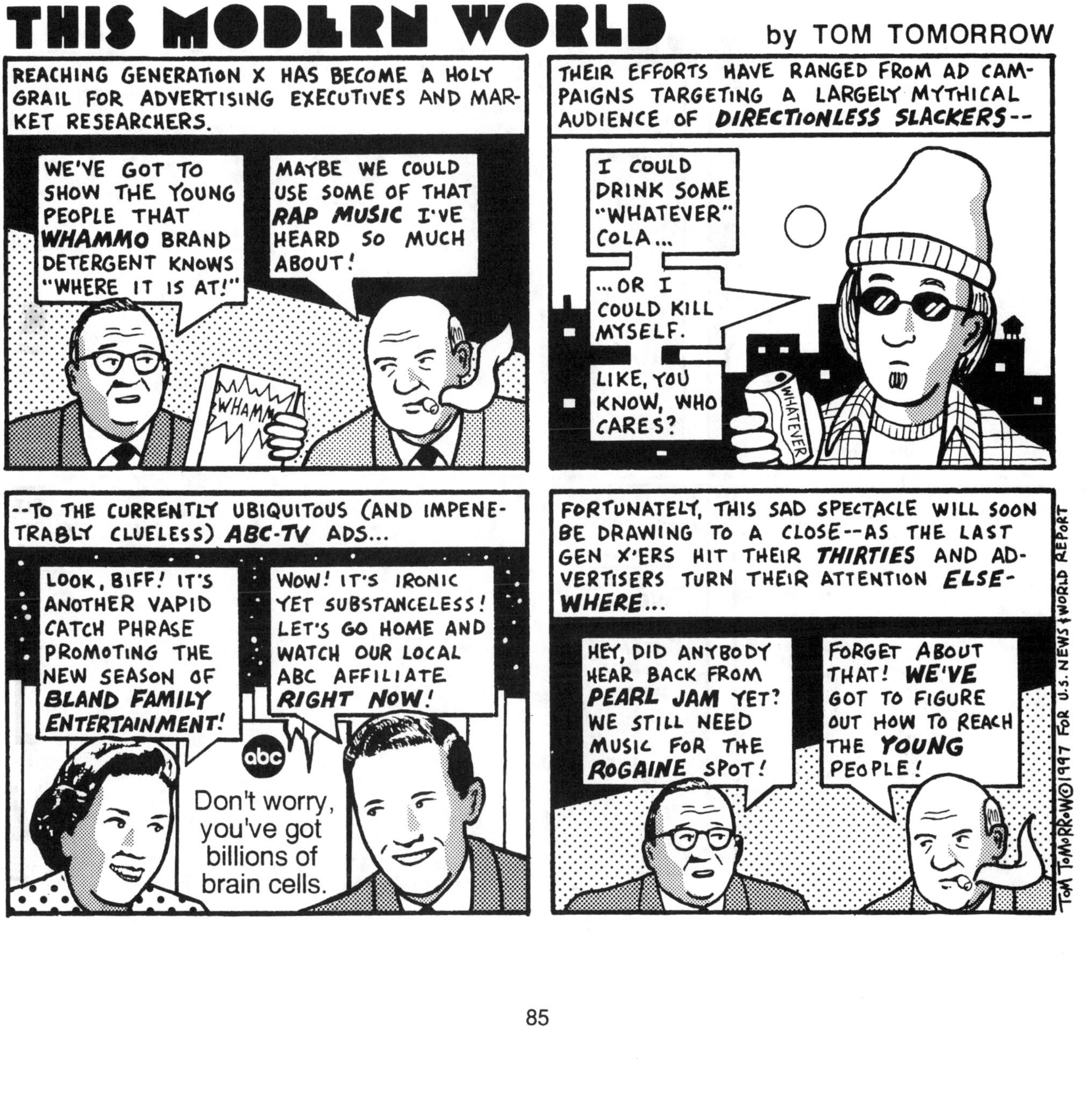
THIS MODERN WORLD
by TOM TOMORROW
REACHING GENERATION X HAS BECOME A HOLY GRAIL FOR ADVERTISING EXECUTIVES AND MARKET RESEARCHERS.
WE'VE GOT TO SHOW THE YOUNG PEOPLE THAT WHAMMO BRAND DETERGENT KNOWS "WHERE IT IS AT!"
MAYBE WE COULD USE SOME OF THAT RAP MUSIC I'VE HEARD SO MUCH ABOUT!
WHAMM
THEIR EFFORTS HAVE RANGED FROM AD CAMPAIGNS TARGETING A LARGELY MYTHICAL AUDIENCE OF DIRECTIONLESS SLACKERS--
I COULD DRINK SOME "WHATEVER" COLA...
...OR I COULD KILL MYSELF.
LIKE, YOU KNOW, WHO CARES?
WHATEVER
--TO THE CURRENTLY UBIQUITOUS (AND IMPENETRABLY CLUELESS) ABC-TV ADS...
LOOK, BIFF! IT'S ANOTHER VAPID CATCH PHRASE PROMOTING THE NEW SEASON OF BLAND FAMILY ENTERTAINMENT!
WOW! IT'S IRONIC YET SUBSTANCELESS! LET'S GO HOME AND WATCH OUR LOCAL ABC AFFILIATE RIGHT NOW!
abc
Don't worry, you've got billions of brain cells.
FORTUNATELY, THIS SAD SPECTACLE WILL SOON BE DRAWING TO A CLOSE--AS THE LAST GEN X'ERS HIT THEIR THIRTIES AND ADVERTISERS TURN THEIR ATTENTION ELSEWHERE...
HEY, DID ANYBODY HEAR BACK FROM PEARL JAM YET? WE STILL NEED MUSIC FOR THE ROGAINE SPOT!
FORGET ABOUT THAT! WE'VE GOT TO FIGURE OUT HOW TO REACH THE YOUNG PEOPLE!
TOM TOMORROW©1997 FOR U.S. NEWS & WORLD REPORT

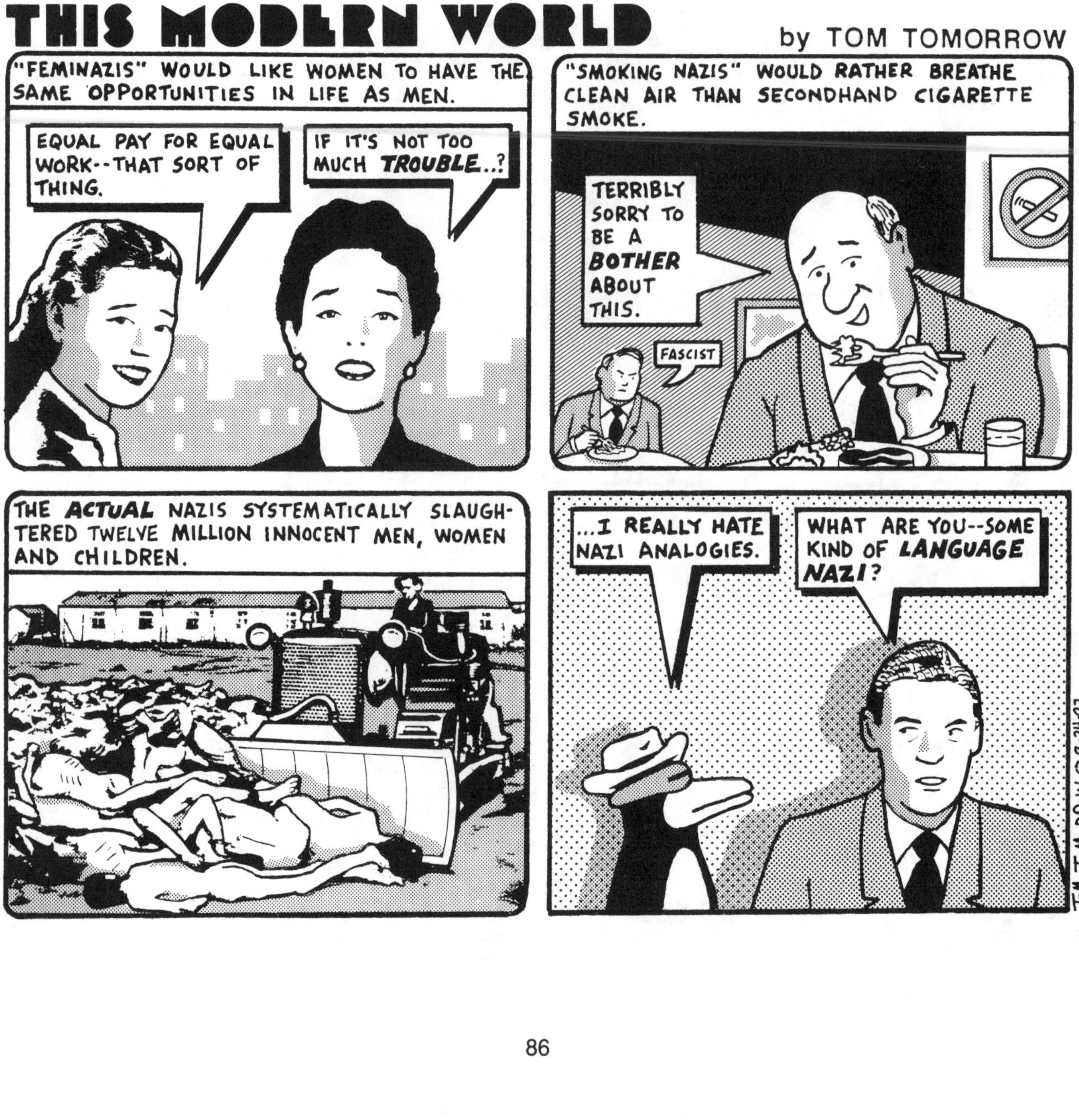
THIS MODERN WORLD
by TOM TOMORROW
"FEMINAZIS" WOULD LIKE WOMEN TO HAVE THE SAME OPPORTUNITIES IN LIFE AS MEN.
EQUAL PAY FOR EQUAL WORK--THAT SORT OF THING.
IF IT'S NOT TOO MUCH TROUBLE..?
"SMOKING NAZIS" WOULD RATHER BREATHE CLEAN AIR THAN SECONDHAND CIGARETTE SMOKE.
TERRIBLY SORRY TO BE A BOTHER ABOUT THIS.
FASCIST
THE ACTUAL NAZIS SYSTEMATICALLY SLAUGHTERED TWELVE MILLION INNOCENT MEN, WOMEN AND CHILDREN.
...I REALLY HATE NAZI ANALOGIES.
WHAT ARE YOU--SOME KIND OF LANGUAGE NAZI?
TOM TOMORROW © 9-24-97

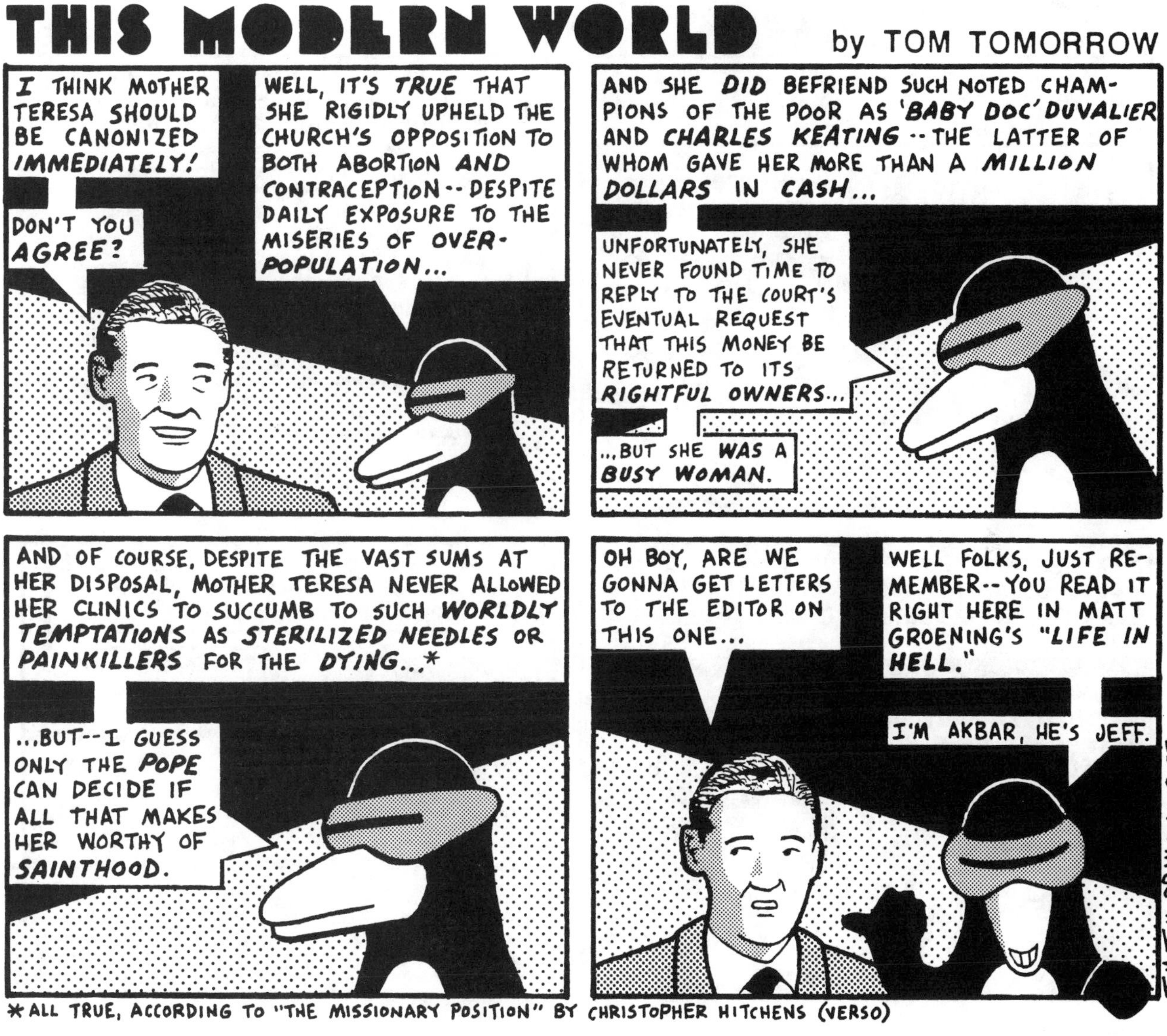
THIS MODERN WORLD
by TOM TOMORROW
I THINK MOTHER TERESA SHOULD BE CANONIZED IMMEDIATELY!
DON'T YOU AGREE?
WELL, IT'S TRUE THAT SHE RIGIDLY UPHELD THE CHURCH'S OPPOSITION TO BOTH ABORTION AND CONTRACEPTION -- DESPITE DAILY EXPOSURE TO THE MISERIES OF OVER-POPULATION...
AND SHE DID BEFRIEND SUCH NOTED CHAMPIONS OF THE POOR AS 'BABY DOC' DUVALIER AND CHARLES KEATING -- THE LATTER OF WHOM GAVE HER MORE THAN A MILLION DOLLARS IN CASH...
UNFORTUNATELY, SHE NEVER FOUND TIME TO REPLY TO THE COURT'S EVENTUAL REQUEST THAT THIS MONEY BE RETURNED TO ITS RIGHTFUL OWNERS...
...BUT SHE WAS A BUSY WOMAN.
AND OF COURSE, DESPITE THE VAST SUMS AT HER DISPOSAL, MOTHER TERESA NEVER ALLOWED HER CLINICS TO SUCCUMB TO SUCH WORLDLY TEMPTATIONS AS STERILIZED NEEDLES OR PAINKILLERS FOR THE DYING...*
...BUT--I GUESS ONLY THE POPE CAN DECIDE IF ALL THAT MAKES HER WORTHY OF SAINTHOOD.
OH BOY, ARE WE GONNA GET LETTERS TO THE EDITOR ON THIS ONE...
WELL FOLKS, JUST REMEMBER--YOU READ IT RIGHT HERE IN MATT GROENING'S "LIFE IN HELL."
I'M AKBAR, HE'S JEFF.
TOM TOMORROW©10-8-97
* ALL TRUE, ACCORDING TO "THE MISSIONARY POSITION" BY CHRISTOPHER HITCHENS (VERSO)

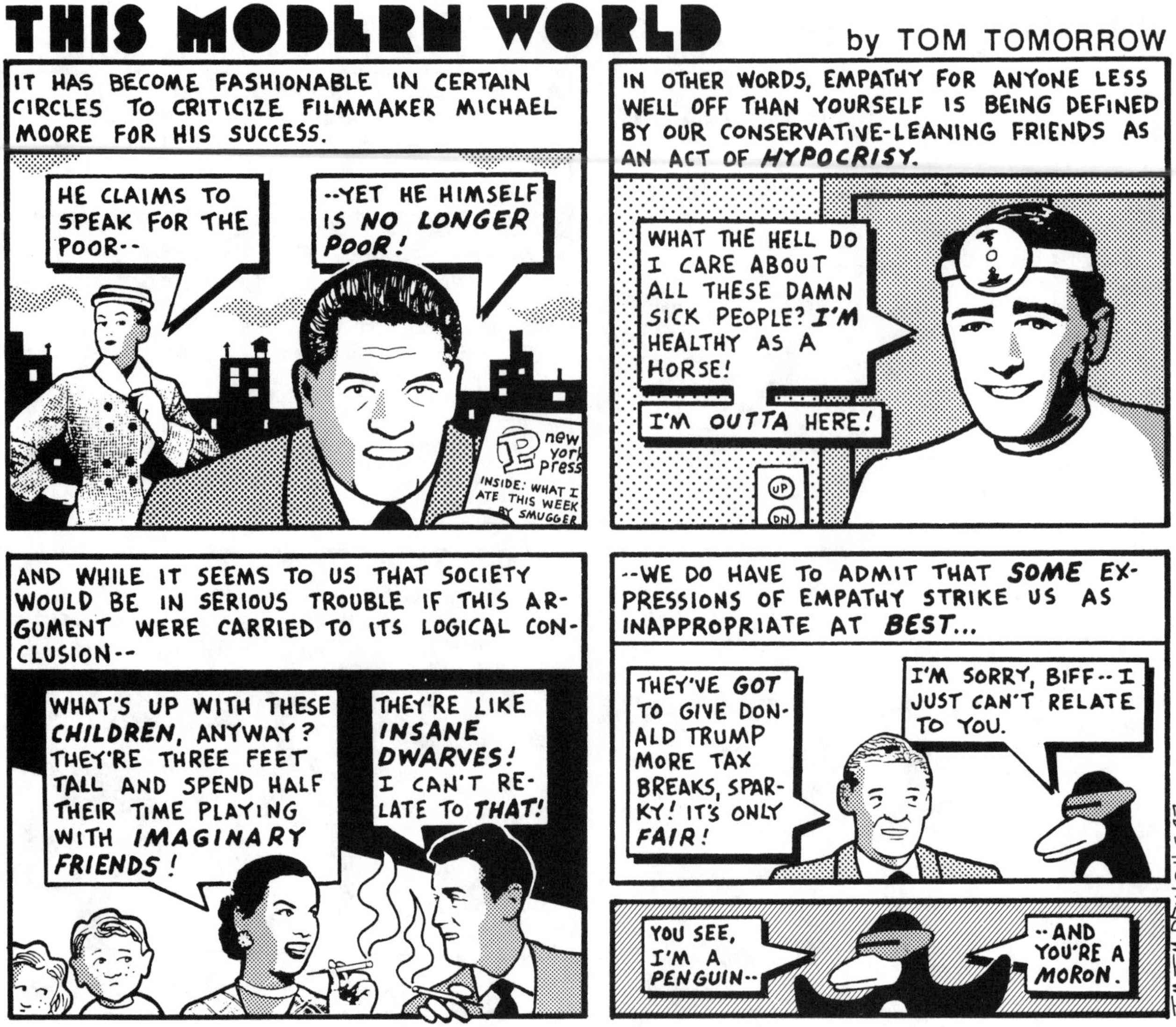
THIS MODERN WORLD
by TOM TOMORROW
IT HAS BECOME FASHIONABLE IN CERTAIN CIRCLES TO CRITICIZE FILMMAKER MICHAEL MOORE FOR HIS SUCCESS.
HE CLAIMS TO SPEAK FOR THE POOR--
--YET HE HIMSELF IS NO LONGER POOR!
new york press
INSIDE: WHAT I ATE THIS WEEK BY SMUGGER
IN OTHER WORDS, EMPATHY FOR ANYONE LESS WELL OFF THAN YOURSELF IS BEING DEFINED BY OUR CONSERVATIVE-LEANING FRIENDS AS AN ACT OF HYPOCRISY.
WHAT THE HELL DO I CARE ABOUT ALL THESE DAMN SICK PEOPLE? I'M HEALTHY AS A HORSE!
I'M OUTTA HERE!
UP
DN
AND WHILE IT SEEMS TO US THAT SOCIETY WOULD BE IN SERIOUS TROUBLE IF THIS ARGUMENT WERE CARRIED TO ITS LOGICAL CONCLUSION--
WHAT'S UP WITH THESE CHILDREN, ANYWAY? THEY'RE THREE FEET TALL AND SPEND HALF THEIR TIME PLAYING WITH IMAGINARY FRIENDS!
THEY'RE LIKE INSANE DWARVES! I CAN'T RELATE TO THAT!
--WE DO HAVE TO ADMIT THAT SOME EXPRESSIONS OF EMPATHY STRIKE US AS INAPPROPRIATE AT BEST...
THEY'VE GOT TO GIVE DONALD TRUMP MORE TAX BREAKS, SPARKY! IT'S ONLY FAIR!
I'M SORRY, BIFF--I JUST CAN'T RELATE TO YOU.
YOU SEE, I'M A PENGUIN--
--AND YOU'RE A MORON.
TOM TOMORROW©11-5-97

THIS MODERN WORLD

by TOM TOMORROW

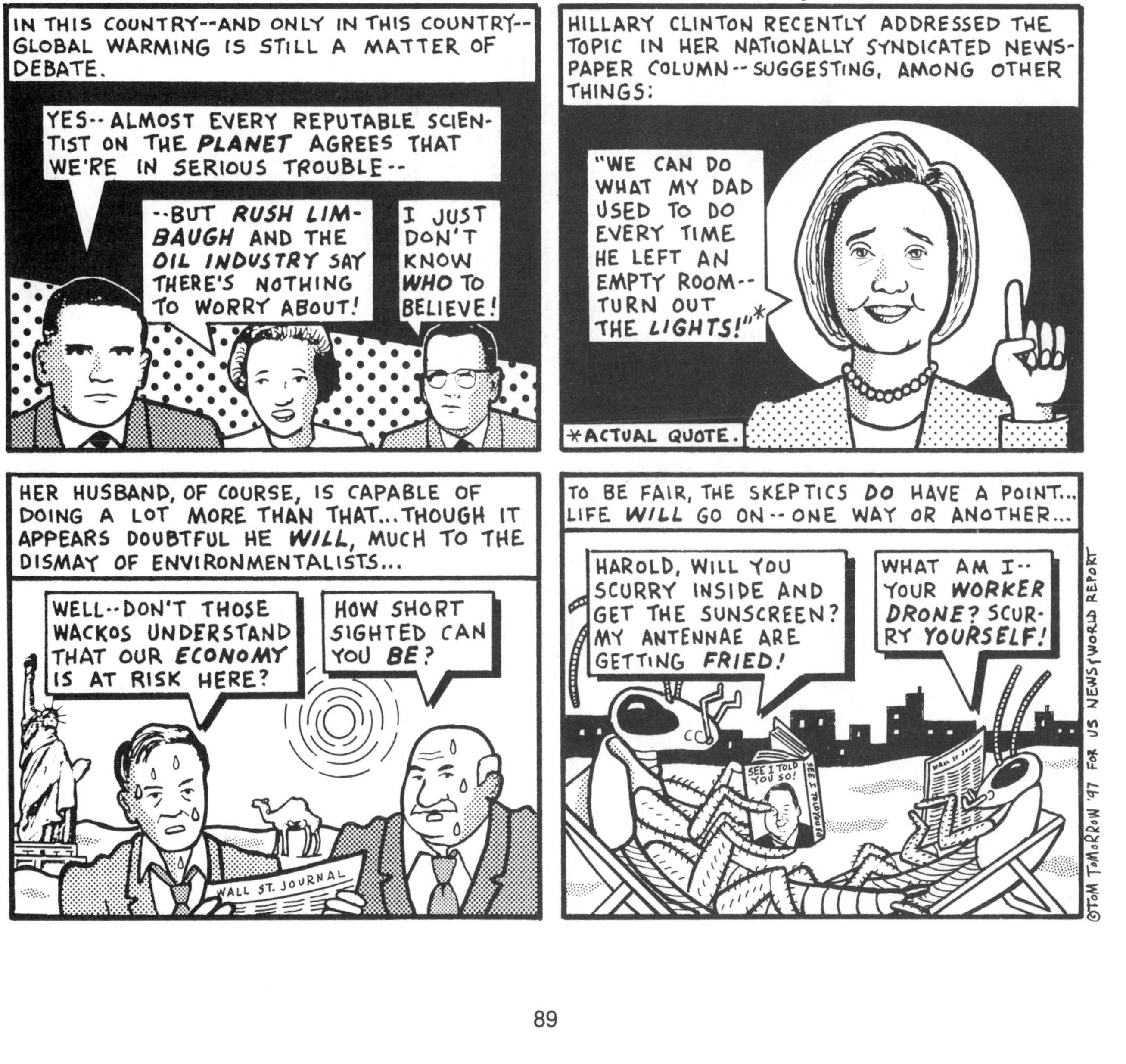
IN THIS COUNTRY--AND ONLY IN THIS COUNTRY--GLOBAL WARMING IS STILL A MATTER OF DEBATE.
YES--ALMOST EVERY REPUTABLE SCIENTIST ON THE *PLANET* AGREES THAT WE'RE IN SERIOUS TROUBLE--
--BUT *RUSH LIMBAUGH* AND THE *OIL INDUSTRY* SAY THERE'S NOTHING TO WORRY ABOUT!
I JUST DON'T KNOW *WHO* TO BELIEVE!
HILLARY CLINTON RECENTLY ADDRESSED THE TOPIC IN HER NATIONALLY SYNDICATED NEWSPAPER COLUMN--SUGGESTING, AMONG OTHER THINGS:
"WE CAN DO WHAT MY DAD USED TO DO EVERY TIME HE LEFT AN EMPTY ROOM--TURN OUT THE *LIGHTS!*"*
*ACTUAL QUOTE.
HER HUSBAND, OF COURSE, IS CAPABLE OF DOING A LOT MORE THAN THAT...THOUGH IT APPEARS DOUBTFUL HE *WILL*, MUCH TO THE DISMAY OF ENVIRONMENTALISTS...
WELL--DON'T THOSE WACKOS UNDERSTAND THAT OUR *ECONOMY* IS AT RISK HERE?
HOW SHORT SIGHTED CAN YOU *BE*?
WALL ST. JOURNAL
TO BE FAIR, THE SKEPTICS *DO* HAVE A POINT... LIFE *WILL* GO ON--ONE WAY OR ANOTHER...
HAROLD, WILL YOU SCURRY INSIDE AND GET THE SUNSCREEN? MY ANTENNAE ARE GETTING *FRIED!*
WHAT AM I--YOUR *WORKER DRONE?* SCURRY *YOURSELF!*
SEE I TOLD YOU SO!
©TOM TOMORROW '97 FOR US NEWS & WORLD REPORT

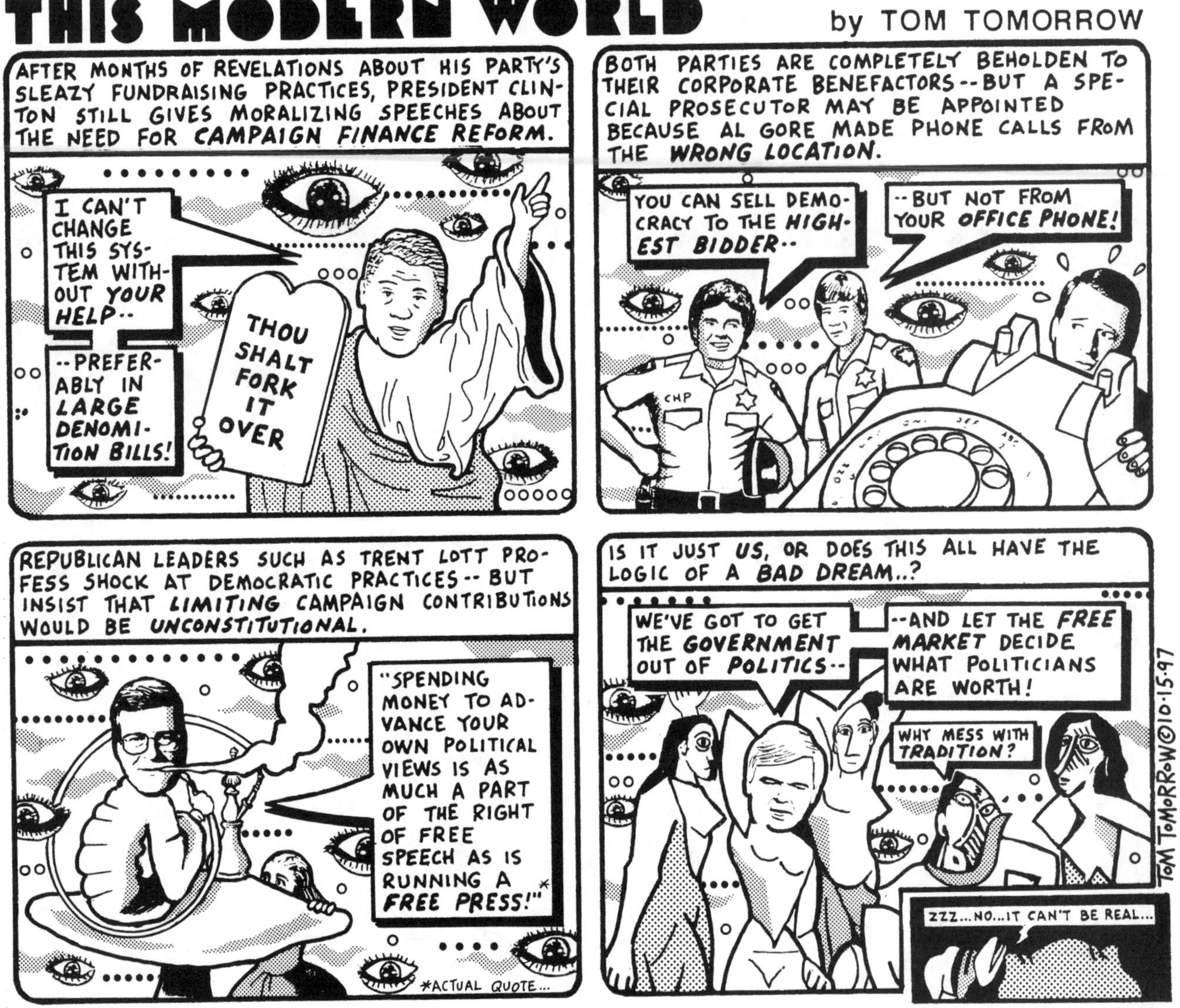
THIS MODERN WORLD
by TOM TOMORROW
AFTER MONTHS OF REVELATIONS ABOUT HIS PARTY'S SLEAZY FUNDRAISING PRACTICES, PRESIDENT CLINTON STILL GIVES MORALIZING SPEECHES ABOUT THE NEED FOR CAMPAIGN FINANCE REFORM.
I CAN'T CHANGE THIS SYSTEM WITHOUT YOUR HELP--
--PREFERABLY IN LARGE DENOMINATION BILLS!
THOU SHALT FORK IT OVER
BOTH PARTIES ARE COMPLETELY BEHOLDEN TO THEIR CORPORATE BENEFACTORS--BUT A SPECIAL PROSECUTOR MAY BE APPOINTED BECAUSE AL GORE MADE PHONE CALLS FROM THE WRONG LOCATION.
YOU CAN SELL DEMOCRACY TO THE HIGHEST BIDDER--
--BUT NOT FROM YOUR OFFICE PHONE!
CHP
REPUBLICAN LEADERS SUCH AS TRENT LOTT PROFESS SHOCK AT DEMOCRATIC PRACTICES--BUT INSIST THAT LIMITING CAMPAIGN CONTRIBUTIONS WOULD BE UNCONSTITUTIONAL.
"SPENDING MONEY TO ADVANCE YOUR OWN POLITICAL VIEWS IS AS MUCH A PART OF THE RIGHT OF FREE SPEECH AS IS RUNNING A FREE PRESS!"*
*ACTUAL QUOTE...
IS IT JUST US, OR DOES THIS ALL HAVE THE LOGIC OF A BAD DREAM..?
WE'VE GOT TO GET THE GOVERNMENT OUT OF POLITICS--
--AND LET THE FREE MARKET DECIDE WHAT POLITICIANS ARE WORTH!
WHY MESS WITH TRADITION?
ZZZ...NO...IT CAN'T BE REAL...
TOM TOMORROW©10·15·97

THIS MODERN WORLD

by TOM TOMORROW

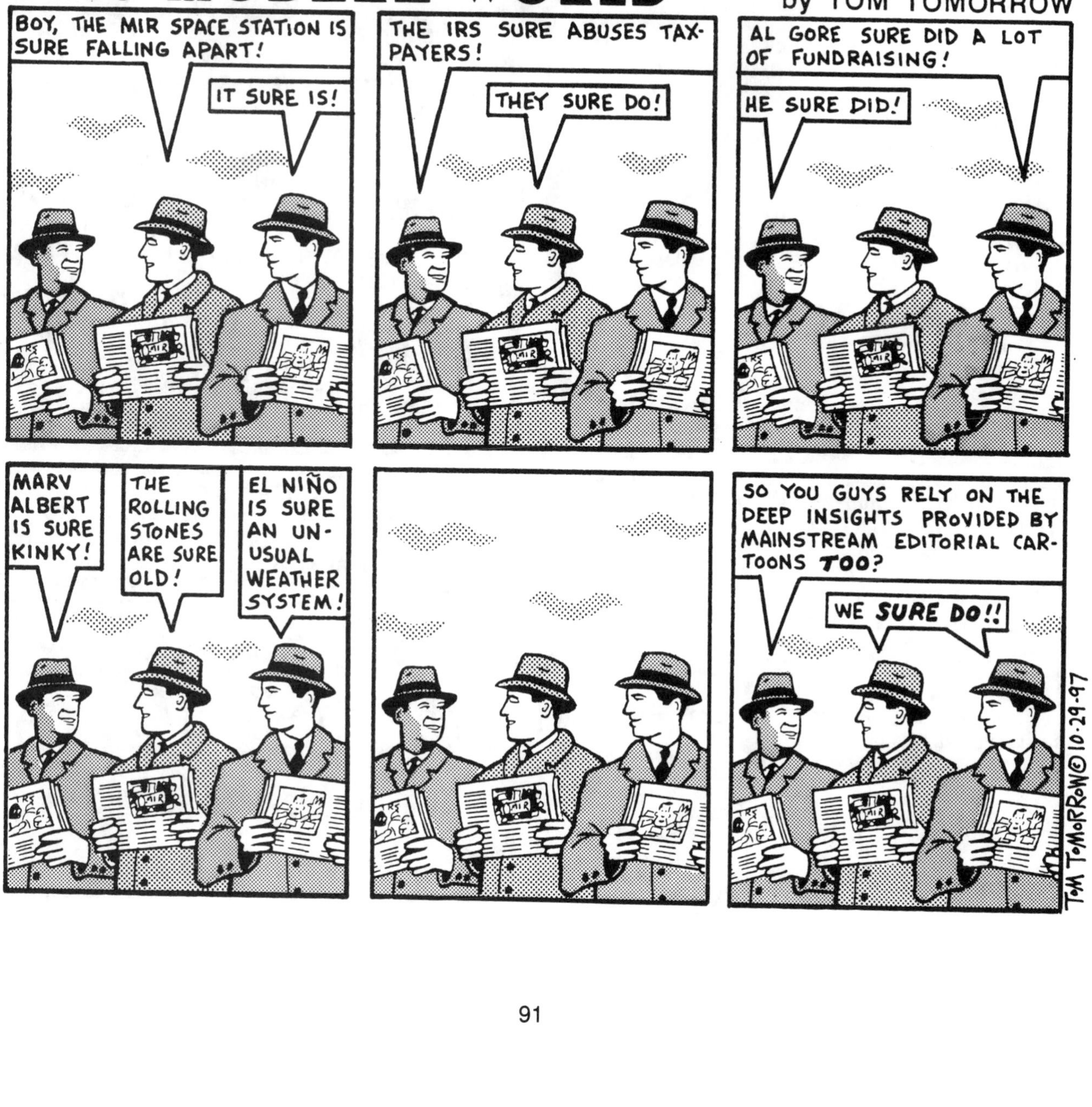

BOY, THE MIR SPACE STATION IS SURE FALLING APART!
IT SURE IS!
THE IRS SURE ABUSES TAX-PAYERS!
THEY SURE DO!
AL GORE SURE DID A LOT OF FUNDRAISING!
HE SURE DID!
MARV ALBERT IS SURE KINKY!
THE ROLLING STONES ARE SURE OLD!
EL NIÑO IS SURE AN UN-USUAL WEATHER SYSTEM!
SO YOU GUYS RELY ON THE DEEP INSIGHTS PROVIDED BY MAINSTREAM EDITORIAL CAR-TOONS TOO?
WE SURE DO!!
TOM TOMORROW © 10·29·97

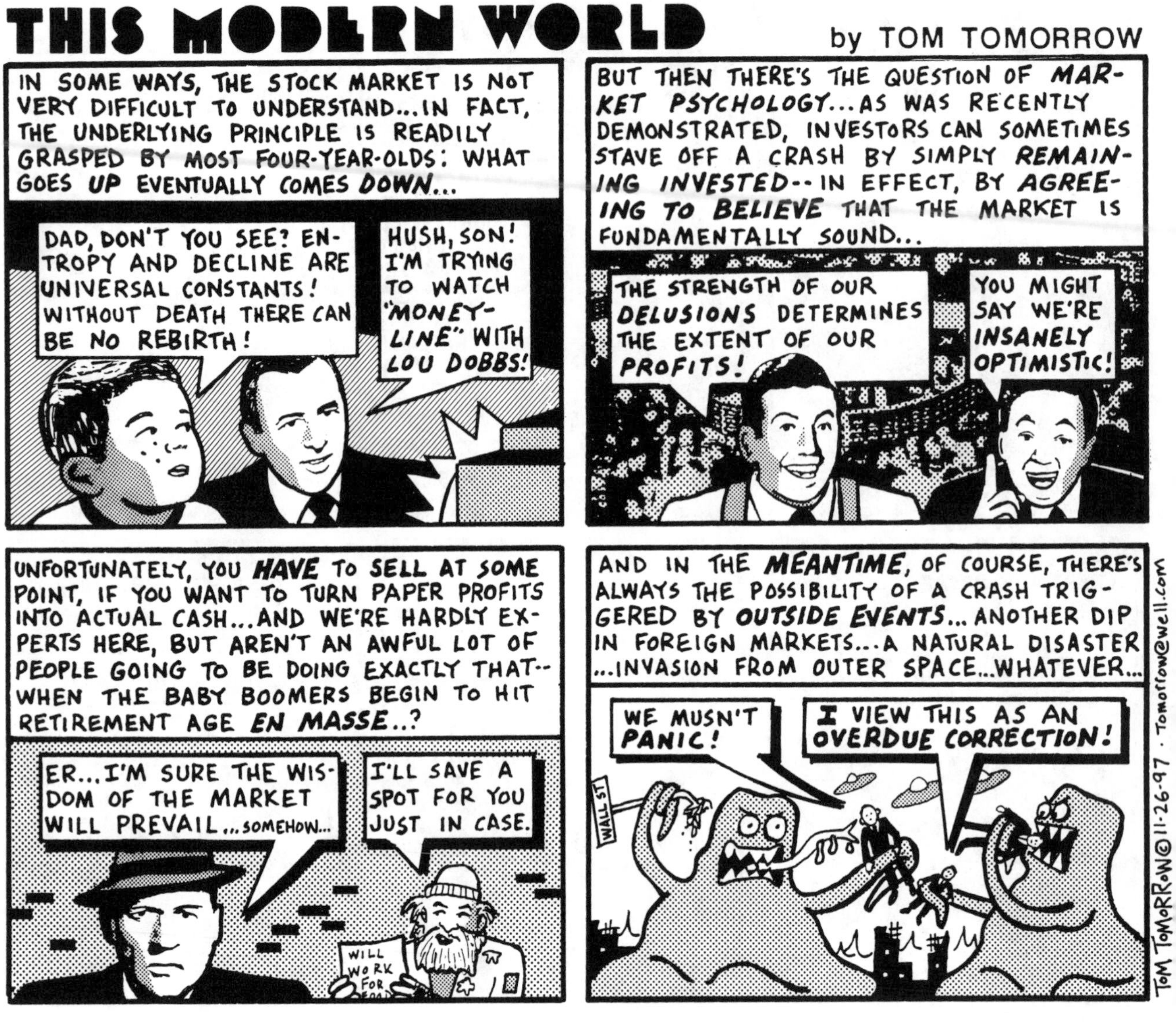
THIS MODERN WORLD
by TOM TOMORROW
IN SOME WAYS, THE STOCK MARKET IS NOT VERY DIFFICULT TO UNDERSTAND... IN FACT, THE UNDERLYING PRINCIPLE IS READILY GRASPED BY MOST FOUR-YEAR-OLDS: WHAT GOES UP EVENTUALLY COMES DOWN...
DAD, DON'T YOU SEE? ENTROPY AND DECLINE ARE UNIVERSAL CONSTANTS! WITHOUT DEATH THERE CAN BE NO REBIRTH!
HUSH, SON! I'M TRYING TO WATCH "MONEYLINE" WITH LOU DOBBS!
BUT THEN THERE'S THE QUESTION OF MARKET PSYCHOLOGY... AS WAS RECENTLY DEMONSTRATED, INVESTORS CAN SOMETIMES STAVE OFF A CRASH BY SIMPLY REMAINING INVESTED-- IN EFFECT, BY AGREEING TO BELIEVE THAT THE MARKET IS FUNDAMENTALLY SOUND...
THE STRENGTH OF OUR DELUSIONS DETERMINES THE EXTENT OF OUR PROFITS!
YOU MIGHT SAY WE'RE INSANELY OPTIMISTIC!
UNFORTUNATELY, YOU HAVE TO SELL AT SOME POINT, IF YOU WANT TO TURN PAPER PROFITS INTO ACTUAL CASH... AND WE'RE HARDLY EXPERTS HERE, BUT AREN'T AN AWFUL LOT OF PEOPLE GOING TO BE DOING EXACTLY THAT-- WHEN THE BABY BOOMERS BEGIN TO HIT RETIREMENT AGE EN MASSE..?
ER... I'M SURE THE WISDOM OF THE MARKET WILL PREVAIL... SOMEHOW...
I'LL SAVE A SPOT FOR YOU JUST IN CASE.
WILL WORK FOR
AND IN THE MEANTIME, OF COURSE, THERE'S ALWAYS THE POSSIBILITY OF A CRASH TRIGGERED BY OUTSIDE EVENTS... ANOTHER DIP IN FOREIGN MARKETS... A NATURAL DISASTER ...INVASION FROM OUTER SPACE... WHATEVER...
WE MUSN'T PANIC!
I VIEW THIS AS AN OVERDUE CORRECTION!
WALL ST
TOM TOMORROW©11-26-97 · tomorrow@well.com

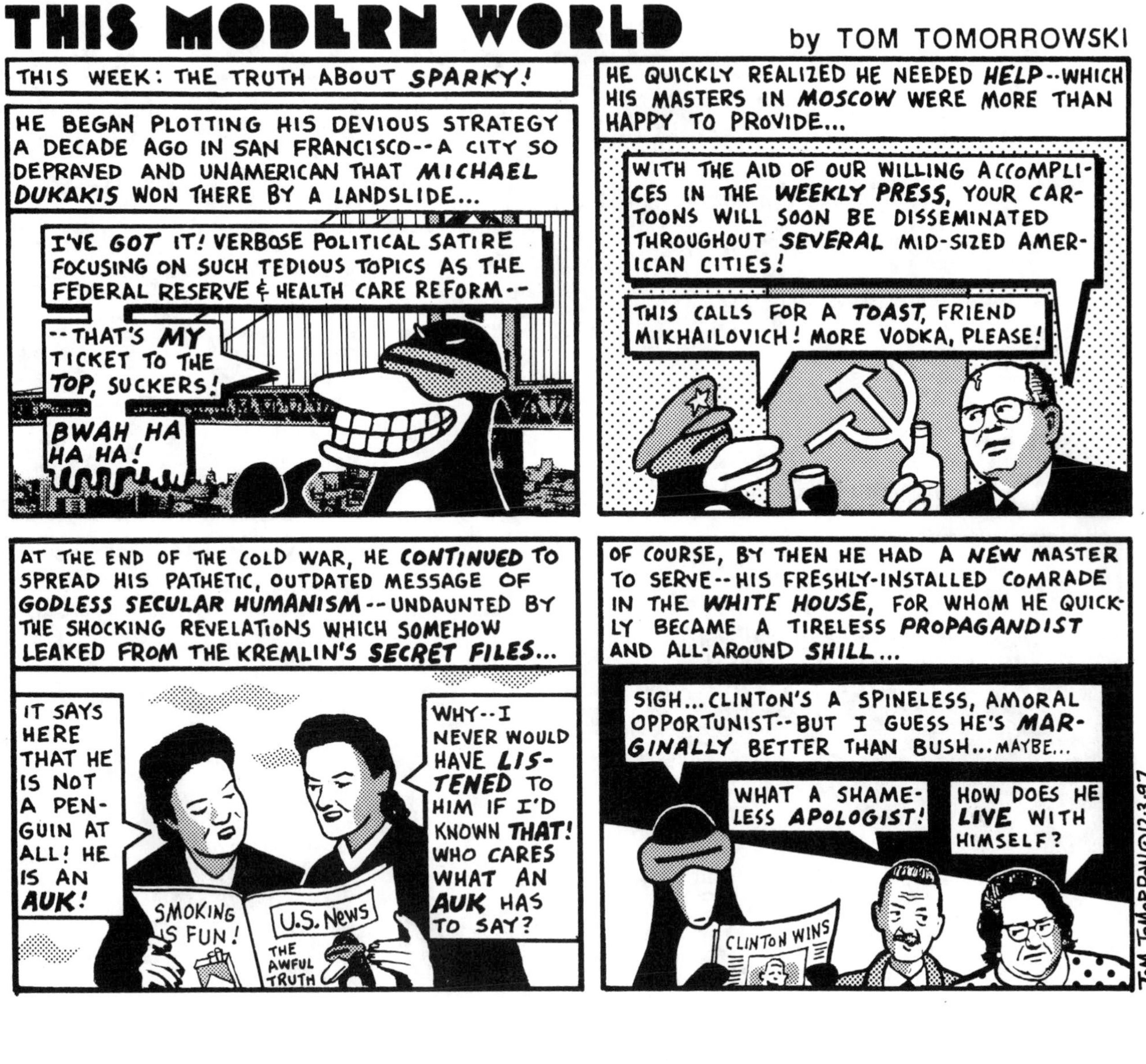
THIS MODERN WORLD
by TOM TOMORROWSKI
THIS WEEK: THE TRUTH ABOUT SPARKY!
HE BEGAN PLOTTING HIS DEVIOUS STRATEGY A DECADE AGO IN SAN FRANCISCO--A CITY SO DEPRAVED AND UNAMERICAN THAT MICHAEL DUKAKIS WON THERE BY A LANDSLIDE...
I'VE GOT IT! VERBOSE POLITICAL SATIRE FOCUSING ON SUCH TEDIOUS TOPICS AS THE FEDERAL RESERVE & HEALTH CARE REFORM--
--THAT'S MY TICKET TO THE TOP, SUCKERS!
BWAH HA HA HA!
HE QUICKLY REALIZED HE NEEDED HELP--WHICH HIS MASTERS IN MOSCOW WERE MORE THAN HAPPY TO PROVIDE...
WITH THE AID OF OUR WILLING ACCOMPLICES IN THE WEEKLY PRESS, YOUR CARTOONS WILL SOON BE DISSEMINATED THROUGHOUT SEVERAL MID-SIZED AMERICAN CITIES!
THIS CALLS FOR A TOAST, FRIEND MIKHAILOVICH! MORE VODKA, PLEASE!
AT THE END OF THE COLD WAR, HE CONTINUED TO SPREAD HIS PATHETIC, OUTDATED MESSAGE OF GODLESS SECULAR HUMANISM--UNDAUNTED BY THE SHOCKING REVELATIONS WHICH SOMEHOW LEAKED FROM THE KREMLIN'S SECRET FILES...
IT SAYS HERE THAT HE IS NOT A PENGUIN AT ALL! HE IS AN AUK!
WHY--I NEVER WOULD HAVE LISTENED TO HIM IF I'D KNOWN THAT! WHO CARES WHAT AN AUK HAS TO SAY?
SMOKING IS FUN!
U.S. News
THE AWFUL TRUTH
OF COURSE, BY THEN HE HAD A NEW MASTER TO SERVE--HIS FRESHLY-INSTALLED COMRADE IN THE WHITE HOUSE, FOR WHOM HE QUICKLY BECAME A TIRELESS PROPAGANDIST AND ALL-AROUND SHILL...
SIGH...CLINTON'S A SPINELESS, AMORAL OPPORTUNIST--BUT I GUESS HE'S MARGINALLY BETTER THAN BUSH...MAYBE...
WHAT A SHAMELESS APOLOGIST!
HOW DOES HE LIVE WITH HIMSELF?
CLINTON WINS
TOM TOMORROW©12-3-97

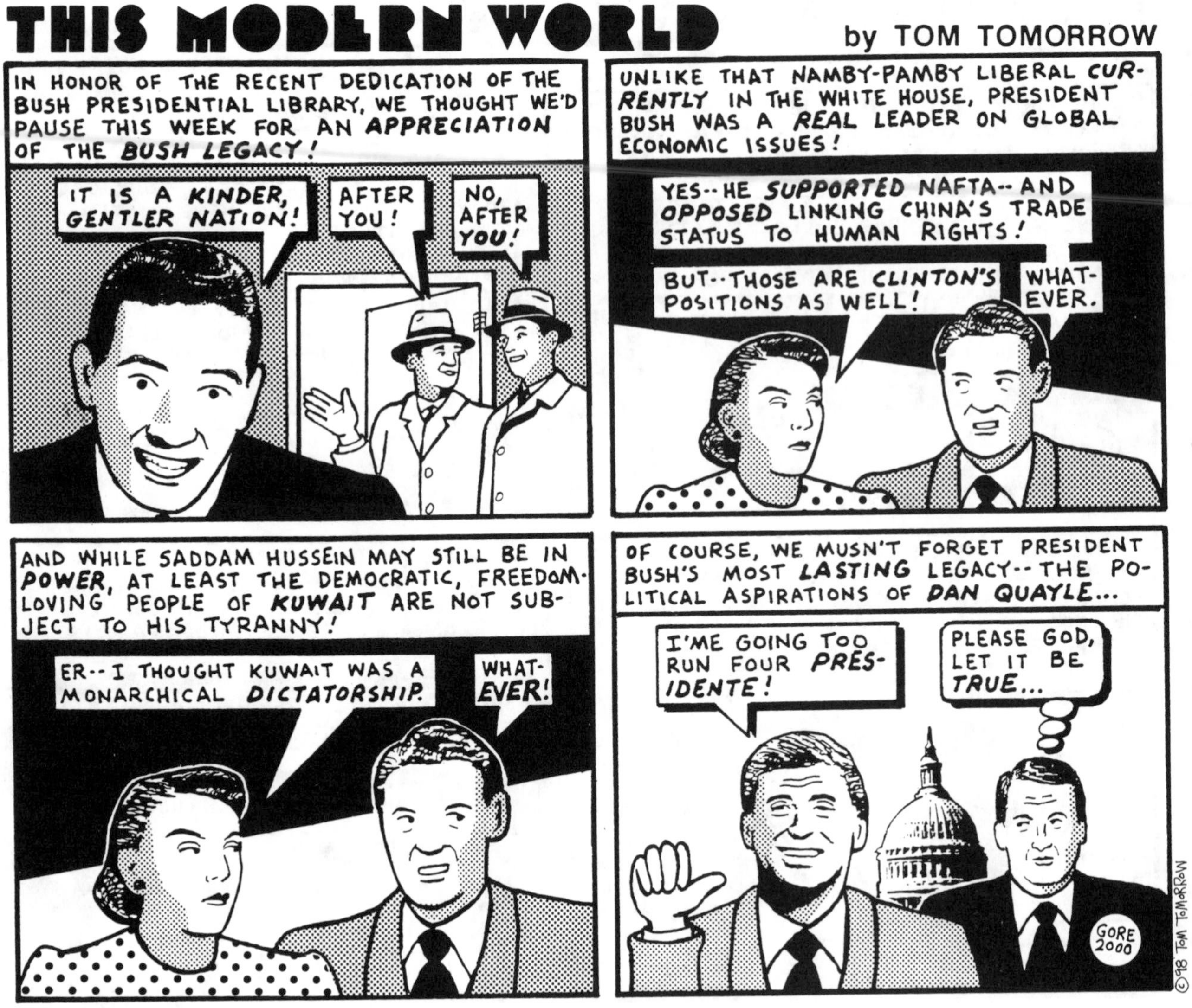
THIS MODERN WORLD
by TOM TOMORROW
IN HONOR OF THE RECENT DEDICATION OF THE BUSH PRESIDENTIAL LIBRARY, WE THOUGHT WE'D PAUSE THIS WEEK FOR AN APPRECIATION OF THE BUSH LEGACY!
IT IS A KINDER, GENTLER NATION!
AFTER YOU!
NO, AFTER YOU!
UNLIKE THAT NAMBY-PAMBY LIBERAL CURRENTLY IN THE WHITE HOUSE, PRESIDENT BUSH WAS A REAL LEADER ON GLOBAL ECONOMIC ISSUES!
YES--HE SUPPORTED NAFTA--AND OPPOSED LINKING CHINA'S TRADE STATUS TO HUMAN RIGHTS!
BUT--THOSE ARE CLINTON'S POSITIONS AS WELL!
WHATEVER.
AND WHILE SADDAM HUSSEIN MAY STILL BE IN POWER, AT LEAST THE DEMOCRATIC, FREEDOM-LOVING PEOPLE OF KUWAIT ARE NOT SUBJECT TO HIS TYRANNY!
ER--I THOUGHT KUWAIT WAS A MONARCHICAL DICTATORSHIP.
WHATEVER!
OF COURSE, WE MUSN'T FORGET PRESIDENT BUSH'S MOST LASTING LEGACY--THE POLITICAL ASPIRATIONS OF DAN QUAYLE...
I'ME GOING TOO RUN FOUR PRESIDENTE!
PLEASE GOD, LET IT BE TRUE...
GORE 2000
©'98 TOM TOMORROW

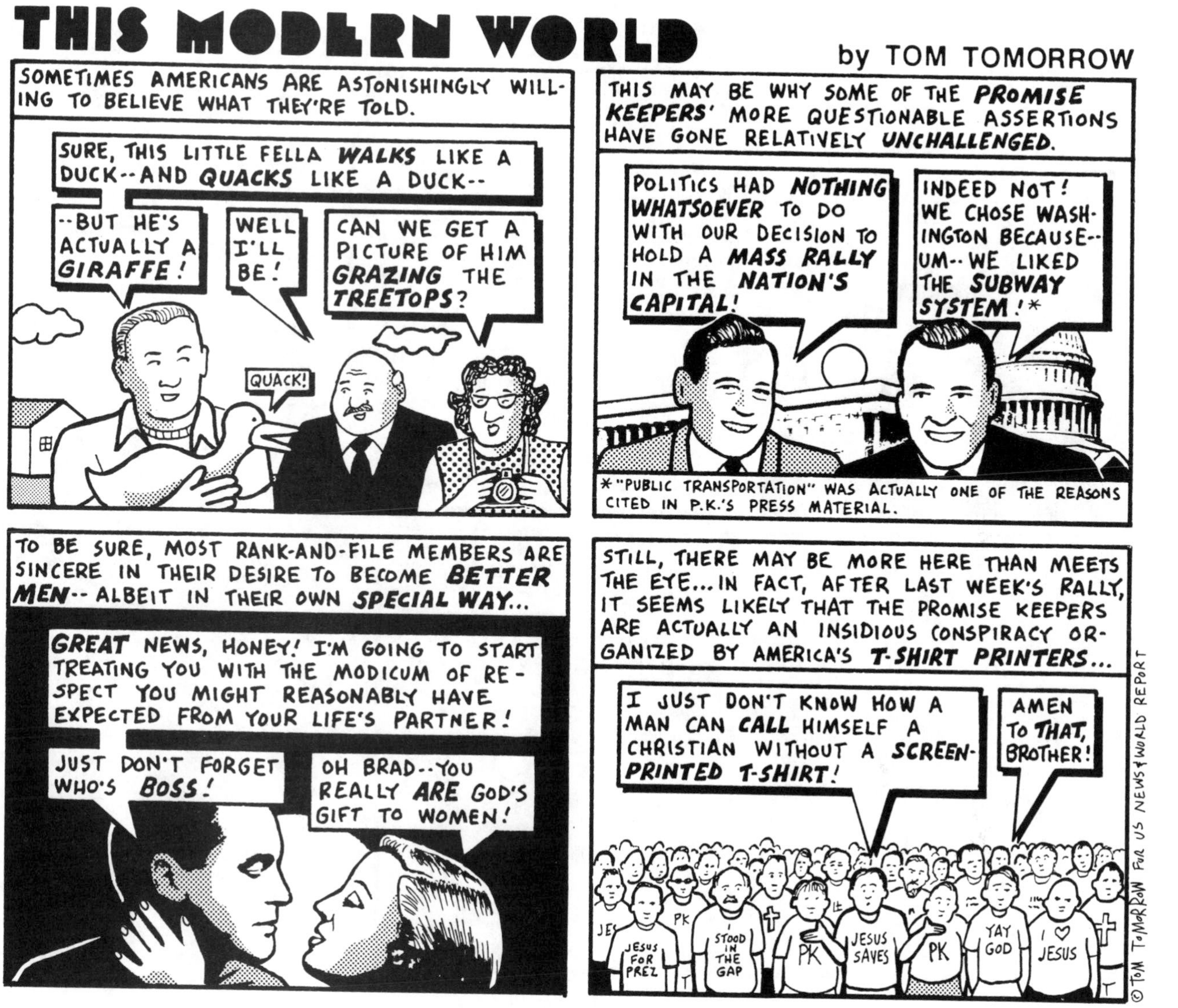
THIS MODERN WORLD
by TOM TOMORROW
SOMETIMES AMERICANS ARE ASTONISHINGLY WILLING TO BELIEVE WHAT THEY'RE TOLD.
SURE, THIS LITTLE FELLA WALKS LIKE A DUCK--AND QUACKS LIKE A DUCK--
--BUT HE'S ACTUALLY A GIRAFFE!
WELL I'LL BE!
CAN WE GET A PICTURE OF HIM GRAZING THE TREETOPS?
QUACK!
THIS MAY BE WHY SOME OF THE PROMISE KEEPERS' MORE QUESTIONABLE ASSERTIONS HAVE GONE RELATIVELY UNCHALLENGED.
POLITICS HAD NOTHING WHATSOEVER TO DO WITH OUR DECISION TO HOLD A MASS RALLY IN THE NATION'S CAPITAL!
INDEED NOT! WE CHOSE WASHINGTON BECAUSE--UM--WE LIKED THE SUBWAY SYSTEM!*
* "PUBLIC TRANSPORTATION" WAS ACTUALLY ONE OF THE REASONS CITED IN P.K.'S PRESS MATERIAL.
TO BE SURE, MOST RANK-AND-FILE MEMBERS ARE SINCERE IN THEIR DESIRE TO BECOME BETTER MEN--ALBEIT IN THEIR OWN SPECIAL WAY...
GREAT NEWS, HONEY! I'M GOING TO START TREATING YOU WITH THE MODICUM OF RESPECT YOU MIGHT REASONABLY HAVE EXPECTED FROM YOUR LIFE'S PARTNER!
JUST DON'T FORGET WHO'S BOSS!
OH BRAD--YOU REALLY ARE GOD'S GIFT TO WOMEN!
STILL, THERE MAY BE MORE HERE THAN MEETS THE EYE... IN FACT, AFTER LAST WEEK'S RALLY, IT SEEMS LIKELY THAT THE PROMISE KEEPERS ARE ACTUALLY AN INSIDIOUS CONSPIRACY ORGANIZED BY AMERICA'S T-SHIRT PRINTERS...
I JUST DON'T KNOW HOW A MAN CAN CALL HIMSELF A CHRISTIAN WITHOUT A SCREEN-PRINTED T-SHIRT!
AMEN TO THAT, BROTHER!
JESUS FOR PREZ
PK
I STOOD IN THE GAP
PK
JESUS SAVES
PK
YAY GOD
I ♡ JESUS
© TOM TOMORROW FOR US NEWS & WORLD REPORT

by TOM TOMORROW

THE *SENATE* CAMPAIGN FINANCE HEARINGS MAY BE WINDING DOWN--BUT THE *HOUSE* INVESTIGATION, CHAIRED BY INDIANA'S DAN BURTON, IS JUST *BEGINNING*...AND HERE TO DISCUSS REP. BURTON'S *QUALIFICATIONS* FOR THE TASK AT HAND IS OUR *SPECIAL GUEST COMMENTATOR*--

THE *FLYING HEAD OF ALEXIS DE TOCQUEVILLE!*

BONJOUR AMÉRICAINS!

ALORS! SLEAZY CAMPAIGN FUNDRAISING *IS* A TOPIC WITH WHICH MONSIEUR BURTON IS *INTIMATELY ACQUAINTED*-- HAVING RAISED *HUNDREDS OF THOUSANDS OF DOLLARS* FROM CONTRIBUTORS INCLUDING *MOBUTU SESE SEKO*, MILITANT *SIKHS*, AND ANTI-CASTRO *CUBAN-AMÉRICAINS*--

--NONE OF WHOM ARE TRADITIONALLY KNOWN FOR THEIR INTEREST IN ZEE STATE OF *INDIANA*...

AND WHILE BILL CLINTON CANNOT REMEMBER IF HE EVAIR MADE FUNDRAISING CALLS FROM HIS OFFICE-- AND AL GORE HAD TO RETURN CONTRIBUTIONS TO A BUDDHIST TEMPLE--

WHA--?

--*DAN BURTON* CANNOT REMEMBER IF *HE* EVAIR MADE SUCH CALLS FROM *HIS* OFFICE-- AND HAD TO RETURN CONTRIBUTIONS TO AT LEAST TWO *SIKH* TEMPLES!

THERE IS SO MUCH *COMMON GROUND* IN YOUR DEMOCRACY!

DAN 2000

AND FURTHER--MONSIEUR BURTON IS UNLIKELY TO ACCEPT THINGS AT, HOW YOU SAY, *FACE VALUE!* WHY, HE ONCE RE-ENACTED ZEE DEATH OF VINCENT FOSTER IN HIS *BACK YARD*--BY FIRING BULLETS INTO WHAT HE DESCRIBED AS A--A--*ZUT ALORS!*--

DAN 2000

--A "HEADLIKE OBJECT"..!

MON DIEU!

AU SECOURS!

POW! POW!

HALP!

WELL--LOOKS LIKE THAT'S ALL FOR *NOW!*

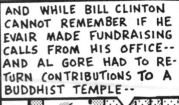

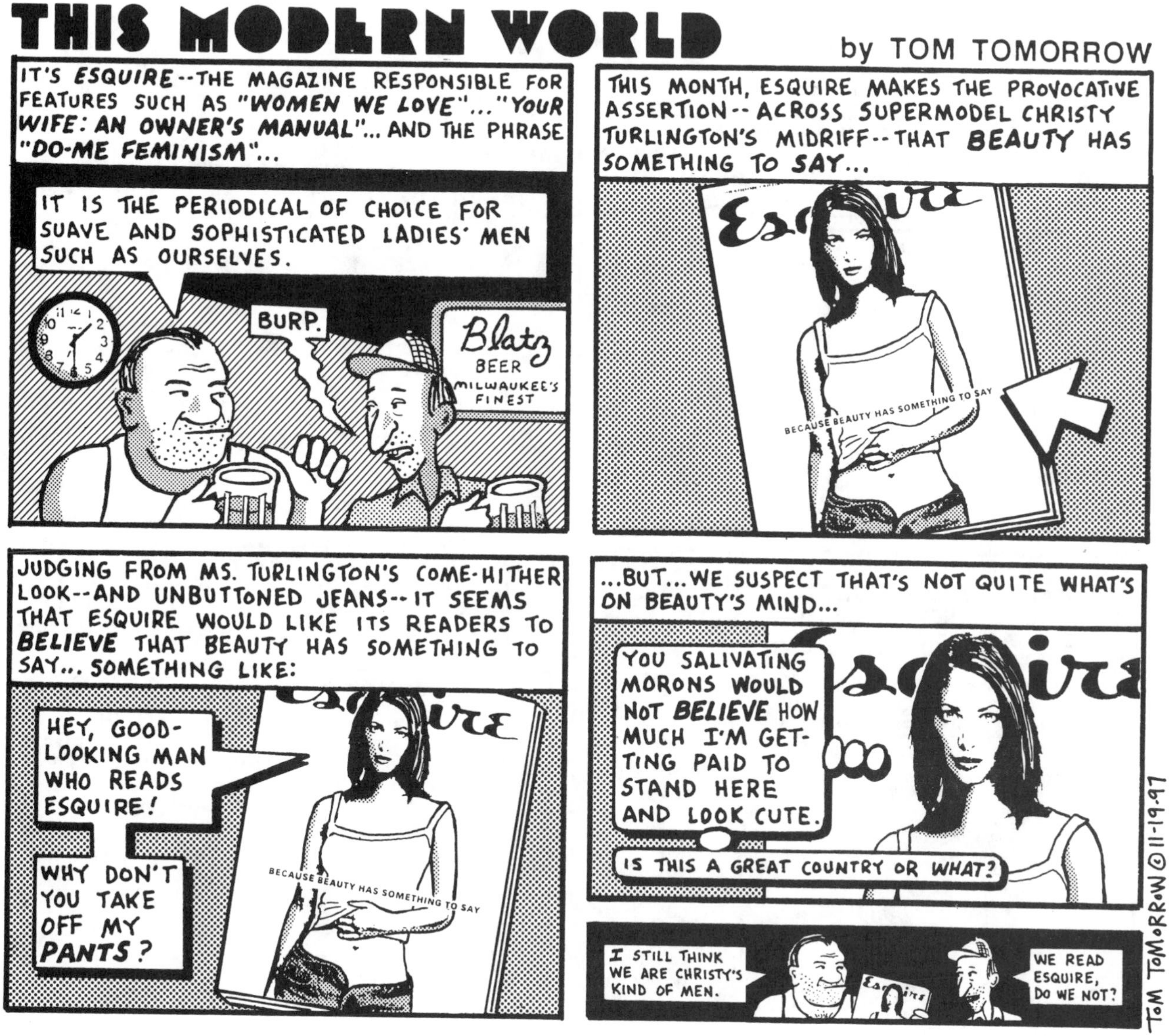
THIS MODERN WORLD
by TOM TOMORROW
IT'S ESQUIRE--THE MAGAZINE RESPONSIBLE FOR FEATURES SUCH AS "WOMEN WE LOVE"..."YOUR WIFE: AN OWNER'S MANUAL"... AND THE PHRASE "DO-ME FEMINISM"...
IT IS THE PERIODICAL OF CHOICE FOR SUAVE AND SOPHISTICATED LADIES' MEN SUCH AS OURSELVES.
BURP.
Blatz BEER MILWAUKEE'S FINEST
THIS MONTH, ESQUIRE MAKES THE PROVOCATIVE ASSERTION--ACROSS SUPERMODEL CHRISTY TURLINGTON'S MIDRIFF--THAT BEAUTY HAS SOMETHING TO SAY...
BECAUSE BEAUTY HAS SOMETHING TO SAY
JUDGING FROM MS. TURLINGTON'S COME-HITHER LOOK--AND UNBUTTONED JEANS--IT SEEMS THAT ESQUIRE WOULD LIKE ITS READERS TO BELIEVE THAT BEAUTY HAS SOMETHING TO SAY... SOMETHING LIKE:
HEY, GOOD-LOOKING MAN WHO READS ESQUIRE!
WHY DON'T YOU TAKE OFF MY PANTS?
BECAUSE BEAUTY HAS SOMETHING TO SAY
...BUT...WE SUSPECT THAT'S NOT QUITE WHAT'S ON BEAUTY'S MIND...
YOU SALIVATING MORONS WOULD NOT BELIEVE HOW MUCH I'M GETTING PAID TO STAND HERE AND LOOK CUTE.
IS THIS A GREAT COUNTRY OR WHAT?
I STILL THINK WE ARE CHRISTY'S KIND OF MEN.
WE READ ESQUIRE, DO WE NOT?
TOM TOMORROW © 11-19-97

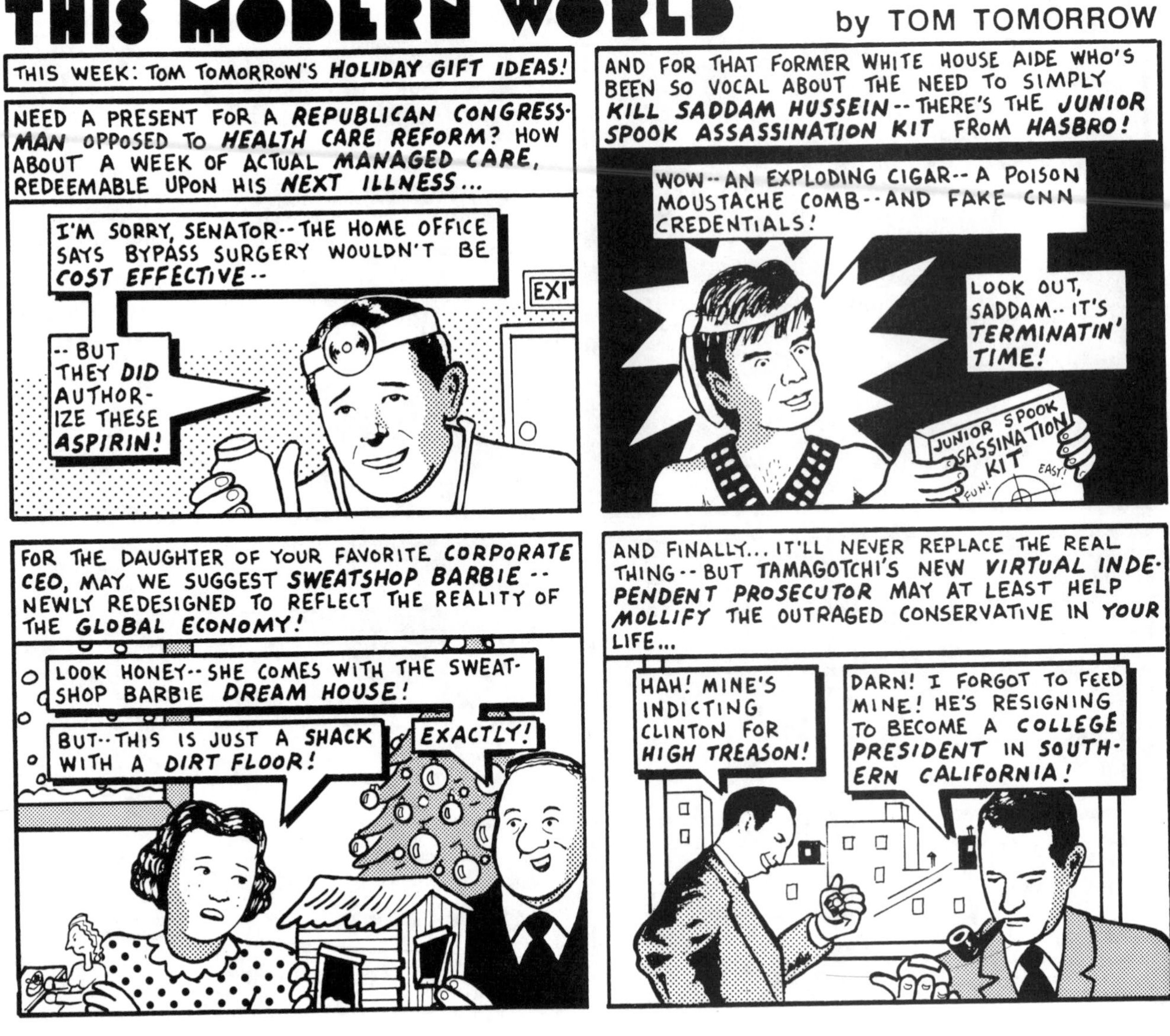
THIS MODERN WORLD
by TOM TOMORROW
THIS WEEK: TOM TOMORROW'S HOLIDAY GIFT IDEAS!
NEED A PRESENT FOR A REPUBLICAN CONGRESSMAN OPPOSED TO HEALTH CARE REFORM? HOW ABOUT A WEEK OF ACTUAL MANAGED CARE, REDEEMABLE UPON HIS NEXT ILLNESS...
I'M SORRY, SENATOR--THE HOME OFFICE SAYS BYPASS SURGERY WOULDN'T BE COST EFFECTIVE--
--BUT THEY DID AUTHORIZE THESE ASPIRIN!
EXIT
AND FOR THAT FORMER WHITE HOUSE AIDE WHO'S BEEN SO VOCAL ABOUT THE NEED TO SIMPLY KILL SADDAM HUSSEIN--THERE'S THE JUNIOR SPOOK ASSASSINATION KIT FROM HASBRO!
WOW--AN EXPLODING CIGAR--A POISON MOUSTACHE COMB--AND FAKE CNN CREDENTIALS!
LOOK OUT, SADDAM--IT'S TERMINATIN' TIME!
JUNIOR SPOOK ASSASSINATION KIT
FUN! EASY!
FOR THE DAUGHTER OF YOUR FAVORITE CORPORATE CEO, MAY WE SUGGEST SWEATSHOP BARBIE--NEWLY REDESIGNED TO REFLECT THE REALITY OF THE GLOBAL ECONOMY!
LOOK HONEY--SHE COMES WITH THE SWEATSHOP BARBIE DREAM HOUSE!
BUT--THIS IS JUST A SHACK WITH A DIRT FLOOR!
EXACTLY!
AND FINALLY... IT'LL NEVER REPLACE THE REAL THING--BUT TAMAGOTCHI'S NEW VIRTUAL INDEPENDENT PROSECUTOR MAY AT LEAST HELP MOLLIFY THE OUTRAGED CONSERVATIVE IN YOUR LIFE...
HAH! MINE'S INDICTING CLINTON FOR HIGH TREASON!
DARN! I FORGOT TO FEED MINE! HE'S RESIGNING TO BECOME A COLLEGE PRESIDENT IN SOUTHERN CALIFORNIA!
TOM TOMORROW©1997 FOR U.S. NEWS & WORLD REPORT

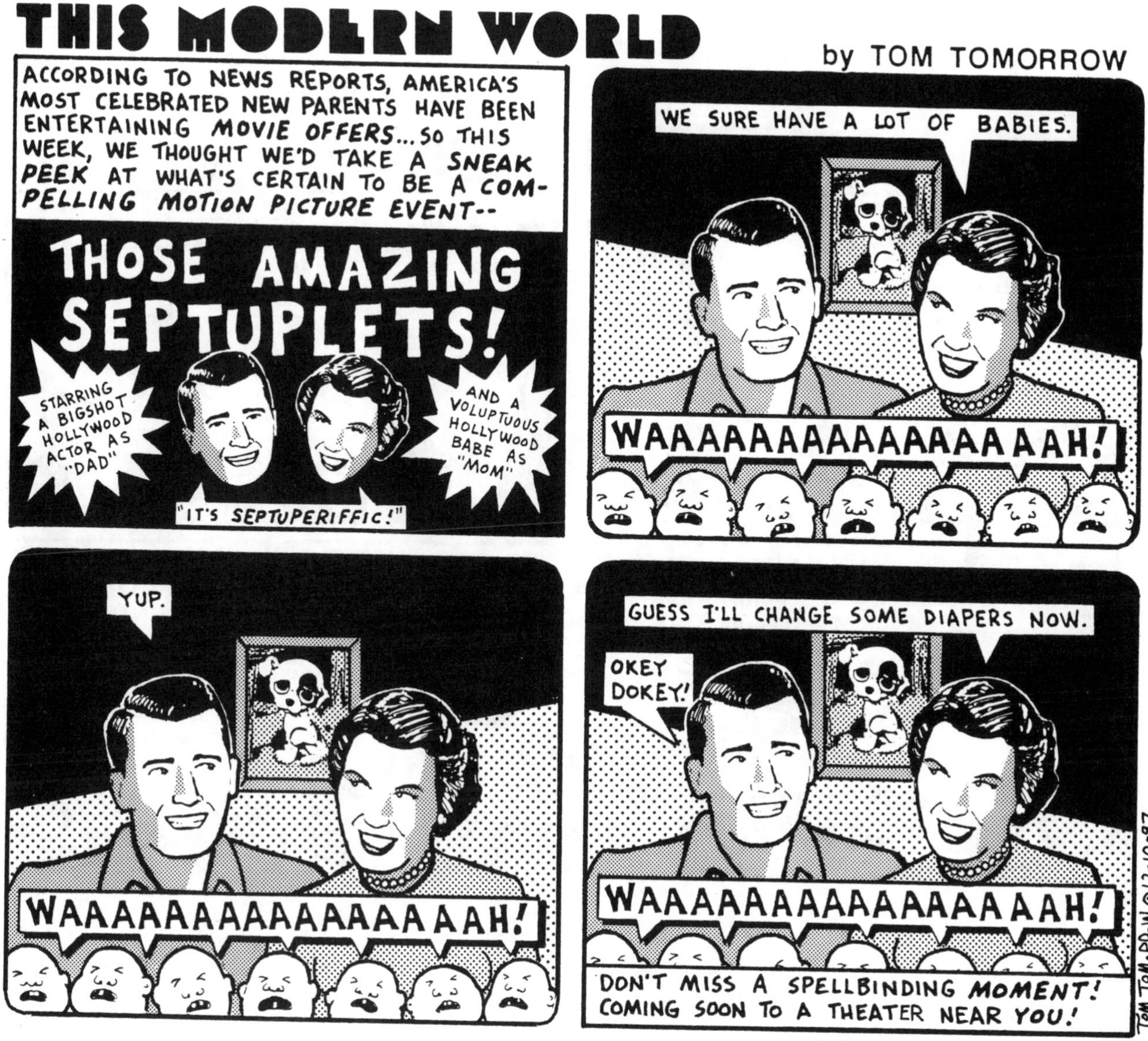
THIS MODERN WORLD
by TOM TOMORROW
ACCORDING TO NEWS REPORTS, AMERICA'S MOST CELEBRATED NEW PARENTS HAVE BEEN ENTERTAINING MOVIE OFFERS... SO THIS WEEK, WE THOUGHT WE'D TAKE A SNEAK PEEK AT WHAT'S CERTAIN TO BE A COMPELLING MOTION PICTURE EVENT--
THOSE AMAZING SEPTUPLETS!
STARRING A BIGSHOT HOLLYWOOD ACTOR AS "DAD"
AND A VOLUPTUOUS HOLLYWOOD BABE AS "MOM"
"IT'S SEPTUPERIFFIC!"
WE SURE HAVE A LOT OF BABIES.
WAAAAAAAAAAAAAAAAH!
YUP.
WAAAAAAAAAAAAAAAAH!
GUESS I'LL CHANGE SOME DIAPERS NOW.
OKEY DOKEY!
WAAAAAAAAAAAAAAAAH!
DON'T MISS A SPELLBINDING MOMENT! COMING SOON TO A THEATER NEAR YOU!
TOM TOMORROW ©12-10-97

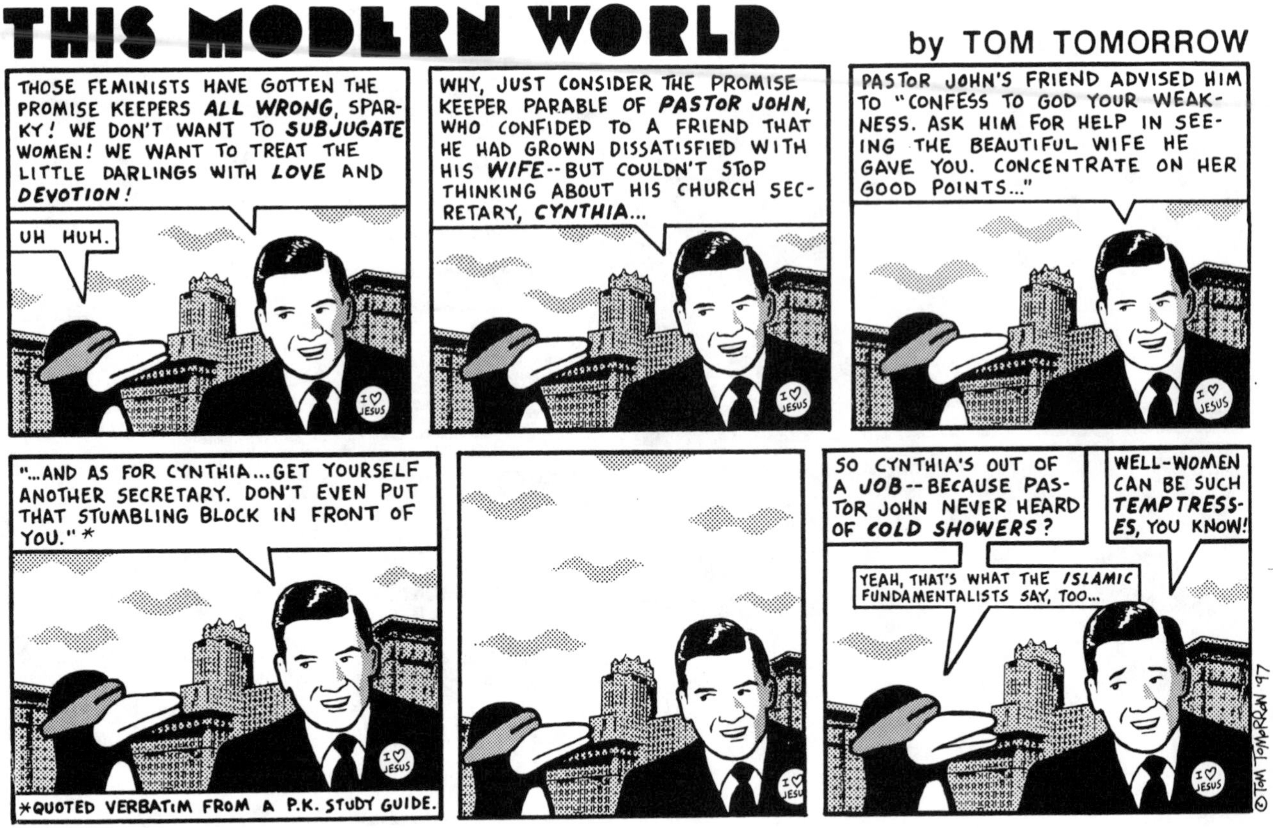
THIS MODERN WORLD
by TOM TOMORROW
THOSE FEMINISTS HAVE GOTTEN THE PROMISE KEEPERS ALL WRONG, SPARKY! WE DON'T WANT TO SUBJUGATE WOMEN! WE WANT TO TREAT THE LITTLE DARLINGS WITH LOVE AND DEVOTION!
UH HUH.
I ♡ JESUS
WHY, JUST CONSIDER THE PROMISE KEEPER PARABLE OF PASTOR JOHN, WHO CONFIDED TO A FRIEND THAT HE HAD GROWN DISSATISFIED WITH HIS WIFE--BUT COULDN'T STOP THINKING ABOUT HIS CHURCH SECRETARY, CYNTHIA...
PASTOR JOHN'S FRIEND ADVISED HIM TO "CONFESS TO GOD YOUR WEAKNESS. ASK HIM FOR HELP IN SEEING THE BEAUTIFUL WIFE HE GAVE YOU. CONCENTRATE ON HER GOOD POINTS..."
"...AND AS FOR CYNTHIA...GET YOURSELF ANOTHER SECRETARY. DON'T EVEN PUT THAT STUMBLING BLOCK IN FRONT OF YOU." *
*QUOTED VERBATIM FROM A P.K. STUDY GUIDE.
SO CYNTHIA'S OUT OF A JOB--BECAUSE PASTOR JOHN NEVER HEARD OF COLD SHOWERS?
WELL-WOMEN CAN BE SUCH TEMPTRESSES, YOU KNOW!
YEAH, THAT'S WHAT THE ISLAMIC FUNDAMENTALISTS SAY, TOO...
©TOM TOMORROW '97

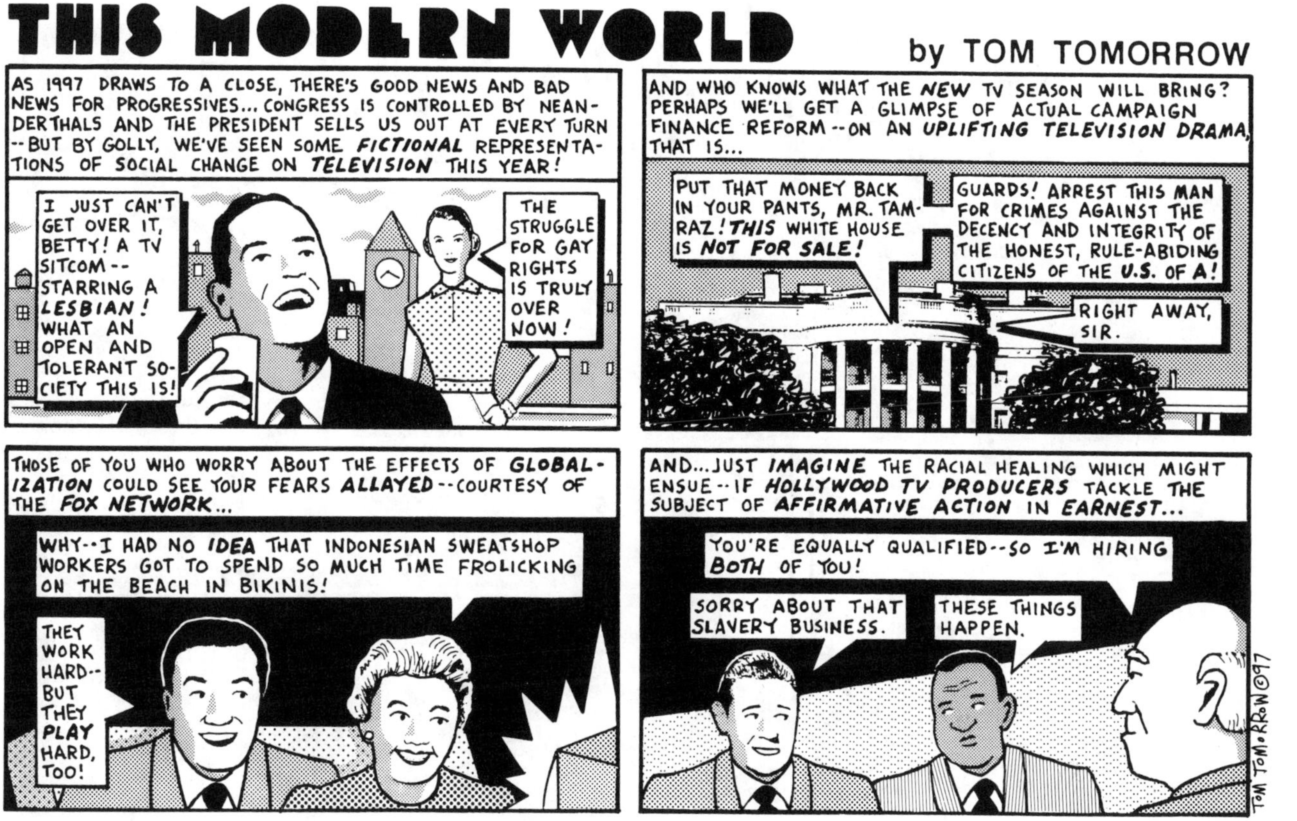
THIS MODERN WORLD
by TOM TOMORROW
AS 1997 DRAWS TO A CLOSE, THERE'S GOOD NEWS AND BAD NEWS FOR PROGRESSIVES... CONGRESS IS CONTROLLED BY NEAN-DERTHALS AND THE PRESIDENT SELLS US OUT AT EVERY TURN --BUT BY GOLLY, WE'VE SEEN SOME FICTIONAL REPRESENTA-TIONS OF SOCIAL CHANGE ON TELEVISION THIS YEAR!
I JUST CAN'T GET OVER IT, BETTY! A TV SITCOM--STARRING A LESBIAN! WHAT AN OPEN AND TOLERANT SO-CIETY THIS IS!
THE STRUGGLE FOR GAY RIGHTS IS TRULY OVER NOW!
AND WHO KNOWS WHAT THE NEW TV SEASON WILL BRING? PERHAPS WE'LL GET A GLIMPSE OF ACTUAL CAMPAIGN FINANCE REFORM--ON AN UPLIFTING TELEVISION DRAMA, THAT IS...
PUT THAT MONEY BACK IN YOUR PANTS, MR. TAM-RAZ! THIS WHITE HOUSE IS NOT FOR SALE!
GUARDS! ARREST THIS MAN FOR CRIMES AGAINST THE DECENCY AND INTEGRITY OF THE HONEST, RULE-ABIDING CITIZENS OF THE U.S. OF A!
RIGHT AWAY, SIR.
THOSE OF YOU WHO WORRY ABOUT THE EFFECTS OF GLOBAL-IZATION COULD SEE YOUR FEARS ALLAYED--COURTESY OF THE FOX NETWORK...
WHY--I HAD NO IDEA THAT INDONESIAN SWEATSHOP WORKERS GOT TO SPEND SO MUCH TIME FROLICKING ON THE BEACH IN BIKINIS!
THEY WORK HARD--BUT THEY PLAY HARD, TOO!
AND...JUST IMAGINE THE RACIAL HEALING WHICH MIGHT ENSUE--IF HOLLYWOOD TV PRODUCERS TACKLE THE SUBJECT OF AFFIRMATIVE ACTION IN EARNEST...
YOU'RE EQUALLY QUALIFIED--SO I'M HIRING BOTH OF YOU!
SORRY ABOUT THAT SLAVERY BUSINESS.
THESE THINGS HAPPEN.
TOM TOMORROW©97

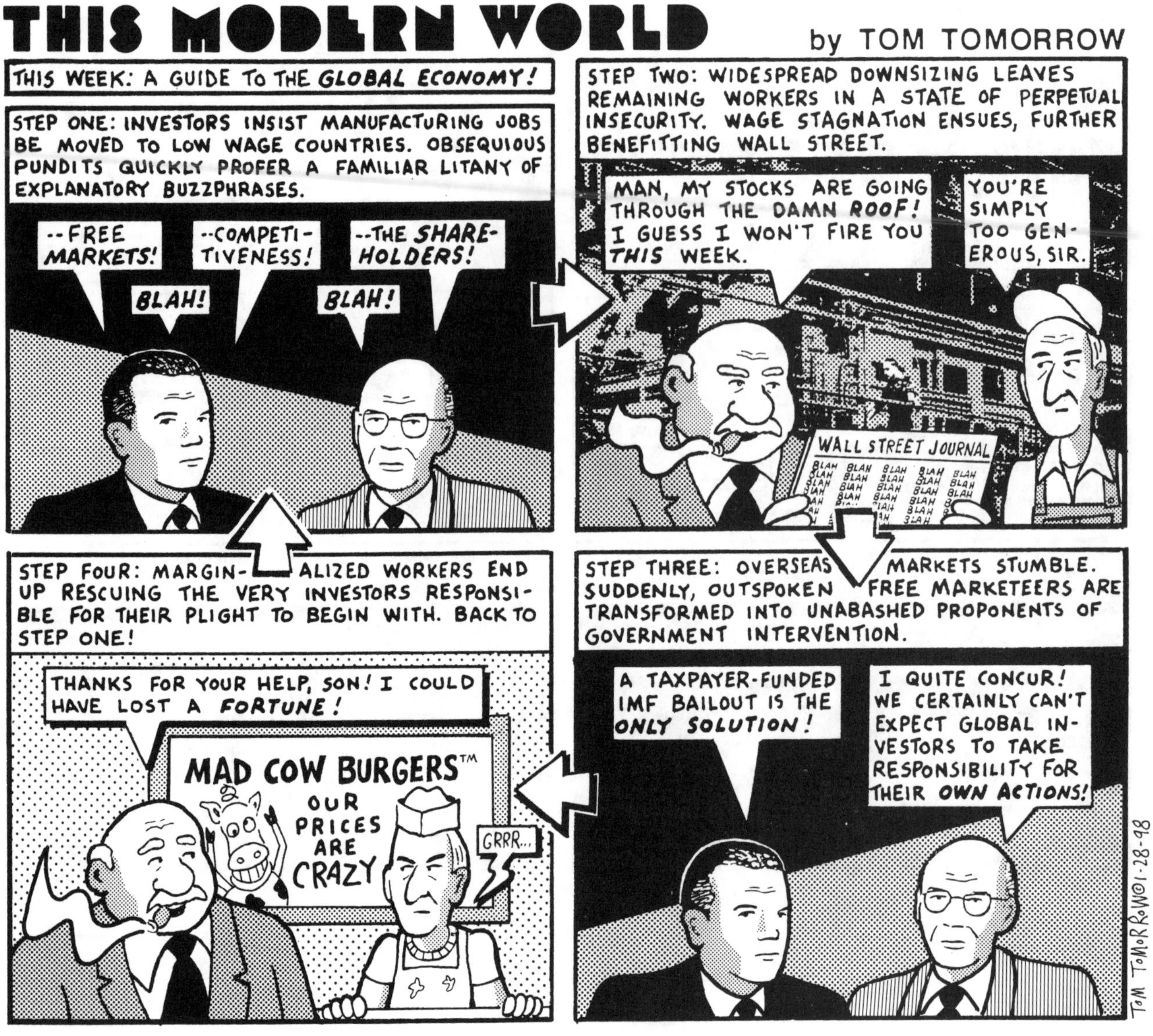
THIS MODERN WORLD
by TOM TOMORROW
THIS WEEK: A GUIDE TO THE GLOBAL ECONOMY!
STEP ONE: INVESTORS INSIST MANUFACTURING JOBS BE MOVED TO LOW WAGE COUNTRIES. OBSEQUIOUS PUNDITS QUICKLY PROFER A FAMILIAR LITANY OF EXPLANATORY BUZZPHRASES.
--FREE MARKETS!
BLAH!
--COMPETITIVENESS!
BLAH!
--THE SHAREHOLDERS!
STEP TWO: WIDESPREAD DOWNSIZING LEAVES REMAINING WORKERS IN A STATE OF PERPETUAL INSECURITY. WAGE STAGNATION ENSUES, FURTHER BENEFITTING WALL STREET.
MAN, MY STOCKS ARE GOING THROUGH THE DAMN ROOF! I GUESS I WON'T FIRE YOU THIS WEEK.
YOU'RE SIMPLY TOO GENEROUS, SIR.
WALL STREET JOURNAL
STEP THREE: OVERSEAS MARKETS STUMBLE. SUDDENLY, OUTSPOKEN FREE MARKETEERS ARE TRANSFORMED INTO UNABASHED PROPONENTS OF GOVERNMENT INTERVENTION.
A TAXPAYER-FUNDED IMF BAILOUT IS THE ONLY SOLUTION!
I QUITE CONCUR! WE CERTAINLY CAN'T EXPECT GLOBAL INVESTORS TO TAKE RESPONSIBILITY FOR THEIR OWN ACTIONS!
STEP FOUR: MARGINALIZED WORKERS END UP RESCUING THE VERY INVESTORS RESPONSIBLE FOR THEIR PLIGHT TO BEGIN WITH. BACK TO STEP ONE!
THANKS FOR YOUR HELP, SON! I COULD HAVE LOST A FORTUNE!
MAD COW BURGERS™
OUR PRICES ARE CRAZY
GRRR...
TOM TOMORROW©1-28-98

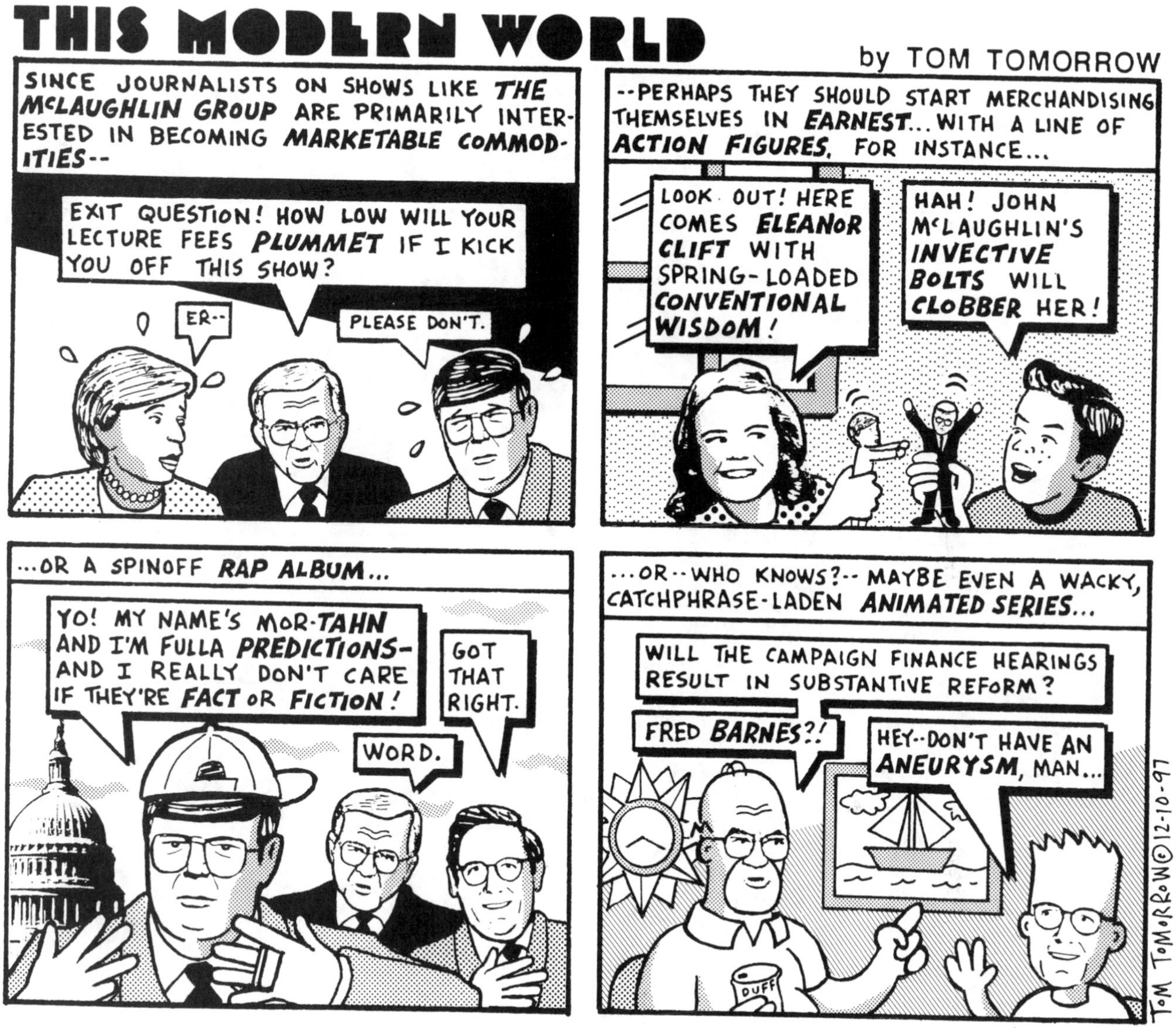
THIS MODERN WORLD
by TOM TOMORROW
SINCE JOURNALISTS ON SHOWS LIKE THE McLAUGHLIN GROUP ARE PRIMARILY INTERESTED IN BECOMING MARKETABLE COMMODITIES--
EXIT QUESTION! HOW LOW WILL YOUR LECTURE FEES PLUMMET IF I KICK YOU OFF THIS SHOW?
ER--
PLEASE DON'T.
--PERHAPS THEY SHOULD START MERCHANDISING THEMSELVES IN EARNEST... WITH A LINE OF ACTION FIGURES, FOR INSTANCE...
LOOK OUT! HERE COMES ELEANOR CLIFT WITH SPRING-LOADED CONVENTIONAL WISDOM!
HAH! JOHN McLAUGHLIN'S INVECTIVE BOLTS WILL CLOBBER HER!
...OR A SPINOFF RAP ALBUM...
YO! MY NAME'S MOR-TAHN AND I'M FULLA PREDICTIONS-AND I REALLY DON'T CARE IF THEY'RE FACT OR FICTION!
GOT THAT RIGHT.
WORD.
...OR--WHO KNOWS?--MAYBE EVEN A WACKY, CATCHPHRASE-LADEN ANIMATED SERIES...
WILL THE CAMPAIGN FINANCE HEARINGS RESULT IN SUBSTANTIVE REFORM?
FRED BARNES?!
HEY--DON'T HAVE AN ANEURYSM, MAN...
DUFF
TOM TOMORROW©12-10-97

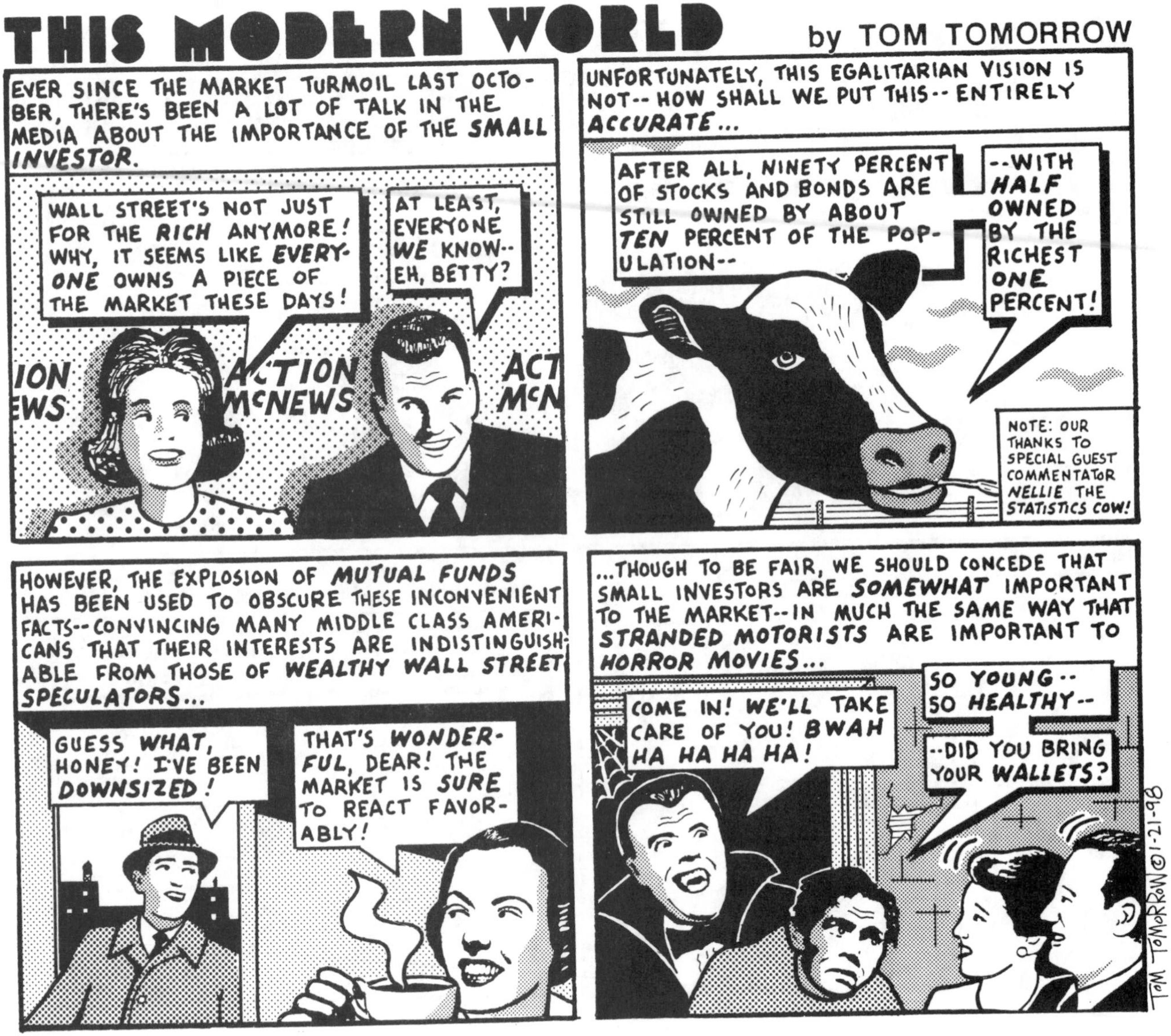
THIS MODERN WORLD
by TOM TOMORROW
EVER SINCE THE MARKET TURMOIL LAST OCTOBER, THERE'S BEEN A LOT OF TALK IN THE MEDIA ABOUT THE IMPORTANCE OF THE SMALL INVESTOR.
WALL STREET'S NOT JUST FOR THE RICH ANYMORE! WHY, IT SEEMS LIKE EVERYONE OWNS A PIECE OF THE MARKET THESE DAYS!
AT LEAST, EVERYONE WE KNOW-- EH, BETTY?
ACTION McNEWS
UNFORTUNATELY, THIS EGALITARIAN VISION IS NOT-- HOW SHALL WE PUT THIS-- ENTIRELY ACCURATE...
AFTER ALL, NINETY PERCENT OF STOCKS AND BONDS ARE STILL OWNED BY ABOUT TEN PERCENT OF THE POPULATION--
--WITH HALF OWNED BY THE RICHEST ONE PERCENT!
NOTE: OUR THANKS TO SPECIAL GUEST COMMENTATOR NELLIE THE STATISTICS COW!
HOWEVER, THE EXPLOSION OF MUTUAL FUNDS HAS BEEN USED TO OBSCURE THESE INCONVENIENT FACTS--CONVINCING MANY MIDDLE CLASS AMERICANS THAT THEIR INTERESTS ARE INDISTINGUISHABLE FROM THOSE OF WEALTHY WALL STREET SPECULATORS...
GUESS WHAT, HONEY! I'VE BEEN DOWNSIZED!
THAT'S WONDERFUL, DEAR! THE MARKET IS SURE TO REACT FAVORABLY!
...THOUGH TO BE FAIR, WE SHOULD CONCEDE THAT SMALL INVESTORS ARE SOMEWHAT IMPORTANT TO THE MARKET--IN MUCH THE SAME WAY THAT STRANDED MOTORISTS ARE IMPORTANT TO HORROR MOVIES...
COME IN! WE'LL TAKE CARE OF YOU! BWAH HA HA HA HA!
SO YOUNG-- SO HEALTHY--
--DID YOU BRING YOUR WALLETS?
TOM TOMORROW ©1-21-98

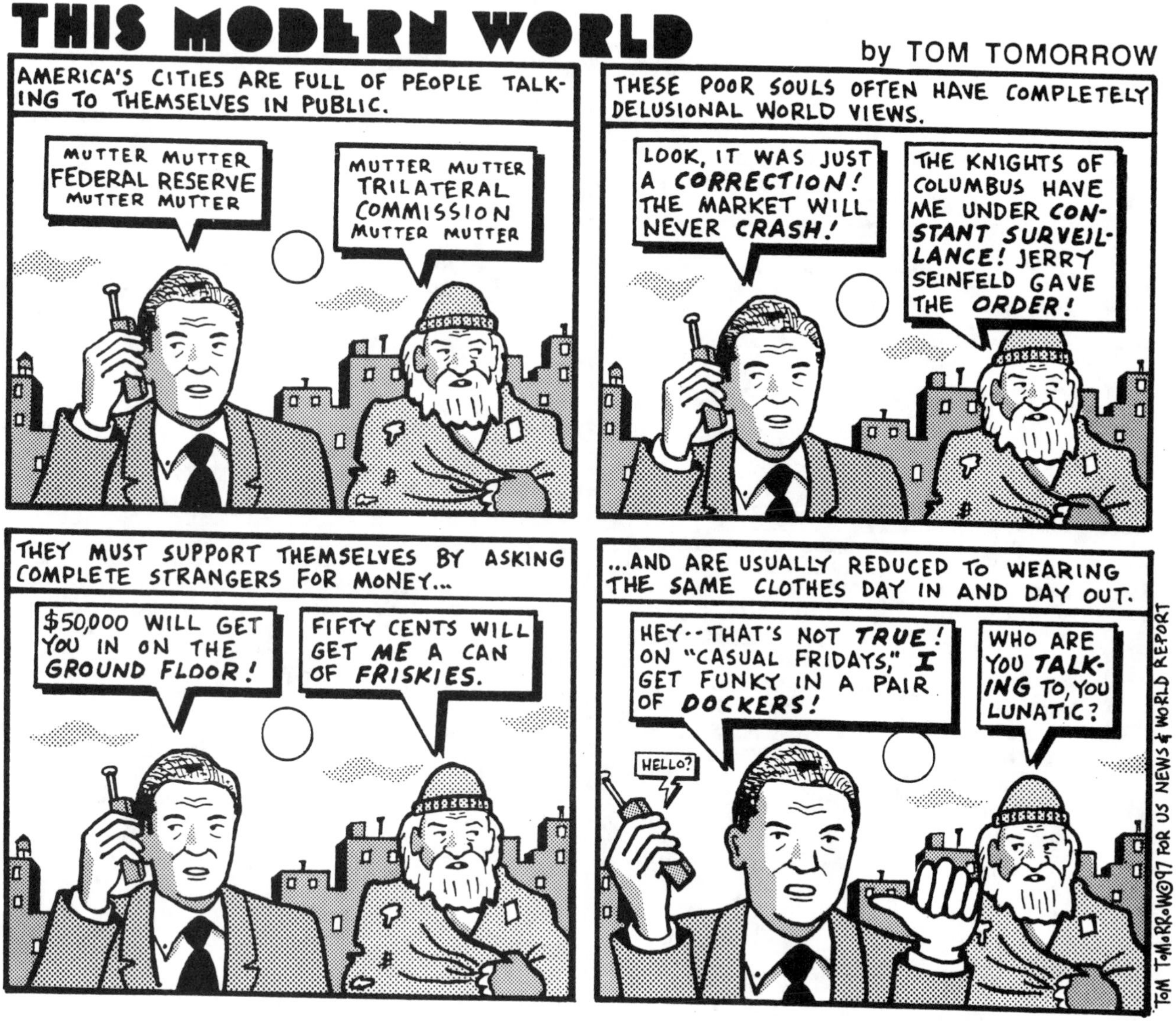
THIS MODERN WORLD
by TOM TOMORROW
AMERICA'S CITIES ARE FULL OF PEOPLE TALKING TO THEMSELVES IN PUBLIC.
MUTTER MUTTER FEDERAL RESERVE MUTTER MUTTER
MUTTER MUTTER TRILATERAL COMMISSION MUTTER MUTTER
THESE POOR SOULS OFTEN HAVE COMPLETELY DELUSIONAL WORLD VIEWS.
LOOK, IT WAS JUST A CORRECTION! THE MARKET WILL NEVER CRASH!
THE KNIGHTS OF COLUMBUS HAVE ME UNDER CONSTANT SURVEILLANCE! JERRY SEINFELD GAVE THE ORDER!
THEY MUST SUPPORT THEMSELVES BY ASKING COMPLETE STRANGERS FOR MONEY...
$50,000 WILL GET YOU IN ON THE GROUND FLOOR!
FIFTY CENTS WILL GET ME A CAN OF FRISKIES.
...AND ARE USUALLY REDUCED TO WEARING THE SAME CLOTHES DAY IN AND DAY OUT.
HEY--THAT'S NOT TRUE! ON "CASUAL FRIDAYS," I GET FUNKY IN A PAIR OF DOCKERS!
HELLO?
WHO ARE YOU TALKING TO, YOU LUNATIC?
TOM TOMORROW©97 FOR US NEWS & WORLD REPORT

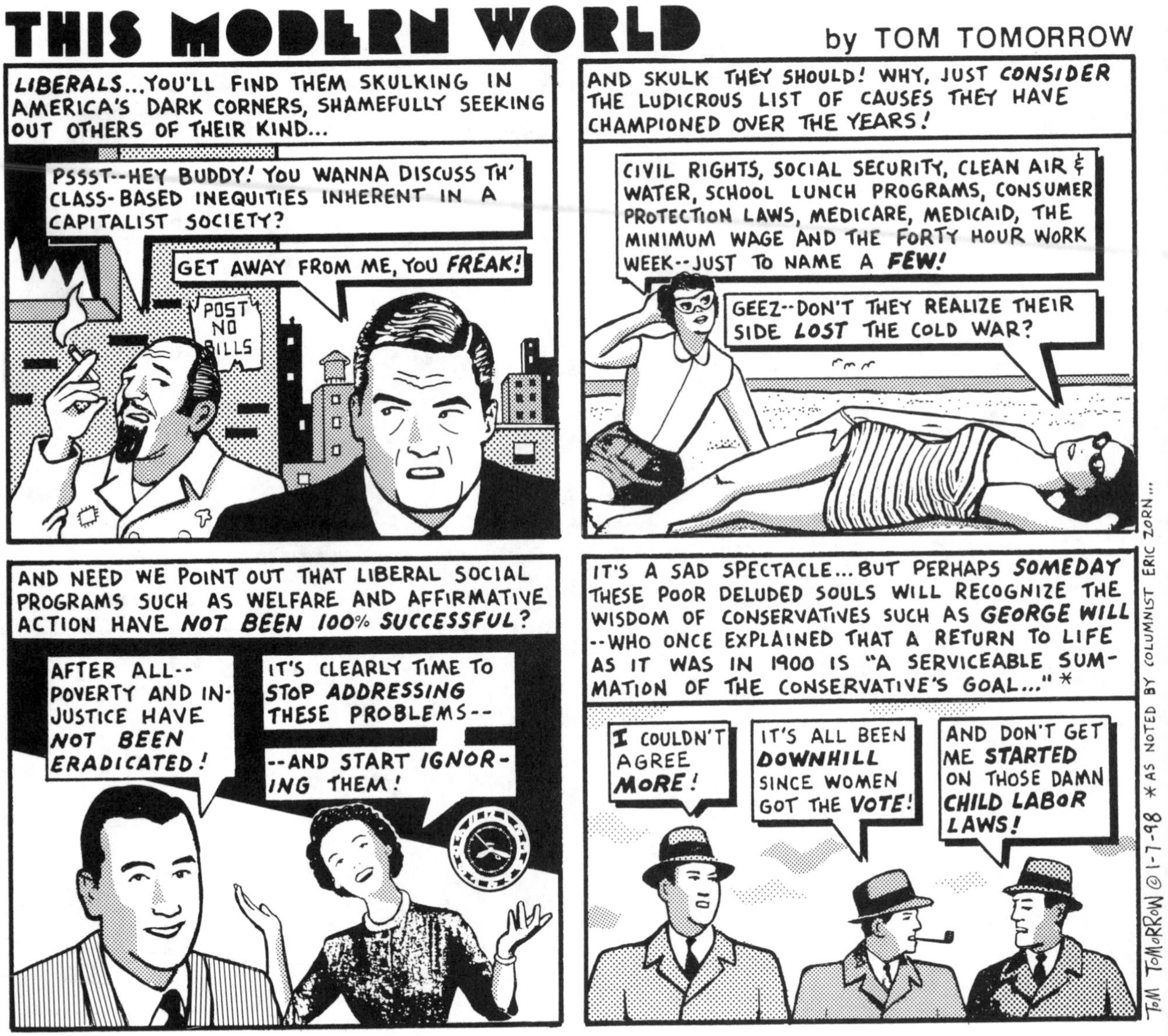
THIS MODERN WORLD
by TOM TOMORROW
LIBERALS... YOU'LL FIND THEM SKULKING IN AMERICA'S DARK CORNERS, SHAMEFULLY SEEKING OUT OTHERS OF THEIR KIND...
PSSST--HEY BUDDY! YOU WANNA DISCUSS TH' CLASS-BASED INEQUITIES INHERENT IN A CAPITALIST SOCIETY?
GET AWAY FROM ME, YOU FREAK!
POST NO BILLS
AND SKULK THEY SHOULD! WHY, JUST CONSIDER THE LUDICROUS LIST OF CAUSES THEY HAVE CHAMPIONED OVER THE YEARS!
CIVIL RIGHTS, SOCIAL SECURITY, CLEAN AIR & WATER, SCHOOL LUNCH PROGRAMS, CONSUMER PROTECTION LAWS, MEDICARE, MEDICAID, THE MINIMUM WAGE AND THE FORTY HOUR WORK WEEK--JUST TO NAME A FEW!
GEEZ--DON'T THEY REALIZE THEIR SIDE LOST THE COLD WAR?
AND NEED WE POINT OUT THAT LIBERAL SOCIAL PROGRAMS SUCH AS WELFARE AND AFFIRMATIVE ACTION HAVE NOT BEEN 100% SUCCESSFUL?
AFTER ALL-- POVERTY AND INJUSTICE HAVE NOT BEEN ERADICATED!
IT'S CLEARLY TIME TO STOP ADDRESSING THESE PROBLEMS--
--AND START IGNORING THEM!
IT'S A SAD SPECTACLE... BUT PERHAPS SOMEDAY THESE POOR DELUDED SOULS WILL RECOGNIZE THE WISDOM OF CONSERVATIVES SUCH AS GEORGE WILL --WHO ONCE EXPLAINED THAT A RETURN TO LIFE AS IT WAS IN 1900 IS "A SERVICEABLE SUMMATION OF THE CONSERVATIVE'S GOAL..." *
I COULDN'T AGREE MORE!
IT'S ALL BEEN DOWNHILL SINCE WOMEN GOT THE VOTE!
AND DON'T GET ME STARTED ON THOSE DAMN CHILD LABOR LAWS!
TOM TOMORROW © 1-7-98 * AS NOTED BY COLUMNIST ERIC ZORN...

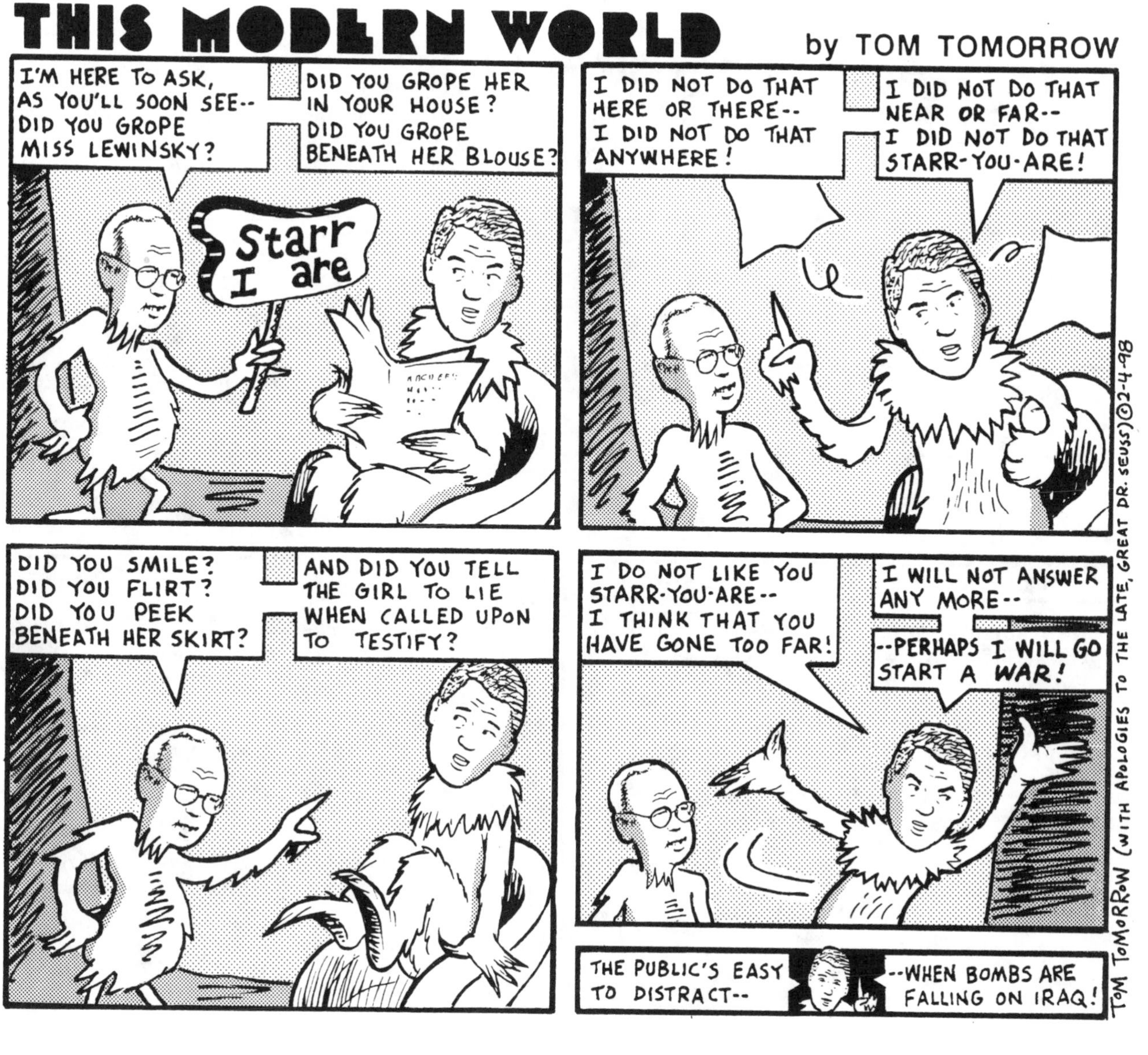
THIS MODERN WORLD
by TOM TOMORROW
I'M HERE TO ASK, AS YOU'LL SOON SEE-- DID YOU GROPE MISS LEWINSKY?
DID YOU GROPE HER IN YOUR HOUSE? DID YOU GROPE BENEATH HER BLOUSE?
Starr I are
I DID NOT DO THAT HERE OR THERE-- I DID NOT DO THAT ANYWHERE!
I DID NOT DO THAT NEAR OR FAR-- I DID NOT DO THAT STARR-YOU-ARE!
DID YOU SMILE? DID YOU FLIRT? DID YOU PEEK BENEATH HER SKIRT?
AND DID YOU TELL THE GIRL TO LIE WHEN CALLED UPON TO TESTIFY?
I DO NOT LIKE YOU STARR-YOU-ARE-- I THINK THAT YOU HAVE GONE TOO FAR!
I WILL NOT ANSWER ANY MORE--
--PERHAPS I WILL GO START A WAR!
THE PUBLIC'S EASY TO DISTRACT--
--WHEN BOMBS ARE FALLING ON IRAQ!
TOM TOMORROW (WITH APOLOGIES TO THE LATE, GREAT DR. SEUSS) ©2-4-98

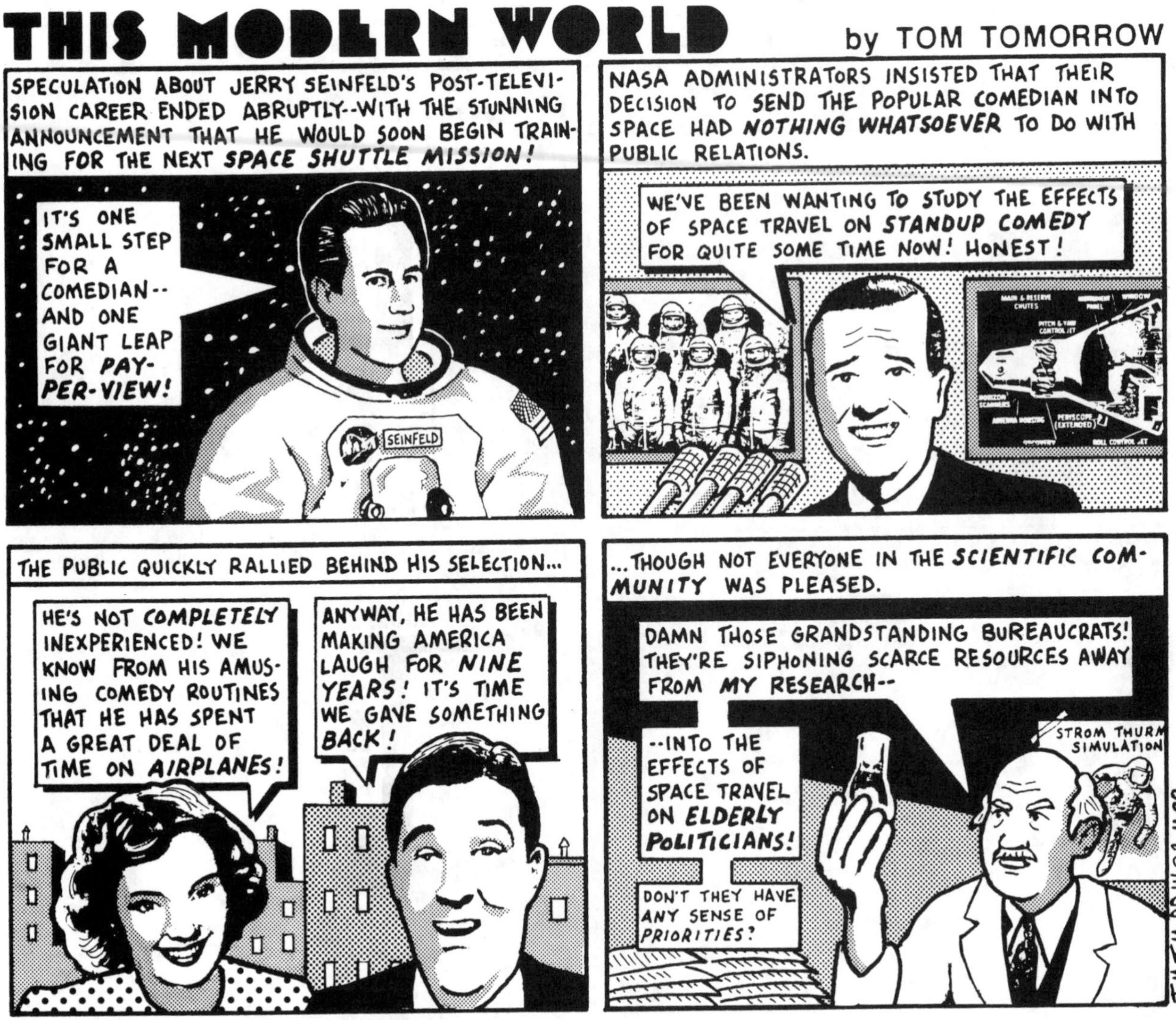
THIS MODERN WORLD
by TOM TOMORROW
SPECULATION ABOUT JERRY SEINFELD'S POST-TELEVISION CAREER ENDED ABRUPTLY--WITH THE STUNNING ANNOUNCEMENT THAT HE WOULD SOON BEGIN TRAINING FOR THE NEXT SPACE SHUTTLE MISSION!
IT'S ONE SMALL STEP FOR A COMEDIAN-- AND ONE GIANT LEAP FOR PAY-PER-VIEW!
SEINFELD
NASA ADMINISTRATORS INSISTED THAT THEIR DECISION TO SEND THE POPULAR COMEDIAN INTO SPACE HAD NOTHING WHATSOEVER TO DO WITH PUBLIC RELATIONS.
WE'VE BEEN WANTING TO STUDY THE EFFECTS OF SPACE TRAVEL ON STANDUP COMEDY FOR QUITE SOME TIME NOW! HONEST!
THE PUBLIC QUICKLY RALLIED BEHIND HIS SELECTION...
HE'S NOT COMPLETELY INEXPERIENCED! WE KNOW FROM HIS AMUSING COMEDY ROUTINES THAT HE HAS SPENT A GREAT DEAL OF TIME ON AIRPLANES!
ANYWAY, HE HAS BEEN MAKING AMERICA LAUGH FOR NINE YEARS! IT'S TIME WE GAVE SOMETHING BACK!
...THOUGH NOT EVERYONE IN THE SCIENTIFIC COMMUNITY WAS PLEASED.
DAMN THOSE GRANDSTANDING BUREAUCRATS! THEY'RE SIPHONING SCARCE RESOURCES AWAY FROM MY RESEARCH--
--INTO THE EFFECTS OF SPACE TRAVEL ON ELDERLY POLITICIANS!
DON'T THEY HAVE ANY SENSE OF PRIORITIES?
STROM THURM SIMULATION
TOM TOMORROW ©2-11-98

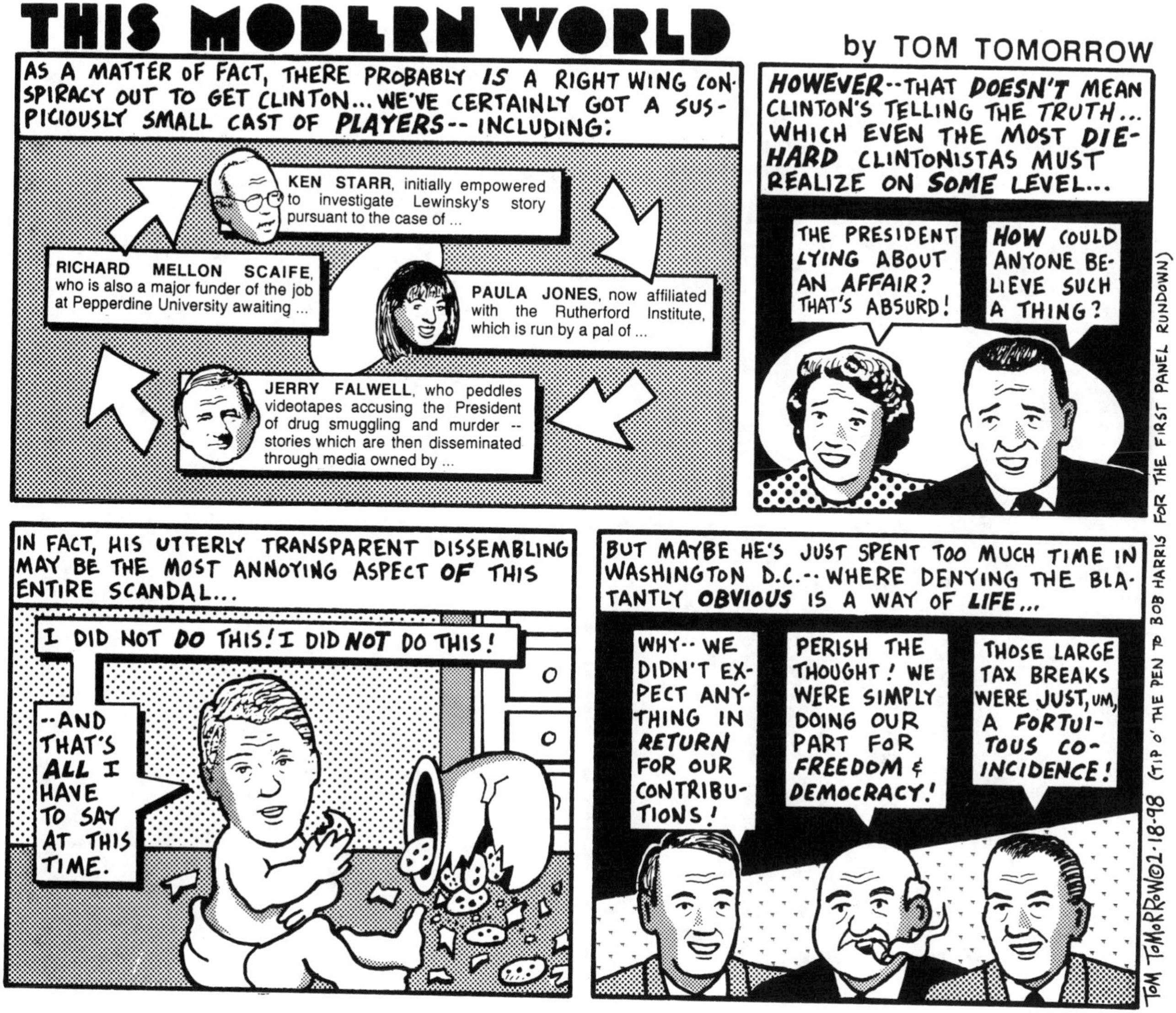
THIS MODERN WORLD
by TOM TOMORROW
AS A MATTER OF FACT, THERE PROBABLY IS A RIGHT WING CONSPIRACY OUT TO GET CLINTON... WE'VE CERTAINLY GOT A SUSPICIOUSLY SMALL CAST OF PLAYERS-- INCLUDING:
KEN STARR, initially empowered to investigate Lewinsky's story pursuant to the case of ...
PAULA JONES, now affiliated with the Rutherford Institute, which is run by a pal of ...
JERRY FALWELL, who peddles videotapes accusing the President of drug smuggling and murder -- stories which are then disseminated through media owned by ...
RICHARD MELLON SCAIFE, who is also a major funder of the job at Pepperdine University awaiting ...
HOWEVER--THAT DOESN'T MEAN CLINTON'S TELLING THE TRUTH... WHICH EVEN THE MOST DIE-HARD CLINTONISTAS MUST REALIZE ON SOME LEVEL...
THE PRESIDENT LYING ABOUT AN AFFAIR? THAT'S ABSURD!
HOW COULD ANYONE BELIEVE SUCH A THING?
IN FACT, HIS UTTERLY TRANSPARENT DISSEMBLING MAY BE THE MOST ANNOYING ASPECT OF THIS ENTIRE SCANDAL...
I DID NOT DO THIS! I DID NOT DO THIS!
--AND THAT'S ALL I HAVE TO SAY AT THIS TIME.
BUT MAYBE HE'S JUST SPENT TOO MUCH TIME IN WASHINGTON D.C.-- WHERE DENYING THE BLATANTLY OBVIOUS IS A WAY OF LIFE...
WHY-- WE DIDN'T EXPECT ANYTHING IN RETURN FOR OUR CONTRIBUTIONS!
PERISH THE THOUGHT! WE WERE SIMPLY DOING OUR PART FOR FREEDOM & DEMOCRACY!
THOSE LARGE TAX BREAKS WERE JUST, UM, A FORTUITOUS COINCIDENCE!
TOM TOMORROW©2-18-98 (TIP O' THE PEN TO BOB HARRIS FOR THE FIRST PANEL RUNDOWN)

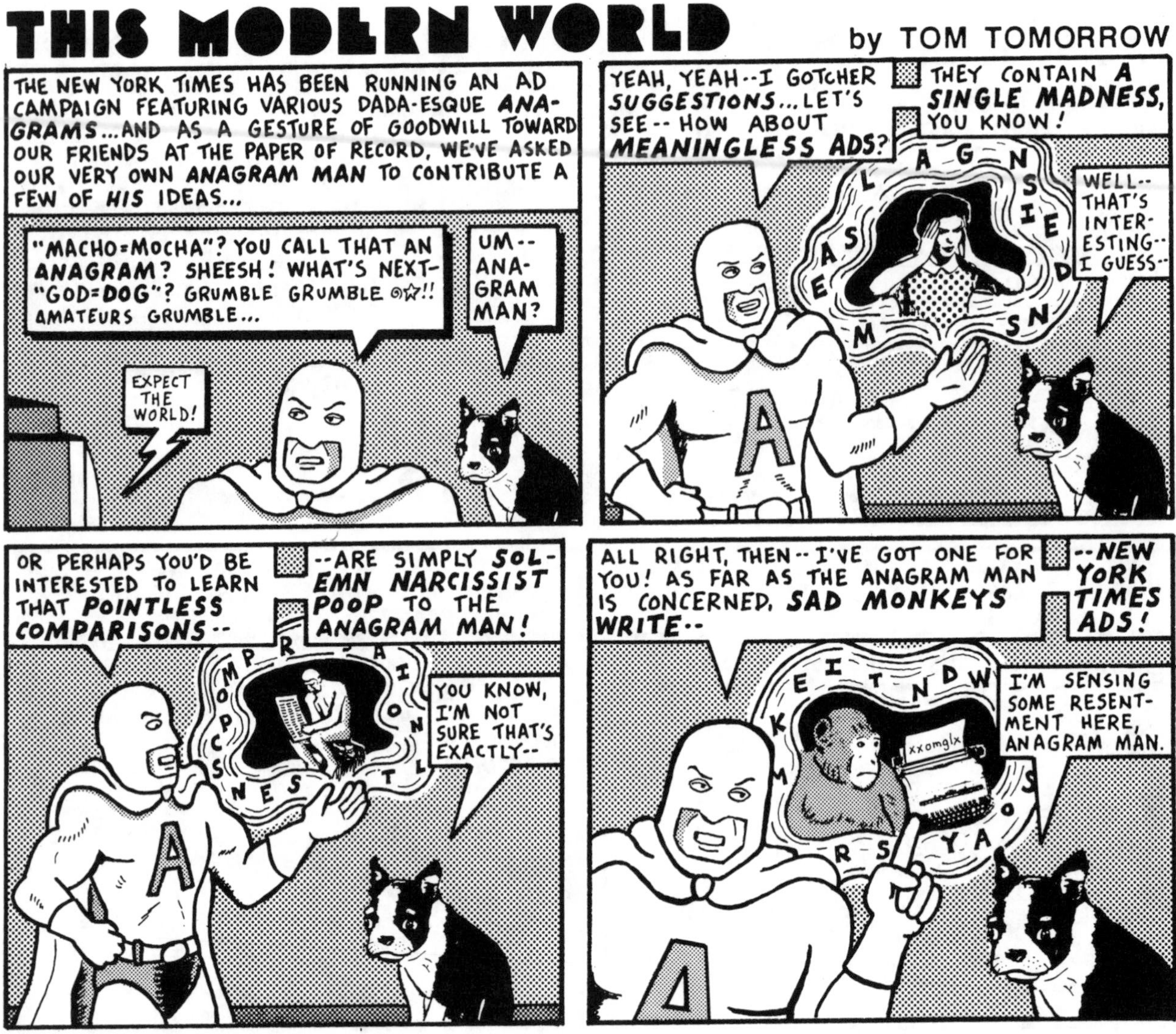
THIS MODERN WORLD
by TOM TOMORROW
THE NEW YORK TIMES HAS BEEN RUNNING AN AD CAMPAIGN FEATURING VARIOUS DADA-ESQUE ANAGRAMS...AND AS A GESTURE OF GOODWILL TOWARD OUR FRIENDS AT THE PAPER OF RECORD, WE'VE ASKED OUR VERY OWN ANAGRAM MAN TO CONTRIBUTE A FEW OF HIS IDEAS...
"MACHO=MOCHA"? YOU CALL THAT AN ANAGRAM? SHEESH! WHAT'S NEXT- "GOD=DOG"? GRUMBLE GRUMBLE @☆!! AMATEURS GRUMBLE...
UM-- ANAGRAM MAN?
EXPECT THE WORLD!
YEAH, YEAH--I GOTCHER SUGGESTIONS...LET'S SEE-- HOW ABOUT MEANINGLESS ADS?
THEY CONTAIN A SINGLE MADNESS, YOU KNOW!
WELL-- THAT'S INTERESTING-- I GUESS--
OR PERHAPS YOU'D BE INTERESTED TO LEARN THAT POINTLESS COMPARISONS--
--ARE SIMPLY SOLEMN NARCISSIST POOP TO THE ANAGRAM MAN!
YOU KNOW, I'M NOT SURE THAT'S EXACTLY--
ALL RIGHT, THEN--I'VE GOT ONE FOR YOU! AS FAR AS THE ANAGRAM MAN IS CONCERNED, SAD MONKEYS WRITE--
--NEW YORK TIMES ADS!
I'M SENSING SOME RESENTMENT HERE, ANAGRAM MAN.
xxomglx
TOM TOMORROW©3-18-98

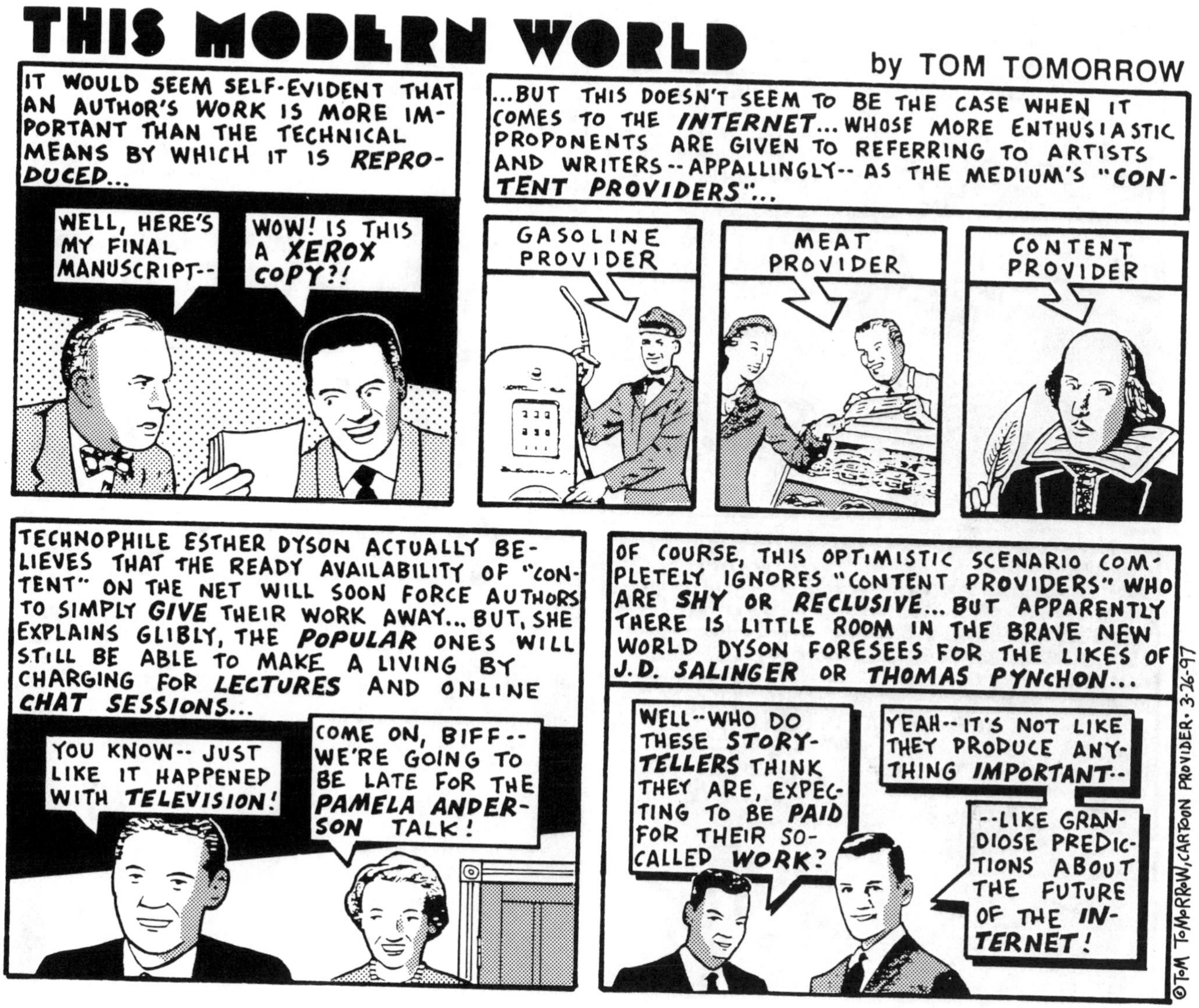
THIS MODERN WORLD
by TOM TOMORROW
IT WOULD SEEM SELF-EVIDENT THAT AN AUTHOR'S WORK IS MORE IMPORTANT THAN THE TECHNICAL MEANS BY WHICH IT IS REPRODUCED...
WELL, HERE'S MY FINAL MANUSCRIPT--
WOW! IS THIS A XEROX COPY?!
...BUT THIS DOESN'T SEEM TO BE THE CASE WHEN IT COMES TO THE INTERNET... WHOSE MORE ENTHUSIASTIC PROPONENTS ARE GIVEN TO REFERRING TO ARTISTS AND WRITERS--APPALLINGLY--AS THE MEDIUM'S "CONTENT PROVIDERS"...
GASOLINE PROVIDER
MEAT PROVIDER
CONTENT PROVIDER
TECHNOPHILE ESTHER DYSON ACTUALLY BELIEVES THAT THE READY AVAILABILITY OF "CONTENT" ON THE NET WILL SOON FORCE AUTHORS TO SIMPLY GIVE THEIR WORK AWAY... BUT, SHE EXPLAINS GLIBLY, THE POPULAR ONES WILL STILL BE ABLE TO MAKE A LIVING BY CHARGING FOR LECTURES AND ONLINE CHAT SESSIONS...
YOU KNOW--JUST LIKE IT HAPPENED WITH TELEVISION!
COME ON, BIFF--WE'RE GOING TO BE LATE FOR THE PAMELA ANDERSON TALK!
OF COURSE, THIS OPTIMISTIC SCENARIO COMPLETELY IGNORES "CONTENT PROVIDERS" WHO ARE SHY OR RECLUSIVE... BUT APPARENTLY THERE IS LITTLE ROOM IN THE BRAVE NEW WORLD DYSON FORESEES FOR THE LIKES OF J.D. SALINGER OR THOMAS PYNCHON...
WELL--WHO DO THESE STORYTELLERS THINK THEY ARE, EXPECTING TO BE PAID FOR THEIR SO-CALLED WORK?
YEAH--IT'S NOT LIKE THEY PRODUCE ANYTHING IMPORTANT--
--LIKE GRANDIOSE PREDICTIONS ABOUT THE FUTURE OF THE INTERNET!
©TOM TOMORROW, CARTOON PROVIDER. 3-26-97

THIS MODERN WORLD

by TOM TOMORROW

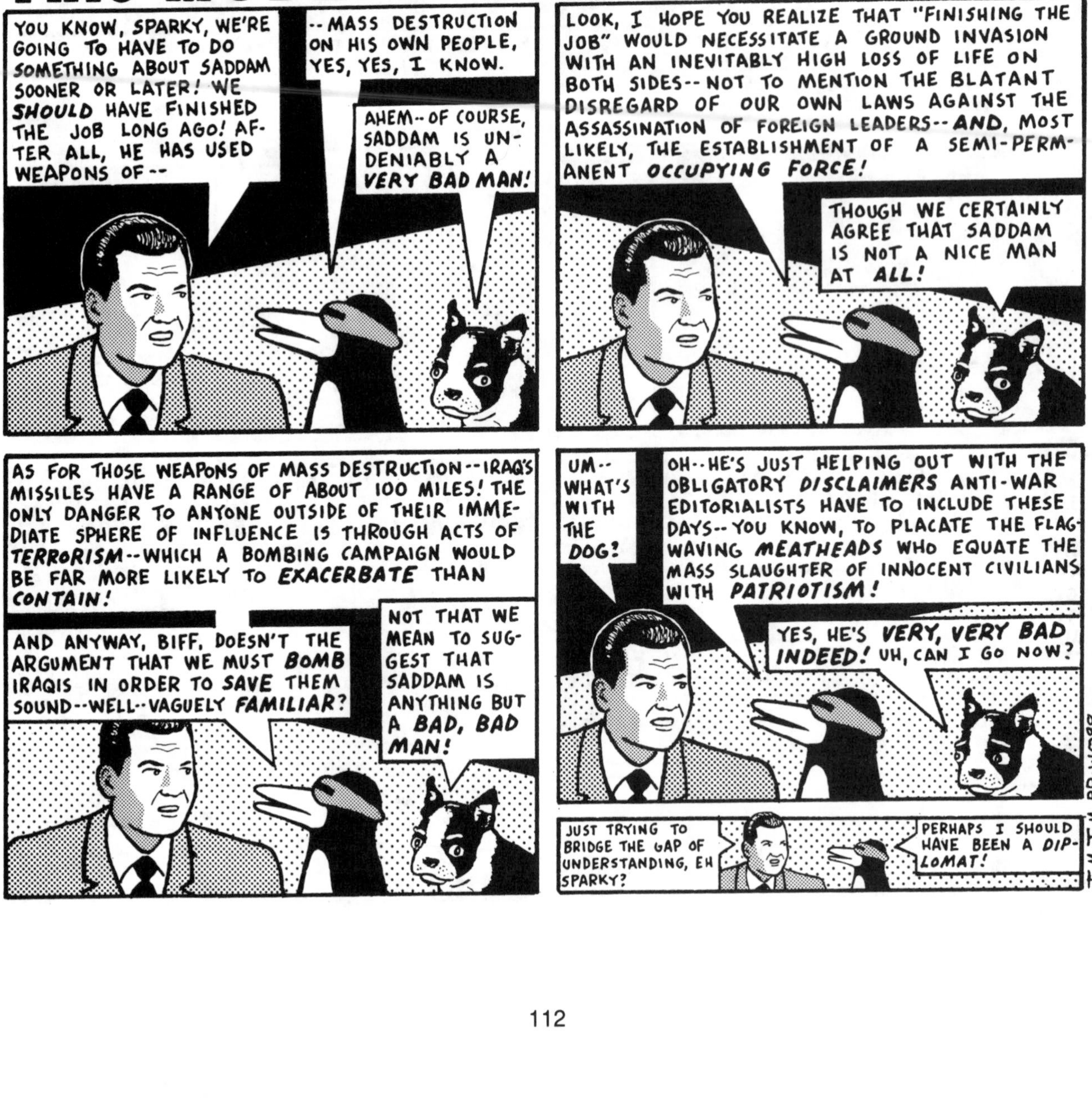

YOU KNOW, SPARKY, WE'RE GOING TO HAVE TO DO SOMETHING ABOUT SADDAM SOONER OR LATER! WE SHOULD HAVE FINISHED THE JOB LONG AGO! AFTER ALL, HE HAS USED WEAPONS OF--
--MASS DESTRUCTION ON HIS OWN PEOPLE, YES, YES, I KNOW.
AHEM--OF COURSE, SADDAM IS UNDENIABLY A VERY BAD MAN!
LOOK, I HOPE YOU REALIZE THAT "FINISHING THE JOB" WOULD NECESSITATE A GROUND INVASION WITH AN INEVITABLY HIGH LOSS OF LIFE ON BOTH SIDES--NOT TO MENTION THE BLATANT DISREGARD OF OUR OWN LAWS AGAINST THE ASSASSINATION OF FOREIGN LEADERS--AND, MOST LIKELY, THE ESTABLISHMENT OF A SEMI-PERMANENT OCCUPYING FORCE!
THOUGH WE CERTAINLY AGREE THAT SADDAM IS NOT A NICE MAN AT ALL!
AS FOR THOSE WEAPONS OF MASS DESTRUCTION--IRAQ'S MISSILES HAVE A RANGE OF ABOUT 100 MILES! THE ONLY DANGER TO ANYONE OUTSIDE OF THEIR IMMEDIATE SPHERE OF INFLUENCE IS THROUGH ACTS OF TERRORISM--WHICH A BOMBING CAMPAIGN WOULD BE FAR MORE LIKELY TO EXACERBATE THAN CONTAIN!
AND ANYWAY, BIFF, DOESN'T THE ARGUMENT THAT WE MUST BOMB IRAQIS IN ORDER TO SAVE THEM SOUND--WELL--VAGUELY FAMILIAR?
NOT THAT WE MEAN TO SUGGEST THAT SADDAM IS ANYTHING BUT A BAD, BAD MAN!
UM--WHAT'S WITH THE DOG?
OH--HE'S JUST HELPING OUT WITH THE OBLIGATORY DISCLAIMERS ANTI-WAR EDITORIALISTS HAVE TO INCLUDE THESE DAYS--YOU KNOW, TO PLACATE THE FLAG-WAVING MEATHEADS WHO EQUATE THE MASS SLAUGHTER OF INNOCENT CIVILIANS WITH PATRIOTISM!
YES, HE'S VERY, VERY BAD INDEED! UH, CAN I GO NOW?
JUST TRYING TO BRIDGE THE GAP OF UNDERSTANDING, EH SPARKY?
PERHAPS I SHOULD HAVE BEEN A DIPLOMAT!
TOM TOMORROW©98

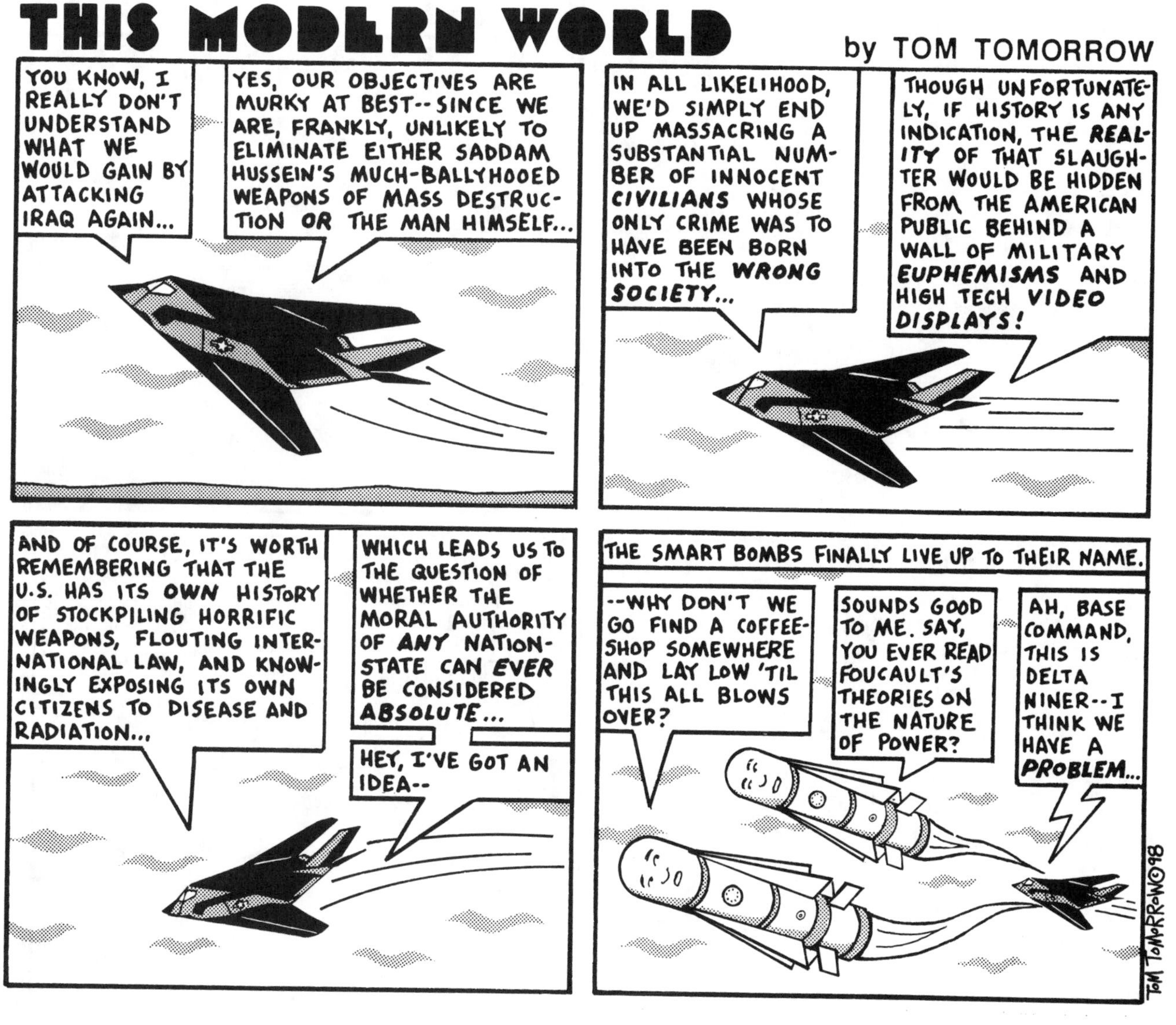
THIS MODERN WORLD
by TOM TOMORROW
YOU KNOW, I REALLY DON'T UNDERSTAND WHAT WE WOULD GAIN BY ATTACKING IRAQ AGAIN...
YES, OUR OBJECTIVES ARE MURKY AT BEST--SINCE WE ARE, FRANKLY, UNLIKELY TO ELIMINATE EITHER SADDAM HUSSEIN'S MUCH-BALLYHOOED WEAPONS OF MASS DESTRUCTION OR THE MAN HIMSELF...
IN ALL LIKELIHOOD, WE'D SIMPLY END UP MASSACRING A SUBSTANTIAL NUMBER OF INNOCENT CIVILIANS WHOSE ONLY CRIME WAS TO HAVE BEEN BORN INTO THE WRONG SOCIETY...
THOUGH UNFORTUNATELY, IF HISTORY IS ANY INDICATION, THE REALITY OF THAT SLAUGHTER WOULD BE HIDDEN FROM THE AMERICAN PUBLIC BEHIND A WALL OF MILITARY EUPHEMISMS AND HIGH TECH VIDEO DISPLAYS!
AND OF COURSE, IT'S WORTH REMEMBERING THAT THE U.S. HAS ITS OWN HISTORY OF STOCKPILING HORRIFIC WEAPONS, FLOUTING INTERNATIONAL LAW, AND KNOWINGLY EXPOSING ITS OWN CITIZENS TO DISEASE AND RADIATION...
WHICH LEADS US TO THE QUESTION OF WHETHER THE MORAL AUTHORITY OF ANY NATION-STATE CAN EVER BE CONSIDERED ABSOLUTE...
HEY, I'VE GOT AN IDEA--
THE SMART BOMBS FINALLY LIVE UP TO THEIR NAME.
--WHY DON'T WE GO FIND A COFFEE-SHOP SOMEWHERE AND LAY LOW 'TIL THIS ALL BLOWS OVER?
SOUNDS GOOD TO ME. SAY, YOU EVER READ FOUCAULT'S THEORIES ON THE NATURE OF POWER?
AH, BASE COMMAND, THIS IS DELTA NINER--I THINK WE HAVE A PROBLEM...
TOM TOMORROW©98

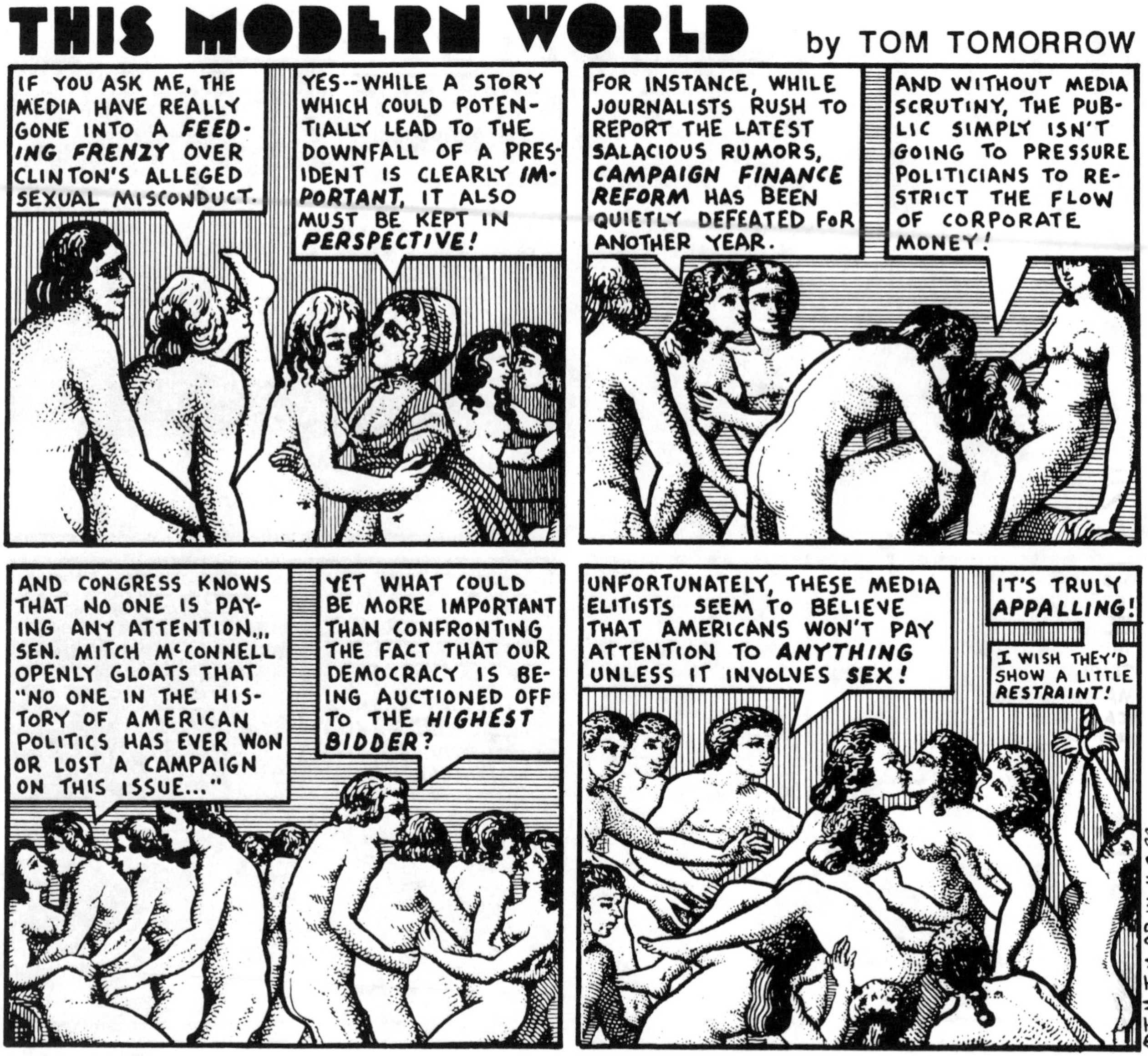
THIS MODERN WORLD
by TOM TOMORROW
IF YOU ASK ME, THE MEDIA HAVE REALLY GONE INTO A FEEDING FRENZY OVER CLINTON'S ALLEGED SEXUAL MISCONDUCT.
YES--WHILE A STORY WHICH COULD POTENTIALLY LEAD TO THE DOWNFALL OF A PRESIDENT IS CLEARLY IMPORTANT, IT ALSO MUST BE KEPT IN PERSPECTIVE!
FOR INSTANCE, WHILE JOURNALISTS RUSH TO REPORT THE LATEST SALACIOUS RUMORS, CAMPAIGN FINANCE REFORM HAS BEEN QUIETLY DEFEATED FOR ANOTHER YEAR.
AND WITHOUT MEDIA SCRUTINY, THE PUBLIC SIMPLY ISN'T GOING TO PRESSURE POLITICIANS TO RESTRICT THE FLOW OF CORPORATE MONEY!
AND CONGRESS KNOWS THAT NO ONE IS PAYING ANY ATTENTION... SEN. MITCH McCONNELL OPENLY GLOATS THAT "NO ONE IN THE HISTORY OF AMERICAN POLITICS HAS EVER WON OR LOST A CAMPAIGN ON THIS ISSUE..."
YET WHAT COULD BE MORE IMPORTANT THAN CONFRONTING THE FACT THAT OUR DEMOCRACY IS BEING AUCTIONED OFF TO THE HIGHEST BIDDER?
UNFORTUNATELY, THESE MEDIA ELITISTS SEEM TO BELIEVE THAT AMERICANS WON'T PAY ATTENTION TO ANYTHING UNLESS IT INVOLVES SEX!
IT'S TRULY APPALLING!
I WISH THEY'D SHOW A LITTLE RESTRAINT!
©TOM TOMORROW 4-8-98

THIS MODERN WORLD

by TOM TOMORROW

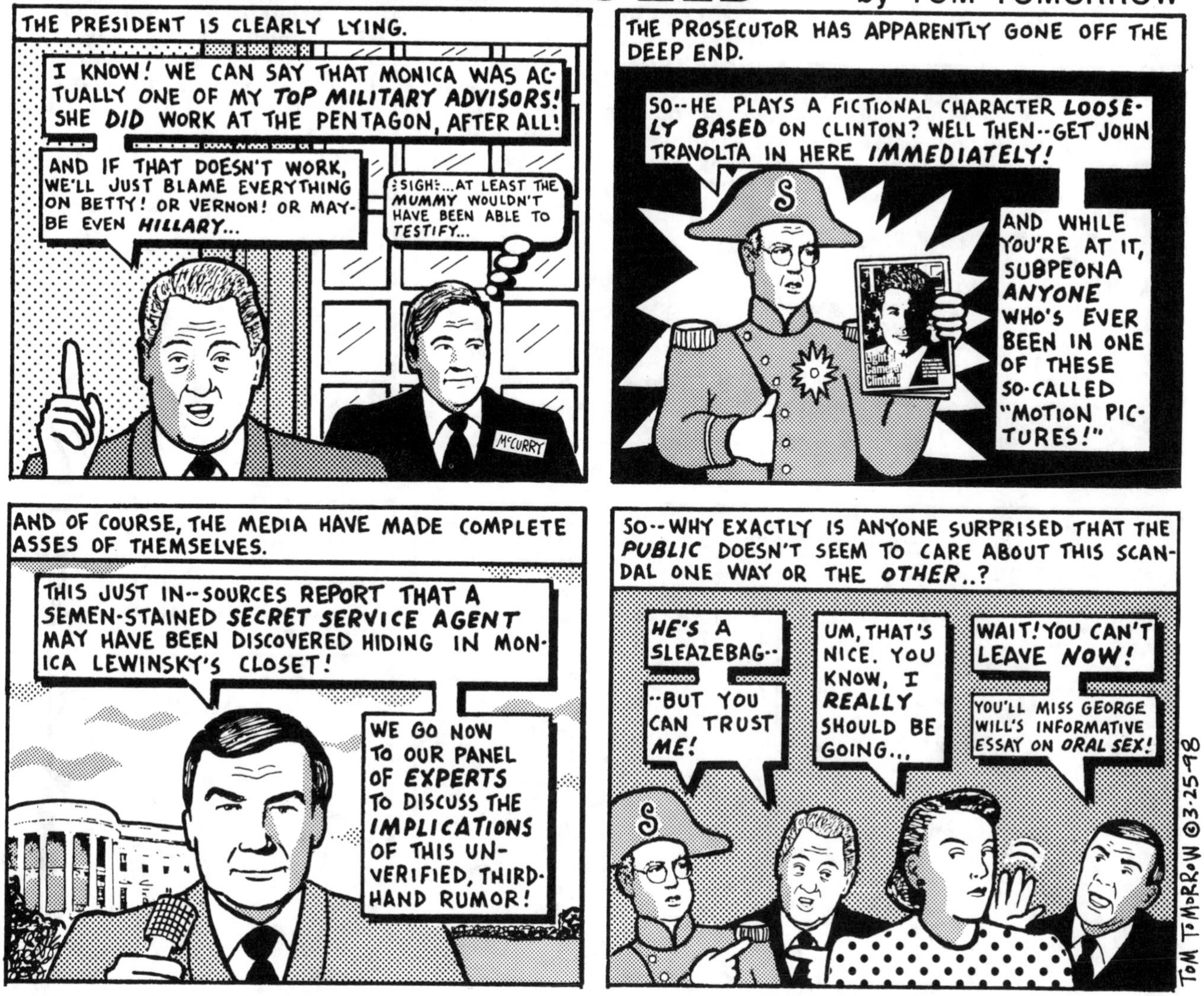

THE PRESIDENT IS CLEARLY LYING.
I KNOW! WE CAN SAY THAT MONICA WAS ACTUALLY ONE OF MY TOP MILITARY ADVISORS! SHE DID WORK AT THE PENTAGON, AFTER ALL!
AND IF THAT DOESN'T WORK, WE'LL JUST BLAME EVERYTHING ON BETTY! OR VERNON! OR MAYBE EVEN HILLARY...
:SIGH:...AT LEAST THE MUMMY WOULDN'T HAVE BEEN ABLE TO TESTIFY...
McCURRY
THE PROSECUTOR HAS APPARENTLY GONE OFF THE DEEP END.
SO--HE PLAYS A FICTIONAL CHARACTER LOOSELY BASED ON CLINTON? WELL THEN--GET JOHN TRAVOLTA IN HERE IMMEDIATELY!
AND WHILE YOU'RE AT IT, SUBPEONA ANYONE WHO'S EVER BEEN IN ONE OF THESE SO-CALLED "MOTION PICTURES!"
Lights! Camera! Clinton!
AND OF COURSE, THE MEDIA HAVE MADE COMPLETE ASSES OF THEMSELVES.
THIS JUST IN--SOURCES REPORT THAT A SEMEN-STAINED SECRET SERVICE AGENT MAY HAVE BEEN DISCOVERED HIDING IN MONICA LEWINSKY'S CLOSET!
WE GO NOW TO OUR PANEL OF EXPERTS TO DISCUSS THE IMPLICATIONS OF THIS UNVERIFIED, THIRD-HAND RUMOR!
SO--WHY EXACTLY IS ANYONE SURPRISED THAT THE PUBLIC DOESN'T SEEM TO CARE ABOUT THIS SCANDAL ONE WAY OR THE OTHER..?
HE'S A SLEAZEBAG--
--BUT YOU CAN TRUST ME!
UM, THAT'S NICE. YOU KNOW, I REALLY SHOULD BE GOING...
WAIT! YOU CAN'T LEAVE NOW!
YOU'LL MISS GEORGE WILL'S INFORMATIVE ESSAY ON ORAL SEX!
TOM TOMORROW ©3-25-98

THIS MODERN WORLD

by TOM TOMORROW

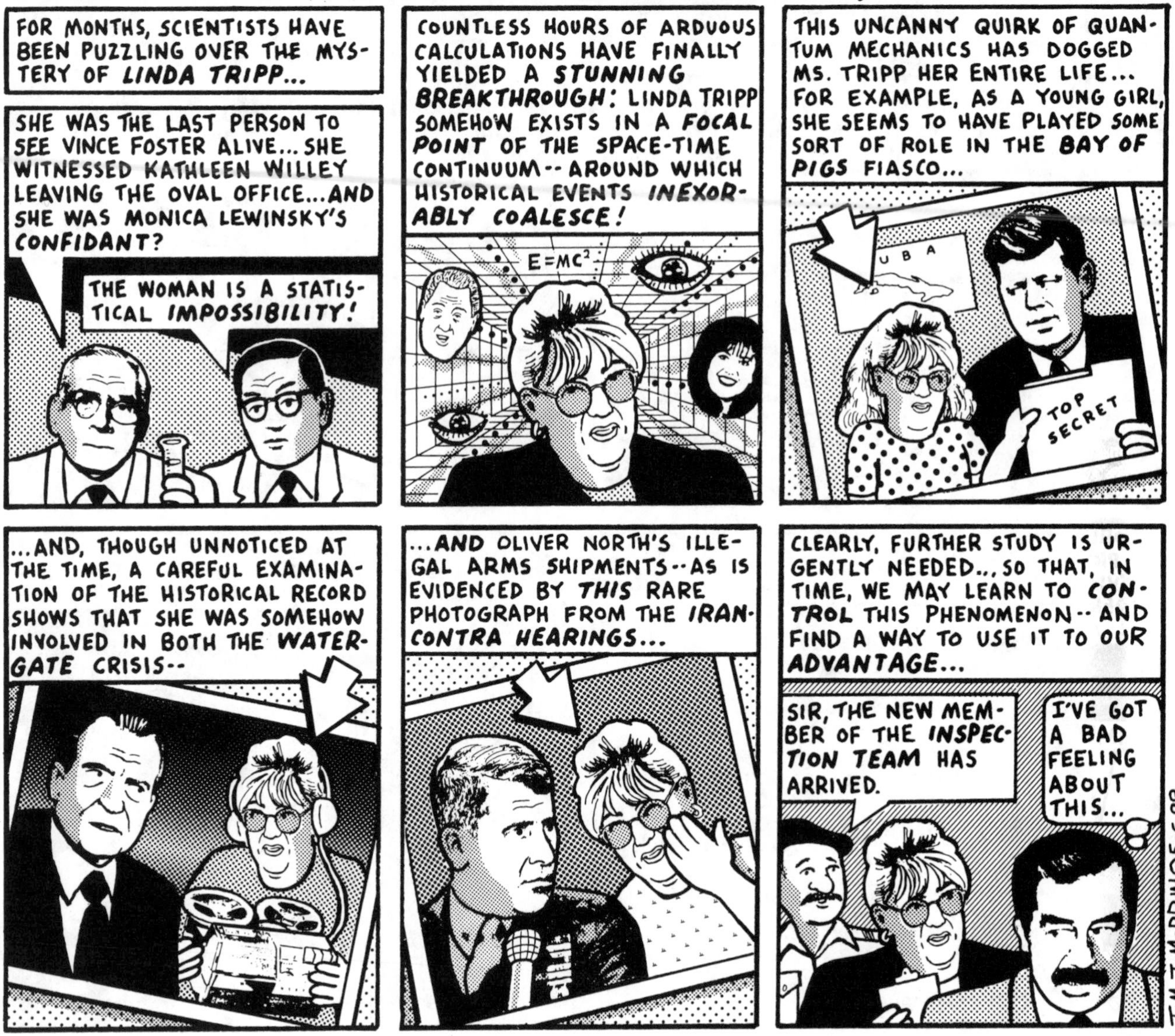

FOR MONTHS, SCIENTISTS HAVE BEEN PUZZLING OVER THE MYSTERY OF LINDA TRIPP...
SHE WAS THE LAST PERSON TO SEE VINCE FOSTER ALIVE... SHE WITNESSED KATHLEEN WILLEY LEAVING THE OVAL OFFICE... AND SHE WAS MONICA LEWINSKY'S CONFIDANT?
THE WOMAN IS A STATISTICAL IMPOSSIBILITY!
COUNTLESS HOURS OF ARDUOUS CALCULATIONS HAVE FINALLY YIELDED A STUNNING BREAKTHROUGH: LINDA TRIPP SOMEHOW EXISTS IN A FOCAL POINT OF THE SPACE-TIME CONTINUUM -- AROUND WHICH HISTORICAL EVENTS INEXORABLY COALESCE!
E=MC²
THIS UNCANNY QUIRK OF QUANTUM MECHANICS HAS DOGGED MS. TRIPP HER ENTIRE LIFE... FOR EXAMPLE, AS A YOUNG GIRL, SHE SEEMS TO HAVE PLAYED SOME SORT OF ROLE IN THE BAY OF PIGS FIASCO...
UBA
TOP SECRET
...AND, THOUGH UNNOTICED AT THE TIME, A CAREFUL EXAMINATION OF THE HISTORICAL RECORD SHOWS THAT SHE WAS SOMEHOW INVOLVED IN BOTH THE WATERGATE CRISIS--
...AND OLIVER NORTH'S ILLEGAL ARMS SHIPMENTS -- AS IS EVIDENCED BY THIS RARE PHOTOGRAPH FROM THE IRAN-CONTRA HEARINGS...
CLEARLY, FURTHER STUDY IS URGENTLY NEEDED... SO THAT, IN TIME, WE MAY LEARN TO CONTROL THIS PHENOMENON -- AND FIND A WAY TO USE IT TO OUR ADVANTAGE...
SIR, THE NEW MEMBER OF THE INSPECTION TEAM HAS ARRIVED.
I'VE GOT A BAD FEELING ABOUT THIS...
TOM TOMORROW ©5-6-98

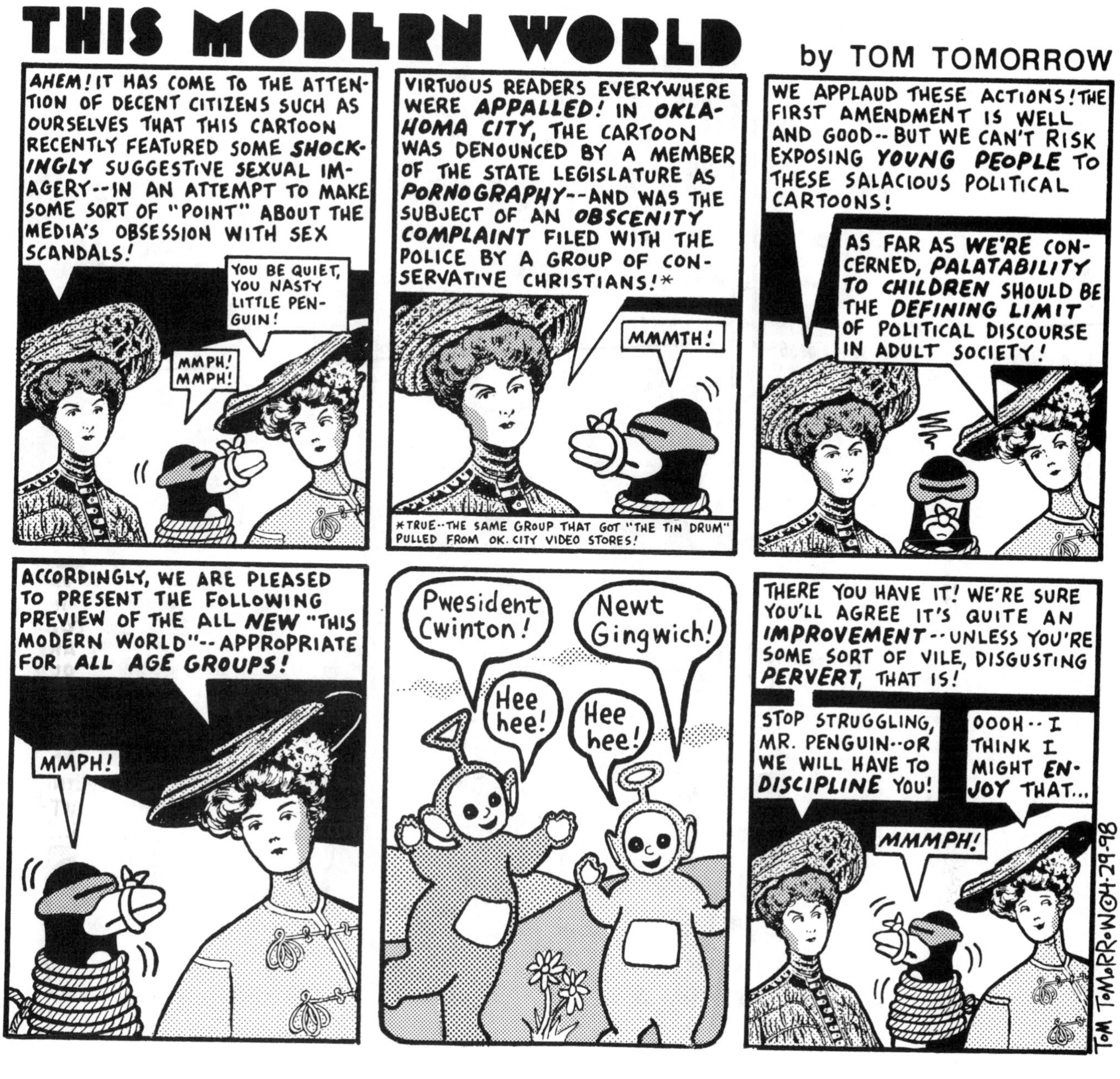
THIS MODERN WORLD
by TOM TOMORROW
AHEM! IT HAS COME TO THE ATTENTION OF DECENT CITIZENS SUCH AS OURSELVES THAT THIS CARTOON RECENTLY FEATURED SOME SHOCKINGLY SUGGESTIVE SEXUAL IMAGERY--IN AN ATTEMPT TO MAKE SOME SORT OF "POINT" ABOUT THE MEDIA'S OBSESSION WITH SEX SCANDALS!
MMPH! MMPH!
YOU BE QUIET, YOU NASTY LITTLE PENGUIN!
VIRTUOUS READERS EVERYWHERE WERE APPALLED! IN OKLAHOMA CITY, THE CARTOON WAS DENOUNCED BY A MEMBER OF THE STATE LEGISLATURE AS PORNOGRAPHY--AND WAS THE SUBJECT OF AN OBSCENITY COMPLAINT FILED WITH THE POLICE BY A GROUP OF CONSERVATIVE CHRISTIANS!*
MMMTH!
*TRUE--THE SAME GROUP THAT GOT "THE TIN DRUM" PULLED FROM OK. CITY VIDEO STORES!
WE APPLAUD THESE ACTIONS! THE FIRST AMENDMENT IS WELL AND GOOD--BUT WE CAN'T RISK EXPOSING YOUNG PEOPLE TO THESE SALACIOUS POLITICAL CARTOONS!
AS FAR AS WE'RE CONCERNED, PALATABILITY TO CHILDREN SHOULD BE THE DEFINING LIMIT OF POLITICAL DISCOURSE IN ADULT SOCIETY!
ACCORDINGLY, WE ARE PLEASED TO PRESENT THE FOLLOWING PREVIEW OF THE ALL NEW "THIS MODERN WORLD"--APPROPRIATE FOR ALL AGE GROUPS!
MMPH!
Pwesident Cwinton!
Newt Gingwich!
Hee hee!
Hee hee!
THERE YOU HAVE IT! WE'RE SURE YOU'LL AGREE IT'S QUITE AN IMPROVEMENT--UNLESS YOU'RE SOME SORT OF VILE, DISGUSTING PERVERT, THAT IS!
STOP STRUGGLING, MR. PENGUIN--OR WE WILL HAVE TO DISCIPLINE YOU!
OOOH--I THINK I MIGHT ENJOY THAT...
MMMPH!
TOM TOMORROW©4-29-98

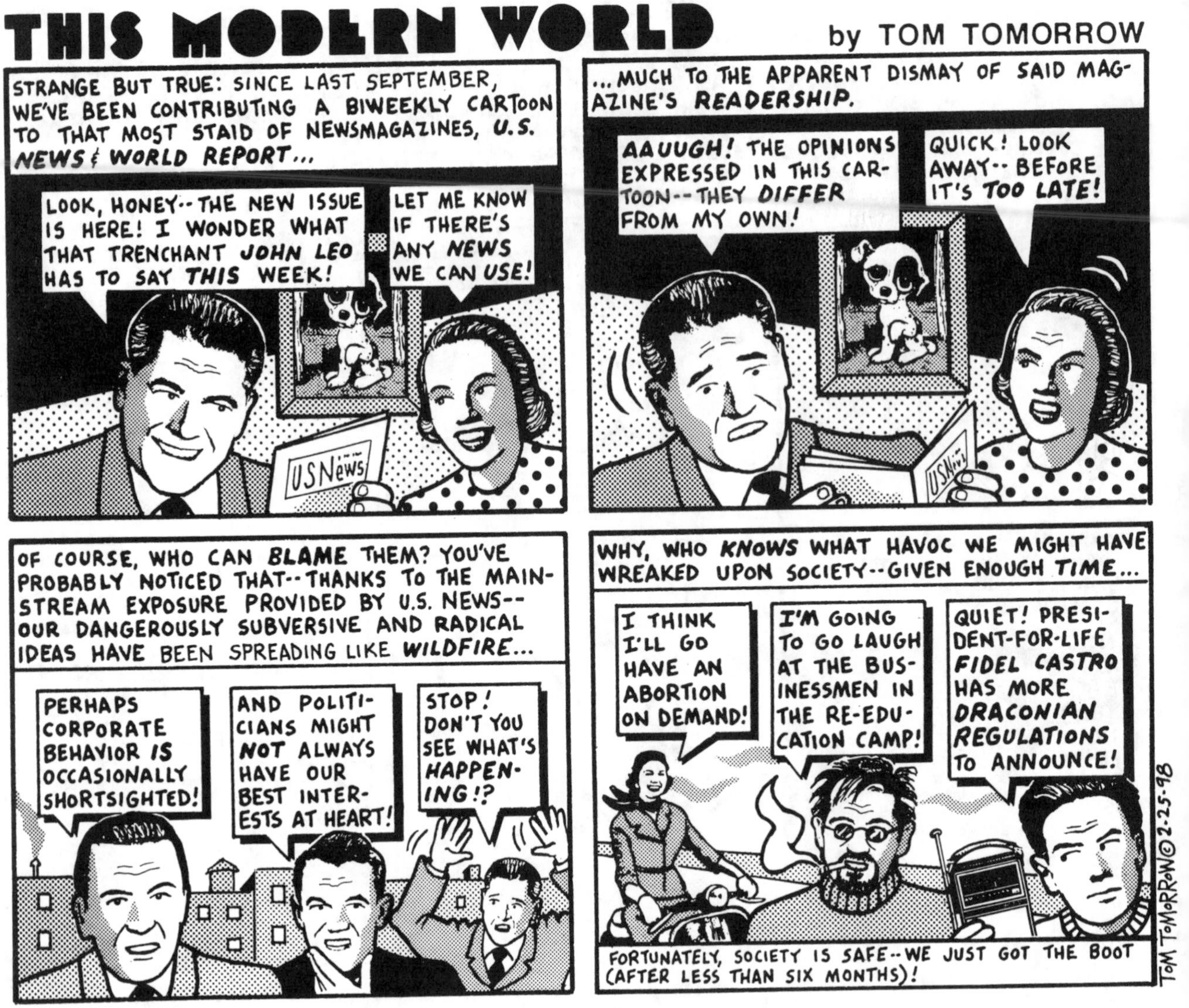
THIS MODERN WORLD
by TOM TOMORROW
STRANGE BUT TRUE: SINCE LAST SEPTEMBER, WE'VE BEEN CONTRIBUTING A BIWEEKLY CARTOON TO THAT MOST STAID OF NEWSMAGAZINES, U.S. NEWS & WORLD REPORT...
LOOK, HONEY-- THE NEW ISSUE IS HERE! I WONDER WHAT THAT TRENCHANT JOHN LEO HAS TO SAY THIS WEEK!
LET ME KNOW IF THERE'S ANY NEWS WE CAN USE!
USNews
...MUCH TO THE APPARENT DISMAY OF SAID MAGAZINE'S READERSHIP.
AAUUGH! THE OPINIONS EXPRESSED IN THIS CARTOON-- THEY DIFFER FROM MY OWN!
QUICK! LOOK AWAY-- BEFORE IT'S TOO LATE!
OF COURSE, WHO CAN BLAME THEM? YOU'VE PROBABLY NOTICED THAT-- THANKS TO THE MAINSTREAM EXPOSURE PROVIDED BY U.S. NEWS-- OUR DANGEROUSLY SUBVERSIVE AND RADICAL IDEAS HAVE BEEN SPREADING LIKE WILDFIRE...
PERHAPS CORPORATE BEHAVIOR IS OCCASIONALLY SHORTSIGHTED!
AND POLITICIANS MIGHT NOT ALWAYS HAVE OUR BEST INTERESTS AT HEART!
STOP! DON'T YOU SEE WHAT'S HAPPENING!?
WHY, WHO KNOWS WHAT HAVOC WE MIGHT HAVE WREAKED UPON SOCIETY-- GIVEN ENOUGH TIME...
I THINK I'LL GO HAVE AN ABORTION ON DEMAND!
I'M GOING TO GO LAUGH AT THE BUSINESSMEN IN THE RE-EDUCATION CAMP!
QUIET! PRESIDENT-FOR-LIFE FIDEL CASTRO HAS MORE DRACONIAN REGULATIONS TO ANNOUNCE!
FORTUNATELY, SOCIETY IS SAFE-- WE JUST GOT THE BOOT (AFTER LESS THAN SIX MONTHS)!
TOM TOMORROW © 2·25·98

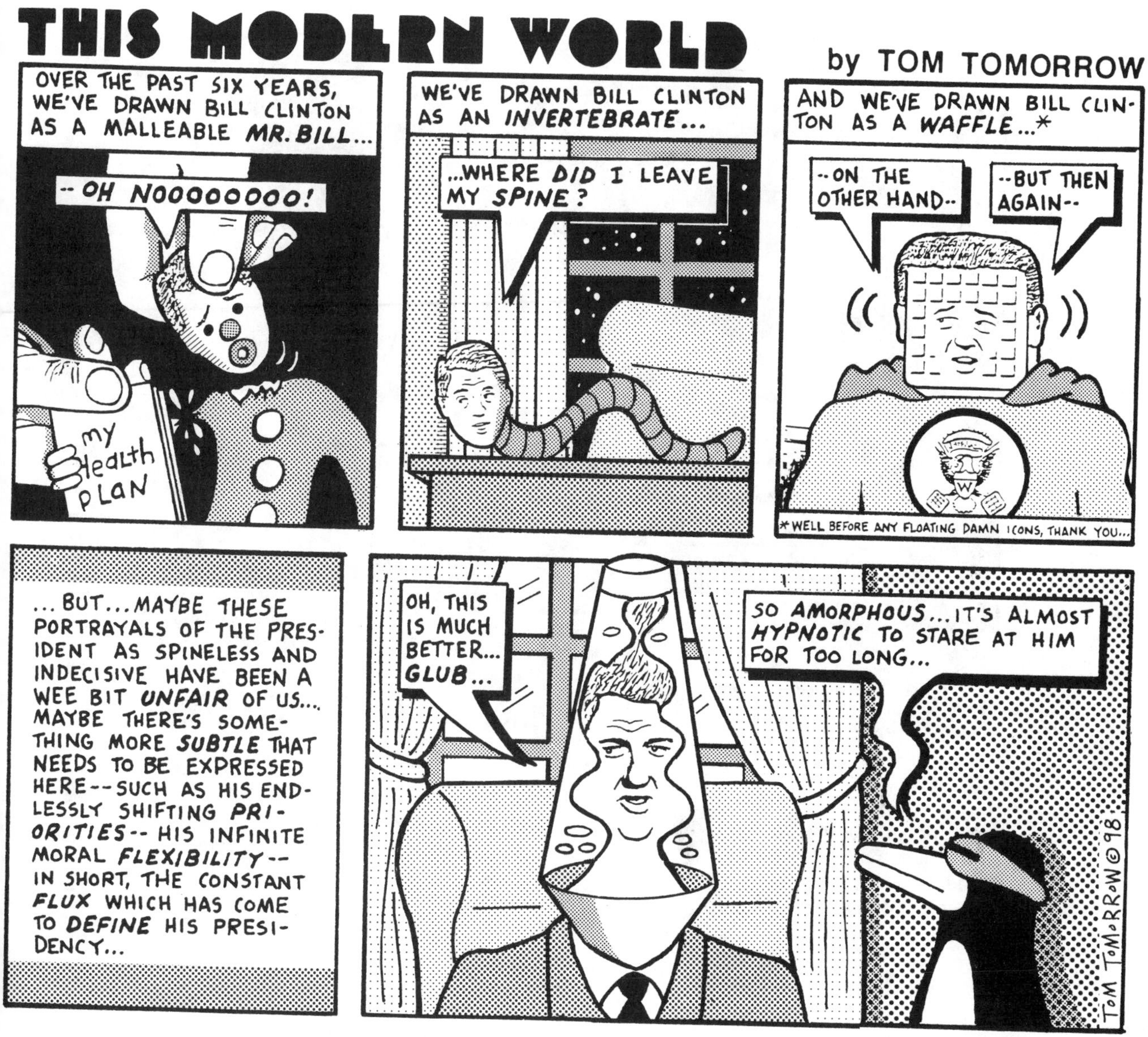
THIS MODERN WORLD
by TOM TOMORROW
OVER THE PAST SIX YEARS, WE'VE DRAWN BILL CLINTON AS A MALLEABLE MR. BILL...
-- OH NOOOOOOOO!
my Health plan
WE'VE DRAWN BILL CLINTON AS AN INVERTEBRATE...
...WHERE DID I LEAVE MY SPINE?
AND WE'VE DRAWN BILL CLIN-TON AS A WAFFLE...*
-- ON THE OTHER HAND--
-- BUT THEN AGAIN--
*WELL BEFORE ANY FLOATING DAMN ICONS, THANK YOU...
... BUT... MAYBE THESE PORTRAYALS OF THE PRES-IDENT AS SPINELESS AND INDECISIVE HAVE BEEN A WEE BIT UNFAIR OF US.... MAYBE THERE'S SOME-THING MORE SUBTLE THAT NEEDS TO BE EXPRESSED HERE-- SUCH AS HIS END-LESSLY SHIFTING PRI-ORITIES-- HIS INFINITE MORAL FLEXIBILITY-- IN SHORT, THE CONSTANT FLUX WHICH HAS COME TO DEFINE HIS PRESI-DENCY...
OH, THIS IS MUCH BETTER... GLUB...
SO AMORPHOUS... IT'S ALMOST HYPNOTIC TO STARE AT HIM FOR TOO LONG...
TOM TOMORROW©98

About the Author

Tom Tomorrow (shown above with close personal friend Marilyn Quayle) is the creator of the nationally syndicated cartoon *This Modern World*, which appears in approximately one hundred newspapers each week. His work has also appeared in *The New York Times, U.S. News & World Report, Esquire, The Nation, Spin,* and numerous other publications. In 1998 he was awarded the Thirtieth Annual Robert F. Kennedy Journalism Award for Cartooning.